PRAISE FOR UNDER-EDUCATION IN AFRICA

A collection of essays from an educator-activist that take us back to one of the richest periods of African intellectual debate about knowledge and colonization, the early 1970s at the University of Dar es Salaam, with valuable lessons for today. **Budd L Hall**, *PhD, Professor Emeritus, UNESCO Co-chair in Community-Based Research and Social Responsibility in Higher Education, University of Victoria, Canada.*

This is a timely, broad ranging, provocative series of essays about under-education in Africa. The author's lived experiences, particularly in Tanzania, form a rich base for much of the critical contextual analysis. New generations of scholar-activists in Africa and elsewhere are urged to learn from history, to debate, to question and strive, with passion and hope, to attain a just, more egalitarian world. **Shirley Walters**, *Professor Emerita, University of Western Cape, South Africa.*

An inspiring collection of vivid stories and profound critiques of education from a committed scholar-activist who draws upon a lifetime of engaged learning, teaching, research and debate. Revealing how *under-education* has been spawned by global capitalism, it also inspires hope and offers strategies for educational and social change in Africa and beyond. **Pat Saul**, *UDSM graduate, teacher and community activist for social change, Toronto.*

A dedicated and passionate educator and scholar activist, Karim Hirji explores the connection between education and a dependent economy, and the systematic de-education of the Tanzanian and African masses during the colonial and post-colonial periods up to the present day. Broad structural analysis of underlying factors such as social and economic injustice, political accountability and neoliberal policy is combined with concrete investigation of the challenges facing students and teachers at all levels of the education system and ends on a positive note, "dare to dream." An enjoyable work; a valuable resource for all concerned about advancing education in Africa. **Marjorie Mbilinyi**, *Professor of Education, University of Dar es Salaam (1968-2003), independent researcher and writer.*

UNDER-EDUCATION IN AFRICA

UNDER-EDUCATION IN AFRICA

FROM COLONIALISM TO NEOLIBERALISM

Karim F Hirji

Daraja Press

Published by Daraja Press
https://darajapress.com
© Karim F. Hirji 2019
All Rights Reserved

Cover Design: Kate McDonnell
Cover Photos: Yusuf Ahmad and Christina Mfanga

Library and Archives Canada Cataloguing in Publication
Hirji, Karim F., author
Under-education in Africa: from colonialism to neoliberalism / Karim F. Hirji.
Includes bibliographic references.
Issued in print and electronic formats.
Identifiers: Canadiana (print) 20190136235. Canadiana (ebook) 20190136251
ISBN 9781988832357 (softcover). ISBN 9781988832364 (ebook).
Education—Tanzania. Education and state—Tanzania.
Education—Africa. Education and state—Africa.
Classification: LCC LA1841 .H57 2020 | DDC 370.9678—dc23

To

The People of Tanzania

++++++++++
Each day be open to the world,
be ready to think;
each day be ready not to accept
what is said just because it is said,
be predisposed to reread what is read;
each day investigate, question, and doubt.
Paulo Freire
++++++++++

Contents

	ACRONYMS	*xiii*
	PREFACE	*xv*
	INTRODUCTION	*xvii*
1.	EDUCATION AND COLONIALISM	1
2.	EDUCATION AND UJAMAA	27
3.	EDUCATION AND DEMOCRACY	51
4.	EDUCATION AND DEPENDENCY	59
5.	EDUCATION AND VIOLENCE	77
6.	EDUCATION AND PRIVATISATION	87
7.	EDUCATION AND COMPUTERS	103
8.	EDUCATION AND AMERICA	115
9.	EDUCATION AND DEBATE	131
10.	EDUCATION AND HISTORY I	145
11.	EDUCATION AND HISTORY II	169
12.	EDUCATION AND READING	187
13.	EDUCATION AND EDUCATORS	217
14.	EDUCATION AND ACTIVISM I	229
15.	EDUCATION AND ACTIVISM II	243
16.	EDUCATION AND LIBERATION	261
	REFERENCES	269
	AUTHOR PROFILE	293

ACRONYMS

AKU	Aga Khan University
CPU	Common People's Uganda
DS	Development Studies
EASE	East African Society and Environment
ESR	Education for Self-Reliance
FRELIMO	Frente de Libertação de Moçambique
HEUA	How Europe Underdeveloped Africa
MCT	Media Council of Tanzania
MNP	Mkuki na Nyota Publishers
MUHAS	Muhimbili University of Health and Allied Sciences
PAC	Pan Africanist Congress
TANU	Tanganyika African National Union
TSh	Tanzania Shilling(s)
TYL	TANU Youth League
UDSM	University of Dar es Salaam
USARF	University Students' African Revolutionary Front
WUS	World University Service

PREFACE

Education means breaking free.
Abhijit Naskar
++++++++++

IN THE COURSE OF TEACHING for over four decades, I wrote a number of essays on the different facets of the education systems in Tanzania and the USA. They were based on my classroom experience as well as wider investigations. The main issues that interested me were:

- What is the purpose of education, for individuals and society?
- Are educational curricula what they should be?
- Whose interests does the education system serve?
- Should educational institutions be run on a democratic footing?
- What is role of teachers in the education system?
- What is meant by good quality and poor quality education?
- How can education serve the interests of the common people and contribute to the development of a just, humane society?

These questions were explored in relation to varying phases of history and different components of the systems of education. This book brings together, in edited and revised versions, sixteen essays in the belief that what they contain is not just of historic interest but is also of relevance to the present times. In revising them, I have tried to maintain the essence of what was in the initial versions, though in several cases, I have added new material. Four essays are new to this book.

While the essays can be read in any order, it is best to tackle them in the sequence given. What appears earlier sheds light on what appears later. The spelling in this book follows US English.

In the course of initially writing the essays, I gained much from my colleagues and students. It is not possible to name them here. Yet, they have my profound thanks. I also thank Christina Mfanga for research and typing two essays, Yusuf Ahmad for photography, Firoze Manji for his comradely and professional support in the production of the book, Rosa Hirji for useful advice, and Farida Hirji for editing assistance and enduring love and encouragement.

Karim F Hirji
July 2019

INTRODUCTION

Don't limit a child to your own learning,
for he was born in another time.
Rabindranath Tagore
++++++++++

EDUCATION, FORMAL AND INFORMAL, elementary and advanced, is the means by which a society transmits its accumulated knowledge, skills and values from one generation to the next. The teacher, a central player in this process, bears the responsibility of molding the growing human along ways consonant with social needs and values. A good education fosters the growth of creative, intellectually mature and astute individuals who prize critical thought and freedom of expression as well as service to fellow human beings.

That, in theory, is how it is supposed to be. Modern societies are not homogeneous entities but are based on economic class divisions. The interests of the many at the bottom do not coincide with those of the few at the top. In such societies, social institutions function in accord with the interests of the dominant class. Education here has a dual role, a technical role and an ideological role. Besides training people who can competently undertake the tasks in the various sectors of society, it also inculcates values and an outlook that conform to the *status quo*. Its role is to produce loyal citizens, not rebels who question why things are the way they are. Imbued with a narrow, occupation and locality oriented intellectual horizon, their critical faculties are accordingly circumscribed. Even highly knowledgeable scientists who do state of the art research or respected intellectuals who are the products of such education lack the ability to view issues in an interconnected fashion or critically appraise the functioning of the social and economic system. I denote such a process of education as **miseducation**. The broad-minded individuals who dare to pose fundamental, troubling questions emerging from this system are but a few exceptions to the rule. As Noam Chomsky puts it:

The whole educational and professional training system is a very elaborate filter, which just weeds out people who are too independent, and who think for themselves, and who don't know how to be submissive, and so on — because they're dysfunctional to the institutions. Noam Chomsky

BASIC TERMINOLGY

The essays in this book generally employ a Marxian (political economy) framework for analyzing the development of society and education. Seven basic ideas used in this approach and which relate education to the local and global economy and society appear throughout. Here I give a brief definition of each.

Capitalism: A capitalist society is a society permeated by commodity production and exchange in which the means of production, economic resources and financial institutions are owned or controlled by a small class. Surplus value (wealth) created through the labor of workers, small scale producers and others (the vast majority) is appropriated by the capitalists. The state and social institutions like the media and education system effectively function to promote and protect the interests of the dominant class.

Imperialism: The direct or indirect domination of one nation by another, essentially by exercising economic control, is called imperialism. Often, economic domination is augmented by political, cultural and military domination. The key feature of imperialism today is the presence of giant multinational corporations based in the dominant nations exercising overall economic control over a large number of dominated nations. It utilizes global financial and political institutions as well as state security agencies and armed forces to reinforce this international order.

Colonialism: Colonialism is a system whereby one nation exercises total (economic, political, military and social) control over another nation. The colonized nation is unable to exercise sovereignty at any level. It is a specific form of imperial domination. Today, it exists only in a few places.

Neocolonialism: The main feature of neocolonialism is the economic domination of nominally independent nations by one nation or a group of powerful nations. It usually entails cultural and diplomatic domination as well. It is another form of imperialism.

Neoliberalism: This term represents the current stage of capitalism whose main features are domination of national and global economies by mega-corporations and financial firms, liberalization and privatization, defunding of social services, low tax for the wealthy, weakening of labor unions and popular movements, and enhanced economic and cultural dependency of the poor nations on the industrialized nations. This system generates extreme levels of economic inequality across the world and generates intense social antagonisms within nations.

Socialism: A socialist society is characterized by emphasis on equality, mutual support and cooperation, grass-roots democracy, control by the common people of the means of production, exchange and finance, and a striving of decent existence for all.

Ideology: An individual's overall conceptual framework for viewing and making sense of the world around him or her is his or her ideology. In a class-based society, the dominant ideology represents an inversion of reality; the people come to believe and accept the opposite of what prevails. Capitalist ideology values the individual, not the community, and stresses competition, not cooperation and presents the existing economic order as the only viable system for humanity. In reality, the individuals who are valued by the system are those from the top 1%.

It is important to note that these terms do not represent emotive labels but empirically grounded and logically formulated concepts that are of use in understanding the broad dynamics of societal development in the past and the present.

EDUCATION AND UNDER-DEVELOPMENT

In a society that is not only class-based but is also dominated by another nation, the education system is further constricted. The notion of underdevelopment popularized by Walter Rodney in his magisterial work *How Europe Underdeveloped Africa* is apropos here. His book regards development as a process that generally improves the modes of life and communication, and the levels of health, contentment and education of the people. It gives more freedom to the people to participate in cultural activities and a greater choice in how they live their lives. In sum:

> [D]evelopment implies an increasing capacity [of a people] to regulate both internal and external relationships (Rodney 1972, page 3).

According to Rodney underdevelopment and undevelopment are not the same concepts. The latter denotes a low level of economic and social progress. Underdevelopment, on the other hand, is characterized by the progressive loss by a people of the ability to control their destiny. That loss is caused by the installation of structures of external dependency in the economy, health, education, culture and state organs, transfer of societal wealth to external entities, and a vast gap between the dominant and dominated nation in terms of technological capacity, infrastructure, social amenities and standard of life. It induces a pattern of stratification whereby the local economic and political elites together with foreign elements prosper at the expense of the masses. Underdevelopment generates extensive poverty, social tensions and conflict, yet makes the people believe that without the external savior, they would be worse off.

The corresponding concept for education in dependent, class-based societies is under-education. It does not mean lack of education as such or miseducation at a purely ideological level. Under-education can occur even when the nation sees an expansion of the number of schools and colleges and their enrollment. It can occur even when more and more of the youth acquire university degrees. It is characterized by the following features:

- A disconnect between the education system and the economy.
- A rapid, poorly regulated expansion of the education system, especially of private schools and colleges.
- Dependence on external sources for funds for facilities, instruction, curriculum development and planning.
- Proliferation of low quality education programs.
- Inculcation negative attitudes towards all that is local, and worship of all that is foreign.
- An extreme level of educational inequality.
- Superficial and memory based learning devoid of critical thought even at the discipline level.
- Prevalence of unprofessional conduct among the educators and unethical practices among the students.

Under-development in Africa began in the days of pre-colonial contact with Europe, gained a firm footing in the colonial era, and was further entrenched, in a somewhat different form, in the neocolonial, neoliberal times. The establishment and dynamics of systems of under-education in the continent reflected that underlying political-economic process.

The basic aim of this book is to uncover, describe and critique, over this historic period, the diverse facets of under-education in one nation of Africa, Tanzania. Starting from the German colonial era in the late 1890s to the post-Independence period, especially the days of *Ujamaa* style socialism and onto the current neoliberal times, it interrogates the school and higher education systems in this nation in terms of content, relevance, social function, fair access, quality of instruction, depth of scholarship, use of modern technology, inculcation of humane values and fostering the spirit of independent inquiry. Disharmonies within the education system and between it and the rest of society are explored as well. Particular attention is paid to the efforts in the post-Independence days that critiqued under-education and sought to replace it with more relevant and appropriate education. Two essays point to the existence of under-education in the minority, deprived neighborhoods of the US.

The 1960s saw emergence of valiant efforts to confront the system of miseducation in Europe and North America. It was a part of an overall struggle against the inequities and injustices of the capitalist, imperialist system. The US aggression against Vietnam was a major catalyst in this struggle. Correspondingly, there were similar efforts to confront under-education in Africa, Asia and Latin America as a part of the broader struggles against imperial domination. The University of Dar es Salaam in the 1960s and 1970s was a leading light in that effort. What transpired in these endeavors is the focus of several essays in the book. In the light of frequent misleading narrations of that history, I also tackle the crucial issue of accurate representation of history.

While the approach of the essays is a critical one that exposes the major shortfalls in the existing system, they also suggest possible ways of confronting under-education and establishing an educational structure to help generate well-grounded, intellectually astute persons who are committed to the transformation of the flawed system and the neoliberal society it serves.[1]

Under-education and under-development are two sides of the same coin. The struggle against one has of necessity to be a struggle against the other. Mental liberation must be contemporaneous and coordinated with social and material liberation.

---

1. Unless otherwise stated, the material and comments in each essay are circumscribed in terms of the conditions prevailing at the time it was written. For example, what is written about computers in education in Essay 4 reflects the types of computer technology and communication avenues available in Tanzania in the early 1990s while what is written about the same issues in Essay 7 reflects the situation around the year 2010. When going through these essays, the reader is advised to keep such historic specificities in mind.

1

EDUCATION AND COLONIALISM

SUMMARY: This essay deals with the missionary education system in the pre-colonial and German colonial periods, and the German colonial governmental system of education in mainland Tanzania. Key features of the present day education system in Tanzania – external dependency, dismal quality education for the majority, inequality and deficient integration between the economy and education – are seen to have been instituted in those earlier days when the foundation of an under-developed economy were also laid. Under-education has long and deep roots and can only be tackled with sustained efforts on all fronts, political, economic, social and educational.[1]

*

---

1. This essay was first published as Hirji KF (1980) Colonial ideological apparatuses in Tanganyika under the Germans, in MHY Kaniki (editor) (1980) *Tanzania Under Colonial Rule*, Longmans, London. This is a shortened and extensively edited version.

> *There were a few farsighted Europeans*
> *who all along saw that*
> *the colonial educational system would serve them*
> *if and when*
> *political independence was regained in Africa.*
> Walter Rodney
> ++++++++++

A PRELIMINARY REMARK

THE DOMINANT VALUES and perspectives on life and society held by the people in a society constitute the ideology of that society. The varied institutions, formal and informal, that generate, elaborate, sustain and disseminate the ideology are called the **ideological apparatuses** of the society. This essay deals with the ideological apparatuses operating in mainland Tanzania just prior to and during the era of German colonial rule from 1885 to 1914. They were the Christian missions and schools, Islamic schools and government schools. I describe their evolution and function, and relate them to the broader economic and social conditions and conflicts in the colony.

PRE-COLONIAL MISSIONARY EDUCATION

Before the influx of missionaries in the latter half of the nineteenth century, some European and American companies were already trading along the East African coast. Based on the island of Zanzibar, they bought ivory and gum, and sold guns, cloth, brandy, etc. British gunboats patrolled the coastal line to halt the export of slaves. The slave trade had become an impediment to the development of capitalism. Africa no longer was to be the source of cheap labor for American and West Indian plantations. Capitalist industry required raw materials and markets for its manufactured goods.

It was at this historical juncture that European missionaries appeared on the East African scene. The first missionaries came from Britain, the most advanced capitalist nation of the time. Missionaries prepared the groundwork for the complete colonization of the area. It is not that all of them were consciously allied with imperial ambitions; they held differing views (Wright 1971, page 7). But whether they did or not is not the point. History is rarely preconceived. Very few people act with an awareness of their objective historical roles. Yet, the missionary pioneers did possess a degree of clarity about their historical mission. David Livingstone, the inspirational architect of missionary endeavor portrayed Africa as a place of suffering souls to be saved from sin and damnation. His conception of redemption was, however, material and spiritual. Africa was in need of commerce as well as Christianity. Influenced by him, the dignitaries of the Anglican Church founded the University Mission to Central Africa (UMCA) to establish *'centers of Christianity and civilization for the promotion of true religion, agriculture and commerce.'* (Oliver 1969, page 13).

It was a view supported by the merchant class in Britain. After his death, a group of Glasgow businessmen raised UK pounds 10,000 to finance such ventures. Two missions were set up near Lake Nyasa and a steamer was commissioned to stimulate trade. The Livingston Central African Trading Company was established by James Stevenson of Glasgow, *'with the dual object of supplying the two missions and bringing out ivory at a price which would undercut the Arab merchants.'* (Oliver 1969, page 13).

Livingstone's death provided a further impetus to missionary effort. The UMCA and the Church Missionary Society (CMS) spread inland and the French Cardinal, Lavigeri, toured European capitals to promote a similar movement in the Catholic Church. The Holy Ghost Fathers (HGF) set up a mission station at Bagamoyo in 1868. By 1872, it comprised twenty-four European priests and nuns and 324 ex-slaves, including 251 children. By 1885, five missionary societies had established themselves in Tanzania, namely the UMCA, CMS, HGF, the Lutheran Missionary Society (LMS), and the White Fathers (WF). At the outset, they stayed in the coastal areas but later went inland and established their respective spheres of influence.

Idealized versions of missionary settlements depict a picture in which missionaries encountered a friendly reception from the *'suffering natives'* and their chiefs who then fell under their *'civilizing'* influence and adopted Christianity. In reality:

> *The missionary who set out with a few dozen porters and tried to settle in a native village had to set up what amounted to a small independent state. He was recognized as a kind of chief by the headmen round about and to a greater or lesser extent the Sultan of Zanzibar and the British or French consul were felt to be behind him, as they were felt to be behind any other caravan manned with porters from the coast.* (Oliver 1969, page 50).

The early missionary followed the established trade routes and settled in the proximity of a trading center. A more or less self-contained station grew its own food, had its own laws and a rudimentary police force to maintain order and for defense. The chief European missionary was the supreme authority at the station. By 1890, the WF station at Kibanga on the shores of Lake Tanganyika had vast plantations growing rice, maize, oil palms, sweet potatoes, bananas, sugar cane and vegetables. The work was done by the converts who worked three days a week on the mission plantation. The rest were spent on their own plots. They received a few pieces of cloth as wages.

The main aim of the missionaries was to propagate their faith. Most of their initial converts were ex-slaves who had no choice but to adopt Christianity. Freed by the British, they had been passed on to the mission for cultural enslavement. The fear of recapture and the lack of means to return to his home area forced the ex-slave to remain in the mission. And many were young children. A few missions bought slaves to swell the ranks of their converts! Once on the station, he or she was required to accept the Gospel and follow the rules governing life there. The villages which sprung up in the vicinity of the early mission station were often started by former slaves or refugees from the tribes in the area. Besides learning the elements of the gospel, the potential converts helped in building the station and maintaining production.

After settling down, the missions sought converts beyond the adjacent areas. They gained their foothold in various ways. The initial reception accorded and their success depended on the economic and political situation at these places. In areas ravaged by famine or disease, or where the population had been dislocated by inter-tribal conflict, they had an easier time. It was more arduous to make headway into the prosperous tribes that had maintained good links with coastal traders. In Mahenge, the first missionaries faced vigorous opposition, and their mission was ransacked by the people.

Converting the local chief was a key goal, as it removed a major impediment and allowed them to work more freely. Presents chosen with care sufficed at times to win them over. Elsewhere, the chiefs wanted a mission for reasons of diplomacy. The superior technology and tools from the missionary reinforced his standing among his own and nearby populations.

Provision of basic education was a useful tool to speed up the rate of conversion. A literate congregation absorbed religious ideas by reading the Bible and participated better in activities like hymn-singing. (Mgonde 1966, page 2). Health and education facilities attracted people and were used to spread religious ideas. At the Kipalapala station where no public preaching occurred until 1885, every opportunity was taken to talk to the adults individually at the dispensary and elsewhere. Some missions provided a sanctuary in times of tribal conflict as well.

The WF mission near Tabora in the 1890s gives a representative picture of the evolution of the early stations. The initial years were spent in building a church, a school and residential houses for the white priests. The African Christians and their families lived close by and regularly took part in church activities. They also did construction work and cleared the areas for farming. Gradually a complex emerged where evangelical work, literacy training, farming, construction activities and nursing sick patients were done. The missionaries went to the adjacent villages to invite the chiefs to come to the mission.

Missionary educational activities evolved in this context. Literacy was a means to impart Christian beliefs and rudimentary education gradually became the main tool for conversion. Manual work and training for practical jobs became integral features of mission schooling. The pupils engaged in productive and construction activities. For example, at the HGF station in Bagamoyo, the pupils spent five and a half hours a day in the classroom and five and a half hours in practical work which was either farm work or craftsmanship. Some were trained as carpenters or masons to meet the need for skilled labor. Some children, categorized as unfit for literary training, had only one hour of elementary studies; the rest of their day was spent in the field. (Nolan 1971, page 51).

Without local manpower, the missionaries could only cover small areas and influence few people. The need for local *'priests'* was acutely felt as mission activities expanded. And it was not just a matter of numbers. In area where the chiefs were hostile to the Fathers, visits by a couple of local `*priests'* made friendly relations possible. Communication problems were also eased. (Nolan 1971, page 52).

Missionaries emphasized catechist training right from the early days. Many ex-slave converts were trained to carry Christianity to the people. The best pupils at the HGF school in Bagamoyo were dispatched to the seminary in Zanzibar. At the WF mission near Tabora, catechists were trained over a period of four years. Their training comprised elementary literacy, Bible study and productive work on the mission. On completion, they were sent to distant villages to spread the Gospel, representing a qualitative change in missionary endeavor. Conversion via direct contact with Europeans was augmented with local effort. Local church workers who had internalized the Christian ideology now diffused it and turned it into a wider phenomenon.

In the process of adopting Christianity and memorizing Biblical texts, the catechist came to reject his tribal customs and beliefs. He was told to be a self-sacrificing, devoted Christian not concerned about material rewards and comforts but about propagating the faith. Hard work was for a greater cause. But pay was meager; the WF missions paid TSh 6 a month to local priests in 1919. Yet, they were among the first Africans to receive regular cash remuneration for work not just of a manual labor kind.

Missionary teachings went against local customs and traditions. Their effort to neutralize such beliefs led to conflicts with the locals. The tactics varied from place to place. At times, they partly adapted to local beliefs at the outset. It minimized alienating the chiefs and the villagers. A few missionaries interpreted local views in Christian terms. Some deployed their scientific knowledge to mystify the people or disprove their beliefs. In other areas they attempted to directly suppress traditional practices. In the Ungoni area, for example, the head of the Peramiho mission ordered the destruction of Nkosi Mputa's *mahoka hut*. Mahoka worship was seen as mere idolatry. (Mapunda and Mpangara 1968, page 14).

Whatever the tactic, the discordance with age-old customs and ideas which did not reflect Christian precepts could not be wished away. They had a concrete basis in tribal societies. External interference generated intense hostility. Catechists were a major instrument in overcoming this hurdle. Looked upon by the people as one who knew the ways of the white man, he was their future image. Being a local, he worked among them with relative ease. His session would be a combination of recitation of holy verses and singing hymns with denunciation of customs frowned upon by the missionaries. They included polygamy, folk dances, and `superstitious' practices. His objective role was to de-culture the people and imbue them with a foreign ideology.

In areas where Muslim influence prevailed, the missionaries had a harder time. It was the case along the coastal areas as well as in places like the shores of Lake Tanganyika where the LMS had constructed its stations. Besides the ideological conflict, a deep-rooted material conflict also existed. Muslim traders from the coast had entrenched themselves in many parts of the country. In places, they were allied with chiefs who commanded a large following. The traders, backed by the Sultanate of Zanzibar, dominated the territory's internal and external trade.

The coastal traders and European merchants needed each other's services at the outset and so did not interfere in each other's domain. The European traders brought commodities to Zanzibar for exchange with goods from the interior. The inland import of manufactured goods and export of local items was monopolized by the coastal traders, who used porter caravans to carry the goods. The contention was over the export of slaves being curbed by the British navy. But now ivory trade was more profitable than slave trade. The porters in the caravans were mostly wage-workers, not slaves.

The penetration of missionaries into the interior slowly upset the détente between the two merchant classes. Their activities undermined the ideological, economic and political positions of the coastal traders. In the final analysis, the missionaries represented interests of European capital. (Arnold 1979).

> [The missionaries] *were employers of labor and therefore dispensers of calico and trade goods. For the erection of their stations, even the simpler ones, they required the assistance of hundreds of Africans, and for their daily existence they needed food and firewood, cooks, gardeners, and many other services. The transport of their supplies alone became quite an industry. Hore employed more than 1,000 porters to carry an open steel boat overland to Ujiji in 1882; a figure of two or three hundred was quite common for the routine caravan bringing up tinned food and missionaries' chattels, European building material and barter goods.* (Oliver 1969, page 69).

Weakening of the monopolistic positions of the coastal traders occurred jointly with the erosion of their political standing *vis-a-vis* the chiefs in the interior. The missionaries now supplied the imported goods previously supplied by them. They employed the chiefs' subjects. And when they managed to convert a chief or his subjects, their position was enhanced.

To cap it all, the missionaries were followed by the European trading companies which had operated from Zanzibar since 1849. By the early 1870s about a quarter of `Zanzibar's trade was with Germany.' (Lubetsky 1972, page 7). These firms now penetrated inland to establish trading outposts. As a result, the contradiction between them and the missionaries on the one part and the coastal traders on the other sharpened. (Oliver 1969, page 117). In places it became violent. For example,

> Karonga in 1891 was like an armed fort, with three cannons and a garrison of over a hundred men, its stockade being guarded by watches of four men each night to warn of the attacks from Mlozi, the Swahili trader with whom the African Lake Company had a commercial feud. (Wright 1971, page 44).

The struggle broadened after the German East Africa Company was granted the charter to administer Tanganyika. Besides the ruthlessness of the company's agents, the conflict between the merchant classes was a basic cause behind the 1889 uprising against the company. Centered in coastal districts, it was led by Bushiri, a prosperous merchant, and Bwana Heri, a major trading chief. Its leaders were `town notables'. (Lubetsky 1972, page 8). Company posts and missions thought to be its outposts, such as the Benedictine mission at Pugu, were attacked.

The suppression of the uprising finally relegated the coastal traders to a subordinate position in relation to the colonizers. Bushiri had led a popular movement against the German invaders, but it ended with a compromise between the local commercial class and the Germans. The colonialists realized that they could not totally dispense with the service of the coastal traders.

> As [the resistance] collapsed, the Germans negotiated with a peace party of Omani aristocrats, who then became the agents of a bureaucratic system of government, providing each major coastal town with a liwali (governor) and the hinterland with subordinate administrators called akidas. (Iliffe 1972, page 13).

Company rule was abolished and the era of direct German colonialism over mainland Tanzania began.

COLONIAL CONSOLIDATION, 1885-1905

The first two decades of German colonial rule were marked by efforts to consolidate political hegemony over the territory. They were also the years which witnessed the inception of the fundamental elements of the colonial socioeconomic structure. (Rodney 1980). Land alienated from the people in various parts of the colony was given to the missions, the incoming tide of settlers, the German enterprises or appropriated by the administration. Production of cash crops on a large scale commenced. Taxes were imposed. The people were, directly or indirectly, compelled to work on plantations for extremely low wages. An infrastructure and communication network to serve the colonial enterprise was constructed. The colonial state took shape and entrenched its authority.

The basic problem was to establish law and order. The *'recalcitrant natives'* must submit. But they did not submit readily and fiercely resisted the imposition of colonial rule. First against the German East Africa Company and later against the government, the struggle raged in many areas, culminating in the *Maji Maji* war of 1905. The German army was made up of *askaris* recruited from the coast and other parts of Africa who were led by German officers. Bloody battles with resisting tribes ensued. A common tactic used by the Germans was to play off one chief against another to conquer both.

Pacification did not occur purely through force. It was facilitated by the judicious utilization of the ideological apparatus in the colony. They used both the missionary and Muslim religious educational systems and elements of the tribal social structure to consolidate their rule. Missionary effort continued to create the psychological climate for colonization and the Islamic school system facilitated the administration of the colony. We first examine the role of latter.

ISLAM AND COLONIALISM

The Germans did not utilize the Islamic institutions as a result of a liking for Islam, but for political expediency and practicality. It was a classic example of how an emergent social formation can modify the social and political elements of the previous formation to serve its own needs. When later the political conditions which had made the Germans utilize Muslim personnel from the coast were no longer in operation, Islamic elements had become a part and parcel of the colonial administrative machine.

As the uprising against the German East African Company was put down and a compromise with coastal traders reached, the colonialists realized that they needed not only commercial service but also political assistance from the coastal *'aristocrats'* in their campaign to pacify and govern the interior. The social and political institutions which had existed along the coast before their arrival were employed to serve colonial ends. In coastal town, the *liwalis* continued to be the civil administrators. But now they reported to the German governor. As available Europeans were too few, Swahili-speaking personnel from the coast were recruited as junior administrators, tax collectors, clerks and interpreters. The coastal elements associated with the traders became *liwalis* and *akidas*, while the commoners swelled the ranks of the *askaris*. Many of them were products of the *Quran* schools which had long functioned along the coast.

These schools had pioneered the provision of literacy training in the territory. In the process of reciting the *Quran* in Arabic, the pupils learnt how to read and write and do simple arithmetic. Their literacy skills and knowledge of the interior areas proved of benefit to the Germans. (Iliffe 1972, page 181).

The importance of the *Quran* schools declined rapidly after the colonial government started its own school system. (AR 1901/1902, page 19). Though the *akidas* and *liwalis* continued to be recruited mostly from the coast, they now had passed through government schools.

The use of Swahili speakers to man the colonial administration had important consequences. Not least was the emergence of Swahili as the *lingua franca* of the territory. Swahili had evolved over centuries as a result of fusion of Arabic and Bantu languages. It was the main language along the coast. The decision of the colonialists to use it as one of the two official languages accelerated its spread into the interior. In the long run, it promoted the secularization of the language. Most of the official correspondence was conducted in Swahili. The colonial administrator had to learn Swahili at the Orientiale Seminar in Berlin before taking up a post in Tanganyika.

The Germans made use of three components of the Islamic social apparatus: personnel, political institutions and language. An inevitable corollary was the spread of Islam. Conversion to Islam thereby gathered momentum in the German era. Besides other forces propelling it, the German policy indirectly became a contributing factor.

Inevitably, the Christian missionaries and the colonial government came into a prolonged conflict over the issue. The missionaries accused the government of favoring Islam, an allegation it flatly rejected. They opposed the importance accorded to Swahili, and gave preference to German or local vernacular languages. But there were a few exceptions. Some missions had adopted Swahili from the early days and produced Swahili dictionaries (Smith 1963, page 99; Abdulaziz 1972, pages 156-157). Disputes over such issues, however, did not derail the foundational unity between the missions and colonial authorities. Their long run goals were complementary. We now turn our attention to the relationship between the missionary ideological apparatus and colonialism.

CHRISTIANITY AND COLONIALISM

The upsurge of oversees activities of the German missionary societies had coincided with Germany's attempts to acquire colonial possessions. In Tanganyika, a number of German missionary societies had followed in the footsteps of the German East Africa

Company. The Benedictine mission was founded in 1885 with the financial assistance from Freiherr von Gravenreuth—a principle shareholder of this company. After setting up its first station in Dar as Salaam, it ventured inland as far as Peramiho and Madibara. Berlin III, a German missionary foundation, was established around this period. One of its aims was to teach the *'natives'* to work on the plantations. Accordingly, its penetration *'followed exactly the line of colonial occupation'*. (Oliver 1969, page 96). The Moravians went towards Lake Nyasa while the Leipzig Missionary Society replaced the British CMS on the slopes of Mount Kilimanjaro after the latter was accused of inciting the Chaggas against the German administration.

The lead spokespersons for colonialism in Germany had rather crude views about the colonial project and the role of the missions. Preferring strong-arm tactics to *'discipline the natives,'* they had a pragmatic stand. Count Pleil, a founder of the German Colonization Society, advised a missionary congress in Germany in 1886 that in the colonies, *'they should teach less of the dangerous doctrine of brotherhood and equality and give all instructions in practical tasks.'* (Smith 1963, page 99). That is, their only role was to train the colonized people to work for the government and the settlers.

The missionaries did not accept such a crude characterization of their *'civilizing mission.'* The director of Berlin III sharply criticized Count Pleil. They took a border view. Thus the congress resolved that:

> German missions, Evangelical and Catholic alike, should be encouraged to take an active part in the realization of a national colonial program; in other words, they should not restrict their activities to mission work but should help to establish German culture and German thought in the colonies. (Helbert 1965, page 92).

The missionaries' role was not just to make the colonized person work but to make him *consent* to work for the colonizers; to make him accept the colonial system. Ideological enslavement was essential for smooth colonial economic exploitation. The *kiboko* (whip) had to be augmented by a mental weapon. Here lay the fundamental tasks of the missionary system: to ensure the spread and reproduction of the colonial ideology; to justify and rationalize colonialism as *'a will of God'*; to inculcate Christian morality and preach submissiveness and humility as prime virtues. Karl Marx's depiction of religion as *'the sigh of the oppressed creature, the sentiment of a heartless world and the soul of a soulless condition'* aptly sums up the manifestation of religion under colonial rule. (Bottomore and Rubel 1967, page 41).

In the field, the missions and the administrators soon realized their identity of interests. (Oliver 1969, page 178). In the Ungoni area, for example, the missions were on good terms with the district authority from the early days. Where the people put up vigorous opposition to colonial rule, missionaries were used to win them over. To subdue the militant Wahehe, *'the governor (Von Soden) urged the Berlin mission to penetrate the Uhehe to make peaceful contact'* (Wright 1971, page 50). But under Mkwawa they fought bitterly until they were defeated by the better armed and organized German forces. This struggle affected the mission in terms of its areas of operation (Wright 1971, page 67).

In those areas where missions had been operating before the advent of colonial rule, the German forces found it relatively easier to establish their authority. The people did not find the demands made completely new, as they had partly been conditioned to work for and accept *'the white man's ways.'* Life became more arduous but they had already been influenced to participate in the commercial culture.

> At a time when law and order, the introduction of currency, the promotion of local trade and the beginning of taxation were the main preoccupations of government, mission employees and adherents stood out from the rest as prosperous and orderly. They paid their taxes and understood the new regime. (Oliver 1969, page 171).

The missionaries derived many benefits from their alliance with the authorities. Where they came into serious conflict with the local chiefs or when the missions took over large tracts of land, the backing of the colonial officials was critical. On occasion, the district authorities enlisted them to carry out land survey and vaccination campaigns. It enhanced their prestige and provided direct contact with a large number of people. The Evangelical mission in Tanga, a predominantly Muslim area, was permitted in 1903 to preach the gospel regularly *'to prisoners in the Boma'*. (AR 1901/1902, page 20; Wright 1971, pages 55-56, 72, 78, 101).

Some district authorities accepted work on mission lands as a substitute for payment of taxes. (Wright 1971, page 102). The catechists were exempted from paying *corvee*. In carrying the *'Word of God'* to the *'native'*, the catechist was also assisting in making him submit to the rule of capital. He often `assumed leadership in civil and political affairs in the village'*. (Nolan 1971, page 56). In areas like Mahenge and Bukoba, the district commissioners assisted the growth of mission schools. Under the protective umbrella of colonial rule, missions and missionary activities grew rapidly, and their influence spread proportionately.

At times, differences between the missionaries and the authorities did arise. The exercise of political power by the missionaries was a key bone of contention. The administration could not accept the unlimited authority exercised by some missionaries at their stations. (Wright 1971, pages 78-80). Eventually, all the missions accepted the imperative of operating under the colonial administration.

The missionary education system experienced a rapid growth. The increasing output of catechists led to a rapid expansion of *'bush school'* – which were open to all and run by low paid catechists – in villages beyond the mission. Often, it was no more than a gathering under a tree. The bush schools fed the central mission schools, many of which were boarding schools. With pupils under supervision all the time, these schools were more effective than day schools. Local teachers and church workers assisted in running the schools and the mission. The Lutheran mission in Iringa, for example, employed African aides to conduct sermons in the villages and teach in the school. Besides, they:

> help the missionary in carrying out the station orders; they mediate in the intercourse between the missionary and natives (Christians and pagans) residing in the area of the stations; they collect donations to the church and keep accounts on them, at the acceptance of applicant for baptism and their eligibility for admission to the church by baptism, these aides are being consulted. (AR 1901/1902, Supplement A.IV, page 26).

The mission schools gradually developed into fully fledged primary schools which also imparted vocational education. The subjects taught were religion, Bible history, hymn singing, reading, writing and arithmetic. Instruction was mostly in the vernacular though some missions also taught German and Kiswahili. Catechists and primary school teachers were trained. The promising pupils were ear-marked for priesthood and sent to the main seminary. Practical skills taught included agriculture, carpentry, masonry and shoe-making, and in one school, printing work. Crafts education helped meet the need for artisans at the missions and the settler farms. Basic literacy qualified the recipient for a clerical job with the government or the plantation. (Smith 1963, pages 100,108, Schadler 1968, page 111).

The pupils served the mission. (AR 1901/1902, AR 1902/1903). They undertook road construction; built schools, churches and missionary houses; manned the large commercial farms growing coffee, cotton, and vegetables; and looked after cattle and poultry. According to the Trappist Mission:

> The black people must be taught through work and prayers. The natives must learn that work and prayers are essential for them, they must realize that work is an honor, that they cannot prosper without it and the necessary education. The one who does not work will be chased away and will never get the benefit of Christening. (AR 1901/1902, Supplement A.IV, pages 39-40)

By one estimate, 171 mission stations scattered over mainland Tanzania operated in 1912 with a European staff of 616, and 1,694 African aides. The latter included catechists and primary school teachers. The missions also ran 1,119 schools, including bush schools, with the total number of pupils at 105,197. (Smith 1963, page 107).

GOVERNMENT SCHOOLS

In addition to the mission and *Quran* schools, a government system of education evolved during the colonial era. The former could not satisfy the administrative demand for literate and skilled personnel. Much of the output of the mission school remained within its own ambit as catechists, teachers and mission workers. A portion went to the plantations and the settlers. Only a small percentage was left for the state, and there too the Swahili requirement posed a problem for the mission-educated clerk in the early days. The *Quran* schools had more limitations.

The governmental demand for trained manpower was basically of two types; artisans and white collar workers. The latter manned the lower and middle ranks of the administration. Skilled craftsmen worked *'in the workshops of the `Kaiseriche Flottille', the imperial navy, the railways where cooper-smiths, boiler makers, turners and casters were employed.'* (Schadler 1968, page 52). Also required were blacksmiths, masons, leather workers and carpenters.

The colonial economic policies led to a decline of traditional crafts and skills along the coast and in the interior. And the traditional craftsmen who were utilized proved to be insufficient or unqualified to meet the demand. In the early years, it was met through importation, mostly from the Indian sub-continent. They were also employed in the government schools to teach their respective trades. (AR 1901/1902, page 5). It took some time for the government and mission schools to produce sufficient numbers of skilled artisans.

The first government schools were started along the coast where the administrative apparatus was better set up and demand for manpower, the greatest. Schools were set up in Tanga and then in Bagamoyo, Dar as Salaam and Lindi. Most pupils were Swahili speakers. An official circular spelled out the aims:

> a) *To enable the native to be used in Government administration.*
> b) *To inculcate a liking for order, cleanliness, diligence and dutifulness and a sound knowledge of German customs and patriotism.* (Cameron and Dodd, 1970, page 56).

With Swahili the language of instruction, the curriculum included Swahili, German, Arithmetic, Geography, Natural History, Drawing, Singing, Music and Gymnastics. The education was functional, directly related to the job the pupils were expected to take up after completing the school. Thus:

> *Each pupil in the first grade must be capable of independent compilation of lists and tables concerning payments, taxes, etc.* (AR 1901/1902, page 61).

The pupils had to do manual work as well. A brief review of the evolution of the Tanga School illustrates these points. In 1892, it comprised a single room, a few pupils and a teacher, a German who spoke fluent Swahili – the outcome of training at the Orientiale Seminar in Berlin. As determined by the need for clerks and interpreters, only reading, writing and the German language were taught at first. It was enlarged as the school had to supply a diverse category of office personnel and junior administrators. By 1897, it had 96 pupils and was made into a boarding school. The pupils were given basic necessities and shelter but cooked their own food. Construction of new buildings, done largely by the boys, began in 1890. They brought beach stones on their heads to the site. At high tide, they waded into the sea to get them. (Hornsby 1962, page 148).

The school started to train *fundis* In 1899. The following year, more than 400 pupils attended classes in standards I to VI. A teacher training and a technical department were established. By 1904, the latter was bringing out carpenters, printers, bookbinders, tailors, blacksmiths and bricklayers.

By 1902, there were three main government schools (Bagamoyo, Dar es Salaam and Tanga) and three subsidiary schools (Kilwa, Pangani and Lindi). Their set-up was similar. A few hinterland make-shift 'schools' run by the district authorities also operated.

An important feature of the government (and the mission) schools was the contribution of pupils towards the cost of their education and the development of the colonial economy. (AR 1908/1909, page 189). The value of the work they did while at school matched the expenses in the construction, teaching materials, maintaining school facilities, paying the teachers, etc. In coastal townships, special levies were imposed to meet costs not covered by the pupils' labor. The direct financial contribution of the government towards developing and running the education system was insignificant. The hinterland schools in Tanga district were allotted a coconut plantation so that the

> pupils acquire already from their youth an interest in and liking of plants and soil; and the revenues enabled the schools to obtain financial means for their equipment and enlargement. (AR 1901/1902, page 56).

The annual report of the crafts school in Kilwa for the year 1907-8 notes:

> All expense for material and so on, wages for colored workers, as well as the living expenses of the apprentices could be covered by its own revenues. (AR 1907/1908, page 95).

What remained was the salary of one European teacher which was paid for by the residents of Kilwa town. In the same year, residents of Lindi contributed some 5,500 rupees to meet the expenses of the government school. (AR 1907/1908, page 96). The contribution of the Technical School in Dar as Salaam to the colonial economy during the year 1908-1909 was given as:

> the completion of furniture of various styles, also the repair of buildings,

> *furniture; turning and wagon building; also the construction of a bridge over the Simbosi at Kissarawe, three bridges on the Kissarawe to Kassi road and a bridge on the road to Magogoni.* (AR 1908/1909, page 189).

And this was accomplished by 19 pupils! The contribution of the Tanga School pupils was greater. Besides working in the school farm, they transported, with their hands and feet, timber, stones, limestone, sand and clay from the source to building sites. Some pupils went daily to the local meteorological station to record instrument readings, and others assisted in *'the administration of the saving bank and town library. Seven senior pupils ably lent assistance in accountancy, book-keeping and stocktaking.'* (AR 1908/1909, page 189). To cap it all, by this time all the government printing was done at Tanga School. Further, in 1902, 12 pupils of this school were trained to join the heliography unit of the colonial armed forces. (AR 1901/1902, page 55).

The pupils of this school played a major role in the expansion of the state education system. They printed books and made equipment for other schools. The carpentry apprentices were sent to interior schools.

> *There, they have to furnish the school building and the teacher's flat, according to their own plan and specifications, with professionally constructed doors, windows, tables, school-benches, and with everything else the school needs in wooden utensils.'* (AR 1901/1902, page 56).

A balance-sheet of the efforts of the pupils would explode the myth that colonialism was an *'educational enterprise.'* Not only was education meant to assist economic exploitation of the colony, but it was the pupils who put up a large part of the educational edifice.

OUTPUT OF MAIN GOVERNMENT SCHOOLS, 1908[2]

SCHOOL	EMPLOYMENT
Kilwa School	3 telegraphists, 1 postman, 1 clerk and 2 sent for craftsmen training.
Lindi School	5 clerks, 3 assistant teachers, 2 houseboys.
Tanga School	6 assistant teachers, 2 writers with district administrators, 1 with meteorological station, 4 as assistants in hospital, 6 postmen, 2 with railways, 11 as clerks with planters, merchants and a*kidas*, 8 carpenters, 7 compositors and 7 printers.

At the outset, African teachers got a salary of one rupee per month, and an annual increment of one rupee per month. They were

---

2. Source: AR 1907/1908.

accorded the status of a qualified teacher and a salary of twelve rupees per month after some years of teaching (Hornsby 1962).

Life in the government schools was tough. Discipline was strict and punishments, including flogging, severe. When some pupils at the Tanga School protested for being kept there by force, the authorities put them *'in the chains'* for a week. The scale of punishment at this school was: minor offences – six strokes, major offences – twelve strokes. Here as in other schools, African teachers found absent from duty were thrashed *'in front of the whole school'*. (Hornsby 1964, page 89).

The teaching methods reveal the oppressive character of the colonial rule. The following example is a case in point. Bishop Weston of the UMCA visited the Lindi government school in 1903 where the boys were being trained to be minor government officials. One of the lessons he watched dealt with *'the laws governing the action of native magistrates'*.

> I heard small boys recite the laws dealing with the powers of majumbe or village magistrates, and the master showed me the book itself, a most formidable volume which each boy must get by heart. Then on Wednesdays and Saturdays the school attends the Government Court, listens to all the cases, witnesses all the flogging. (Hornsby 1964, page 85).

Some combination of education in the theory and practice of oppression!

By 1902, some 4,000 pupils attended the government schools across the territory. During the entire period of German rule in Tanganyika not a single girl studied in any of the government schools.

Initially, the children of the colonial administrators and settlers received their education in Europe. Two schools for the Europeans were established later in Dar as Salaam and Meru areas.

THE MAJIMAJI WAR

The colonial invaders had encountered resistance wherever they had gone. For two decades from 1885, the colonial forces had faced battles in one place or another virtually each year. But the struggles had been localized. It changed in 1905 with the outbreak of freedom struggles in almost the entire southern part of Tanzania. It was the *Maji Maji* war.

The immediate cause was the cotton scheme implemented along the coast and in the south. (Iliffe 1972, page 23). Each village had to cultivate cotton in an allocated area. It was funded by a group of German textile manufactures who sought an alternative to the high priced cotton from America. Payment was meager and treatment, harsh. Beginning in the Rufiji area, the people said no more and fought back. Once kindled, it spread like a prairie fire in the south.

Colonial officials, the *akidas*, traders and missionaries closely identified with the state were attacked.

The rural peasant formed the backbone of struggle but the leadership came from dissident elements of the traditional ruling groups and the lower sections of the emergent African middle class. (Iliffe 1972, page 23). The uprising was suppressed with utmost brutality; the leaders were executed. In some areas, only prolonged famine, caused by the war and reinforced by deliberate measures of the authorities, sapped the fighting spirit. The mobilizing ideology was based on superstition. But the defeat stemmed mainly from inferior technology and lack of organization.

The unfolding of this struggle underscored a key historical truth: To perpetuate economic exploitation it is essential to complement physical repression with ideological obfuscation. The colonial ideological system, especially the mission system, had not functioned in vain. In the affected areas, missionaries were in general spared. Further, `several mission-educated groups refused to participate in the uprising'. (Mbilinyi 1972, page 40).

Lubetsky comprehensively shows that the areas more fully integrated into the colonial socioeconomic network did not participate in *Maji Maji*. The chiefs who sided with the colonialists were generally those who had exhibited greater enthusiasm for Christianity and education. In areas like Iringa district which earlier had put up a prolonged fight, the leadership had been decimated, subservient chiefs installed, the people demoralized and firm colonial administration imposed. These factors had prevented their participation in *Maji Maji*. The material and ideological forces set in motion by colonial rule were in operation (Lubetsky 1972, page 14).

The war did not spread into the north. The potential leaders had been co-opted into the system; colonial economic policies had transformed the mode of life; and the people were more responsive to its demands. Cash crop production was extensive and a greater presence of the missionary schools prevailed. Having had the 'benefit' of education, Christianization and the crumbs from the rulers, the middle class elements did not lead the masses against them. Although the intensity of exploitation in areas like Kilimanjaro was higher, the colonial ideological system neutralized the potential leaders. (Iliffe 1972, page 153). This important lesson of the war was not lost on the colonial policy makers.

POST MAJI MAJI ECONOMIC POLICY

The *Maji Maji* struggle was the last major battle in the fight against the establishment of colonialism. The reverberations from its suppression ushered in of a new phase of colonial rule. Political stability and a virtual absence of violent opposition prevailed. The people were convinced, by the gun, that it was `futile' to oppose the outsiders. They had to live and struggle within the system. (Lubetsky 1972, page 15).

And they generally came to terms the three major symbols of colonial domination, education, Christianity and Islam. Famine had made many rely on the missions. People in areas where cotton cultivation had been fiercely opposed spontaneously began to cultivate the crop. A rapid conversion to Christianity occurred, particularly in the south. In some places, substantial conversion to Islam was seen. (Iliffe 1969, page 131; Oliver 1969, pages 197-198; Wright 1971, page 108).

Support for mission education became official policy. Attendance in both mission and government schools rose. Demand exceeded supply. In Usagara and Ugogo, people asked for more schools and teachers. The chiefs and villagers in Tabora and elsewhere built schools on their own initiative and sought teachers from the missions or paid for the teachers. (AR 1908/1909, pages 12-13).

An increasing segment of the population became involved in cash crop production and the migrant labor system. People became entwined into the colonial system as the economy of Tanganyika became more integrated into the global capitalist system. Adaptation to the subordinate colonial way of life was witnessed across the territory.

The struggle between major German companies and the European (mainly German) settlers was an important aspect of the post-*Maji Maji* changes. The main banks, industrial enterprises and commercial houses in Germany saw colonies as fields for lucrative investment, an expanding market and reliable suppliers of raw materials and food. The latter also helped meet Germany's balance of payments problem. Despite the maximal exploitation of local labor and resources, deficits had continued because of the subsidies for military campaigns and establishing the administrative infrastructure. The German policy makers and firms now wanted `sound economic management' to fully fund colonial costs and secure profits (Pierard 1967, page 34). The principal issue in this regard was whether Tanganyika should have a mainly settler and plantation based economy or one mainly based on small holder peasant farming.

In 1907, there were 479 adult male settlers in Tanganyika, 70% of them, Germans. By 1913, their number had risen to 882. They had come to establish agricultural enterprises and had acquired large tracts of the best lands. Until the final years of German rule, their economic role was marginal. The plantations and settler farms did not perform. To secure a better and reliable source of revenue and generate political stability, the major German capitalists and their representatives in the state were in favour of developing a mostly peasant based economy. (Lubetsky 1972, page 18).

The settlers and their spokesmen in the parliament bitterly opposed this policy. They sought to restrict peasant production in order to reduce competition and get cheap labor for their farms.

They did not like the move to encourage Indian traders and wanted to impose strict-Apartheid like controls on Africans. After intense debates, they were overruled by the interests of the big banks and commercial concerns. (Iliffe 1972, pages 40, 91, 97; Pierard 1967, pages 31, 36).

In 1907, the Colonial Director and ten prominent businessmen toured Tanganyika. The post-*Maji Maji* Governor, Baron von Rechenberg, was given the mandate to implement the new policy which emphasized the need to make the colony financially self-sufficient, rapid construction of railways and better treatment of local people. He oversaw measures to foster small peasant production and utilize Indian and Arab traders as the middlemen. The traders were agents of the German East Africa Company and enterprises. The central railway line was built to transport crops to the port and manufactured goods to the interior, and facilitate the movement of troops in times of trouble. It also eased *'the existing labor shortage'* by reducing the need for caravans. (Iliffe 1972, page 73, 97, 106-107; Pierard 1967, pages 35-36; Lubetsky 1972, page 15; Wright 1968).

In the eyes of the German government and monopoly capitalists the new policy was a success. Not only did political stability prevail but also subsidies from the metropole were reduced. In the later years, even the plantations prospered. But it was the big banks and the main capitalist firms who reaped the largest profits. (Iliffe 1972, page 73).

By 1914, *'no less than 32 per cent of local revenue was used to service loans for the railway construction.'* (Iliffe 1972, page 76). Between 1905 and 1912, textile imports more than doubled while the total value of foreign trade trebled. A large share of profits from the increased trade went to the German East Africa Company which had

> the widest trading network, the only land concession, and the largest plantation, and which controlled the only two banks and conducted most mortgage business. From 1906 to 1908 it paid dividends of 5 per cent; in 1909, in 1910 and 1911, 8 percent and in 1912, 9 per cent. (Iliffe 1972, page 97; Rodney 1980).

The settlers, strengthened by the rubber boom, attempted a comeback after 1910 but the policies instituted by Rechneberg were not reversed. (Wright 1971, pages 628-629). And, it was all made irrelevant by the outbreak of the First World War in 1914.

The struggle between the settlers and the monopoly capitalists, and the economic policies of the post-*Maji Maji* era have been described at length because of their importance in determining the form, organization, function and content of the ideological apparatuses in Tanganyika. Had the struggle gone in favor of the settlers, the reformist policies would not have been implemented. The settler sector would have grown at the expense of small-holder peasant cultivation, further land alienation with stricter labor laws would have occurred. The educational policies and role of the missions would have been oriented to meet the needs of a settler economy. A stronger repressive arm of the state would have emerged as direct force, not economic incentives and pacification through ideology would have been the prime means of implementing colonial policies.

COLONIAL CLASS STRCTURE

Before the advent of colonial rule Tanganyika was not a unified entity—economically or politically—although the process of unification had commenced as a result of commercial penetration long before colonial rule. Mostly, there were scattered tribal groupings comprising communal cultivators or pastoralists where little differentiation had taken place. No group dominated the means of production. But some communities had undergone significant differentiation. In a few places, a semi-feudal type of social structure had emerged. For example, among the Bahaya an institution resembling serfdom enabled the chiefs to expropriate surplus from others (Sheriff 1980).

Along the coast Arab, Indian and Swahili traders had, from their base in Zanzibar, dominated the scene for a time. Their penetration into the interior for slaves, ivory, and gum to exchange with manufactured goods from Europe hastened the process of differentiation in the societies with which they came into contact. It also began the process of integration of the societies into the commercial network of global capitalism. The import of large quantities of guns consolidated the power of indigenous ruling strata who by this time had formed alliances with the coast traders, and the Western companies operating along the coast. Most of the slaves were sent to European plantations overseas (Lubetsky 1972, page 3).

This arrangement was threatened when the European companies and missionaries penetrated inland. The economic position and political power of the coastal traders and their chiefly allies were in jeopardy. A violent struggle ensued. Culminating in the Bushiri uprising, the outcome was a victory for European capital. At the same time, Germany strove to establish political hegemony over the territory and impose its designs. Though helped by some chiefs, in general it faced vigorous resistance wherever it went. The *Maji Maji* war of 1905, in which imperialism emerged triumphant, climaxed the conflict. After *Maji Maji*, the conflict between German monopoly capital and the settlers intensified. Initially, the big capitalists secured the dominant position but just prior to World War I the latter seemed to be regaining lost ground.

The main features of the social structure which evolved in Tanganyika in this period were dominance by a foreign ruling class, emergence of middle level classes and the formation of the oppressed classes. This process did not occur overnight. It continued after the demise of German colonialism as well. The growth of the colonial ideological apparatus assisted the evolution of this class structure.

The ruling class in the territory was the metropolitan capitalist class. The ideological apparatus functioned to serve its interests and justify its rule. As this ruling class resided abroad, its interests were protected by local managers of the German firms, civil servants, military officers and the missionaries. Considering the lands they alienated and labor force they employed, the missionaries were settlers in their own right as well.

The European settlers, a potentially dominant class, remained in a subordinate position. Their influence on education was insignificant. In fact, they generally displayed backward attitudes towards education for not only the local population but also their own children.

The most exploited classes in the colonial society were the peasantry, the plantations workers and other local people engaged in manual work. Colonialism accelerated the process by which the peasant produced crops for the world market and food crops for the towns and plantations, and was involved in the money economy. Exploited through unequal exchange, his fate was decided by the world market. Introduction of taxation as well as direct compulsion hastened this process.

Prior to colonialism wage labour had existed in the form of thousands of porters working in caravans to transport goods to and from the coast. With the onset of the colonial rule, cheap labour was required for the plantations, railways, construction, the few manufacturing enterprises and workshops. This emergent working class was mostly composed of unskilled migrant labourers who were forced to seek wage employment in order to pay taxes, and a small skilled labour force, the *fundis*, the products of mission and government schools. The reforms increased the size of the work force so that by 1913 there were about 146,000 wage labourers in Tanganyika. (Lubetsky 1972, page 5, 18, 24).

The educational and mission systems served to make the dominated classes submissive and live with the capitalist mode of production, to make him believe the limitations imposed by it were unchangeable. After the end of colonial rule, it was these aspects of ideological domination which were preserved and further developed.

During the genesis of capitalism in Europe, force was used to deprive the producer of his means of production and turn him into a seller of labour power. At the genesis of colonialism, brute force ensured the subordination of the colonised person to imperial capital. In metropolitan capitalist formations, `the organization of the capitalist process of production, once fully developed, breaks down all resistance .... The dull compulsion of economic relations completes the subjugation of the labourer to the capitalist'. (Marx 1971, page 689). In peripheral capitalist formations, however, the capitalist mode of production does not become the universal mode of production. It is this enforced co-existence of the various modes of production which impedes the *'automatic'* reproduction of the relations of production through *'the dull compulsion of economic relation.'* (Amin 1974). The state thus played an active role throughout the colonial period to ensure that producer served the interests of the metropolitan bourgeoisie.

These quantitatively different roles of the state and the difference in the level of development of productive forces determine the different modes of operation of the ideological apparatuses in the two formations. Under colonial rule, the apparatuses are restricted in scope and mainly operate at a political level. Their basic function, namely to subordinate the producer to the rule of capital is, however, the same. Paraphrasing Marx:

> *The advance of* [colonialism] *develops* [working and peasant classes] *which by education, tradition, habit look upon the conditions of* [peripheral capitalism] *as self-evident laws of nature.* (Marx 1971, page 689).

In this connection it is not surprising to note that the stated purpose of the first taxation ordinance issued by the Germans in Tanganyika was *'educational'* in nature. As Iliffe says *'it was intended to oblige Africans to accept paid labour and accustom themselves to European administrative discipline'*. (Gwassa 1972; Iliffe 1972, page 160).

The emergent African elite was central to the ideological apparatus. Not only was it a product of the apparatus, but it also played a major role in it. Imbued with the colonial ideology, the elite facilitated the ideological and political domination of the other classes in the colonial society.

Benefitting from colonial education, its members received a regular income without doing manual labour. Its growth was fostered by the development of cash crops production, and the expansion of the colonial state apparatus and the missionary and education systems. It had two sub-strata: (i) The upper stratum consisted of the *liwalis, akidas* and other higher civil servants as well as the chiefs and the kulak farmers. (ii) The lower stratum comprised church workers, teachers, clerks, interpreters, lower ranks of the armed forces, etc. The upper level was recruited mostly from chiefly or well-to-do families. (Iliffe 1972, page 149). In the early years, many came from the coastal areas, and the wealthy families. Later, the recruitment occurred on a wider basis.

There were many mission schools for, or mainly for, sons of chiefs in this period. (Lubetsky 1972, page 12; Oliver 1969, page 13; Mapunda and Mpangara 1968, pages 28-29; Illife 1972, pages 176-179; Wright 1968, page 626). Even before *Maji Maji*, the Governor had encouraged education for the sons of the chiefs; after *Maji Maji*, literacy was made compulsory for them and their sons (Wright 1968, page 627). Some government schools gave preference to children from chiefly and wealthy families (AR 1901/1902, page 19; Wright 1971, page 124). These families also secured more benefits from commercial agriculture. (Lubestsky 1972, page 13; Iliffe 1972, pages 170-171).

For now, the African elites struggled for betterment of their status within the system. African priests and church workers fought for better pay and status. They formed self-help associations, mainly along tribal lines. And they gave voice to the grievances of the people towards Asian traders operating in their areas. (Wright 1971, page 124; Iliffe 1971, pages 179, 206-207; Shivji 1976; Lubetsky 1972, page 24).

These struggles were precursors of the struggles for independence that were to unfold during British rule. The colonial educations system was thus inadvertently producing the grave diggers of colonial rule. Shaaban Robert, the prominent nationalist poet and author, was a student of Tanga School in 1914, and Martin Kayamba, a key political activist in the 1930s, was a graduate of St. Andrew's College.

The local commercial class, as an agent of the European firms, played a major role in facilitating the expropriation of economic surplus from the colony. But its role in the education system was minimal. Though, about a third of the pupils in the government schools in Dar es Salaam in 1908 were of Indian origin (AR1908/1909, page 187). By 1910, there were 6,923 Indians in Tanganyika, mostly traders and many recent migrants from the Indian subcontinent. The few who owned large business concerns forged solid links with the European companies and the administration. They also engaged in charitable activities, donating money to schools and financing urban hospital construction. Governor Rechenderg considered them indispensable `*commercial intermediaries between Europeans firms and the natives.*' But they faced strong hostility from the settlers who regarded them as competitors. (Iliffe 1972, pages 94-96; Wright 1968, page 626).

There was a significant overlap between class and race divisions in the colonial era. Europeans (business managers, government officials, settlers and missionaries) formed the dominant class, merchants (Indian and Arab) populated the upper middle layer, and Africans, the lower middle and lowest layers.

The colonial society was fundamentally divided along gender lines as well. The inferior position of women and girls, inherited from Europe and the traditional societies, was further cemented in this era. In particular, not a single girl was educated in the governmental schools and it is not likely that any was educated in the Islamic or Mission schools either.

EDUCATION POLICY AFTER MAJI MAJI

While many aspects of the past educational policy were carried over, the changes therein after *Maji Maji* reflected the changes in the political and economic spheres. A comprehensive survey of the education system in German colonies was conducted by Martin Schlunk in 1911. His report, which has been regarded as representative of both the official and missionary opinions, shows an illuminating picture of the system. (Schlunk 1964; Scanlon 1964, page 29).

He endorsed the idea that the African must be educated for work. The German government had no interest in education for its own sake. Its primary aim was to turn the colonies into useful economic dependencies. Hence vocational training was to be emphasized (Schlunk 1964, pages 34, 47). But functional education was not to exclude character training.

> *Colonial schools are the cradle of German culture in Africa...... The true process of civilization has to be internalized if it is to be effective. The purpose of the schools cannot be merely to teach a trade to a few people. Rather it must be to bring up a new generation that will have accepted the new civilization internally as well as externally* (Schlunk 1964, page 32).

What was taking place in the drawing classes of the government school in Pangani was in accord with this vision. The pupils drew '(i)*llustrated pictures of German history from Germany's greatest era* (which) *deepened their grasp of Germany's strength and greatness.*' (AR 1908/1909, page 12). Colonial education must also stress the training of leaders since the pupils graduating from colonial schools constituted

> *a special class between us and the rest of the natives* [and] *those natives who have received education will then become leaders of their people in the struggle against us. The only chance of averting this is to use schools for character training.* (Schlunk 1964, page 43).

The lessons of *Maji Maji* had been assimilated. The potential leaders must not come into contact with subversive ideas, especially socialist ideas. With Marxist literature clearly in mind, he advocated the complete exclusion of '*that undesirable literature which preaches internationalism instead of patriotism.*' (Schlunk 1964, page 42).

Appointment of educated leaders was implemented in the Ungoni area where the traditional political system and ruling groups had been destroyed by the colonizers. Those who had been educated in mission schools were now favored for such positions. The new *akida* had usually passed through a government or mission school. School teachers were also made *akidas*. (Mapunda and Mpangara, 1968, pages 28-29; Iliffe 1972, pages 183, 186).

A reduction in harsh punishments meted out to the pupils was seen. The Governor forbade the use of the *kiboko* on Africans under sixteen, and Arab and Indian pupils and African teachers (Hornsby 1964, page 89). The education related co-operation between the missions and government improved after *Maji Maji*. Rechenberg encouraged school attendance and advocated the raising of the standard of mission schools to match those of the government schools. The missions gradually shed the hostility to Swahili as the medium of instruction. Instead, they worked to Christianize it. Axenfield, a pre-Rechenberg era missionary, later to be the director of Berlin mission, was straightforward: *'The new classes could be captured positively by full missionary participation in the Swahili medium education.'* By the end of 1906, both the Berlin mission and the Moravians had instruction in Swahili. The other missions gradually came to adopt it as well. (AR 1908/1909, page 14; Lubetsky 1972, page 15; Oliver 1969, page 206; Wright 1972, pages 83, 113-115, 122-133).

In 1910, the government made it mandatory for all chiefs and their progenies to learn to read and write. Enrolment in the mission schools thus grew. By 1913, the state began granting subsides to missions for training pupils for government posts. (Lubetsky 1972, page 18; Smith 1963, page 100).

BASIC FUNCTION

The main ideological apparatuses during the German colonial rule were the missions, and the mission and government school systems. Their basic function was to support the colonial economic and political systems. This was done through:

- Using the labour of the pupils to construct and fund the schools.
- Spreading the ideology of the colonizers.
- Training the cadres for the colonial administrative apparatus.
- Assisting the growth of the colonial economy by training craftsmen, imparting agricultural education and spreading the cash crop economy.
- Sustaining their own growth by training priests and teachers.

The schools and missions contributed significantly to the evolution of the colonial class-structure as well. And inadvertently, they produced the future leaders of anti-colonial struggles. But these products of colonial education were also qualified to man the neocolonial state apparatus. (Hirji 1973).

2

EDUCATION AND UJAMAA

SUMMARY: In February 1967, Tanzania adopted the policy socialism (*Ujamaa*) under the guiding document The Arusha Declaration. A few months on, President Julius Nyerere brought out the related education document, Education for Self-Reliance (ESR). These policies were seen as socialistic ways to combat under-development and under-education. This essay examines the impact of ESR on primary and secondary schools in mainland Tanzania during the years 1967 to 1973. The principal conclusion is because of the continued neocolonial, dependent trends in the economy and the dearth of committed socialist cadres, the transformation in the education system envisaged by ESR did not materialize. If anything, under-education was reinforced as the content, quality and organization of the education system went into a decline. Words did not match the deeds.[1]

*

---

1. This essay was first published as Hirji KF (1973): 'School education and underdevelopment in Tanzania,'*MajiMaji* (University of Dar es Salaam), 12:1-23. This is a shortened and extensively edited version. I have modified the rigid terminology of the original, rectified some archaic arguments and rearranged the material. But in essence and conclusion, the contents are the same as before.

> *Let our students be educated to be members
> and servants of the kind of just and egalitarian
> future to which this country aspires.*
> Julius Nyerere

++++++++++

WITHIN A DECADE OF INDEPENDENCE, the education system in Tanzania had expanded substantially. In 1961, there were 41 public and private secondary schools in the nation. With a teaching staff of about 760, their total enrolment was 12,000. By 1971, 141 public and private secondary schools enrolled 43,352 students with the teaching force at 2,111. More teacher training colleges were built and institutions of higher education like the University College of Dar es Salaam came into being (Tanzania 1972, page 131). Primary education grew at a faster pace. The funds for the expansion of secondary schools were secured through loans, mostly from the World Bank (Daily News 1973; Hunter 1972).

By 1967, though some communal and private schools still operated, education in Tanzania was more or less under the control of the state. Despite a series of bottlenecks in the system, the standard of instruction as measured by the conventional criteria was generally satisfactory. Graduate teachers from the university did a fine job in science and arts subjects. Quite a few students excelled and went for further studies. In sum, teachers and students were in good numbers engaged in a relatively efficient though traditional type of learning process.

The *Arusha Declaration* of 1967 directed the nation onto the path of socialism and self-reliance. In the same year, President Julius Nyerere issued a corresponding document for education, *Education for Self-Reliance* (ESR). Hailed by domestic and external education experts as a visionary paper, it promulgated measures to qualitatively transform the content, orientation and methods of education in the nation (Resnick 1968).

The fundamental premise of ESR is that Tanzania is striving for a social order based on socialist principles, namely,

> ... *equality and respect for human dignity; sharing of resources which are produced by our efforts; work by everyone and exploitation by none.* (Nyerere 1967, page 5).

Accordingly, the education system is to be transformed so that it serves

> .... *to foster the social goals of living together, and working together for the common good.* (Nyerere 1967, page 8).

This aim of this essay is to assess the theory and practice of ESR and discuss how schools in the nation have fared since its inception.

I restrict myself for the most part to primary and secondary education in mainland Tanzania.

SOCIETAL ANALYSIS

Before examining ESR, a word on the methods of analyzing society and history is in order. I divide them into three categories, idealism, realism and scientific method.

Idealism: This approach holds that ideas and intentions are the primary agents of social stability and change. Competition between diverse ideas is the main driver of history. An enlightened, charismatic leader with a bold vision plays a major, often decisive, role. For an idealist, societal change is a process of realization of an ideal state. Good ideas promote positive change; bad ideas lead to social stagnation.

Realism: This approach emphasizes a factual study of social conditions, past and present, as the main device for understanding why things are the way they were and are, and what the future can possibly be. Do not speculate, look at the facts. It generally lacks an explicit model to justify why some facts, not others are gathered, or to explain what is observed. Thus the explanations it presents from these facts takes the fundamental features of the existing social system for granted.

Scientific Method: The scientific approach employs a cohesive blend of facts and theory to understand the past and the present, and formulate the prospects for minor or structural change in the social system. Facts are gathered systematically using a study design based on the theory. The theory is not sacrosanct, but amenable to minor or major alteration depending on how it conforms to what is observed. Thereby, this method reflects an interplay between theory and practice (facts, experiment, observation or experience). Logical consistency and reproducibility by other investigators are fundamental tenets of the scientific method.

THE DEBATE ON ESR

Of recent, nearly six years after the introduction of ESR, the primary and secondary schools have been the subjects of a vigorous public debate. Students, teachers, parents, journalists, politicians and citizens — all have voiced their opinions through various channels. The debate centers on the implementation of the policy of ESR. A feeling that our schools are in a state of crisis prevails. But opinions as to the nature of this crisis, its causes and the methods for resolving it vary. From the diverse ideas and proposals aired, I discern two basic schools of thought, namely, apologetic idealism and cosmetic realism.

The idealists take the socialistic aims of ESR as their ideal frame of reference. They hold that with its noble intent, humane values and exemplary objectives, ESR has the power to not just resolve the current shortfalls in the system of education but also establish an alternative, effective, socialist education system in the nation.

They see the recent stresses and strains in our schools as transitional problems arising in the process of realizing of these ideals. Thus, we find Ndimara Tegambwage stating:

> [T]hose who cannot follow the socialist tide desperately shout that our educational standards are falling drastically. (Tegambwage 1973).

Further on he says:

> I believe we are still in the transitional period and what is happening now is quite inevitable. (Tegambwage 1973).

The idealists plan to bring about the desired changes through changes in attitudes and values of the students, and re-organize the school set up and curricula to serve those social goals (Raza 1973). But they offer scant empirical evidence to support their views. As such, they confuse the ideal with the actual and objectively, their stand provides an apology for the existent situation (Lema 1973a). And succumbing to political opportunism, they beat both sides of the drum. Thus, while Lema (1973a) sees the old attitudes among school students in a state of rapid decline, Lema (1973b) makes the opposite case.

Their opponents, the realists (pragmatists), base their conclusions on the reality as it immediately appears to them. Viewing the world through a superficial, fragmented looking glass, they pick on obvious flaws here and there, and propound the thesis that the school system is in shambles (Ndamagi 1973). Despite its good intentions, the new policy is not working. They also imply that it cannot work. Forget philosophizing; address the real issues. What is needed is to improve not alter the pre-ESR school system. Improve academic standards and administration of schools. Give more incentives to teachers, increase their salaries and benefits, make the Ministry of National Education function in an efficient manner, and impose a strict code of conduct in the schools (A Correspondent 1973; True Patriot 1973). That is their stand.

Their realism is founded on isolated details and on a tacit acceptance of the neocolonial, capitalist realty. Factual as it may be, it is not a substitute for an interconnected picture of the system, does not give a consistent explanation of its problems, or present viable proposals for change.

Employing unscientific approaches, both sides produce

conclusions that are not much further than where they began. What is required is a concrete analysis under which the ideal is related to the real and their interrelationship elucidated. The analysis of the education system should reveal the main bottlenecks in the system, trace their socio-historic roots, and connect them to general societal problems. This essay is a venture in that direction. First, a review of the historical background is in order.

EDUCATION UNDER COLONIALISM

The present day system of education in Tanzania has its roots in the colonial era (Cameron and Dodd 1970; Rodney 1972). Its foundations were laid at the end of the 1800s by Christian missionaries. Their major goals were to propagate Christianity and train African priests. By the early 1900s, more than 600 mission schools held literacy and Bible study classes for about 50,000 pupils across the land. As elsewhere in Africa, the Bible preceded the gun and set the stage for formal colonial rule. Subjectively, the missionaries may have viewed their work as a civilizing mission on the `dark continent.' Objectively, their role was to prepare the ideological groundwork for the subsequent imperialist penetration. Missionary education facilitated the separation of the African from the traditional society for absorption into the colonial socioeconomic system (see Essay 1 for details).

Education was not a priority for the colonialists. When the Germans took over Tanganyika, their chief concern was to establish law and order and open up the country to commerce. But because a junior, local civil service was required for these goals, they were forced into creating an education system to staff it (Cameron and Dodd 1970, page 55). They pursued the task in a methodical manner. Alongside missionary schools, a government school system was set up. An official circular stated the aims.

> a) *To enable the native to be used in government administration.*
> b) *To inculcate a liking for order, cleanliness, diligence, and dutifulness and a sound knowledge of German customs and patriotism.* (Cameron and Dodd 1970, page 56).

A distinctive feature of the government schools was that the medium of instruction was Swahili. It was a part of a strategy to consolidate colonial political domination throughout the territory in a rapid manner. Initially, the lower ranks of the colonial administrative machine were manned by Swahili speaking personnel from the coast. By the start of World War I, the official correspondence in the territory was mostly conducted in Swahili.

The advent of the British rule after the War led to many changes in this set up. Swahili lost its prominent place. Knowledge of and instilling loyalty to the British crown became the central goals. More direct links with missionary education were established, and a racially organized system evolved. But the essential function of education was unchanged, namely to facilitate the smooth operation of the colonial system.

Colonialism had a profound impact on the economy of the country. Its natural resources were exploited using cheap local labor. Production of raw material for industries in the metropole and creation of a protected market for their manufactured goods were the key priorities. A rail and road network to transport goods from the interior to the coast and vice versa was built. In due course, the economy of Tanzania became integrated into the underdeveloped segment of the world capitalist system.

The changes in the economic base produced changes in the social structure. The communal or nascent feudal societies in existence were rendered asunder by production for the world market and the system of migrant labor. Stratification within the peasantry and emergence of a working class in the plantations and urban areas was directly linked to the development of production and processing for export. The mainly Asian shopkeepers formed an essential link between peasant producers and foreign capital, and enabled the appropriation of the economic surplus to the colonizing nation (Shivji 1973).

Corresponding political and ideological mechanisms, including an education system enabled this economic system operate in a stable manner. The resources devoted to education, though, were minimal and it was developed in a restricted way. A map of colonial Tanzania shows that the main cotton and coffee growing areas were mostly the areas where education was available (Rodney 1972, pages 266–267). The expanding state apparatus increased the demand for local personnel. To be a clerk or a teacher, or get a skilled job you needed education. Accordingly, its output comprised clerks, tax collectors, primary school teachers, junior administrators, interpreters, priests, policemen as well as artisans and craftsmen. The policy of indirect rule used the traditional rulers to entrench colonial domination. Hence the children of chiefs were accorded preferential access to public schools. Numerically, these children were a small proportion of those who got an education and joined the lower ranks of the colonial administration.

The colonial social structure was a four-stage structure with the ruling class of the European colonizers and business elite at the zenith. They were followed by the upper middle class (the Asian business community) and the lower middle class (the educated Africans). At the bottom were the mainly African manual workers and rural peasants, herders and others.

Accordingly, the colonial school system was a race-based system in which European children had the best facilities. The Asian children were next in line, and the African children, at the bottom. The inequalities were vast. In the year 1961, the annual expenditure per pupil and pupil-teacher ratio respectively were Tsh 3,320/= and 16 for the first group, TSh 460/= and 28 for the second, and for

Tsh 200/= and 54 for the last (Van de Laar 1972b). And, only a tiny fraction of African children attended school. The education disparity was manifested in job allocation: the top state and managerial positions were for Europeans; the Asians were at the next level, and the Africans at the bottom. Similar gaps were observed in housing quality, residential areas and health services.

The colonial vision of African education deemphasized traditional academic type of education for the majority. As noted in the legislative council proceedings for the year 1928:

> (I)n any vision of future development, agriculture must occupy the foremost place. ...Everything, therefore points to agriculture as the basis of our educational system in the elementary stages. (Cameron and Dodd 1970, page 69).

The 1953 primary school syllabus was more specific:

> In the teaching and education in school it would be wrong to consider the pupils and their individual progress alone, we must consider also their responsibility in the community and the environment, so that their lessons may lead them to actions which will benefit their country. ... it is obligatory that every primary school should have a sufficient farm. ...The purpose of this farm is educational, that is to show the practice of good farming and to accustom them to follow these practices. (Cameron and Dodd 1970, page 109; Tanganyika 1953).

Two years later, the middle school syllabus reiterated the same theme:

> The middle school course is designed to be complete in itself so that those who pass through it, whether they proceed further or not, will have received an education which assists them to follow in a more intelligent and capable manner whatever pursuits they take up and, generally, to play a more useful part in the development of the locality to which they belong. (Cameron and Dodd 1970, page 109; Tanganyika 1955).

Beneath the flowery words of the colonial educationists lay the real aims. Farming and manual work were for African schools only. They had to learn that their place was in the rural, not urban areas. Their task was to produce agricultural goods for export overseas. Under this system, a complementary development of agriculture and industry on a scientific foundation was not in the cards (Rodney 1972, page 276).

The European and Asian children received education modelled on that obtainable in the UK. This system ensured that the manual tasks were the preserve of Africans while most of the upper level white collar jobs were for the others.

The few Africans who obtained a slightly better education were set apart, socially and economically, from the communities from which they originated. They morphed into a stratum that embraced a foreign culture, exhibited a spirit of subservience to the colonizers, and reflected elitist values like individualism and desire for material acquisition. But this process had a paradoxical aspect. Education brought them into contact with liberal ideas like democracy, freedom and even socialism which led them to consider possibilities of life beyond colonial rule.

Sandwiched between two antagonistic worlds, that of resolute power and that of powerlessness, the lot of the African semi-elite was not a happy one. It daily worked near the center of political power, yet could only do what it was ordered to do. What it saw up close bred discontent with just having a slightly better economic level than before. It wanted more. Education unleashed these aspirations by opening up a new window to the world. But the race-based system could not satisfy them. Thus, as a result of sharpening of the contradictions between the colonizer and the colonized, and in the context of unfolding anti-colonial struggles across the world, it was not surprising then that leadership of the struggle for freedom from colonial rule emerged for the most part from the enlightened segment of this educated semi-elite (Iliffe 1972, page 14).

Better access to education was a key demand in the struggle for Independence. Sensing that demand, TANU had set up and run primary schools under the umbrella of the Tanganyika Parents Association. Local communities in several regions also established their own schools.

In sum, missionary and public education provided under colonial rule legitimized the imperialist intrusion in Africa in religious and cultural terms, spread the spirit of humility and submission amongst the people, created the agents for spreading the colonizers' ideology, and generated the skilled personnel required for the colonial system. It facilitated the bonding of the economy to the global market and led to the formation of a new class structure. And dialectically, it generated the grave diggers of colonial rule as well.

EARLY POST-INDEPENDENCE PERIOD

Formal independence did not alter the status of the Tanzanian economy in the world capitalist system. If anything, the channels for siphoning the economic surplus were increased through multilateralization of external links and greater reliance on foreign capital, markets and technology. Not just British capital but also capital from other places could operate in the nation with incentives like tax concessions and the right to repatriate profits. The policy priority was to expand the activities established under colonial rule, principally the extension of agriculture production for export and the related infrastructure. Industrial growth focused on export processing and final stage import substitution. Unequal exchange was a major roadblock to development. For example, from 1967 to 1972 the money prices of Tanzania exports remained nearly constant but those of the imports rose about one third, with the real loss running at about US $80-90 million per year. The main driver of the post-Independence economic strategy was the World Bank. This economic strategy fostered the development of an underdeveloped neocolonial economy (Seidman 1972).

Yet, *Uhuru* did entail major changes in the social set up. Political power now rested in the hands of a new set of rulers. At the outset, Africanization of the senior positions and skilled personnel in the public and private sectors was a core aspect of the national policy. Recruitment in the civil service expanded the numbers of the African elite. Although national political leadership exuded militant nationalism, its status was connected to the continued expansion of external economic linkages. Through control of the state, it became the new middleman for external economic entities. As in the other former colonies, a confrontation with the existing middlemen, here the Asian business stratum, ensued. The colonial legacy of race-based preferences meant that this confrontation had racial as well as economic overtones (Shivji 1973).

A key arena where the conflict played out was education. Among the steps taken after *Uhuru*, steps that were necessary and important, were to make the system merit-based rather than race-based, abolish school fees and establish a Ministry of National Education to oversee the entire system of education system. Both public and private schools fell under its purview. The administration of school system was stream lined by the establishment of a unified teaching service. Emphasis on the teaching of Swahili, making subjects like history and literature Africa oriented and infusing patriotic ideas into the curriculum were the main changes made at the outset. In other aspects, the contents of primary and secondary education remained basically unchanged (Nyerere 1967).

The demand for education intensified. Now qualified personnel were needed to fill the posts left vacant by the departing colonialists and the new, higher level posts created in the expanded state apparatus. But the lop-sided nature of the economic expansion implied that the demand was mainly for white collar personnel.

Consequently, the growth of technical education lagged behind. The following table gives the relevant details.

Growth of Education, Tanzania[2]

Level	1961	1966	%
Primary School	486,470	740,991	52%
Secondary School	11,832	23,836	101%
Teacher Training	909	2,560	182%
Technical Education	2,697	2,095	-22%
University Education	811	1,719	112%
Total	502,919	771,201	53%

In terms of meeting manpower needs, the education system achieved a fair measure of success. While reliance on expatriates in key jobs went on, the proportion of local personnel in most sectors rose. Tanzanians formed 38.5% of 4,723 senior and middle grade civil servants in 1962. By 1971, of the 10,723 civil servants at this grade, a full 90.5% were Tanzanians (Tanzania 1972, page 133).

EDUCATION AND SOCIETY

In the policy document ESR, Mwalimu Nyerere states that the purpose of education in society is:

> …. *to transmit from one generation to the next the accumulated wisdom and knowledge of the society, and to prepare the young people for their future membership of the society and their active participation in its maintenance or development.* (Nyerere 1967).

Further, education should make the student develop:

> *…an inquiring mind; an ability to learn from what others do, and reject or adapt it to his own needs …* (Nyerere 1967).

In modern times, the state plays an important, though varied role in education. It lays down the structure of the system, sets the rules and regulations that govern its operation and has organs that oversee inspections, criteria for teacher qualifications and set examinations. Many schools and colleges are publicly owned. The state is seen as a neutral entity whose role is to maintain education quality and fairness, control fraud, and ensure that the system caters to the manpower needs of the society.

While this liberal depiction of education and education systems

---

2. Van de Laar (1972a).

has elements of validity, it rests on a major omission. In a society divided into classes, the state and education, as we saw under colonial rule, are not socially neutral entities. They fundamentally cater to the interests of the class which owns and controls the means of production. This class requires political power to guard and increase its wealth. Control of the interlocking state institutions like the legislative organ, law enforcement agencies, the armed forces, the judiciary and the prisons is thereby its fundamental priority.

That control however does not suffice for the long term stability of the system. Discontent from below cannot be suppressed by purely resorting to institutions ultimately based on coercion. To maintain social stability, the 99% at the bottom have to be convinced that there is no ruling class; that the people chose and change their rulers through a fair democratic process, that the state is a neutral and just arbiter for the entire citizenry; that if there are glitches, they are transient, individual failings and not systemic flaws; that the current social arrangement is the best there can be and no viable alternative exists.

Years of implicit and explicit conditioning instill such conformist ideas into the minds of the citizens. Parents, peers, the mass media, the major entertainment and literary venues, religious bodies, national role models (the ideological apparatuses) and the fear of being isolated or ostracized play a key role in the process of assimilation into the dominant mind set. And the education system is a major player in this process. It teaches the young minds to accept the existent state of affairs, disciplines them into obedience and imbues them with the spirit of respect for authority. Further, by transmitting and expanding knowledge and skills, it helps to augment the economic surplus appropriated by the ruling class (Althusser 1971; Engels 1968).

The statements from ESR quoted above do not fully capture the role of education in a class based society. They can be construed to mean that education is a neutral process benefiting all members of society. That was definitely not so under colonial rule and it is not so today as well.

There is also a built-in transformative facet in the education system. Despite its limitations, education opens up a person's mind to new ideas and instils a spirit of inquiry. Else its role as a custodian of the intellectual wealth of society and producer of knowledge would be compromised. In the process, some individuals apply their skills of logical inquiry beyond their narrow fields of specialization to the social reality as a whole. In so doing, they puncture the prevailing ideological mystifications and invoke the possibility of structural change. The education system has its own internal contradictions. Through expression of different class interests, it partakes in the general societal contradictions. The interplay of these contradictions and the development of productive forces affect the manner and direction of education and social change.

The social function of the education system is susceptible to change. In times of social stability, when the social and political supremacy of the ruling class is unchallenged, it functions mostly to preserve the status quo. But when struggles from below begin to take the center stage, the dominant ideology falls under scrutiny from the educators and students. From being a rationalizer of the rule of the rulers, the education system turns into a battle-ground for generation of new social horizons.

ESR: THEORY AND PRACTICE

Seven years after *Uhuru*, the economy of Tanzania was showing signs of severe strain. Foreign investment and loans had been inadequate; the prices of export goods, especially sisal, fell sharply. State revenue was insufficient and job growth poor. Unequal terms of international trade further drained national resources. Economic growth, even within the limits imposed by the neocolonial framework, was severely retarded.

Similar problems occurred in the other African nations as well. Each nation devised its own strategy to tackle them. In Tanzania, that strategy was enshrined in the Arusha Declaration of 1967. Its main feature was the expansion of the direct role of the state in economic affairs. Through nationalization, large portions of the trade, financial and industrial sectors were brought under the ownership of the state. Infrastructure development and provision of social services were already mostly under the state. And a program of establishing collective (*Ujamaa*) villages was initiated.

The main effect of the new measures was to modify the linkage of the Tanzanian economy to the world capitalist system. The colonial era middle men, the Asian commercial stratum, were displaced by the state. British capital lost its monopoly position. Instead, through joint ventures, management agreements, lines of credit, loans and direct investments, links with and dependency on foreign capital from wider sources were expanded.

Yet, the essence of the economic policy remained unchanged. The emphasis remained on production of primary commodities for export, and industrial development was confined to processing for export and import substitution. The *Ujamaa* villages grouped isolated peasants to further bring them into the cash economy through production of export crops. The post-Arusha changes did not include plans for laying the foundation of a nationally integrated economy through comprehensive planning and mass mobilization, as a genuinely socialist transformation would have. These changes occurred under a framework laid down by the World Bank and formed the basis for a neocolonial state-capitalist economy. While nominal ownership of industries was in the hands of the state, control was largely exercised by foreign management firms. These firms employed unfair pricing and other devices to benefit their parent companies (Shivji 1970, 1973; Thomas 1972).

The problems in the economy acutely affected education. In the early colonial days, four to six years of primary education sufficed for a clerical job in the public sector. By the 1950s:

> (t)he days when education up to standard VI was the gateway to paid employment had ended. Indeed, in a very short time, the gateway open to those with 8 years education was also to close. (Cameron and Dodd 1970, page 103).

School enrollment expanded rapidly after *Uhuru*. But job prospects for school leavers grew at a tepid pace. A primary school certificate no longer sufficed for any job, let alone a decent one. The situation became progressively worse. In 1964, 23 per cent of those completing primary school found places in secondary schools. By 1968, while the output of these schools had increased by nearly two-and-a-half times, only 13 per cent was absorbed into secondary schools. The rest were lucky to get low-paid, temporary casual jobs. Their plight is aptly depicted in the following:

> Urban children will stay in town and try to get work; their aim may certainly be a white collar job, or entry into a regular form of training. But since only a very small proportion will succeed, the rest will probably be prepared to take casual manual work — on a building site, in a sisal plantation, at a petrol pump, behind the bar in a hotel or cafe. This, at least a first in a stop gap measure, until the hoped-for job — perhaps as a messenger in a government office — comes along.

> For the boys with rural homes, the main pattern is the same, but more difficult. They will, if they can, first stay with a relative in town and hunt for work. For those who went to a boarding primary school, the tie with home has already been weakened. If their first try fails, they may get a bus fare from a relative and try the next town, or a big plantation which may need casual labor. They can earn a few shillings by any possible means which comes to hand. After this trial period, if they are getting desperate they may return to their home village for a while. If they earn a little money working for a neighboring farmer or in other ways — they may well set off on their travels again, once more take casual employment and again return home. (Hunter 1972, page 251).

A similar problem affects those with four years of secondary education. A larger and larger proportion do not either get a place in Form V, find a venue for technical training, or secure direct employment. Soon we will have a Form VI-leavers problem and graduate joblessness. Where to allocate science graduates who lack teaching credentials is already a key concern of the manpower planners.

The plight of primary school leavers is the major issue addressed by ESR. Based on the assumption that after primary school they would pursue secondary schooling, the first seven years of education did not equip them with skills for any job. Unable to secure further education or training, get a job or make a decent living in the rural areas, these school leavers in large numbers head to urban centers to find ways to make a living. The migration from rural to urban areas is now more like a one way exodus, and has increased congestion and unemployment in the towns. Economic opportunities in towns, even for menial, minimum wage jobs or petty self-employment are limited. The 'revolution of rising expectations' induced by education has become a reality of rising frustrations. The plight of the fifty per cent or so of the children who never obtain any schooling is a yet grimmer story (von Freyhold 1972).

To solve this critical societal dilemma, ESR proposed that:

> (i)nstead of primary school activities being geared to the competitive examination which will select the few who go on to secondary school, they must be prepared for the life which majority of the children will lead. (Nyerere 1967, page 17).

In that regard, it was assumed that:

> Tanzania will continue to have a predominantly rural economy for long time to come. (Nyerere 1967, page 7).

The similarity between the colonial policy statements about education for Africans quoted earlier and the reforms proposed in ESR is striking (see Essay 1 for the German era stress on practical education). And it is not accidental but points to the continuity of a fundamental economic reality, that of dependency and persistent low economic progress. The colonial education policy was designed to install and buttress the mechanisms of dependency. ESR and the Arusha Declaration, the related basic policy document, assume a continuation of Tanzania's existent position within the world capitalist system.

ESR represents an admission by the political rulers that even trying to transform this situation is not on the agenda. There is no plan to create a nationally integrated economy, to develop a multitude of small scale plants based on intermediate technology, to harmonize education with the new forms of manpower requirement created by such a scheme, and so on. Instead, the direction of economic development will be that set-forth by the World Bank. The peasant in the *Ujamaa* villages will continue to focus on production of the usual types of cash crops for export.

ESR thus proposes to fit education to an existing reality, rather than to revolutionize it and establish a revolutionary education process. And it ignores the powerful social and economic forces propelling the formation of classes in Tanzania. It is thus caught up in the contradiction of trying to eliminate the class structure of society without tackling the structures of underdevelopment that generate the class structure. It is an idealist policy as it aims to recreate the egalitarian societies of the pre-colonial era primarily by instilling new values among the school goers.

Education is an essential weapon in transition towards socialism, an important tool for changing values. But that change has to occur in the context of an overall transformative process. Imbued with an economic bias and caught up in a maze of contradictions characteristic of utopian radicalism, it is not surprising to find the practice of ESR littered with major shortcomings on all fronts. We consider these below.

ESR AND EMPLOYMENT

The output of the education system in a dependent economy usually outpaces the growth of the job market. The large numbers of educated unemployed plagues the satellite nations of Asia, Africa and Latin America and is a key driver of unrest in their education institutions and urban centers. When the years spent for getting a diploma lead only to emptiness, frustrations multiply. A rising crime rate in the urban areas is one consequence.

In such an economy, the demand for labor is basically composed of two components. First, workers are required for low paid, low skill jobs in the farms, mines, the transport and construction sectors, and the few factories in operation. Formal education contributes little to the productive work force. The education system mostly caters to fill white collar posts in the administrative apparatus.

Manpower planning done in Tanzania since *Uhuru* has focused on replacement of expatriate personnel and growth of jobs like the existing ones. The service sector and the state bureaucracy have grown rapidly. The demand for office workers; typists, secretaries, phone operators, messengers, clerks, cleaners, drivers, accountants, supervisors and managers – has gone up. By the early 1970s, the public sector comprising mostly of unproductive personnel accounted for 65% of the wage employment. Development of communication and the construction of luxury offices for ministries and parastatals have absorbed a large slice of the investment funds (Bienfeld 1972).

The growth of bureaucracy has occurred unevenly. In some areas, there is a shortage whilst other areas are overstaffed. Nor has allocation of personnel always conformed to type of training received. A graduate with a degree in botany is likely to find himself or herself shuffling papers rather than in an agriculture station. Unpredictable transfer of personnel hinders improvement of efficiency through accumulation of experience. In some areas, the expansion of the work force and facilities has resulted in declining efficiency.

ESR recognizes the unproductive, white collar bias of the current system of education. But its stated goal of ending such bias and making education more practical faces the fact that economic and manpower planning is geared towards generation of such jobs. White collar employees usually enjoy higher income and status. This basic mismatch between rhetoric and reality prevents the measures in ESR from being adopted in a rational manner. Moreover, the contents and ways of instruction used for practical education are seriously flawed as well.

PRACTICAL EDUCATION: THEN AND NOW

In the colonial era, the attempts to introduce a so-called practical and relevant curriculum in Africa schools met with vigorous resistance from the people. That the colonialists meant to keep Africans at the bottom was clear. Academic education, a passport to good jobs and higher income, was not for them. Combining education with manual work was correctly regarded by them as inferior education. And, as Rodney points out, the process of combining the two, especially in the British times, was fraught with serious deficiencies:

> (i)n many colonial schools agriculture became an apology for a subject. It was part of the drudgery of the institution. The teachers received no agricultural education and therefore, they could not teach anything scientific. Children acquired nothing but distaste for the heavy labor of shamba work, and in fact it was used as a form of punishment. (Rodney 1972, page 277).

Cameroon and Dodd make a similar observation, though in apologetic terms:

> When later the school began producing more than could be employed in the modern sector which required entrants with more than just a primary education, the educationists naturally redoubled their efforts to make agriculture an integral part of the syllabus in order to cater for the increasing number of pupils who after some education would now have to return to the land. Just as determinedly, the Africans resisted these efforts and demanded more post-primary education. Every family, every kinship group in the areas where Western education had taken root aspired to get at least one of its members away from home into paid employment from which they would all benefit. (Cameroon and Dodd 1970, page 70).

It was popular pressure and the role of education in the rising demand for educated workers that frustrated the aims of the colonialists. Today, a similar phenomenon prompts resistance by students, teachers, parents and educationists towards the practical education proposals in ESR. The manner of implementation of ESR forms a key aspect of their misgivings.

ESR is a policy document. It does not contain details on how the enunciated principles would be actualized in practice. That is the task of the Ministry of National Education. Schools need guidelines on the types of practical activities, their scope, the average number of hours students at different levels are expected to spend in such activities, evaluation of student performance, and funding and supplies for school projects. This crucial follow up step has not yet been taken and there are no signs that it will be.

Instead, what transpired was exertion of strong political pressure on schools to immediately undertake some form of practical work, which in most cases is a school farm. Some schools have a poultry shed, a dairy project, carpentry or some form of handicraft activity. But projects are undertaken on a purely ad hoc, mostly poorly organized basis. It basically depends on what the headmaster and teachers feel about practical education, the resources available, and the time and effort they devote to ensure good implementation. A few schools have projects that are productive. The local politicians use them as demonstration entities for external visitors. But in the majority of schools, a substandard project is maintained to show that the school is not in violation of the national policy.

Rodney's depiction of colonial agricultural education as `apology' and `drudgery' applies to self-reliance projects in most Tanzanian schools today. Often practical work just means taking a broom to school and cleaning the school compound and classrooms. It is hard to see how such activities can inculcate a cooperative spirit or equip students with skills they can use later in life. Most rural children already know more about farming, dairy and poultry from their parents. In the German era, though practical training was brutally enforced, at least it was done systematically and produced trained craftsmen and technicians.

The conflict between the realists and idealists over education noted at the start reflects this reality of generally poor state of ERS projects. The former decry the time wasted in the projects and consequent declining standards of education while the latter stress the notion of relevance in education. The contention is reminiscent of the complaints against inferior education in the colonial era. It is also related to the current system of examination.

ESR AND EXAMINATIONS

Tanzania inherited the British system of reliance on a few hours of written exams at the end of a given stage of education to select the candidates for entry into the next stage. ESR provides an in-depth, enlightened critique of this system. Exams emphasize memorization of facts, not critical reasoning or character. ERS suggests that despite their advantages, they should not be the sole basis for judging a student. Education should not be geared towards passing competitive exams for entry, by a minority, into the next stage of the education ladder. Instead, it should focus on preparing the majority for life after they finish their schooling.

Noble sentiments need plan and action. An objective evaluation scheme, as ESR admits, is essential. It is needed to determine what the student has learned and his or her qualification and capability for later education or work related activities. Without a sieving device, higher education will experience major bottlenecks. It is difficult to avoid nepotism in job or further study allocation without some scheme of assessment. The issue of judging character, though, is an unresolved challenge.

A different type of examination that is fair and adequate and which integrates book learning with assessment of practical activities can be devised. Before exploring that, we first look at the current system of examination in greater depth.

Until the mid-1960s, terminal school examinations in Tanzania were administered under the UK based Cambridge examinations system. Now they are under the purview of the National Examination Authority. But apart from history, English literature, civics and Swahili, the contents of the other subjects, especially science subjects, have hardly changed. In a few, they are an exact copy of the Cambridge syllabus. A national policy on curriculum content has yet to be issued. Schools are uncertain about course material, a matter that generates uncertainty in the setting of exam papers. Subjects like mathematics, physics and chemistry face an unresolved dichotomy between traditional and modern content and methods.

The national examination system has experienced major problems in two areas: administration and progressively declining level of performance.

All the stages of the annual examination exercise, from setting the exam papers, conducting the exams, marking the scripts to the announcement of the results have experienced major glitches. Delayed arrival of question papers and mix-up of papers occur on a frequent basis. Private candidates encounter hurdles from start to finish. In some subjects, a shortage of markers prevails. Less than half, mostly teachers from secondary schools, turn up. They want a larger allowance for the job. The lack of planning and co-ordination compounds the problems.

The performance of candidates in the national exams has generally been poor. In some subjects, the results are appalling. For example, in 1972, of the candidates who sat for the subject mathematics at O-level, nearly 70% got less than 30 marks out of 100. The national mean was around 20 marks with about 1,200 candidates getting less than 4 marks! Poor and declining performance is linked to the standards of instruction in the classroom. Insufficient facilities, shortage of qualified teachers and textbooks, frequent disruptions, poorly set exams and transfers of teachers, all share the blame for the unsatisfactory performance.

A model for an alternative exam system already exists. Secondary technical schools, though handful in number, have functioned for a while now. My secondary education in the years 1963 to 1965 took place at the Dar es Salaam Technical College. In addition to English, history, physics, chemistry, mathematics, we had to do three practical subjects. They were chosen from metal work, electrical repair, auto mechanics, carpentry and engineering drawing. At the end of four years, we sat for the Cambridge exam in the traditional subjects and the City and Guilds exam in the technical subjects. Assessment of the objects we had made in the final year was done for the technical subjects. We had the incentive to seriously attend to both categories of subjects because both had formal curricula, qualified teachers and a recognized certificate for good performance.

Oddly, instead of being emulated and expanded, secondary technical education went into decline after the promulgation of ESR. What is needed is to extend the list of practical subjects to include agriculture, horticulture, poultry and dairy farming, culinary skills, and arts and crafts (making straw baskets, mats etc.). For each subject, an appropriate syllabus, list of books and resources has to be produced, and a teacher training scheme put in place. A national system of examination for the theoretical and practical aspects of the practical subjects is also needed. But this option has not received attention from the Ministry of National Education. It is not a surprise then that practical education continues to be seen as a drudgery of no educational or life improving value.

ESR AND DEMOCRACY

ESR places direct democracy as a key facet of school practical projects. Students should be involved in making decisions in relation to the output and revenue of school farms and should not work under rigid rules from above. Autonomy will instill respect for cooperative manual work and link it with improvement of their conditions. They should also cooperate with nearby communities at a practical level through, for example, irrigation projects.

Currently education institutions in Tanzania function under a strict top-down system. The Ministry of National Education and the Prime Minister's Office issue directives that are transmitted to schools and colleges by the District Education Officers. At the school level, the headmaster is the king. Maintaining discipline is his or her main concern. Any transgression on the part of the students is punished via assignment of manual work, caning, suspension or expulsion. Thus it is common to find a whole class cutting grass in the school yard because it was making noise.

Problems like poor classroom instruction, unqualified teachers, lack of textbooks, teacher absenteeism, frequent punishments, poor state of the dormitories, substandard food and low job prospects demoralize the students. Hypocrisy in the political sphere dampens their morale. In the urban areas, these frustrations and the influence of Western culture drive some to hooliganism.

Maintaining discipline was the main theme of the national

conference of headmasters in May 1973. Though, the conference ended with urging the students to assist adult education work and the African liberation movements. Such grand resolutions are hollow because they are made for reasons of political expediency than anything else. Neither students nor teachers are impressed.

The reality is far from the theory. It is rare to find schools with projects that involve students in deciding what is done and how it is done. In many schools, students complain that the fruits of their labor are being appropriated by the teachers. And working with adjoining communities is a dream yet to be realized.

The *TANU Guidelines* (*Mwongozo*), a path breaking document issued in 1971, makes participation of people in making decisions about things that affect their lives a fundamental requirement. It requires those in positions of leadership to set aside arrogant, heavy-handed behavior and become humble, dedicated servants of the people. Coming on top of the exhortations about democracy in ESR, this call was taken seriously by workers in factories and students in schools, colleges and the university. Material frustrations together with democratic ideals influenced them to rise up in place after place to air their grievances and assert their right to be involved in decision making. Student uprisings occurred at many schools including Pugu Secondary School, Mkwawa Secondary School, Mzumbe Secondary School and Njombe Secondary School. Instead of engaging in a constructive dialog, school authorities reacted with massive force. Hundreds of students were punished and/or expelled (A Sixth Former 1973).

At times, the nature of the punishment meted out was unnerving. Thus in October 1972, after the outbreak of a conflict between students and some teachers at Njombe Secondary School:

> ... pupils were ordered to have a shower while in full uniform, then commanded to roll in the gravel or clay soil, then forced to enter class without changing clothes. The barbarity they also launched was to beat students with clubs on any parts of their bodies. (Mawanafunzi Mfiahaki 1973).

And often, as happened at Mzumbe Secondary School in June 1973, the riot police are called in to control the students. In this case, 187 students were expelled for 'refusing to obey the school rules.' It was as if we were back in the colonial era.

The fine ideals of critical thinking, democracy, cooperative work and community involvement expressed in ESR have thereby become political slogans devoid of content. The leaders and officials say one thing but do the opposite, and those at the bottom have to be content with business as usual.

ESR AND TEACHERS

The growth of the teaching profession in the past decade has exceeded that of most other professions. But it has come with an increase in the problems they experience at work. A primary school teacher earns a little more than the minimum wage; a secondary school teacher has lower salary and benefits in comparison with an employee of a parastatal organization with a similar level of education. Overworked by large class sizes, they are assigned extracurricular work within and beyond the school. They decry the low priority the Ministry of National Education accords to their complaints, the inefficient manner in which it operates, nepotism, frequency of transfers, and say that uncooperative parents and unruly pupils make it difficult for them to discharge their duties well.

The teachers of today feel that in spite of their diligence under difficult conditions, no one is grateful to them. In the course of supervising the teaching practice of UDSM mathematics teacher trainees over a period of three years, I visited many secondary schools across the nation. In the process, I conversed with about a hundred teachers. These talks together with media reports and field studies done by educationists have led me to believe that the morale of the entire teaching profession is at a disturbingly low ebb. (A Correspondent 1973; Affected 1973; Kibwana 1973; Kikubatyo 1973; Mbiru 1973; Mtaita 1973; Mtui 1973; Shikoyoni 1973).

Only a few teachers regard their job a noble calling. Many joined the profession because of the lack of a better opportunity. A high level of unprofessional conduct prevails. They frequently skip class, do not complete the syllabus, neglect student homework, etc.

The relationship between the teachers and students is far from ideal. Each group views the other with hostility. The teachers sublimate their frustrations by treating the students harshly and resort to strong sanction for minor misconduct. The learning environment is then compromised to a serious degree.

The combination of political hypocrisy, work problems, inefficient and uncaring officials, and the dominance of the cash nexus, make the oft heard exhortations on the teachers to serve the nation fall on deaf ears. Moral incentives cannot operate in an environment where individualism and double talk reign supreme. Emanating from the lips of those who exhibit little signs of believing them, they are viewed as little more than deceptive mockery. No wonder, the teachers remain singularly apathetic towards the ideals expressed in ESR.

ESR AND POLITICAL EDUCATION

Political education in Tanzania covers issues like the nation's history and culture, the formation of the union between Zanzibar and Tanganyika, basic facts about East African affairs, the liberation of Africa, African unity, the main documents on the policy of socialism and self-reliance, and the role of our leaders. Its stated aims are to counter individualism and to instill the spirit of patriotism, sacrifice and cooperative endeavor.

In practice, political education faces two stumbling blocks: (i) the large gap between rhetoric and reality and (ii) level of comprehension of the subject matter by, and commitment of, the educators. There has been no program to re-educate the political educators. It is assumed that any teacher can teach *siasa* (politics). A dearth of dedicated, theoretically grounded cadres plagues the ruling party as well. It is filled with opportunists expert at mouthing acceptable slogans.

Accordingly, political education is of poor quality. The emphasis is on memorizing few historical facts and the ruling party declarations, not on a sound understanding of social reality and concepts like socialism and capitalism. A print version of relevant radio broadcasts on the origin and development of world socialism by M Holness, for example, collects dust at the Ministry (Holness 197). ESR declares that there is no political holy book for Tanzania. Yet the books and speeches of Mwalimu Nyerere are treated exactly in that spirit. The atmosphere under which political education is imparted is an artificial one. Pretense is rampant and critical thought is expunged. Teachers and students compete in terms of who best can praise the national leaders and political philosophy. Instead of fostering thought, it dulls the mind. When students see that what their teachers and political leaders practice is the opposite of what they are taught in *siasa*, they are driven to knee-jerk cynicism, a sure recipe for banishing logical thought.

CONCLUSIONS

Despite everything discussed above, the education system in Tanzania is not falling apart. Students go to school and learn the traditional types of academic subjects. Teachers continue to slog before the blackboard to assist the learning exercise. A good number of students do well in the examination and proceed to the next ladder of the education system. There are many qualified, dedicated, competent and well-liked teachers in the system.

Yet, it faces many serious problems. As the realists suggest, much can be done to improve the system. Measures to enhance the quality of instruction, examination performance and administrative efficiency can be devised and put into practice. But these improvements will not occur within a neocolonial economy in which more and more school, college and university leavers do not land a decent job. High levels of corruption and nepotism in the society will affect the education system too. Such realities will invariably undermine the intrinsic value of a certificate, diploma or degree. Like the rest of the society, the education system will become highly unequal. Those with the means will secure a good education and the rest will attend substandard institutions.

ESR proposes the establishment of an alternative education system that will not only address the conventional type of problems but also put the education system on a different, revolutionary footing. In my view, that is the direction the nation needs to follow. But the main obstacle faced here is that overall the national economy is developing not along socialist but along neocolonial lines. The declaration and reality in the society and the education system are completely contradictory. Deeds do not match words.

In comparison, the German colonialists had matched their goals with harsh deeds. With the judicious deployment of the whip, ideological effort and a modicum of material rewards, they had ensured that the government and mission schools produced literate cadres for colonial administration and the missions, and skilled craftsmen for the economy in general and for the state, settlers and missions. They drove the pupils like slaves to work and pay for their education and expand the education system. But in those days, only a limited number could join the schools.

What are need for ESR are efforts to transform the economy into an integrated, self-sustaining economy based on intermediate technology, have a sound plan to combine traditional and practical education, implement the plan in a democratic fashion with the help of committed teachers and political cadres, tame the conservative bureaucracy, make political education an exercise to learn about history, politics and social change, and create confidence among students, teachers and parents with a fair and sound system of evaluation and job allocation and inspire the people though acts of self-sacrifice on the part of the leadership. Instead, ESR is turning into a chaotic exercise where the student takes a broom to school, sweeps the grounds and does a bit of digging in the farm. It has become an exercise that, sooner or later, is bound to fail.

Another stumbling block for ESR is the lack of dedicated, qualified, competent socialist cadres (teachers, administrators and governmental officials) to spearhead path breaking measures in education. Lack of resources can be overcome. With a good number of committed cadres and appropriate planning, no problem is insurmountable.

The central question are: How can the Ministry of National Education as constituted at present and manned by bureaucrats imbued with a neocolonial, conservative mindset, plan and implement the measures to revolutionize the content and quality of education and effectively install an alternative education system, and instill values like serving the nation, fostering equality and cooperative endeavor? Can an alternative examination system function without a corresponding change in the manpower planning and job allocation exercises? Can reliance on World Bank influenced advisors in the Ministry of Planning and elsewhere facilitate this socialistic exercise? Can the Ministry of National Education as it is now design the scheme of training teachers who will effectively and willingly operate in a socialist environment?

Character and values do not derive just from what students hear from their teachers and elders. They derive from life experience. When students do not have role models to inspire them to value equality, cooperation, dedication, deep respect for knowledge and hard work, and when they see what they are told is the opposite of what is done, and when they are harshly punished for the smallest misdeed, most will be drawn towards unruly tendencies and opportunistic and individualistic life style.

There is however a silver lining on the dark clouds. A small group of students in the secondary schools are paying serious attention to the progressive ideas and ideals enshrined in ESR. On their own initiative, they are seriously studying the history of capitalism and socialism. They discuss books and pamphlets on these and related topics. They have joined hands with students elsewhere, especially the radical students at the university, in this effort. Will they be the agents of genuine socialist transformation in the future? With they turn out to be the grave diggers of capitalism and neocolonialism? Perhaps; only time can tell. In that respect, ESR will have made a contribution as a key catalyst for this long term transformative process.

3

EDUCATION AND DEMOCRACY

SUMMARY: This essay looks at the secondary schools and colleges in Tanzania during the 1970s. The topics covered include the relationship between students and teachers, quality of instruction, relevance of the subject matter, the methods of assessing student performance, teacher motivation, administrative efficiency and use of institutional resources. While functioning at a basic level of adequacy, the education system is observed to be rife with features of under-education.

The operating and pedagogic conditions are far from satisfactory. Discontent prevails among the students and teachers. Several measures of a democratic nature are proposed to remedy the situation.[1]

*

---

1. This essay was first published as Hirji KF (A Correspondent) (1980) Democracy and education, *The Transporter*, National Institute of Transport, Dar es Salaam, 4:11-17. An edited version appeared in the appendix of *The Travails of a Tanzanian Teacher* (Hirji 2018).

> *The paradox of education is precisely this*
> *– that as one begins to become conscious*
> *one begins to examine the society*
> *in which he is being educated.*
> James Baldwin
> ++++++++++

NEWSPAPERS ARE LIKE THE TIP OF AN ICEBERG. What they reveal is only a small fraction of what there is. And that too may not be in a proper perspective. But if they are anything to go by, they indicate that many places of learning in Tanzania today are in a state of crisis.

The *Daily News* of 29 August 1979 reported that around 1,000 students of Dar es Salaam Technical College had marched the day before to the office of Ilala District Party Secretary to complain about the intolerable conditions at the college. To quote the report:

> The students' complaints included allegations of food shortage, bad food, bad accommodation, academic problems, bad services and bad leadership at the school.

On 16 August of last year, the same paper had reported a scandal at National Institute of Transport. Of the 38 students who had been asked to sit for supplementary examination thirty students had passed the initial exam. Only eight needed a further exam. The records were mixed up. Attributing this to regular administrative negligence, the report went on:

> Among the many complaints students listed included shortage of books, science laboratory, minimal practical training and general lack of organization.

Last year, eight students of Nyegezi Social Training Center were expelled for leading a protest against one of the lecturers. Eighteen other students were issued with warning letters for boycotting the classes of the lecturer who, they claimed, was not competent (Daily News, 16 November 979). Just a few months ago there were reports of serious disturbances at Mtwara Technical School when students went on a rampage, stoning teachers' houses.

Besides expulsions and suspensions, absenteeism prevails in schools and colleges. Mass punishments also occur. In some secondary schools, students are subjected to severe thrashings. A Radio Tanzania broadcast on 22 October 1979 mentioned the case of three pupils of Ifunda Technical School who had been hospitalized after being caned at school. It was reminiscent of the harsh discipline prevalent during the German colonial era.

Many similar examples can be cited but these suffice to raise serious questions regarding our educational establishments. Schools and colleges are being transformed from a battle-field of ideas into an arena of chaos. What is the cause? Students, teachers, parents, administrators—indeed all concerned with social progress—need to tackle these issues with seriousness they deserve.

THE CLASSROOM

Harmony between students and teachers is vital for the smooth sailing of the ship of education. Learning is a cooperative endeavor. Major tensions between these primary pillars of education propel the ship into stormy seas. They can reverberate not just throughout the educational system but also across the nation. What is the nature of the interaction between them these days?

Now it is like a tug of war. The two groups are pitted against each other in an environment not favorable for appropriate education to take place. Both are victims of circumstances beyond their control. The students see the teachers as just interested in dumping a mass of complex material on them. So they struggle, by means foul or fair, to score a grade which will enable them to get the coveted certificate or diploma on which their future depends.

One source of tension is a new evaluation scheme, continuous assessment, recently introduced for schools and institutions of higher learning. It is supposed to be a progressive system as compared to the inherited British system of gauging a person's knowledge and ability through end-of-the-year three-hour memory testing exercises. But the new scheme has recreated in a continuous form miniature exercises of the same old mold. Emphasis is still on examinations, the difference being that instead of once a year, you do them once a month or once a week. It has turned into a literal nightmare for students and teacher alike. Only the administrators, with their preference for methodical drabness, draw satisfaction from the mass of reports filled in. The students are justified in calling it a system of continuous harassment.

Education then becomes an assembly line process, tailored to produce standardized robots. Creativity is banished to a corner. Any flexibility in teaching or evaluation is viewed with horror: it may lower the standards! Emphasis is on weekly tests with multiple choice questions to facilitate the marking. The talk is of combination of theory with practice. The snag is that either the theory is impractical or the practice is just a formal one.

While students are supposed to undertake project work, teachers lack the experience to guide them. The students are besieged with so many tests that they hardly have time to think about and digest anything well, let alone engage in creative work the projects demand. They memorize current topics only to forget them as soon as they have the required units. Project reports turn out to be an odd assortment of data gathered from here and there interspersed with diffuse ideas from textbooks. For the teacher the system has become a spine wreaking burden he or she has to bear day to day, year to year.

Schools and colleges had shortages of teachers before continuous evaluation was introduced. Teachers were already overburdened. Now their load has increased to an extent that their life has come to resemble that of the fully jammed UDA buses which groan as they crawl along the road, sagging completely on one side and liable to breakdown at any time. A pile of test papers and progress report forms clutter their desks. One can forecast that in future teachers will be spending more time filling forms than preparing lessons.

Many teachers supported the new system at its inception, unaware of what lay in store for them. Now that it is here to stay, they respond by not completing the syllabus, carrying out the assessments in a hurried, superficial fashion and at times, manufacturing marks. The purpose of continuous evaluation is to ensure that the students' heads are immersed in books and the teachers are on their toes all the time. But whether better education is being imparted is something which is yet to be established.

The syllabuses of various subjects being taught at schools and colleges give the impression that we want to set exalted standards for the whole world to emulate. There are too many topics. And some topics are too advanced for the educational level. Only a teacher who rushes through them like a hurricane can cover all the topics. The committees charged with setting syllabi tend to include topics from the advanced courses its members had attended locally or abroad. It is not uncommon to see teachers issuing to students the same handouts and books they got from their professors at the university.

The high turnover in the teaching profession has an adverse effect on the quality of classroom instruction. Most local teachers are fresh from college or university. After a few years at the blackboard they seek better paid, less demanding work. Experienced, qualified local teachers who stick to their profession and work diligently are in the minority. Reliance on expatriate teachers goes on. But they are here today and away tomorrow. Long term improvements cannot come from reliance on transient elements. Besides, many of them are timid yes-men. In the hope of renewing their contracts, they just follow, perhaps conscientiously, the system as it is rather than struggle for a better one.

The teachers and students work in the face of numerous constraints. Books and stationery are in short supply. So are typing and duplicating facilities. Orders are misplaced or delayed; suppliers are not paid in time, etc. Priorities are reversed. An air conditioner for the main office is prioritized over a duplicating machine, teacher handouts are set aside when office correspondence has to be typed, etc.

In spite of the high standards set (or may be because of them) the quality of the students emerging from the education system from the schools to the university is nothing to boast about. In places, when faced with the projects of mass failure, the teachers become lenient and simply pass everyone. At the next step of the educational ladder, these students will have to learn what they are supposed to have mastered already.

This state of affairs frustrates both the students and their teachers. And, in the case of students, it spills over into other areas and causes the types of disturbances we hear about now and again. The academic drudgery they are subjected to is reflected in the fury with which they react.

THE INSTITUTIONAL ENVIRONMENT

As the students and the teachers are the two major pillars of education, the task of the workers and administrators is to provide services to facilitate the learning process. But in many schools and colleges we get the impression that the teachers, students and workers exist to primarily serve the administrators. Institutional resources and facilities are used to firstly to make life comfortable for the administrators.

Some examples have been cited. Take the utilization of vehicles. Many colleges own a couple of vehicles; some have a fleet of cars, vans, trucks and buses. If one investigates their usage, all sorts of revelations emerge. Vehicle meant for academic use are diverted elsewhere. A van may be bought for research but the sole research it may end up doing is around brothels on Saturday nights.

When you seek a vehicle to collect an external tutor, send students on a field trip, or enable teachers to supervise student projects, none is at hand. It takes a major effort to procure a vehicle. But if it is a question of sending the principal's wife for shopping or transporting a bag of cement to the bursar's home, the problem does not exist. The vehicles of some colleges meander around the bars at night for private business purposes. Such practices add to the mounting grievances in the college.

The general services provided to the students and teachers are poor. Often, it is due to lack of organization and neglect. Class rooms lack simple things as dusters forcing the teachers to bring their own rags to clean the blackboard. The purchase of supplies is riddled with scandals. Food is bought at inflated prices and someone pockets the difference. Purchase of books, stationery, lab material and workshop equipment is riddled with similar anomalies. Most schools and some colleges have a shortage of funds. But instead of trying to make the best of it, a few savvy individuals try to make the most of it. Students end up eating rotten beans and maize purchased at high prices and when they complain they are told it is a national problem.

Favoritism is rampant. Student recruitment, employment of cleaners and secretaries, and teacher promotion are tainted by *ndugunization*. The students know who among them are there not through their know-how but know-who. Teachers are not surprised when one of them who has a few achievements to his credit rises fast up the ladder. Favoritism affects the issuance of scholarships. Some international organizations provide scholarships to colleges for advanced training for their teaching staff. But the administrators often taste the cake first. The teachers get the leftovers after the bosses have taken their share.

In places, the administration lacks the foresight and competence to run the institution and plan its long-term development. Narrow horizons govern their decisions, which in most cases are done on a day to day basis. Instead of emphasizing academic excellence, they stress loyalty. Many hesitate to recruit qualified, competent local staff in the fear of being replaced or exposed. Local teachers are frustrated through insufficient incentives, lack of fringe benefits and facilities, and too strict a promotion policy. Some administrators prefer expatriates or local staff with dubious qualifications who are content with being their yes-men.

Many administrators run their colleges like primary schools. Stressing petty issues, they seek a strict control on everything that goes on. Some go to the dining hall at meal times to ensure that the students do not get more than the specified share. They emphasize attendance, obedience and punctuality. Students showing minor violations of the rules are dealt with harshly. The teachers are required to report on duty at 8:00 in the morning and be on the premises for the entire working time irrespective of whether they have classes to teach or not. A teacher is thereby turned into an office clerk. His efficiency inevitably declines because of the lack of flexibility which his work demands.

BUREAUCRACY OR DEMOCRACY

Bookish drudgery reduces student involvement in the extracurricular activities. Participation in sports, students clubs, discussion groups, cultural events, student organization affairs and student magazine declines as they are permanently buried under an avalanche of tests and assignments. But such activities are an important component of education. Without them, the outlook of the students will be shallow and careerist and they will not be able to play their role in social and national development. Instead of being mature, critical thinkers, they will function in their places of work like stunted robots.

A sound education must be based on democratic foundations. The old fashioned bureaucrat for whom students are just an unruly lot has no place in the modern education system. Lack of participation of students in decision making is one of the fundamental causes of the present crisis in the system. Even teachers have little say in what goes on in their places.
Absence of participation and control from below enables individuals in key positions to take advantage of existing problems and magnify them. Wanton practices proliferate when the

bureaucracy has the upper hand. It leads to mounting frustrations among the students, teachers and workers. To prevent explosions and improve the situation in schools and colleges, broad-based democracy, grass-roots control and freedom of information are absolutely essential.

WHAT IS TO BE DONE?

The long term solution to the existing impasse in education is to organize the system on a firm democratic footing. With the involvement of all concerned parties, specific problems can be tackled and resolved. Participation of the students in decision making relating to the affairs of the school or college community is crucial.

The present situation of academic drudgery for students and over work for the teachers must be remedied, and a more rational system of learning and evaluation has to be worked out.

An independent and democratic student organization through which the students can channel their contributions is a key ingredient of that process. The recent announcement of the establishment of the National Union of Students is a welcome one. But the union should not be loaded with bureaucratic controls that would turn it into a student organ in name only. And the students need to elect their leaders with care. Some student leaders are only interested in prestige and running bars, and do not attend to the interests of their constituents. Students should elect committed and bold leaders who exhibit a deep understanding of the society in which they live.

In a similar fashion, a national union of teachers with branches at all the places of learning is an essential, urgent requirement. It should be a democratic, autonomous organization tasked with serving and protecting the teaching profession and promoting academic excellence. Attracting and retaining competent, committed teachers and improvement of their terms and conditions of work should be at the top of its list of priorities.

And there is a need to promote freedom of ideas through free flow of information and unhindered discussion. Members of the school or college community should have the right to access information about the affairs of the school or the college. The present bureaucratic system of locking up even the pettiest detail leads to small problems remaining undetected and not addressed until they assume mammoth proportions. Students and teachers, through their elected representatives, must be informed about community affairs and how institutional resources and finance are used. In case of misuse, they must be empowered to take appropriate measures.

In order to promote debate through which problems can be discussed and resolved, students and teachers must have the latitude to establish their own magazines, journals or newsletters to voice their opinions on academic, institutional and national issues. These magazines must be free from external administrative or political interference.

The policy of Education for Self-Reliance enunciated in 1967 stressed relevance, adequacy and democratic participation in education (Essay 2). Yet, more than a decade on, the implementation of these proposals is far from reality.

ADDITIONAL REMARKS

The problems of the educational system cannot be solved without the participation of the students and the teachers. The reforms suggested here are intended to ensure that this participation occurs on a free and democratic basis. Grass-roots democracy and freedom of debate in the educational institutions are essential components of the struggle against under-education.

The above essay presents a rather bleak picture of the contents, organization and quality of education in the Tanzanian education system of the late 1970s. But in comparison with what prevails today, it was a system that generally delivered the goods. College graduates could read and write in English at a decent level, displayed adequate theoretical and practical knowledge of subjects taught and performed satisfactorily at their work stations. Teachers generally taught well and worked hard. On the other hand, the diplomas and degrees held by the present day output of our colleges and universities are not worth the paper they are printed on. The teachers at such higher learning institutions today, in comparison with their counterparts of yesteryears, do a patently substandard job.

A detailed description of the establishment, operation and problems of one institution of higher learning, the National Institute of Transport, from 1976 to 1980 is provided in Chapter 8 of Hirji (2018). While the situation at this institute reflected the problems described above, there were also notable attempts to overcome aspects of under-education like reliance on external funds and expert manpower. There were also efforts to make the curriculum more relevant to the needs of the transport sector in Tanzania. The achievements and limitations on this score are described as well.

4

EDUCATION AND DEPENDENCY

SUMMARY: Reliance on funds from outside agencies for development of the facilities, sense of direction, teaching, research and other activities is a primary feature of under-education in Africa. This essay explores the nature and consequences of such external dependency on university education in Tanzania. Mainly based on my observation and experience at the Faculty of Medicine, University of Dar es Salaam, from 1989 to 1991, it shows that dependency leads to a deterioration of the quality of teaching as well as of other pedagogic activities and conditions of the academy.[1]

*

---

1. This essay was first published as Hirji KF (1990) Academic pursuits under the Link, *CODESRIA Bulletin*, (Senegal), 2:9-16. An updated version appeared as Chapter 6 in CB Mwaria, F Federici and J McLaren (editors) (2000) *Africa Visions: Literary Images, Political Change and Social Struggle in Contemporary Africa*, Praeger Press, Westport, Connecticut. This is a substantially edited version.

> *There's no such thing as neutral education.*
> *Education either functions as an instrument*
> *to bring about conformity or freedom.*
> Paulo Freire

++++++++++

AFTER AN ABSENCE OF EIGHT YEARS, I returned to Tanzania in January 1989 to take up a teaching position in the Department of Epidemiology and Biostatistics, Faculty of Medicine, University of Dar as Salaam (UDSM). Upon reporting for duty, I was given an office and a teaching assignment. Thereupon I briskly strode down to the office and asked for some stationary—nothing extravagant—just a pen, pencil and writing paper. The looks my request elicited were my first encounter with the LINK.

The head of the department patiently conveyed to me that the annual budget for purchasing such items was inadequate and had been exhausted long ago. I protested. My monthly salary of about fifty US dollars did not even suffice to purchase groceries for my family. Looking around the office I saw a few usable items. Surely, there were some to spare. Just then, the LINK came to my rescue. The secretary opened her drawer and brought out one of the nicest notebooks I have ever seen. On it was inscribed 'Kollegieblock.' It was adorned with other undecipherable symbols as well. Yet, I cherished the book and used it with care for six months. It was a left over from a Scandinavian funded research project. The pen and pencil, though, had to be found elsewhere. The department had a very large supply of computer paper obtained from this and other LINKs. It was the pin-fed type of continuous paper with perforated edges. Yet, I was advised to use it as writing material!

From then on, time after time, I encountered the LINK in all sorts of places, even in the toilet. It is all pervasive, like an Orwellian Big Brother. I have learned that to progress you need to be LINKed. If you march out of tune with it, you are courting a disaster. The academicians blessed by the LINK smile radiantly and prosper; those without a LINKage are perpetually enveloped by an aura of gloom.

Thanks to it, our department has five microcomputers, several laser and dot-matrix printers, photocopiers, computer accessories and supplies. But for almost the whole of 1989, the bread-and-butter items like pens, pencils, writing paper and rulers were in short supply. I say almost, as just a week before the end of the year, each member of the department was blessed with a Christmas present comprising a writing pad, two red pens, and two blue pens. A week earlier some prominent LINK personalities had visited the place. Whether the gift was connected to that visit or not was not known.

Whatever the facet of academic life at the Faculty of the Medicine I look at, I see anomalies of this nature. Can an academic institution discharge its responsibilities in such paradoxical circumstances? What kind of academic activities do they engender? What attitudes towards teaching and research does the presence of LINK foster? These are the issues I examine in this essay.

TEACHING

Biostatistics is a required first-year course for the postgraduate students pursuing the Master of Tropical Diseases Control or Master of Medicine degree in a specialty like community health, microbiology, pathology and internal medicine. And that is what I was assigned to teach. My class had ten enthusiastic students.

It seems trite to state that books are necessary for effective learning. Societies where knowledge passes from generation to generation by the word of mouth are supposed to be found in historical works only. Today even elementary school pupils need books. But between them, my students did not have a single text for their subject. They did not have photocopied material either. The photocopying paper in the department was not for making handouts for students. Consequently, at the outset, a lot of class time was wasted in copying by hand the essential parts of the course notes.

The student book allowance is grossly inadequate. Asking them to photocopy a paper, even an important one, at their own expense can be done rarely. It is a strain on their limited budgets. Yet, the LINK has a role here too. Some books ordered through a British LINK were expected anytime. A stipulation was that only books published in the United Kingdom could be purchased. They arrived a couple of months later. A few were kept in the offices of the lecturers and professors. The rest were sent to the library and placed on special reserve. This offered some respite. But, by the start of the next academic year, half of the books sent to the library had mysteriously vanished. I had learnt my lesson by then. Through my own LINK I had secured sufficient bound volumes of photocopied material and salvaged seven copies of a book procured by the department. These were loaned out so that two students shared a copy of each item. I saw one other lecturer use his LINK to provide books for his class. From then on, the class time was devoted to discussing issues and concepts, not copying notes. What the situation will be next year is at the mercy of the LINK. These remarks also apply to laboratory and other supplies needed for preclinical and clinical training at a medical school. In all these activities, without the blessings of a LINK, students and teachers end up in dire circumstances, able to proceed only with difficulty.

The Faculty of Medicine offers two types of courses. First, there are the regular courses listed in the University catalogue. What I have stated thus far applies to such courses. Then there are the specially funded short courses. I was involved in one such course a few months after my arrival. It was a course on reproductive epidemiology. The participants were drawn from all over Africa.

Funded by the Rockefeller Foundation, it was organized and conducted by our department.

While lecturing in this course, my teaching of the regular course went on. Both were in the same building. My regular class was held in a ground floor room that was never cleaned, where the students had to wipe off the dust from the chairs and tables at the start of each session, where I wrote on a worn out blackboard and used a dirty rag to wipe it, where the window panes were broken and in which all sorts of debris, including rusted air conditioners, lay in the corner. The short course was held in the first story extension built recently with German funding. The place was immaculate, sparkling clean and had new furniture and the latest teaching aides. Swirling ceiling fans warded off the tropical heat.

The short course students had all the required books and supplies. They got decent meals, lodging, transport and a hefty allowance. The instructors and course organizers also secured an allowance. My reward for the five lectures I gave over a period of two weeks amounted to twice my regular monthly salary.

The support staff benefited as well. Consequently, the administrative efficiency associated with it was an order of magnitude higher than that encountered from the same workers in the regular course of duties.

Yet, from an academic point of view, such courses are of little value. What the students get is a hodgepodge of topics. The basic motivation among the instructors and students is financial, related more to travel opportunities than to anything else. But such courses secure the lion's share of attention and devotion. The regular training of postgraduate and undergraduate medical, dental, pharmacy and public health students, on the other hand, is beset with relative neglect and disinterest.

What can one make of a recent short course funded by Swedish Agency for Research and Economic Cooperation (SAREC) that was held at a splendid beach hotel? Its purpose was to instruct the academic and nonacademic staff in the use of word processing and other computer software. A secretary and two instructors from Sweden conducted the course. Surely, there are well qualified Tanzanians who could have done the job. Or was its purpose to provide a paid tropical holiday for the instructors? The allowances they got can only be deemed discriminatory in relation to what the Tanzanian participants were given. The local organizers were given more crumbs.

It is not that such courses should not be held. By all means, where there is a need, let us have them. But they can be organized on a rational basis. If organizations like SAREC want to assist, they must do it on terms that reflect the academic requirements and capabilities of the university.

If the large sums dissipated for the short courses are used to support the regular courses in terms of teaching allowance for instructors and books and supplies for the students, they can markedly help improve the quality of instruction. The professors and lecturers would be encouraged to spend more time on pedagogic pursuit than on growing and marketing pineapples and eggs from their farms. They would also be around when the students need their help. Or is it that agencies like the Rockefeller Foundation and SAREC are locked into supporting inconsequential courses of dubious academic value?

A few regular courses receive special LINK funds. But, a scant portion of the funds filters down to the students. The lecturers are unable to purchase course supplies from the funds; the available facilities are monopolized by the coordinator; no meetings are held to discuss the utilization of the funds; and there is little internal accountability in relation to them. Thereby, even where LINK funds are available, their impact on the regular courses is minimal. An attitude of resignation and frustration prevails among students and concerned academic staff. No one can do anything to resolve the problems.

Therefore, in spite of the multitude of the LINKs at the faculty, the quality of instruction for the regular study programs leaves a lot to be desired. This is one of the principal, though not the sole, reasons behind the poor and declining performance of our students in the university examinations. It is an issue the Faculty is currently grappling with, but no solution is in sight.

BOOKSTORE AND LIBRARY

In the 1960s and 1970s, the university students purchased books and other supplies from the main university bookstore. It was an efficiently managed store well stocked with textbooks and supplementary material required for all study programs. Invariably available at the start of the academic year, the books were eminently affordable. A book loan of about TSh 1,200/= sufficed to purchase the required books, stationery and other books of interest, and still have money left over for sundry items like alarm clocks. Books were in abundant supply throughout the academic year. The students did not get the book allowance in cash. Instead, each had a purchase account at the bookstore. Apart from the book loan, students pursued their studies at the public expense.

Today, that situation has turned upside down. The book allowance is now given in cash. And it is hardly used for books. In the first place, only a few of the relevant books are available. And when they are, they are too expensive. A typical student purchases only one or two books. Some of the cash is used for photocopied parts of the books. Most is diverted to other pressing needs. The days of books in abundance are so distant that most students do not know they ever existed.

Due to years of mismanagement and funding shortfall, this bookstore cannot compete even with street hawkers. A bookseller operating in a dilapidated hut near the Kisutu market has better books on medicine and statistics. When I visited the bookshop, I was horrified to see the pathetic state it had stumbled into. A once first rate store with the latest books and journals on a diversity of disciplines was now a place where one could not find adequate material for a single one of the degrees offered at the university. And it was replete with paradoxes. For a particular course connected to a special LINK, books were not a problem. But for programs bereft of a LINK, the majority, even a single book was not on the shelves.

At one point in time, the bookshop had received a large grant through an exclusive LINK. But orders were not placed in time. Some books were ordered at the last minute. And many were not the needed ones. There is hardly any coordination between the academic departments and the bookstore. Each department seeks its own solution by cultivating its own LINK. Hence, a few departments are well endowed with books and journals, but the rest wallow in a state of intellectual famine.

The university library is a valuable resource for research and teaching material. In the 1960s and 1970s, the UDSM main library was among the best university libraries in Africa. That is no longer the case. Yet, it has retained a modicum of good organization. Its repertoire of journals is better than expected. A LINK, responsible management, and incentives for the staff are the secrets behind its present status. Nonetheless, it is but a shadow of its glorious past.

The medical library, on the other hand, resembles a dusty museum. For most medical specialties, the shelves contain ancient material. The shortages are heightened by frequent disappearance of new material. Here and there, an exception is seen; a state-of-the-art text or complete volumes of a key journal. Basic reference materials are unavailable. For example, the library does not have recent volumes of *Index Medicus*, the major bibliographic Bible for medicine! Previous volumes had been placed in the main library by mistake, and nobody had missed them until I took the trouble to locate them.

Of recent, the world has witnessed an explosive growth of scientific and medical knowledge. With conditions like these we are, day by day, receding further and further away from the frontiers of knowledge. Books and journals are a precious resource. The sum allocated in the internal budget is woefully inadequate. Could a part of the funds wasted in the numerous unofficial trips with official vehicles be used for books? Could the Bank of Tanzania spare more foreign exchange to purchase books and educational material?

What current material the library has is provided by a few LINKs. But that does not amount to much. The library has a computer, but it is not visible to the user. Whether or when they will be able use it to search electronic bibliographies and databases is another question.

RESEARCH

The two activities where the LINK is omnipresent are research and consultancy. A colleague recently said that if you cultivate good LINKs for such endeavors, you can `mine diamonds.' Not everyone can aspire to be a globetrotting consultant like some senior professors or heads of departments. (Some departments are effectively run by junior staff. I wonder at the quality of instruction and supervision imparted to the students.) But, everyone aspires to do research. And research generates data. When the researcher has gathered volumes of data, it is not uncommon for him or her to be at a loss as to how to interpret them. That is when he or she consults a statistician.

Being one of a few statisticians here, I am regularly on call. Students, staff and other researchers are constantly at my doorstep seeking advice on what to do with their data. More often than not, they discover that they should have consulted a statistician prior to embarking upon their study. Either the design or the types of data collected are found to be inappropriate for the question posed. At this stage the researcher may seek a second opinion that may render a more favorable diagnosis of the research effort, or he or she may desire a palliative exercise to be undertaken. Such an experience is common to statisticians in biomedical institutions the world over. At the Faculty of Medicine too, a substantial portion of the research effort is ill-conceived and badly executed, and the results, erroneously interpreted. There are a few exceptions I will note later.

These research projects fall into two categories; undergraduate and graduate student research and faculty research. Undergraduate student research, whether as a group or individual project, is generally of no value. The potential to do good work exists. Adequate preparations and guidance do not. I recall a request to join a class of undergraduate medical students on a weeklong project to evaluate the Essential Drugs Program in Kibaha. I requested the department concerned for a write up on the aims, design and implementation of the project. But none was available; the best I could get was a page of hastily scribbled stuff.

The postgraduate students have a year for dissertation work. They are better placed to conduct research. But as a result of inadequate supervision many flounder for months. By international standards, their budget is meager, less than two or three hundred US dollars. Despite the multiple obstacles they face many, if properly guided, are able to undertake sound research that is relevant to the health needs of the nation. Some work with amazing dedication and perseverance. The work of some postgraduate students in pediatrics in the past year deserves high commendation.

There are also grandiose projects in which senior academics are the principal investigators. Blessed by international agencies, their budgets run into thousands of dollars. Yet, their quality is often inversely related to the size of the budget. When I read the grant proposal of some of these projects, I wonder how they were approved by the funders. If a graduate student had brought such a proposal to me, I would have unceremoniously tossed it out of the window. Or is it that the LINK has a different standard for African nations? Given the paternalistic attitudes prevalent in these organizations, I would not be surprised if it was the case. Sometimes it is a case of you scratch my back and I will scratch yours. To justify their existence to the domestic tax payers, they need to show that they are aiding the poor of the world. And in order to make up for their inability to assist those who truly need it, they end up funding projects for which they derive impressive looking data and glowing reports from the local counterparts to support their charitable claims. No one pays attention to the fact that the data are of dubious quality.

To paraphrase PJ Davis and R Hersh, scientific research is of three types: (1) pure research, which results from the internal dynamics of a specific discipline; (2) applied research, which emanates as a response to specific problems in engineering, medicine, agriculture, or education; and (3) rhetorical research,

which is neither pure nor applied, and whose sole consequence is to generate publications, reports and grant proposals filled with empty verbiage and pretentious obfuscation. (Davis and Hersh 1986).

In the many years that I spent in the United States as a student and an academic at prominent universities, I came across instances of all three types of research. The time, energy and resources devoted to rhetorical research at these famed institutions are mind-boggling. (Broad and Wade 1982). But since my return to Tanzania, I have come across a new category of research, namely, pseudo research.

It camouflages itself as applied research. But its design and execution and the quality of information it generates rule out any applicability of its findings. Lacking a scientific or policy value, it is characterized by the paucity of the scholarly sounding publications that are the hallmarks of rhetorical research. The report may decorate the pages of a conference proceeding, but its existence is soon forgotten even by the authors. The primary motive behind it is pecuniary, including chances for international travel for shopping purposes.

The Faculty of Medicine also hosts a multitude of conferences every year. First, it is the medical association, then the public health association, then the surgeons' association, and so on. From September to December this year, a blue and white banner graced the entrance of the Muhimbili hospital to announce a conference almost every week. The gathering is usually held under the sponsorship of a LINK. Despite the glossy folders and nicely printed material, the quality of the papers presented therein reflects the dubious quality of research done here and at other research establishments in the country and Africa.

The bulk of the papers are either book reviews, summaries of case records, or results of surveys conducted on an ad hoc basis. Once in a while, a scientifically designed and executed investigation appears. And rarer is a report on a sound investigation to address a health problem in the nation. According to the editors of the *World Health Forum*:

> The job of a researcher is not only to publish the results but also to start the process of decision making. Thousands of research papers have, over the years, proved only to be of academic interest. (Editor 1988).

Action based reports are infrequent. At a recent meeting of the Tanzania Public Health Association, a project on the control of filariasis with the use of polystyrene beads in pit latrines was presented. Conducted in Zanzibar, it was a fascinating exercise undertaken by British and local scientists. This relatively cheap method is effective for mosquito control. Its use would impact the transmission of other vector borne diseases as well. But it did not garner publicity in the media. In Dar es Salaam, it has ended as a showpiece project. Do the officials in the Ministry of Health dream of implementing the exercise on a wider scale? Maybe they need a LINK funds to travel to London to learn more about it!

Another concomitant of the multitude of research projects initiated here is the computer boom currently underway. Many departments have, or are in the process of getting microcomputers and related equipment. Other departments are vying for LINK funds to procure them. No doubt computers have a role to play in medical and public health research. But there is a tendency to conflate *scientific praxis* with the use of latest gadgetry. The adage among computer experts 'garbage in, garbage out' seems to have been lost on the researchers here. Research quality is not necessarily improved by the fact that the data have been fed into a computer and the results printed out in a nice format on a laser printer. For a study with a faulty design, or poor conduct, computer use actually creates a false impression. As I have seen, computers and fancy printers are often employed to print flawed grant proposals and research reports in a glossy format.

Where the tradition of scientific rigor is weak, computer use sustains unscientific practice. The training of physicians in most parts of the world does not stress the inculcation of a scientific attitude. They spend the bulk of their time memorizing a huge mass of information. And it is a form of training that promotes reverence of authority. (Pocock 1983). In the Third World nations, weak democratic traditions, poor spirit of critical inquiry in the academia and political submissiveness make the problem worse. An electronic gadget more easily camouflages the shortcomings of existing practices rather than encourage critical investigation in health, agriculture, industry or education.

The use of computer can also add errors. Until recently, computer file data were rarely checked in our department, the department with the largest number of computers at the Faculty. It processes the bulk of the data generated by the studies conducted here. When checking the input data was begun, we found that for some studies, what was on the forms and what was in the computer were two different things! When the data are not checked for accuracy and consistency, the validity of the results can be compromised.

Computers are the academic status symbols of this era. A powerful computer is often used exclusively for word processing. An electronic typewriter with memory or a dedicated word processor, both of which are much less expensive, can suffice. Computer accessories particularly suitable for local conditions are not deployed. An unstable power supply calls for cheap, reliable surge suppressors. But most computer users have not heard of them. They use the costly voltage stabilizers or uninterruptable power supply units. When continuous feed paper is expensive and not easy to obtain, one would think that printers would be fitted with cut sheet feeders. But hardly anyone knows about them.

A reason for this state of affairs is that the decisions about computer equipment are not made locally. Computers and computer supplies are frequently dumped onto the campus by a LINK, and we have to get by with what they give. One department has Swedish equipment with its user guide printed in Swedish, another has Japanese computers with Japanese language books, and so on. Basic facilities for preventive maintenance like disk-drive cleaning kits and print-head cleaners are not provided. They are used as local buses are, without preventive care until they grind to a halt. Then a new LINK is sought. Even crucial tasks like making regular backup copies of the data on the hard disk drives are seldom done.

Computers are not the panacea for improving research quality. First and foremost, what is needed is to inculcate a spirit of scientific inquiry that is rigorous and critical. It would not condone sacrificing professional, ethical and academic standards for the sake of expediency. The credibility of a scientific statement is gauged by the degree to which it conforms with experiment or observation. If computer use at best only helps transform pseudo research into rhetorical research, then it has little scientific value. Further, the consolidation of scientific traditions in order to perform sound, rigorous and relevant research has to be done by ourselves. The LINK is not a substitute.

CONCLUDING REMARKS

Discussions with several lecturers and professors lead me to believe that the above remarks pertain to all the faculties of the University of Dar as Salaam. Has academic life always been like this? If not, what internal and external factors have led to the present situation? What has been the reaction of the academics to symptoms of intellectual atrophy? Is there a way out?

I do not claim to have definitive answers to these basic questions. My purpose is to set the ball rolling and generate a debate. If my views will provoke others to respond, perhaps analyses based on firmer foundations and solid evidence can emerge. If a broad consensus on the basic causes and possible remedies for the academic ailments at our university can be attained, then appropriate preventive and curative therapies to address them can be initiated.

In the early 1970s most departments of the University of Dar as Salaam had been in the existence for about a decade. Yet, one could claim with justification that a graduate from this university had received an education comparable to that at the best universities in the world. A 1971 bachelor's degree graduate from the mathematics department who went for advanced study at a prestigious Canadian university wrote to me that he found most of the required courses quite easy. He had scaled a more arduous terrain in his undergraduate years. Scholars and students from all over Africa and the world taught or studied at this university. During those years, a trend to make university instruction be in accord with the nation's requirements was in evidence. Most of the departments were established with external assistance and staff. But in a short while, qualified Tanzanians manned the upper echelons of the academia. They included prominent economists, lawyers, historians, chemists, surgeons, parasitologists, and so on.

Despite that solid foundation, today the academic life at UDSM is in the doldrums. Despite the efforts to rescue it through the LINK, what was once a beacon of scholarship is now an institution where intellectual mediocrity is rampant. But it is incorrect to only blame the academics for this state of affairs. What we see at the university in general, and at the Faculty of Medicine in particular, reflects the state of and trends in the broader society. The excessive dependence on the LINK at this place parallels the national policies pursued since independence. Despite its political ideology, the government of Tanzania never changed its policy of relying on foreign loans, grants and planners for most of its projects. In the heydays of sloganeering about socialism and self-reliance, Tanzania was the highest per capita recipient of foreign funds in Africa. Projects like adult education or health education campaigns which could and should have been implemented purely with local effort were not undertaken without external backing.

Our political leaders have mastered the art of saying with a straight face exactly the opposite of what they do. While government projects followed plans laid out by foreign consultants, we were said to be deciding over our own future. While local experts were referred to with derision as *wasomi* in their speeches, the foreign *wasomi* were taken at their word. A systematic policy to harness local intellectual resources at the university or elsewhere to promote national development was not put in place. If anything, there was a significant discouragement for such efforts.

The past three decades have seen a vast growth of higher education in Tanzania. New departments and faculties were established at UDSM. The Faculty of Agriculture is now an autonomous university. Many colleges and institutes were started around the country. The variety of advanced training available rivals that in any other African country. But these institutions sprang up as appendages of the state or parastatal bureaucracy. And hardly any has had a notable impact on its respective social or economic sector. In some cases the growth of the educational arm went along with the deterioration of the sector it was to serve. That Tanzania is among a few nations of Africa to have a Cooperative College has not implied that the cooperatives are better run here; that it is the only nation in sub-Saharan Africa with a Transport Institute has not resulted in the bus or rail companies being run on a more efficient basis; the presence of the Ardhi Institute has not meant that land is used in a rational and planned manner; the Institute of Finance Management did not produce healthier financial institutions; the Social Welfare Training Institute did not lead to better services for the disadvantaged, and so on. One can multiply such examples from health, education, agriculture and other sectors, and paint a similar picture for the faculties of the two universities as well.

Educational development has become an end unto itself, not related to social and economic development. Higher education has become a formal exercise. What one learns is not applied at work either because of its unsuitability to the local environment, or because of the resistance towards absorption of innovative ideas. If what one has learned is in line with how things are currently done, then the knowledge is of use. Else, it is of no use. The bureaucracy has little room for creativity. Graduates from the educational institutions have found themselves frustrated if they dared to suggest or implement any innovations at their places of work.

The negative political attitude on creativity and intellectual endeavor has also impacted life within the academy. The administrative arm is now stronger compared to the academic arm; resource are channeled to benefit the bureaucrats; democratic traditions have become weaker, and accountability has been reduced. (The new vice chancellor at UDSM has tried to arrest this trend but faces political opposition.) The quality and originality of research, its applicability to practical problems or excellence in teaching are not the key criteria for advancement. This is another factor that has led to neglect of teaching and decline in research quality. The academic life has stultified to the extent that now exchange of ideas beyond the confines of the classroom has virtually ceased. (Unless, it is in the context of a LINK sponsored conference!) What was once a seminar and discussion room in the Community Medicine Building is used by the nonacademic staff to take a nap. The cupboards lining its walls are full of moldy books and journals that have been untouched for years.

Together with a reduction of overall government budget for education, the university budget has declined in real terms. The departments without a LINK are reduced to a state of penury. With mounting inflation, the salaries of the university staff have reached their present ridiculous proportions. In Tanzania today, what a professor earns is not far from the minimum wage in Kenya. I find it miraculous that in spite of the minuscule paycheck, secretaries still type well, workers keep the toilets clean, and some lecturers give well-researched and thought-out lectures!

Overall, the academics reacted to the decline of their institutions in a way that only led to a further deterioration of the academic environment. Mostly they retreated inwards and sought personal solutions to their problems. Many got involved in external income generating projects that had no relation to their professional work. Others and I found higher paying jobs abroad. Some became globe-trotting consultants or conference attendees. And others kept churning out grant proposals by the month. Since economic gain was the main motivation, academic standards were not upheld. Teaching and research suffered further as a consequence of this search for personal salvation. (Shivji 1988).

Seeking the missing LINK became the sole preoccupation in the academia. Leftists and rightists, engineers or doctors, all looked beyond the national boundaries for a savior. Some wrote papers critiquing foreign investments but did so with foreign assistance. Life within the academy was fragmented. Each department head cultivated his or her own LINK. It was his or her mini empire. The available resources were distributed according to his or her whims. Fair allocation of the benefits derived from a LINK, whether in terms of research fund or trips abroad, is never on the agenda of the otherwise democratic departmental meetings. Hence, planned academic endeavors become next to impossible, and the cohesion of the faculty or department melts away.

As you go around the Faculty of Medicine, you wonder whether about a hundred years after Karl Peters landed here, a second partition of Africa is in progress. The Dental School is run by the Finnish, the AIDS research program by the Swedish, the community health projects by the Germans, with the British, Italians, Danish, etc. functioning in their exclusive zones of influence. International exchange should be promoted. I favor it. But when such an exchange is conducted solely in the framework of a donor-recipient relation, what will assure that it is done on the basis of academic equality and mutual respect? One can only hope that the professors and heads of departments who sign the LINK agreements and control their resources are not the modern day chiefs resembling their historical counterparts who sold out their peoples for a pittance.

What is to be done? There are no simple answers. But there are simple answers as to how to go about finding appropriate solutions.

We need to take steps in a direction that will produce viable solutions. They include a reaffirmation by the academics of the commitment to uphold universal academic and ethical values, and undertake collective and democratic endeavors, rather than individual, *ad hoc* ones.

As a group, they should reassert their commitment to seek the truth and advance the frontiers of knowledge while at the same time finding ways and means of using their know-how to deal with the problems facing society. They should stress commitment to pursue these values in the framework of democracy and respect for human dignity. They need to shed off their cloak of timidity and selfishness and be more audacious in seeking solutions to institutional and societal problems.

Today education and health account for about 5 percent of the national budget but the military gets more than 15 percent. Such World Bank tolerated anomalies should come under critical scrutiny. Does a country like ours need bullets more than medicines and books? Payment of starvation salaries to qualified personnel only promotes corruption, mismanagement, and brain drain, and needs to be thoroughly criticized as well.

Instead of seeking private and unethical solutions like the *Chakula cha Daktari* (food for the doctor) practices rampant at the Faculty of Medicine and Muhimbili Hospital, the academics should address these problems in the open. A patient scheduled for surgery at this hospital is often asked to pay an under-the-table fee. This is inevitable when the monthly income of a well-qualified surgeon does not exceed one hundred US dollars. Everyone is aware of such practices. The politicians maintain their traditional stance of dignified hypocrisy. The academics should not. They should call for a more rational system of payment that will facilitate delivery of efficient service to the patients. For example, a system whereby the surgeon gets a reasonable fee for every operation done can be put in place. The surgeon then has to undertake a required number of cases of non-fee paying patients. The academics must stand against the corruption and waste that prevails in the health sector. They should, for instance, put under the microscope why and how the urban malaria control projects faltered due to misappropriation of resources. That exercise has to go along with finding ways of improving the economic and work conditions of nurses, lab assistants and doctors. They should scrutinize the performance of the Ministry of Health. Why is the health of the typical person in Tanzania is so poor, and the medical services so backward? How trustworthy are the statistics dished out by the Ministry? Do they just paint a rosy picture of worsening situation? Instead of incessantly clamoring for research funds, they should perform well designed, executed research that contribute to knowledge and assist in solving real problems in the health sector. The available LINK funds should be utilized rationally and in a transparent way for the benefit of all in the faculty.

The solutions to our predicament will only emerge from collective and democratic efforts within departments, faculties and the university. The University of Dar as Salaam can enter the twenty-first century as a shining center of scholarship only if the academics are prepared to commit themselves to addressing institutional and social problems without fear or favor.

ADDENDUM (2000)

The preceding sections constitute a stylistically edited version of an article published in 1990. As we begin the new millennium, does it still constitute an accurate portrayal of the academic environment in Tanzania?

I left the University of Dar as Salaam for the University of California Los Angeles (UCLA) in January 1991. A combination of financial, family and professional circumstances propelled the move. Frustrated and broke, I became fully LINKed. I returned to the Faculty of Medicine for five months in 1994. It had a new name: the Muhimbili University College of Health Sciences (MUCHS). There were a few changes here and there. But on the whole, what I had written earlier had not lost its validity. To this day, the LINK reigns supreme at MUCHS and the University of Dar as Salaam. And these institutions have yet to embark on the path of recovery from the academic afflictions described above.

In 1994, the remuneration package of the academics had improved considerably. It allowed you to at least feed your family without engaging in another income raising activity. Unfortunately, that did not mean that the lecturers and professors spent more effort on teaching. The lucrative LINK related activities consumed most of their time. The pedagogical and living environments for the students had declined. I also witnessed further compromises of basic academic integrity. When I unearthed solid evidence of wide-scale examination fraud, no one did anything about it. It was pushed under the rug. The library had more recent books and journals. But a huge pile of LINK donated material lay on a damp, musty floor and was about to rot. The administration had refused to release overtime payment for the library staff; hence the neglect.

A couple of academics had published papers based on well designed and executed research related to HIV infection. But a myopic outlook, and an unwillingness to raise basic questions were as evident as before. The research agenda did not emerge from internal discussion but was patterned from the priorities set by the LINK. Money was available for research on population issues and AIDS but not for much else. No one was interested to examine the vexing issue: why had the multitude of foreign-funded health projects in the past three decades either generated paltry gains or failed miserably? Instead, the academicians were on the lookout for more LINK funds to do more of the same. Ethnic and regional rivalries had risen to prominence in the internal politics. Else, intellectual and social apathy were the order of the day.

Computer use had proliferated in the medical, dental and public health schools. But the seriously ill hospital patients slept on the cold, hard floor. The hospital wards lacked basic supplies like gloves, bandages, syringes, antibiotics, and pain medication.

Corruption and mismanagement were rampant. Yet, the LINK funds kept pouring in. In brief, what I saw at MUCHS was a microcosm of the trends in Tanzania as a whole. Abject poverty and misery were on the ascendance while a minority reaped the rewards of unbridled aggrandizement. We had multiparty democracy and many independent newspapers. But each had its own LINK, and none dared to raise any principled challenge to the external and internal economic overloads. Political conflicts revolved around personality issues. The politicians vied with each other to implement the externally imposed agenda of complete take-over of the economy by multinational firms. Burgeoning joblessness and rapid deindustrialization were of little consequence to the guardians of public welfare.

The academic LINK is but a part of a more basic LINK, the economic domination of Tanzania and other African nations by foreign agencies and corporations. Its features include unequal terms of trade, exploitation of local labor and other resources, minimal reinvestment of profits, absence of protection for nascent local industries, high burden of debt, imposition by the World Bank of economic priorities that lead to more indebtedness, and support for undemocratic regimes. In essence, the LINK is the modern day global imperialism led by the US and economically enforced by the World Bank and IMF.

Both types of LINKs complement one another. Thus, the United States Agency for International Development program to promote condom use to prevent HIV infection is related to the economic agenda imposed on Tanzania by the Western agencies. The latter generates massive layoffs and promotes urban prostitution, and thereby increases the HIV infection rate.

Under World Bank pressure, per university student expenditure in 33 African nations declined from US $6,800 in 1980 to $1,200 in 2002. But after a policy turnaround, once again influenced by external actors, more external funds flowed into the system. About US$1 billion was allotted to higher education in Africa between 2000 and 2005. By the 2010s, all the main universities in many sub-Saharan nations had become highly dependent on foreign grants, especially for doctoral and post-doctoral training for the academic staff and research. But appropriate evaluation of these grant programs is not being well-conducted by the providers or the recipient institutions. Educational priorities continue to be set outside of the continent and under-education persists. (Andoh 2019; Cloete at al. 2011, pages xv-xxiii).

Some see the LINK as a rescuer of Africa from its dire circumstances. Nothing is further from the truth. It is the LINK in its most basic form, and its relation to those who hold the reigns of power, that constitutes the central cause of the problems facing Africa. By keeping in power those who do not have the interests of the people at heart, the LINK undermines genuine democracy and the right of people to self-determination. It is the LINK that prevents Africa from embarking on sustained and sound programs to feed, house, and clothe its people. The charitable aspect of the LINK is just a stopgap remedial measure to try to arrest a catastrophe.

The LINK is not a novel entity. It has been with us throughout the post-Independence period. The forms have been changing. Previously we had the massive, foreign funded, multipurpose development programs that led to nowhere, and now we have the same in a more targeted form. The LINK associated problems are systemic problems. They are not just caused by the mistakes or bad intentions of individuals. There are dedicated persons on both sides. There are diligent local and external university teachers and researchers who do a good job despite the obstacles they face. They get positive results here and there. But often they end up spent and disillusioned. The system promotes anomalous individual behavior. It needs a fundamental overhaul.

The elites in Tanzania and Africa have internalized the ideology of the LINK. Like the slave trading chiefs of yesteryears, they benefit by enforcing the will of imperialism on the people. But valiant challenges to the LINK are also evident. They manifest the desire of the people of Africa to take their destiny into their own hands. In Zaire, the Western-LINKed dictator is no more, although the road to liberation is still a long one. In Nigeria and Kenya, heroic efforts are afoot. In Tanzania, a day is bound to come when the people will want to take control of their own lives. When that day comes, one can only hope that the students and faculty of the University of Dar as Salaam and MUCHS will not be found on the wrong side of the fence.

5
EDUCATION AND VIOLENCE

SUMMARY: This essay provides a comparative perspective on the occurrence of violent incidents in the schools of Dar es Salaam, Tanzania and Los Angeles, USA. In both places, the problem is connected to the economic and social problems in society. Schools in Dar es Salaam and the poor, minority areas of Los Angeles are resource deprived, lack motivated teachers, and are administered badly. The prospects for their students are bleak. In both places, the calls to deal with school violence through a simple punitive, moralizing approach and privatization of the schools are unlikely to achieve much success. Changes at the school level have to go hand in hand with fundamental social reform and tackling the causes and manifestations of under-education.[1]

*

---

1. This essay was first published as Hirji KF (1993) A tale of two cities, *Business Times* (Tanzania), 5 May 1993. This is an extensively edited and augmented version.

*I am afraid we must make the world honest
before we can honestly say to our children
that honesty is the best policy.*
George Bernard Shaw
++++++++++

DAR ES SALAAM, TANZANIA

ON 3 MAY 1993, AFTER THEIR SOCCER TEAM lost a game, students from the Tambaza Secondary School in Dar es Salaam went on a rampage. They assaulted students from the opposing school, harassed school girls around the city and stoned city buses. Some were involved in a fight with a bus conductor that caused his death. Subsequently, 65 students were arrested. In the not too distant a past, there had been two other incidents of hooliganism involving the same school.

Yet, this school has not always had a bad reputation. In 1961, when our nation was transiting from colonial rule to political independence, I joined this school. Run by the Aga Khan Education Board, it reflected the colonial education set-up. The students were mainly of Asian origin; African and Arab students formed a tiny minority.

Discipline was strict. If you were late, talked without permission in class, or littered the school ground, you risked stinging lashes from the assistant principal. Students were terrified by authority. An incident of the type noted above was unimaginable in those days. According to the media, now the situation has been reversed. It is the teachers who are said to be afraid of the students.

This incident occasioned headlines and editorial comment. The editor of the *Daily News* (4 May 1993) posed the query: What is wrong with our society? But he concluded that the problem was localized. The school administration was at fault for failing to control the students. External intervention to impose strict discipline was in order. Being a government paper and Tambaza now a public school, that was not a surprising stand. The Minister for Home Affairs visited the school a few days after this incident and issued a stern warning to the students. On the other hand, *Watu*, an independent biweekly had a different line. The editor called for strict punishment, including the death penalty, for students found guilty of killing the bus conductor (1-15 May 1993 issue). According to him, because Tambaza was not a boarding school, its students were free to mingle with street hoodlums and participate in nefarious activities like use of illegal drugs. In addition to firm disciplinary measures, he suggested that the answer was to privatize all the schools that had been taken over by the Ministry of Education after attainment of national independence. It was implied that indiscipline was a general problem afflicting public schools.

LOS ANGELES, USA

Earlier this year, when I was in Los Angeles, California, several violent incidents in high schools captured public attention. The most shocking one, which raised an outcry, was at Fairfax High School. One student had brought a loaded pistol to school. While he was fingering it in his backpack, it fired accidentally, killing a student nearby. In another incident just outside the school yard, some students bludgeoned a fellow student to death. According to the police, they had argued about a planned robbery of an electronic outlet. A couple were from well-to-do families and had excellent academic records. In schools in the LA area, the teachers were said to be afraid of disciplining the students who were reputed to be gang members. According to the media, the schools in Los Angeles, especially the public schools, were plagued with problems of violence, drug addiction, teenage pregnancies, high dropout rates, and low levels of scholastic achievement. Schools in poor localities with mostly African American and Hispanic American residents were the worst off.

The shooting at Fairfax High school drew a swift response from the Los Angeles School Board. Metal detectors to screen persons entering the school yard were installed. A policy of unannounced random searches for weapons was instituted. Conservative politicians blamed the school problems (and all social problems) on the absence of family values. The movement to break up the Los Angeles public school system gained momentum. One portion would be in the affluent, predominantly white, neighborhoods, and the other, in the mostly lower class, non-white areas.

From the media and the establishment political reactions, it appears that violence in secondary schools in Dar es Salaam and Los Angeles emanate from the same underlying factors. A decline in moral values is leading the youth towards socially harmful conduct. The problems are more acute in public schools. The solution is twofold: stern measures to stem the tide of violence and increased investment in private especially, religious oriented, schools. President Reagan had put prayers in public schools at the top of his agenda. Conservative politicians now stressed that it was high time to take this step. Before accepting such views, a look at history is in order.

HISTORY, TANZANIA

In 1961, the early days of Tambaza, only a small fraction of age eligible children joined secondary schools. They looked towards the future with hope. The prospects for landing a good job or continuing their studies were bright. Teachers got adequate pay, educational supplies sufficed to meet the needs, and an atmosphere of learning was in the air. But, those days were not without tension. In public and private schools students confronted the authorities over quality of food in the cafeteria, living conditions and occasional teacher misconduct.

After 1961, most secondary schools were taken over by the Ministry of Education. And there was a rapid growth of public and private schools. A new policy, Education for Self-Reliance was introduced in 1967. Its aim was to integrate theoretical and practical education so as to meet the social and economic requirements of a developing, socialist nation.

But the political and educational authorities failed to take appropriate steps to implement this program. Political slogans are not a substitute for concrete plans. The same lack of direction was observed in the planning for economic development, transport and social services in the urban and rural areas. Despite the fine rhetoric, actual policies remained within the ambit of the neo-colonial World Bank policies for Africa.

Lacking sound socialist plans and measures, all sectors of society and economy experienced minimal progress. Many state enterprises and rural cooperative villages failed. Incomes of the people stagnated and promised services like water and health failed to materialize. An economic base to absorb the products of the education institutions did not develop. As a result of this fact and the disharmonies introduced in the education system by the flawed implementation of the new policy, the value and quality of education eroded. Despite the rhetoric of self-reliance, projects in education were dependent on external funding. Local initiative suffered. Bureaucratic bungling prevailed. (see Essay 2 for elaboration).

The legacy of the past thirty years of education is a legacy of double talk combined with disregard for real educational development. While the education sector received millions of dollars in external funding, schools and colleges faced major operational problems. Shortages of essential supplies were common. Teacher welfare was neglected. The national examination scheme was poorly administered. Mismanagement and corruption at the institutional and ministerial levels added to the woes of the system.

The ruling political party and the Ministry of Education bear the primary responsibility for the current mess in the education system. The new ethic of capitalism has made lack of scruples and rampant greed a fact of life among the economic and political captains of the nation. Political leaders try to solve social problems by the use of force, not democratic interaction. The youth of today have little hope for a good future. The main cultural activities available to the young glorify violence, greed and immorality.

This is the real context for the problems of violence and indiscipline in secondary schools. There is now a fertile soil for generating such violence. To dream that such problems will be solved by returning to the good old days of strict morality and absence of government interference is to ignore the conditions which give rise to them. Violence and drug abuse in school are reflective of the more basic problems afflicting the system.

HISTORY, USA

The link between educational and societal problem is more pronounced in the USA. The Reagan-Bush policies of the 1980s drastically decreased federal government funding for education and other social services, and allocated more funds for the military and weapons of mass destruction. The leeway granted to the corporate sector catalyzed the formation of an unscrupulous business environment that generated numerous financial scandals like the collapse of many savings and loan associations. Well-paid industrial jobs declined as low paid employment in the service sector mushroomed. A significant section of population experienced a decline in living standards. Homelessness became a common facet of urban life as the governmental policies facilitated an unparalleled transfer of societal wealth to a very small segment of the society. This was the context within which problems like drug abuse, crime and gang violence became a feature of the US landscape.

Consider the issue of violence. The production of weapons of war is an integral component of the US economy. In 1991, this nation US was the top supplier of arms to Third World nations, outpacing the other ten major suppliers combined. Despite the demise of the USSR, there is no move towards conversion to a civilian based economy. The politicians talk of human rights but finance and support murderous death-squad regimes in Central America, and the likes of Mobutu, Savimbi, Siad Barre, Saddam Hussein and Renamo who inflict horrendous pain on their peoples.

On the domestic arena, the number of guns owned by Americans is astounding. The National Rifle Association is one of the strongest political pressure groups in the country. After the riots in Los Angeles in 1992, instead of steps to promote interracial harmony, the sale of firearms went on the upswing. The US has the highest incarceration rate in the world. The construction of prisons is a growth industry. The murder rate in the nation in 1990 was 10.5 per 100,000 making it the most murderous nation in the industrialized world. In 1984, the US Surgeon General declared violence a critical public health issue. The US Centers for Disease Control indicated that the homicide rate among young black men was akin to the fatality rate of a war.

And it is not just a matter of race. There is a high level geographical correlation between the prevalence of homicide and high infant mortality, level of low birth weight, drug use, teenage pregnancy, AIDS and school dropout rates. (Harvard Public Health Review, Winter 1991). Violence is a concomitant of a constellation of social conditions, not a separate problem that can be dealt with on its own. And homicide is an indicator for violence in general.

Violence and drug abuse in Los Angeles high schools, especially those in the deprived neighborhoods, are endemic. Public schools in these areas suffer from the same type of mismanagement and budgetary reduction as in Tanzania. The two books *Savage Inequalities: Children in America's Schools* (Kozol 1991) and *The Shame of the Nation: The Restoration of Apartheid Schooling in America* (Kozol 2006) vividly document the depth of despair and blight affecting public schools in these areas. Segregation is as rampant as it was in the 1960s. Systematic neglect has generated a dramatic decline in the quality of education. Just around the same time the incident at Fairfax High School occurred, it was revealed by a TV news station that the Los Angeles school authorities had been purchasing school supplies at grossly over inflated prices. Alex Kotlowitz, in his book *There Are No Children Here* (Kotlowitz 1991), demonstrates how the vicious cycle of racism, poverty and violence makes it almost impossible for those ensnared in such conditions to aspire to a better life. Through heroic effort, a few manage to escape the ghetto but most remain in abject misery and despair. Is it surprising that under these circumstances they turn to crime, drug use, violence and other antisocial activities?

In terms of violence and drug addiction, Los Angeles is far ahead of Dar es Salaam. In spite of all measures instituted thus far, the problems appear to be on the increase. Unemployment and despair soar, family units break up and crime increases all the while as the conservatives who are backed by the reapers of huge fortunes decry a decline in family values. They decry violence but show utter disregard for improving life in the inner cities. As the infant mortality rates in the poor, African American areas approach Third World levels, they cannot fund a program of childhood immunization. The contempt for basic human welfare displayed by the establishment makes it ludicrous to think that the younger generation will somehow be inspired by a call to uphold family or moral values. The moral bankruptcy of the economic and political system only generates cynicism among those who are the victims of the system. An atmosphere of total hypocrisy towards the value of human life, peace and nonviolence prevails.

When violence in many forms is central to the ethos of the society, talk about a return to moral conduct without addressing the fundamental issues is superficial clap trap. When the mass media continually revel in displaying daily doses of fictionalized and actual violence and gore, and when they favorably report the cheers of the missile factory workers when a weapon of their manufacture strikes a target in Iraq and display no concern for the consequences for the Iraqi people, can such a social and political culture generate a genuine respect for non-violence?

These are the realities of life surrounding the problem of violence in American schools. It is naive to think that this problem can be addressed just by a simple disciplinarian, policing approach.

IN CONCLUSION

In Tanzania, the problem of violence in schools is not as acute as in the US. But the level of disorganization and neglect is greater. It is not an issue of absolute level of deprivation but of economic and social trends. Are they such as to inspire and generate hope among the youth, or are they such as to breed despair and discord? The problem of violence in schools reflects the level of disharmony in society. It has to be viewed in terms of a broader culture of social irresponsibility and disregard for the welfare of the people. A schizophrenic morality whereby in one breadth one abhors violence and in another vigorously supports the death penalty prevails. Violence is tackled by the exercise of state violence. It is a culture of political double talk where only the interests of the rich and powerful generate concrete action. The name of the system is capitalism gone berserk. It cannot inspire the young towards a higher morality.

And it is not an issue of private versus public education. From Taiwan to Canada, many examples of successful, orderly public school systems exist. In the US, the relative performance of public and private schools is dependent on location. Funding for public education mostly comes from local property taxes. As property values in the wealthy areas are high, it generates a larger tax base for schools. Public schools there have adequate resources and facilities, a better paid teaching staff, and more experienced and qualified teachers. The wealthier parents get more involved in school affairs and make larger donations to the schools their children attend. In terms of variety of subjects and activities, educational standards and student performance, these schools outclass the top private schools in the state. According to an education consultant who advises parents on matters of school choice, parents with good income levels tend to prefer public schools because of more qualified teachers, higher test scores, greater diversity and possibility of greater influence of school affairs through donations and parent associations. (Rim 2019). While decrying public education, the conservative politicians who live in such affluent neighborhoods have little problem with sending their children to the well reputed public schools.

In contrast, cities like LA, with large swathes of poor and low property value areas, are unable to raise sufficient local funds to provide good schooling for their large student populations. State and federal subsidies do not make up the shortfall. Decades of neglect produces the dire conditions described above. Qualified teachers are driven away and a downward slide ensues.

Educational quality in the US is ensnared by a capitalist cycle: High property values produce better schools which in turn drive up property values. Low property values beget schools run in dismal conditions that in turn further lower property values. In addition, as the poor areas are predominantly minority populated areas, institutionalized racism factors into this equation as well. Resolution of educational problems cannot be attained without dealing with broader societal issues.

In Tanzania and other African nations, economic dependency, and an irresponsible political establishment have led to a systematic neglect of public education. While there is a wide difference between the schools in Dar es Salaam and the poor areas of LA, the similarities are striking. In both cases, we see symptoms of under-education. In both places, the political rhetoric deviates from reality. In both nations, only a few benefit from the supposedly generally beneficial policies.

There is a veritable decline in morality. But it is the morality of those who economically and politically dominate and lead the society that is in question. Their actions do not reflect the interest of the vast majority but of a privileged minority. There are no lofty moral principles embodied in their practices. This is quite evident to the youth.

Violence in schools is a marker for the underlying problems in the education system and society. It cannot be resolved purely by means of state or legal violence, moral exhortation or privatization. We need to address the underlying issues of social justice, economic disparity, political accountability and responsible government and combat under-education in a comprehensive fashion. We need to act now. Else, years down the line, we will have a bigger problem to deal with.

ADDITIONAL REMARKS (2019)

A comprehensive report dealing with improving school performance in American schools, quoted in Singer (2018), proposed the following set of general targets and measures:

- Reduce the rate of low birth weight children among African Americans.
- Reduce drug and alcohol abuse.
- Reduce pollutants in the cities and move people away from toxic sites.
- Provide universal and free medical care for all citizens.
- Insure that no one suffers from food insecurity.
- Reduce the rates of family violence in low-income households.
- Improve mental health services among the poor.
- Distribute low-income housing units throughout communities more evenly.
- Reduce both the mobility and absenteeism rates of children.

- Provide high-quality preschools for all children.
- Provide summer programs for students from low-income homes to reduce summer losses in their academic achievement.

But the mainstream media and political establishment ignore such recommendations and continue to peddle promote moral exhortations, charter schools, frequent standardized tests and stringent discipline. Instability and indiscipline thus persist in schools in poor areas.

Not surprisingly then that in the twenty five years since this essay was written, incidents of mass shooting in the schools, colleges and public places in America have become the stuff of regular global headlines. Yet, no amount of carnage is too shocking to prompt the politicians to tackle the basic causes and control the proliferation of guns, including high powered automatic weapons. Instead they seek to provide guns to the teachers and citizens to confront potential shooters. Police shooting of unarmed civilians, especially in the African American neighborhoods, has not abated. But hardly any police officer is convicted by the courts, even when the police video provides clear evidence showing the unjustified and uncalled for nature of the act.

While gun violence is extremely rare, assaults within the premises are not unknown in the schools of the UK. In 2010, for example, an ambulance was called to take 44 school staff who suffered injuries to hospital while a further 207 injured teachers needed at least three days off from work to recuperate. (Garner 2010). But instead of adequately investigating such incidents, the responsibility is automatically laid at the feet of the students and calls for stricter discipline, better upbringing and firm control over the youth ensue.

Overall, under the capitalist system, in Africa or America and Europe, there is tendency to avoid dealing with the systemic factors behind the breakdown of discipline in the school environment. It is a tendency that is bound to fail in the face of mounting social problems and inequality under neoliberalism.

6

EDUCATION AND PRIVATISATION

SUMMARY: Private education is often presented as an essential part of the solution to the ills of the education in Africa and the West (Chapter 5). In the year 2007, I first taught Basic Biostatistics to medical postgraduate students at a private university and a public university. Both are in Dar es Salaam. The contents of the course, my approach and the academic level of students at the two places were identical. Yet, the responses I got from my classes and the academics, the pace at which the courses proceeded and the outcomes were miles apart. This essay details my experience at the two institutions and reflects on the reasons behind the disparate reactions. The advantages of privatization of education are unduly hyped. It is not a solution to our educational problems; it is a key constituent of under-education.[1]

*

---

1. This previously unpublished, privately circulated essay written in April 2007 has appeared on the Internet under the title A Tale of Two Universities (Hirji 2007). This is a substantially edited and partly extended version.

Smooth seas do not make skillful sailors.
African Proverb
++++++++++

THE MERITS AND DEMERITS of private and public education have been debated the world over. Covering primary schools to universities, and involving educators, scholars, the media and the public, the voluminous, often acrimonious exchange is far from being resolved. The disputation has a technical and a political (ideological) angle. In Tanzania, it is rekindled each year after the announcement of the results of the national Form IV and Form VI examinations. Upon perusing them in a statistically uniformed manner, the media gurus and political pundits place the blame for the poor showing, especially in science subjects, on public schools, and present privatization as the basic panacea.

I recently taught at a private university, and then at a public university. My experiences in the two settings were so diverse that I am compelled to put my thoughts to paper. Perhaps, there is a lesson to be learned.

LECTURING AT THE AKU

In late 2006, I had the opportunity to teach the Master of Medicine (MMed) degree students at the newly established Aga Khan University (AKU) in Dar es Salaam. The class had three first year and three second year students, all qualified doctors pursuing a further specialization in family medicine. With two decades of dealing with students at this level behind me, it should have been a straightforward task. Sadly, it was not.

It began with a visit I paid, upon the suggestion from a colleague, to the director of the MMed program at the AKU. The campus is adjacent to the Agakhan Hospital, in a pristine beach side environment, shielded from the grime and bustle of the city. Though my visit was unannounced, I was well received, and informed that I had come at an opportune time. For it was in biostatistics and epidemiology, my fields of expertise, that the MMed study program had not made much headway. The second year students, who were about half way into their training, had not had so much as a lecture on this subject.

I was surprised. Biostatistics and epidemiology are not core subjects in basic medical training. But for a postgraduate degree, be it in surgery or pediatrics, they are key subjects, started from day one of the study program and stressed throughout. The students have to read and critique research papers, and design, conduct and write reports on their own research projects. Later, as consultants, they will need to keep up with the latest developments in their fields. Without a good grasp of epidemiological and biostatistical concepts, they will be hard put to plan and undertake scientifically valid research. And, since current journal papers in general medicine and their specialty are infused with such concepts, they will find it difficult to comprehend them.

Feeling that these students deserved better, I volunteered to help out. The director expeditiously organized a meeting. Besides him, the others present were two AKU instructors and an American professor. After the introductions, I was handed a draft of the syllabus for the subject. That was my next element of surprise. The half-a-page document was a copy of the table of contents from a standard text, not something crafted with effort or thought. In this era of email and the Internet, how difficult is it to secure, borrow or copy a decent, detailed syllabus? How can a postgraduate program even begin without one?

Keeping my impressions to myself, I talked about why the traditional approach to teaching biostatistics and epidemiology yields poor results. Unduly crammed with formulae and numbers, it is not integrated with the clinical topics a doctor has to learn. The teaching of biostatistics has to be contextualized within medicine and public health. It has to be infused with relevant examples to make students appreciate that without basic quantitative concepts and statistical logic, their comprehension of health medical issues is deficient. The traditional approach breeds a class of bored students, who memorize this and that fact, and forgets it once the exams are over. A sound biostatistical and epidemiological training, on the other hand, produces critical thinkers able to evaluate the validity and relevance of the large volume of information on medicine and public health doctors come across in their professional lives.

The immediate issue was: What was to be done for the current AKU MMed class? It came to pass that I would give a series of lectures (once a week for an hour and a half) to jump start the teaching of the subject, to give it a sense of direction and to provide a model for the instructor who would take over from me. I was more than happy at the prospect. Teaching is my passion; give me a student and I am ready to roll.

As a part of my preparation, I inspected the classroom. It was a well maintained, small but right-sized, air-conditioned room with fine furniture and all the needed teaching aids. The material I gave for photocopying was efficiently produced by the secretary. I was shown a cabinet full of books in her office. The adjacent room had latest issues of international medical journals. But there was not a single book for my subject, and it was not clear how much access the students had to this material. But on the whole, the stage seemed set for a fruitful pedagogic exercise.

On the first day, and as is usual for me, I was early. As I was mulling over how to begin, the two AKU instructors entered. The students started to trickle in a short time later. Twenty minutes past the start time, five of the six were in. I normally start on time. But this was the first day in a new place, and I wanted all students to begin on the same footing. So I started late. Aiming to review basic concepts and discern the general state of knowledge of my class, my first lecture was more didactic than usual. The ensuing discussion was satisfactory. At the end, I gave out the reading material for the next class, and urged all to be on time.

The handouts for the second class were efficiently produced as well. Again I went early. This time one student, one instructor and the director were there by the start time. Again the other students slowly trickled in. After twenty five minutes, four were finally there. The one who was not present the last time was now there, but the two who were present then were now absent. Though my blood pressure had risen a few notches, I started as I normally would, asking questions about the last lecture, and quizzing the class about the paper on field trials for the polio vaccine that I had given them to read. To my dismay, only one student had taken the trouble to read the whole article.

At this stage, I expressed my annoyance in a forthright manner. This was not what I expected from postgraduate students, I said. And it was not the Kariakoo Market where one did what one wanted. Late arrival, absence without permission or beeping cell phones was unacceptable. Reading the class papers was mandatory, not optional. They seemed taken aback at my firmness, but that is how I teach. I expend due preparatory effort for each lecture. When needed, I extend additional assistance to the students. But no matter where or who I teach, my standards and expectations are invariant. Work hard and you are rewarded; else, you face my wrath. A diligent student will find that my evaluations are fair, but up to the required level.

I then proceeded with the lecture, though I had to go faster to cover the planned topics. Some queries from the class were also addressed. Again I assigned an article to read for the next session, noting the key points they needed to reflect on. Later, I expressed my concerns to the director. He told me that these students were like that. It was as if they were doing everyone a favor by coming to class and doing any work at all. But what was he doing to control this distinctly anti-academic conduct? That he did not say.

A week later, with notes and handouts ready, I went early. This time, the classroom was full, but not with the people I expected. Someone had reserved it for the day for a team of external consultants. Undeterred, I barged in, and told them that they had to leave in two minutes. And with a wry face, they did.

A while later my audience started to trickle in. First, it was the director and the instructors. But no students! It was twenty minutes before the first one showed up. He was not apologetic. He said that his colleagues had been tasked with orienting a group of new interns, and he was unsure how many, if any, would come to class. One other student did pop in later, but soon popped out. And then the two American consultants arrived.

More than half way into the lecture time, I was plainly dejected. My firmness had come to naught. The students were taking matters too lightly. And the director was unable to do anything about it. A teaching hospital must plan the clinical duties and class sessions for the residents and postgraduates in a way that will avoid such conflicts. How can one teach in such a state of anarchy? And who was at fault, anyways?

With just a single student present, I lost all the incentive to give the planned lecture. I was about to leave when the director said, `Since the professor is here, let us pick his brain to see what advice he can give on student research.' The student who was present wanted to undertake a research project related to the WHO guidelines for treatment of asthma. One of the external consultants had given him preliminary advice on the matter. So a discussion on how to formulate his research proposal began.

To put it mildly, the cart was being put miles ahead of the horse. When after one and a half years into the training, the core subject that prepares students for research has not been taught, and when my efforts to correct it have gone nowhere, how can we talk about doing actual research? Or, about getting research funds? The basic subject had to be taught first, period. There was no other way. Yet, all present were oblivious of the elementary proposition. Emotionally drained, I mumbled a few words, posed a question or two, and called it a day. When I walked out, it was with a decisive but silent vow not to put my foot into this place again unless I had convincing evidence that things had changed for the better.

My experience at the AKU had left me crestfallen. For the first time in a teaching career spanning three and a half decades, I felt I had failed utterly. It had been a sheer waste of time, for me and the students. Perhaps I was too old; maybe my pedagogic skills had dulled over time; maybe it was time I retired from teaching.

LECTURING AT MUCHS

A few months later, I taught short courses on evidence-based medicine to medical postgraduates and research fellows at the University of California, Los Angeles, and at the University of Oslo, Norway. At both places, the courses were a resounding success (and I am not bragging). The feedback from the students and the course organizers was highly positive. At both places, I was requested to return the following year.

My spirits revived, I was ready for another plunge into the challenging tendrils of the Tanzanian academia. That I did in January 2007, when I got a chance to teach at the Muhmibili University College of Health Sciences (MUCHS) in Dar es Salaam. The class had 32 first year postgraduate public health, medical, pharmacy and dental students. The medical students, who were in the majority, came from fields ranging from internal medicine and pediatrics to surgery and microbiology. Their level was the same as those at the AKU. Over a six week period, I was to cover similar material, that is, basic aspects of the design, conduct and analysis of clinical trials. These students had been given several lectures on basic biostatistics.

When preparing for my much larger class, I was told that there were no funds for photocopying any material except examination papers. The usual thing to do was to give a copy of each handout to the class representative. Each student would then make his or her own copy. I did that for some supplementary material. But for the class notes, I made 16 copies of each set at my own expense. Two students shared a copy. In my talks with the previous instructors, it was not clear exactly what topics had been covered. The physiology laboratory served as the class room, just adequate, but with too small a writing board. It was not a room designed for lectures. The needed books were in short supply; the library had old titles. Yet, I was keen to begin.

My first class began, as at the AKU, in an exploratory fashion, seeking to know what the students knew and what they did not. I went over some basic concepts, framing issues in health related terms to motivate them. Twenty nine students were present. Two walked in late. Some did not seem to be paying attention. I ended with an emphasis on punctuality, reading the class material ahead of time, doing the set assignments and putting in required effort.

A week went by. The second session did not begin well. Only 17 of the 32 students were present. Some were late. Only a few had done the tasks set. Their answers showed they had not put in much effort either. As I queried them, I found that not many had read the assigned article (the same as the one given to the AKU students). Those who had read it had done it superficially. Predictably, I turned livid and thundered that I would not tolerate such behavior in my class. We were not at the Kariakoo Market. I worked hard to teach them and I expected them to do the same. As at the AKU, the students were surprised at my outburst. Here they were, qualified doctors and future specialists, being bullied like primary school kids.

But now they became attentive, and the session proceeded in earnest. We parted our ways after the material and assignments for the following week were given. At the next class, I was earlier than usual. This time a few students had preceded me. In no time the room had 28 fully attentive students. Most had read the assigned material. Some posed thoughtful questions and a fruitful discussion ensued.

The responses of these students reflected maturity and responsibility. From then on, the lectures proceeded smoothly. At the end, I gave a test and set questions for the final exam. Despite a shaky start, progress was made. Despite my sternness, the students were respectfully grateful that they had learned things that were important to their specialty. At the end of this exercise, I was in a mood to redo it.

In a subsequent discussion with the MUCHS Principal, my opinion about the quality of the students was elicited. My response was unequivocal: they can, I said, compete with students from anywhere provided we, the teachers, take the time and trouble to instruct them well, and lay a solid foundation for further study.

WHY THE DIFFERENCE?

The AKU is a well-endowed private institution. The MMed class size was small enough for productive individualized instruction. Though recently established, it is an extension of a larger and older medical university in Nairobi. And the latter is linked with the prestigious Agakhan University in Pakistan, which in turn has ties with a major Western university. By Tanzanian standards, AKU students get a comparatively high stipend. With the personal financial needs better addressed, they can devote more time to their studies than their MUCHS counterparts.

At MUCHS, a public institution, the resources for teaching are scarce. The class size is not only much larger but has doubled of recent. MUCHS lecturers complain about the additional work load. Here too, I found a lack of coordination among the staff and an initial lethargic atmosphere in the class.

In one place, my effort to remedy the situation roundly backfired; in the other, the students came to their senses in no time. At AKU, I walked out dejected; at MUCHS, I emerged elated. At MUCHS, the students and staff appreciated my efforts; at AKU, I am not sure if I was missed at all. How does one explain the difference?

The typical answer blames the students, as I heard at AKU. At MUCHS as well, some lecturers talk about disinterested, unresponsive students. If there is truth to this claim, one has to ask why they are like that. Only ineffective teachers and poor administrators blame students as a group. Students will always be students: a few work hard and excel, some hardly care, but most usually fall somewhere in between. Blaming them is not an explanation or a solution for any major problem in the academy.

While there is no simple answer to this critical query, the key reason relates to the presence of a sound academic tradition and accountability. At the AKU, I did not encounter either. That in the director's presence the students got away with what they did spoke volumes about the structure and standards of the academic program. There seemed to be no incentive to adhere to basic academic discipline. If the prevailing sense is that you will pass, get the degree and secure research funds with minimal effort, why bother to expend extra effort?

At MUCHS, such attitudes are not totally absent. In fact, the teaching and assessment of biostatistics is tainted with them. But they were totally unacceptable to me. So I firmly rallied against them. And since the aura and tradition of an academy were in existence, the students soon got my message. If they continued to goof around, there would be real consequences. They may fail my exam and not get the degree. A sense of academic responsibility prevailed. They came to realize that matters of value to their professional lives were being taught. If someone was taking the trouble to teach that kind of stuff, they were willing to play their part.

Let me be clear: I do not want to romanticize the situation at MUCHS. It is a vast institution; my current experience was a limited one. It too has major problems. The time, emphasis and resources devoted to teaching are far from adequate. The level of academic integrity among the students is not satisfactory. Two students in my MUCHS class exhibited a degree of intellectual misconduct. But when I took note of it, they were truly sorry and apologized.

Despite the multiplicity of problems, a sound academic tradition of four decades remains alive at MUCHS. At AKU, despite its international connections, the drive to adhere to academic standards was lacking. That, in my view, explains why my experiences in the two places were so distinct.

PRIVATIZATION IN PERSPECTIVE

The AKU is a private university; MUCHS is a college of a large public university. Are there any valid implications from my saga for the debate on private and public universities? As a statistician, I know the dangers of generalizing from a limited, selective experience. But, it is not bereft of value. A specific event or experience, if placed in context and history, can produce hypotheses for future investigation and reasonable conclusions of a cautionary nature.

We live in the World Bank initiated era of privatization. Privatization is now the remedy for the problems of Africa. State interference is the root of all evil. When everything is finally privatized, an economic, pedagogic paradise will descend on planet Earth. If you doubt this truth, you need a psychiatric checkup. That is what the powers based in the USA and their minions have decreed.

Yet, I have my doubts, both for education in general and for university education in particular. Many of the large public universities in Africa were founded as national universities some half a century ago. Colonial rule had restricted the level and quality of education for the majority. The basic aim of these institutions was to meet the urgent demand for highly educated manpower in the nation. In their heyday, they delivered, even by the august Western standards, quality education. In no time, Africa had many local secondary school teachers, managers, economists, doctors, engineers, scientists and university lecturers and professors. Virtually all the universities in Africa then were public universities.

These institutions experienced a precipitous decline just two decades on. It was caused principally by the dependency entrenching economic policies installed by the World Bank for

Africa. External debt skyrocketed and economic growth stalled. Qualified personnel found it hard to get a job, especially one attuned to their training. The brightest obtained work beyond the national boundaries. The IMF/World Bank structural adjustment programs of the 1980s specifically called for large reductions in the funds for higher education. The lack of democratic accountability at the national and institutional levels played a role in the decline of the African university. The education system cannot flourish in isolation. If the nation faces difficulties, it too will be affected.

Enrollment in African universities has grown rapidly in the recent times. But it has occurred without the required addition of funds, facilities and staff. The students are from a markedly inferior school system. They now face overcrowded dormitories, substandard cafeteria food, shortage of books and institutional disorganization. Classes are too large and too many to be handled by the staff. Lecturers complain about excessive work load, the poor background of the students and low salaries and benefits. At times, the students go on strike. These problems affect both private and public universities (Chapter 10).

An unsavory aspect of this era is corporate style showmanship. In the name of public relations, significant attention is devoted to creating and maintaining an elegant public image. Private and even public institutions, in education or other sectors, have come under the spell of that ethos. In the haste to be viewed as marketable, reputable entities, they generate an image that overshadows actuality. The reality of academic destitution is masked by the glitz and glamour of elaborate graduation ceremonies. Students get degrees but not rigorous, quality education. Yet, no one complains. The students get what they want. The institution acquires prestige. More students enroll. The so-called donors, owners, and the public are satisfied.

It takes a while for the reality to sink in. Eventually things begin to fall apart. Rumors abound. When, for jobs needing skills and responsibility, graduates from elsewhere are preferred, people wonder why?

I observed an inkling of corporatized glitz at the AKU. On the surface, things were immaculate and efficient. But the pedagogic reality beneath was another story. With an intake of three to four students a year, it was no big deal to provide each one a good textbook on biostatistics and epidemiology. If a key subject has not been taught, a book fills a part of the vacuum, and gives the students something they can use for years. The university has the funds and facilities to procure books from abroad. But someone has to do the needed groundwork first.

Institutions provide a learning environment. Teachers guide students over an arduous terrain. But ultimately, the student must take charge. Education is your work. It is about books and practice, about thinking and doing, over and over. It is about being creative and critical. Be it in law or physiology, medicine or engineering, you need to burn the candle through the night. You have to reflect on complex issues, grasp intricate concepts and master practical tasks. You need to integrate the skills and strands of knowledge, combine theory with practice. And you need to ponder on the limitations of what you are being taught. That is the ABC of education. No computer or gadget can be a substitute for such effort. If a scholar or an expert has to emerge at the end, education has to occur the old fashioned way (Stoll 1999).

CONCLUSION

To date, Africa has educated hundreds of thousands of its daughters and sons in varied areas of science, technology, social science, medicine and the arts. Yet, in ways more than one, the era of intellectual servitude has not passed. Despite some heroic efforts, the educated generation of the past failed to live up to its historic challenge to break that bondage. Hence today what the `donors' and international bankers say to Africa is the final word on matters of health, agriculture, industry, communication, trade, governance and education. This word is never about making fundamental changes but about small solutions which do not challenge their dominant position. The educated in Africa sing the tune of the `donors.' As the continent goes from one crisis to another, one temporary fix to a bigger problem, it remains mired in an endless cycle of mass poverty, disease, ignorance, alienation, and eventually, societal violence.

The recipe of blanket privatization is not a solution to Africa's woes. In fact, in the name of privatization, the wealth of Africa is being plundered, left and right, by foreign firms and local tycoons. In Tanzania, the hastily conducted post-1990 privatizations and liberalization seriously damaged the industrial sector. The new owners did not adhere to the contract terms to revive the factories. The local capacity to make basic consumer items was diminished and reliance on imports grew. Export processing plants closed down, reducing the value of exported items. Banks and other state enterprises were sold off at astonishingly low prices, causing heavy losses to public coffers. Privatizations of water services and the railways led to such reductions in the quality of services, chaos, financial scandals, worker unrest and higher rates that intense outcries from the public ensued. And they were repossessed. Privatization had entailed a loss of organizational memory and experienced personnel. Revitalization was made difficult after renationalization. Foreign and local investors and the political bigwigs were the sole beneficiaries of this exercise.

A one-sided promotion of private universities in Africa leads to a greater neglect of public universities. African governments are reducing financial support for public universities. Increased student fees have led to strikes and protests in Ghana, Madagascar, Sierra Leon, South Africa, Togo and Uganda. In the aftermath, the authorities advocated a greater role for the private sector in higher education (Kavuma 2011).

For education (and services like water, health and transport), reliance on the private sector is a historically flawed idea. If you take the case of any nation that is at an advanced level of development based on science and technology, you find that it was achieved on a foundation of a strong public education system. The nations of Europe, USA, Canada, UK, Australia, Japan, Korea, Taiwan and China illustrate the indispensability of a broad based, state funded system stretching from elementary schools to universities. African nations had also developed sound public education systems soon after Independence.

The University of California is a state-wide, public university with a series of semi-autonomous universities spread across the state. These institutions, like UC Berkeley, UCLA, UC Irvine and UC Santa Cruz are among the top-notch universities in the US and rank with elite private universities like Stanford University and Princeton University.

The spell of American style showmanship that has emerged with private education will facilitate the trivialization of university education. Africa needs universities that will generate bold thinkers and experts who will not hesitate to query the conventional wisdom dished out from external experts and strive to develop the directions and strategies to take it out of its quagmire. That is the urgent responsibility of African universities, public and private.

I do not argue against private educational facilities. They are here to stay. Well run private universities do exist. There is room for cooperation between private and public universities. But what I saw going on at the AKU was not university level education. There is little chance that such education can generate the type of specialists the nation needs. When a place is called a university, it has to function like one.

As a student at the University of Dar es Salaam four decades ago, I struggled under a rigorous curriculum. It was a demanding venture but worth it. There were concerns about relevance of the education to local conditions. Efforts to remedy the deficiency were under way when the institution (like the nation) was beset by one crisis after another. Now it needs to reclaim that glory, and achieve even loftier goals. And other universities need to follow suit.

In conclusion, all our universities must uncompromisingly strive for academic excellence and produce professionals, experts, writers, artists, teachers, planners, researchers and thinkers with the inclination and ability to address the serious health, educational, economic, social and other problems facing the continent. They need to be nurtured and valued, and held up to a high standard of scholarship and relevance. In the zeal to privatize, let us not neglect public universities. Let us not conflate image with reality, or confuse imitation with academic training. If we do, it will be at our own peril, as we may then end up with the worst of both the worlds.

ADDENDUM

Since April 2007, a vast expansion of higher educational institutions has occurred. By July 2019, there were 15 public and 34 private universities and university colleges in Tanzania. The number of students admitted into Bachelor's degree programs rose from about 45,000 in 2012/2013 to about 64,000 in 2017/2018 (www.tcu.go.tz).

But quality has not accompanied quantity. If anything, it has declined. New institutions were set up without adequate qualified staff. An acute shortage of lecturers with doctoral degrees prevails. The slightly higher salaries and benefits offered by private universities attracted experienced academics from the public universities. Those who did not move over gave lectures on a part-time basis, neglecting their teaching duties at their home institutions. A good number of professors took up administrative positions in private universities. In the recent year, many professors have been given ministerial level or other top posts in the government and the ruling party. An unplanned expansion of the study programs and enrollment compounded the problems. The academics of today are more inclined to spend their time on consultancy work with externally funded NGOs and research. Teaching is their last priority. Shortages of books, lab supplies and class room space are common.

Indicators are that the education offered in the Tanzanian universities is hollow and shallow, requiring minimal effort on the part of the students and the instructors. Most degrees are essentially worthless. In 2017, after inspecting the universities and university colleges in terms staffing level, facilities and supplies, the Tanzania Commission for Universities (TCU) stopped 19 institutions from enrolling new students for any degree program. And 22 other universities were told not to enroll students for 75 specific study programs (Kamagi 2017). These inspections did not cover what was being taught, at what level, student performance and standards of the degree examinations. If that had been done, the ban may have been an almost total one. In terms of educational quality, the private universities are at bottom of the ladder.

Even such limited efforts to improve educational standards, however, face opposition from prominent politicians and the media. With their material and ideological bondage to privatization, they put pressure on TCU to relax the restrictions placed on especially the private universities. (Editorial 2019).

Yet, the same media often report outcries from potential employers about the low levels of basic skills exhibited by local graduates. Articles on the issue abound. My personal experience at the Muhmibili University of Health and Allied Sciences (the new name for MUCHS) from the years 2007 to 2012 amply validated the complaints. Most postgraduate students could not write a logical, grammatical paragraph in English, and had a hard time grasping papers from medical journals. The quality of research papers written by undergraduate and post-graduate students was poor in the utmost sense. The students in the Master of Nursing program showed the poorest performance in my class. And most of them had obtained their bachelor's degree from AKU.

I also met many students from UDSM who had completed or were in the process of completing bachelor's degrees in mathematics, statistics, engineering, journalism and law, and conversed with the new academic staff in these departments. To some, I posed direct questions to gauge what they knew and what they did not. Most spoke English of a strange kind and were unable to tackle even high school problems related to their study areas. The assistant lecturers displayed major deficiencies in the topics they should have learned in undergraduate and post-graduate training. Yet, the band wagon goes on. Year after year our universities pump out degree holders into the market. A large portion remains unemployed for years. Some go into petty trading or drive taxis.

Private universities and schools are for-profit entities. Their owners, seeking to recoup their investment in a short time, expand student intake without adequate groundwork. Rapid expansion of private universities has occurred throughout the Third World. And in many places, it has generated veritable scandals.

The situation in Peru is emblematic. Compared to the 1980s, the number of universities has grown more than four-fold to 140. Most are private universities. But the degrees they offer are of a sub-standard variety and are not recognized outside of Peru. The image they present belies the pedagogic reality. The Telesup University in this nation is an extreme case.

> From the street, the newest site of the Telesup university in Lima appeared to be a gleaming, glass-fronted 7-story tower. Inside, however, students were surprised to find the stairs only reached the fourth floor. Drone photos published this week revealed that the top three floors were just a façade supported by metal struts ... (Collyns 2019).

The upper three floors were `fake floors.' It was closed in June 2019 after education inspectors found serious deficiencies in the programs. Yet, despite the lack of accreditation, it had managed to enroll about 20,000 students. In the words of Ricardo Cuenca, the Director of the Institute of Peruvian Studies:

> It's a symbol of the facade that is the Peruvian university system. It was presenting an image with nothing behind it. (Collyns 2019).

An audit conducted by the educational authority in India revealed that in June 2019, there were 24 fake universities operating in the country. In early 2018, the Nigerian National Universities Commission identified a total of 58 fake universities operating in the nation. For a global listing of hundreds of unaccredited institutions of higher education, see *Wikepedia* (2019).

Despite the high fees, private universities in Nigeria short change the students in terms of availability of water and electricity supply and living facilities. Bypassing the set admission requirements, private institutions give preferential treatment to students from wealthy families. Under payment for lecturers and employing unqualified lecturers are normal. Yet, their pass rates are unusually high. Privatization is fueled by reduction of state funds for public education and pro-business bias in the national regulatory authority. Academic freedom is curtailed though a few egregious incidents of neglect of student wellbeing have generated to violent protests. High handedness and neglect on the part of the authorities has led to staff strikes. While public universities also face similar problems, the private ones present an extreme situation. (Ibrahim 2012).

Commercialization and privatization also affect educational systems in the US and UK. Publicly subsidized charter (private) schools in the US, which mostly operate in the minority neighborhoods are accused of profiteering at the expense of educational quality and have been found by the courts to be mistreating students with disabilities. Unaccredited trade colleges and online universities have duped many students with diplomas of little market value. According to one estimate, in 2012, there were more than a hundred blacklisted universities in the USA (Ajay 2012; Ravitch 2014).

The neoliberal assault on education includes reducing the number of teachers in public schools, lower salaries and benefits, and weaken the teacher unions. Thus in the US at present:

public schools employ 250,000 fewer people than they did before the recession of 2008–09. Meanwhile enrollment has increased by 800,000 students. Singer (2018).

As school nurses, counselors and librarians are laid off, the teachers who get lower salaries compared to other professionals with similar education are burdened with higher class sizes, grading tests on a more frequent basis and dealing with general problems their students face. And when test performance declines, as it would be expected to decline, teachers and public schools are blamed, and private schools receive further political impetus.

A similar trend affects higher education. As state funding declines, universities increase fees, have higher student-staff ratios and place a greater emphasis on research to increase funding. Promotions are more tilted towards research and academic staff come under greater pressure to secure research funds from corporate sources and foundations. In the UK, other than at a few top-notch universities, overcrowding and decline of instructional quality and grade inflation are emergent features of undergraduate education. (Collini 2012).

The mushrooming of private universities under such circumstances compounds these problems. In the UK, of the about 130 universities in 2011, 80 were less than twenty years old. Their focus is on business studies and job related degrees, not the traditional subjects. By providing more opportunities to those who can afford the higher fees, private universities function more to reproduce existent class structure rather than as avenues for social mobility. (Head 2011).

Commercialization and privatization are making universities adopt a business model as the basis for their operation. Some universities in the US now keep a profit and loss account for each faculty. Their salaries depend on revenue generation from teaching, research and publication record. Often even distinguished professors are found in the red. Use of contingent staff who can be hired and fired at will and made to teach flexible work hours fosters a low wage workshop type of environment in the academy. (Head 2011).

Garth Sturdy, a seasoned academic and commentator, is disturbed by the trend towards commercialization of university education in the UK. An undergraduate degree now easily lands the student with a debt in the region of 50,000 UK pounds. Yet, intellectual rigor and challenge are not stressed. The quality of teaching is on the decline. In his view, both the universities at the top and those at the bottom of the academic ladder are affected.

> The question of what is of value in a modern university is an important one. Faculties and departments do everything they can to sell their wares on promises of higher wages, glamorous careers, foreign travel and exclusive professional networks. They aggressively target foreign students in particular because of the higher revenue they bring in, while subject courses are often drawn up not on the basis of their academic value but of their commercial viability. (Sturdy 2019).

Decrying the emergence of `Mickey Mouse' education in the new private universities, he cites cases of students who have sued these institutions and won large damages. (Sturdy 2019). In July 2019, the agency in charge of higher education in the UK deprived The Bloomsbury Institute, a private university offering degrees in accountancy, management and law, further access to student loans. And the Institute was deregistered. Low quality of the degrees and high dropout rates were cited as the reasons. It was the first time such a step had been taken. (Turner 2019).

After reviewing the history and state of his nation, and noting the large scale theft of public coffers, astounding inequality, persistent poverty, social instability and economic stagnation in his nation, AM Lopez Obrador, the new president of Mexico surmised: `Privatization is theft.' (Lopez Obrador 2018). This observation is pertinent to Africa. In particular, for profit entities have no role in the essential services like health, education, water, power and public transport. In education, they create inequalities that leave the majority of the students with abysmal quality education and an uncertain future. Privatization is a recipe for cementing under-education, not for enhancing relevant, quality education.

In conclusion, I note that a substantial body of work on the issue of public versus private education at the school and university levels exists. My discussion has just scratched the surface. For an excellent overview of this question and the effects of modern educational `reforms', role of teachers, standardized testing and other related issues in the Canadian context, I recommend the five comprehensive articles by Rick Salutin in *The Toronto Star*, Salutin (2011a, 2011b, 2011c, 2011d, 2011e). He also provides a comparative perspective on what in many respects is an exemplary public education system, namely that in Finland.

7

EDUCATION AND COMPUTERS

SUMMARY: Almost every university student has a computer these days. In Tanzanian universities, the use of textbooks and printed material has, however, declined remarkably. It is possible to get a bachelor's degree without having read a single book from cover to cover. This essay reflects on the pedagogic and social implications of that condition. While a judicious utilization of computers and the Internet can assist in dealing with under-education, the current manner in which they are employed is counter-productive. Instead of sound learning and critical engagement, modern technology is promoting superficial discourse that is presented in a glitzy style. Computers in higher education in Africa are, for the most part, serving to entrench under-education.[1]

*

---

1. This essay was first published as Hirji KF (2009) Books, bytes and higher miseducation, *Chemchemi: Fountain of Ideas*, 1:13-20, April 2009, University of Dar es Salaam. This is an edited version. It should be read in conjunction with the sections on computers and books in chapters 4 and 12.

How is it we have so much information,
but know so little?
Noam Chomsky
++++++++++

THEN AND NOW

A MUNDANE FACT FROM DAYS PAST: In the year 1971, a course in botany, education, mathematics, economics, sociology, law or another discipline at the University of Dar es Salaam (UDSM) typically had at least one textbook, and a supplementary text or more. At the start of the academic year, the university bookstore had state of the art works in the relevant fields. Some courses had bound course readers on sale. The student bookstore account of about 1,200 shillings sufficed to purchase the required material and left a decent balance for books and other items that caught your fancy. The library shelves were lined with academic and general books, journals and reports. The Muhimbili medical campus was not far behind.

Two decades on, the situation had changed drastically. In 1990, the bookstore was in a pathetic state. Only a few subjects were represented on its shelves, and in numbers unrelated to the need. Most courses were taught without a textbook; the book allowance had not kept pace with inflation; the library had few inexplicably selected new journals and books. The quality and rigor of education, once at par with the best in the world, had gone down precipitously (Hirji 1990).

Today, two and half decades ahead, the scene has changed again, in some respects in a fundamental way. The shortage of quality books has been alleviated to a small degree. But new sources of scholarly material exist. Students and staff acquire, read and present educational material mainly via the electronic medium. Access is instantaneous. Several schemes enable the African universities to freely access a wide variety of the latest issues and archives of journals, and other scholarly items from all over the world. The Internet abounds with information. Course syllabi, lecture notes, presentation slides, question papers, essays, and relevant papers exist for download, free of charge.

Computers and the Internet have the potential to enhance the quality of academic instruction in a significant manner, even in the challenging setting of Tanzania. That is the theory. What is the practice?

POTENTIAL AND PRACTICE

At first glance, the new medium appears to have had a positive impact on the academy. The academician has fervently embraced electronic technology. Computers are ubiquitous. Lectures are adorned with Power Point projections. Students and staff regularly resort to the Internet. Plans are afoot to provide course material on the web. An avalanche of research by staff and students is under way. Their data are entered and analyzed on a computer. Bulky and glossy reports are churned out. Like his or her counterpart in Europe and the US, the lecturer spends most of the work hours and beyond glued to the screen. Only the unpredictable power outages disrupt the monotony. Then, in a reminder of the ancient days, but now as if in a daze, the mousepad bound scholar is seen chattering or wandering aimlessly in the hallways.

That, however, is a superficial impression. The reality is far from rosy. This essay reflects on this issue. My case is developed with illustrations from the one year Master of Public Health (MPH) degree program at the School of Public Health and Social Sciences (SPHSS) of the Muhimbili University of Health and Allied Sciences (MUHAS). For the most part, I focus on the research projects done by students pursuing this program.

MPH

With an intake of about twenty five, the well-endowed MPH program attracts professionals from the various parts of the health sector. It has a computer friendly classroom and a networked computer room. External funds enable the lecturers to be paid a teaching allowance. The students get tea and snacks on a daily basis. Most students also have their own laptop computers.

A fast paced program, it covers a range of health related subjects. Organized in thematic modules, each is taught by a team of in-house and external experts. In addition to the module and university exams, students write a dissertation based on a three month field project. Performance is evaluated by internal and external examiners, and with a rare exception, all generally obtain good grades and the coveted degree.

Mid-way into the year, students present their research proposals over two to three days to other students and members of the academic staff. Each student outlines the objectives, design, and methods of his or her study, and gets feedback from the audience.

Sitting through these sessions during the academic year 2007/2008 gave me an insight into what they learn. The better looking Power Point presentations were in contrast to the haughty scribbles of the past. The range of topics, though, reflected more donor fund availability than local public health priorities. Topics on HIV/AIDS thus dominated the scene.

In terms of conceptualization, design and methods, a lot was amiss. The uniformity of misguidedness was striking. The project titles were not clearly formulated. The objectives were too many to be tackled in a time and resource limited first-time exercise. And most were mechanically stated. Some were incompatible with the design of the study. The study sample was uniformly declared random, but a query revealed otherwise. The actuality of sampling was unclear, or it was a convenience sample. All deployed the same formula for sample size computation, even as the design and types of effect measures varied. All stated identical methods of data analysis. But for many, the methods were either inappropriate or incomplete. The background survey reflected an ad hoc choice of the papers reviewed; no one cited a systematic review of his or her topic.

On reading some of the proposals I saw that they had picked portions of papers from an Internet search, and pasted them into the write-up. The questionnaires were too long, as if all the knowledge on the topic were to be gained from a single project. Basic ideas like delineation of mutually exclusive categories, not asking leading questions, especially in a way that biases the later responses, logically ordering the questions, and the choice of and focus on essential matters were not thought through. The crucial issues of interview fatigue and errors of multiplicity were generally ignored.

The knowledge of statistical methods was just a step beyond that in a ritualistically taught undergraduate course. Under this staid approach, scientific research is narrowly framed in terms of rejecting or accepting a null hypothesis using the artificial cut-point of $p < 0.05$. A subject matter grounded approach to design, analysis and interpretation takes the back seat. Take one example: One study of the impact of anti-retroviral drug use on risky sexual behavior showed a statistically significant effect. Three different ways of measuring risk and adjusting for the effects other factors confirmed it. Yet, the explanatory power of the fitted models was poor; none of them explained more than 7% of the variability in the data. The findings were statistically significant but practically dubious. Further data dredging could have produced a better non-linear model; but what would it mean? Instead of seeking practically oriented interpretation, the focus is on the p-value. But it is not their fault. The mechanical style of teaching does not encourage a genuinely scientific outlook; all that seems to matter is the `significance' of the hazily understood p-value.

Though they get lectures on research methods, they do not evaluate research papers. No instructor in community health, biostatistics, or epidemiology dissects a paper from head to toe and critically reviews its aims, substance, methods and conclusions with them. Few, if any, recent journal papers are read. No subject has a course reader or a text book. When writing the dissertation, the students do not know what goes to the methods section and what into the discussion. In their initial drafts, material belonging to one section is strewn all over the place.

I worked for a month with a student I unofficially supervised to transform her diffuse write up into a coherent and focused proposal. It took many sessions to pin down the objectives, define the relevant data items, frame the questions well, relate them to the objectives, separate response and explanatory factors, exactly define the sampling frame and scheme, and drive home the key distinction between a comparative and a descriptive study. The questionnaire was trimmed down to a single printed page with a set of clearly categorized pertinent queries framed in a uniform way. Often, I ended up spoon feeding her. Yet, she was one of the top students in the class.

Such deficiencies point at both the weak background of the students of today and at what should have been covered in their MPH courses. A post-graduate program without a single required textbook was unheard of in 1970. They provide the core material each student must learn. Research papers and articles supplement that with more nuanced ideas, and display methodological variations, exceptions, contrasting views, practical hurdles, and recent work in the field. General lectures on the methods do not convey the essence of research. A student needs to read and digest papers from diverse areas to get a basic understanding of the purpose and methods of research.

The responsibility for ensuring this lies with the instructor, whether he or she is expounding on malaria, breast feeding, or the organization of health services, and the module coordinators. I asked students in the Master of Science in Tropical Disease Control degree a question relating to the latest WHO report on malaria that is accessible on the Internet. But they had not heard of it. Our students rely on the Instructor's Power Point slides, class notes and Google searches for instant learning. Essay type assignments are rare; multiple choice or short questions dominate the tests. Memorization skills, not reflection and originality of expression are assessed. When students with profound deficiencies in such skills are taught along lines that de-emphasize them, and are then required to conduct research that cannot be done well without them, can the consequences be other than what we see?

The MPH students have about six weeks for field work for research, and a month or so to analyze and write it up. During this phase, practical matters like printing questionnaires, interviewer recruitment and training, selection of the subjects, actual interviews, quality control, data entry, checking, analysis and interpretation have also to be done. The budget is modest. Much of the work is done or supervised by the student. They obtain data analysis assistance from the programmers on the campus. Having dealt with many research projects in various capacities for nearly forty years, I view this as an impossible task, at least if it has to be done within a modicum of standards that protect the scientific validity of the research endeavor.

Yet, student after student here does it; and year after year. Often five hundred or more subjects are said to have been interviewed, with hardly any non-responder and almost no missing data. And all that is rapidly entered into the computer files, generating impressive tabulations, chi-square tests, logistic regression and p-values. Ultimately, patently weighty conclusions are drawn from the work.

Yet, what does that mean? A typical graduate student, who cannot write a proper sentence in the English language, whose numerical skills are sadly deficient, and who is unable express himself or herself in a logical and coherent manner, whose knowledge of key areas of public health is substandard, produces an elegant dissertation that is usually accepted with minor comments by the supervisor and the internal and external examiners. Again, I ask, what does that really mean?

At times, remarkable stuff is seen. One data analysis table reported the coefficients of partial correlation. Three weeks earlier she did not know why linear regression, not logistic regression, was appropriate for the outcome variable in her study. Everyone else was doing logistic regression. Why? While not knowing the ABC of logistic regression, they do it just because the program coordinator has said so. After all, one only needs to click the right icon on the screen. It took quite a while for me to explain to her that it was not relevant in her context. Now, lo and behold, a major intellectual leap has occurred. The intricate coefficients are reported. Where did they come from? Well, other papers in the field, located over Internet, report them. So they were found in the computer output, and put in! What do they mean? Are they relevant in this table? If anything, they were out of place, not related to the analytic objectives set, and thereby, had to be removed. When you interrogate the student, he or she cannot explain what the research report contains.

The ubiquitous computer permits a seemingly rapid learning time and produces fast turnaround times. I discuss an aspect of the questionnaire, and study design with her. In a few hours, an email attachment with the modifications comes in. But not much thought has gone into it; this word or that section is touched up mechanically and instantly transmitted. All things happen at the speed of light. The key is to make an impression. To carefully weigh the matter and go beyond what was discussed are not in fashion any more.

Computerization and the Internet provide a fantastic avenue to make a work lacking rudimentary standards of scientific quality appear as sound scholarship. Form triumphs over substance; critical scrutiny is minimal. The comments of the external and internal examiners on the dissertations pertain to style, structure, a detail here and there, and so on. The public health significance of the topic, research design, data quality, soundness of analytic strategies, intricacies of interpretation and general implications are hardly commented on.

COMPROMISED INTEGRITY

Research occurs in a social context. Ours world abounds with cynicism, disinformation, mistrust, and dishonesty in all aspects of life. Money and inequality have mangled human discourse and relations. In industrialized nations, the process is astutely camouflaged until the bubble bursts now and then. In the poor nations, the decimation of social integrity is directly evident. Can the academia and research be immune from the malady? This is a broad issue that cannot be well covered in a short essay. There is ample evidence that compromised, flawed or fraudulent research occurs at higher than acceptable rates even at the globally distinguished academic centers in the West. Corporate funding and associated conflict of interest have resulted in publication of contorted research as well as suppression of important research. (Altman 2002; Angell 2005; Chan 2008; DeAngelis 2006; Kassirer 2005).

Cheating by students is a global concern. The Cambridge University in the UK is ranked among the top ten universities in the world. Yet, in a recent survey, about half of its students admitted to have plagiarized at some point in time (Anonymous 2008; Garner 2008; Llanos 2008). In June 2017, the examination board in the UK had to withdraw papers in Further Mathematics, Statistics and Economics. They had leaked on the Internet (Weale 2017). In June 2019, Serbian children staged street protests after the mathematics paper for the primary school examination had leaked on the social media. It had been posted by an employee of the printing company. In India, cheating is a well-organized, perennial and expansive exercise involving tens of thousands students at all the levels of the education system. Judicious use of cell phones and the Internet make the process more efficient and geographically wider (Safi 2018).

To return to the local scene: One marker of the academic integrity at SPHSS is the scale of plagiarization in the written work of the students. No hard data exist, but my experience is that most students plagiarize. Even if one cannot trace the source, the changing style from paragraph to paragraph, the crude manner in which that is done, the mixture of grammatically impeccable sentences with garbled ones make its presence obvious. Instructors complain about it. But no concrete steps are taken. The scale is just too large. Like a boat propelled by a powerful wind, it seems unstoppable. Computers and the Internet are the prime facilitators of the expanded scale of this practice today.

Cheating in tests and examinations is another marker. Though a long standing concern, no hard data exist. Year after year, I confront it; in each of my biostatistics classes for postgraduate students for the past three academic years, I had solid evidence of copying in the class tests. Even after taking stringent measures like separate class rooms, extra invigilators, keeping distance between students, permuting and slightly modifying questions, informing students that they may not be doing the same test as their neighbor, the practice continues. When such steps are not taken, it can happen on a large scale, as was the case with the two post-graduate epidemiology continuous assessment tests in 2008. When it became public, one test had to be reset. When supervising an undergraduate test last year, I saw several students clearly itching to get help from those next to them; the moment one turned around, the deed was done. It was an eerie feeling. During the final exams, a lot of hullabaloo about leaked papers occurred. No investigation was done, though stricter rules for handling the question papers were instituted.

As we saw earlier, these problems are global in scope. And electronic technology plays a major role in enabling and identifying the practice. Fake certificates and transcripts augment this conundrum. Cheating is not new; what is new is the scale on which it occurs and the casual way in which it is talked about. A rare event in the past that would elicit a flood of indignation is now accepted as a fact of life.

Does this relate to research? The same students in the same social environment are doing demanding research. The supervisors have too many students. Their priority, anyway, is on their lucrative donor funded projects. They spend minimal time improving and monitoring student research. In the end, though, students bring in seemingly impeccable and voluminous data which, once fed into the computer, assume a distinct status. Now they are hard data, a collection of facts, not opinions which are subjected to intricate statistical analysis. Even that is often flawed, yet passes undetected. Ponderous conclusions are drawn. Bound in impressive volumes, they are the gateway to the degree, and the world beyond; all made possible by the incredible computer and the fabulous Internet.

As an old fashioned fellow, I harbor my doubts. Is this a wonderland where things are not what they seem to be? Research seeks the truth, requires reflection and planning, demands a good foundation in the subject matter and methodology, and needs meticulous implementation, careful analysis and prudent interpretation. At all its stages, it must proceed at a measured pace that is subject to quality control. Research, indeed, is a quintessential act that embodies a combination of personal, institutional and social responsibility.

With basic norms among students in short supply and academic irresponsibility at a high level, our universities are in a constant state of turmoil. Without a direct financial reward, the tasks are done at a snail's pace. The pursuit of intellectual excellence through research seminars and scholarly exchange is not in evidence. If a foreign visitor requests it, a seminar is instantly held; otherwise, you wait for years to see a regular faculty seminar. Yet, it is in this very environment of profound anti-intellectualism that an abundance of student and staff research occurs. Yet, I cannot but view with skepticism the elegantly printed, computer generated research report, be it from an international agency, a professor or a student. With a high prevalence of poor quality research in major biomedical journals, I need solid evidence that the task was carried out under rigorous standards and good quality control measures in all its stages before I take its data, p-values, and findings seriously.

In truth, nobody does. Once it has passed muster, the dissertation just graces the shelf of the MPH program office; it does not even appear in the library or in an electronic format for access by others. New students do not consult it. No seminar to discuss an important and well done project is held. The fine oratory at the initial presentation about its significance for a key public health problem has blown away in the wind. It is, as they say, time to move on.

A COMPLEX CONUNDRUM

When I was a student, we took a book or a printed paper to bed or the dining table. It came alive when we felt the paper, turned it page by page. Often we fell asleep doing so. Notions flawed logically, one sentence at a time, with a picture here and there. We pondered; spent much time on the puzzling sections; got frustrated and more. Yet, in the end, it made sense and produced a clearer vision of the subject.

Now students are wedded to the electronic medium. Instead of books and papers, they carry around laptops and flash drives. Access is fast, information is abundant, and hyperlinks enable one to scramble all over the planet while reading a single article. One hardly looks at the same stuff twice; and even then, it is a fast visit. The joy of intense involvement with the printed page is an uncommon experience; indeed, reading is now branded a subversive activity (Carr 2008; Morford 2008; Pitts 2008). While there is much of intellectual and real advantage in this electronic era, there are grave dangers associated with it as well.

Prominent neuroscientists, psychiatrists and psychologists claim that the Internet and the computer are changing, for the worse, the way in which people think and behave. While the ability to speak has a genetic basis, to read or write does not. The latter have developed recently and are socially acquired through an intense process in the childhood when the neural circuitry is more pliant and absorbent (Greenfield 2008; Small and Vorgan 2008). In the Western world, a generation is growing up immersed in television, video games, cell phones, MP3 players, computers and the Internet. Diminished skills in writing, logical expression and arithmetical operations are common features of this era of smart phones and the computer. One commentator, discussing the situation in the UK, observes:

> We check our phones every 12 minutes, often just after waking up. Always-on

behavior is harmful to long-term mental health, and we need to learn to the hit the pause button. (Griffey 2018).

In the Third World nations, poverty keeps the majority of the children away from such gadgets. But in the urban areas, that trend exists. And in the universities, combined with an acute shortage of books, extreme commercialism and donor worship prevalent among the academic staff, computers and the Internet only give us the worst of both the worlds. The MUHAS library has a new immaculately constructed floor — the new computer center for the students. This is in addition to the several others computer rooms on the campus. Everything is ready to go; machines and all. Yet, the place has remained closed for two years now. There is no money to connect the generator for the center. Another white elephant graces the campus while the lower dusty floors of the library are stocked with ancient books. What if even a tenth of that money had gone into good quality and relevant books?

The Internet can widen our intellectual horizon. I am regularly amazed at the vast variety of scholarly and teaching material one can find on any subject, for all the levels of the educational ladder. The academy has a real chance to do wonders, to challenge the students, flood them with good material and train them with rigor and inculcate a broad theoretical and practical horizon. Yet, subjects are team taught without ensuring rigorous standards. Many lecturers give their four or so hours of lectures on the same topic with the same slides in very different settings without modification. The students have to memorize these slides to pass the exam. And that is it.

But it could be otherwise. Take an instance: in the past, it took effort to get relevant journal papers from the library and photocopy them for the students. Often the funds were lacking, or the photocopier was not working. Just when it was needed, electrical power was cut off. Now, one just has to locate the papers over the Internet, download them, and put them on a flash drive. You give that and the course notes to the class representative at the start of the semester. All students get it from him or her. Lo and behold, they have all the needed class material. Yet, no other instructor I talked to does that. All react as if it is a Nobel Prize winning idea, while all the time they share material in a similar fashion while working on their donor funded projects.

Funds from such projects can finance purchase of books, institutional software licenses, and other academic material that are in short supply. Small steps can have a large impact, if the material is used as required. MUHAS has now placed an order with the British Medical Association for medical books; I was able to secure Norwegian funds for books to set up a class library and for use by the academic staff. How about using project funds to produce academic course readers, and putting them on flash drives or CDs for the students?

The possibilities are many. But we need take the challenges

facing us seriously. Some members of the academic staff do a good job. But they face institutional barriers and feel isolated. Other than for formulating symbolic five year plans to procure funds from abroad, enlightened and bold leadership is sorely lacking in the academy.

CONCLUSIONS

Every seasoned academic one talks to says educational standards have declined of recent. That is my impression also. In particular, the quality of postgraduate training at MUHAS and UDSM is not at a satisfactory level. A scientific study is needed. Form has triumphed over substance; ease of access has bred intellectual blight. What transpires reflects the worst of the new and old eras. Instead of a thoughtful discourse, the classroom scene is dominated by superficial presentations adorned by graphics and dynamic images. Collections of minor factoids and routine schematic formulations dominate over ground-up derivation, in-depth reasoning, challenging exercises, enhancement of knowledge, and the pursuit of applications to serve broad based local needs. Academics say that the background of students is poor, and they lack motivation. So we teach to the lowest common denominator. Most get a passing grade, perpetuating a vicious cycle. We complain that the student intake is too high, and teachers too few. But instead of taking up this issue seriously with the administration, we teach as if on a go slow strike. Indeed, circumscribed intellectual horizons seem to be a signal feature of this age of information.

Have the computer and Internet improved the situation? Just a little bit. Have they helped worsen it? Quite a lot, I surmise. The promised potential of the computer to revolutionize education is not evident. A decade ago, a computer expert sounded the alarm for the US and other industrialized nations (Stoll 1999). That is what I see occurring here as well.

Yet, this is not inevitable; it is a choice we have made, or agreed to have made for us. And, it is also a situation we ourselves need to and can change. As Mao Tse Tung said, we need to walk on both legs; to combine the good of the past with the best of the new. We need to revive book based education, rigorous standards, deeper discourse, realistic practical work, reading a range of theory and applied papers, and critical discussion and combine that with a prudent utilization of computers and the Internet. Staff seminars, a rare entity now, have to be revived; and good student research projects presented therein, not just shelved. The attitude of commercialism has to be curtailed. Greater intellectual engagement is needed, among both the staff and students. To think that powerful computers, faster Internet access, latest anti-virus and other software and cell phones with email capability are, in and of themselves, the gateway to an academic Nirvana is to live in a fantasy world. If we do not counter the current trends, we will surely end up with authentically certified but essentially fake higher education.

The context also counts. These negative trends have occurred in a culture of almost complete `donor' dependency. Commitment towards teaching courses that do not pay extra allowances is low. Much research is done. But research seminars are not held until a foreign academic comes for a visit. If donor or other funds for a weekend retreat in a beach side hotel are not at hand, work on curricular development is not done. The world of ideas has been taken over by an ethos of greed. In regional or national level projects not much is undertaken without a foreign funder in the background.

We must set priorities that reflect the needs of the nation and promote quality education. Undue reliance on charity cannot bring sustainable development, be it at the national or university level. Total dependence on so-called donor funds is a cause of the current quagmire. President Nyerere's government paid lip service to self-reliance but sidelined it in practice. Self-reliance, not to be confused with isolationism, begins with intellectual self-reliance. We must decide for ourselves where we need to go and how to get there. Using our own resources, we can work on curricular reform, restart seminars, conduct public discussions of health issues, write and publish books, evaluate teaching and research with appropriate standards, use the joint student research as educational and public health promoting tasks, and conduct institutional affairs in a democratic and transparent manner.

Only our own efforts can enhance excellence and responsibility. Nobody can do that for us. In the sole School of Public Health in a nation facing tremendous health problems, the urgent challenge is to play a role, by example and scientific discourse to confront these problems. Staff and student research must be a vital segment of that effort. Their findings need to be discussed at MUHAS and disseminated to the public and relevant bodies. Our job is not to turn out degreed bureaucrats and quasi-competent functionaries who carry on business as usual but well trained professionals who are critical thinkers committed to dealing with the problems at hand.

There is no technological quick fix out of the quagmire. The way out, in the most practical sense of the term, lies in our hearts and brains; let us deploy them well.

8

EDUCATION AND AMERICA

SUMMARY: This essay recounts three aspects of my teaching at the University of California, Los Angeles: (i) the challenges of teaching medical statistics to trainee doctors; (ii) manifestation and impact of affirmative action in higher education; and (iii) the existence of subtle censorship in the academy and society. It underscores the presence of miseducation and racial bias even at reputed universities in the US.[1]

*

---

1. Aspects of the first part of this essay were discussed in Chapter 9 of *The Travails of a Tanzanian Teacher* (Hirji 2018). Otherwise, it has not been published before.

Blind belief in authority is
the greatest enemy of truth.
Albert Einstein
++++++++++

TO STUDY MEDICINE OR DENTISTRY in the US, you need a bachelor's degree. In the time I taught at the UCLA School of Medicine, there were a hundred and fifty medical students in each entering class. In the first two years, they had basic science courses like Anatomy, Physiology and Microbiology that were complemented by a modicum of clinical exposure. Medical Statistics, a semester-long course, was done in the first year and was taught by faculty from the Department of Bio-Mathematics. During the late 1980s and 1990s I was one of the five instructors involved in teaching this course.

The class of 150 was divided into five sections with roughly 30 students in each section. Each instructor was assigned his or her own section. We shared the services of two teaching assistants who helped with grading course assignments and giving individualized assistance to students during the course office hours.

To teach medical statistics to trainee doctors in an effective manner you first have to overcome a major attitudinal obstacle. The majority have the view that statistics has little bearing on their future work as doctors. In the case of anatomy or biochemistry, for example, the issue does not arise. They need to know some statistics to pass the first part of their licensing exam at the end of the first two years; that is all. Apart from the few who plan to pursue a research-based career, the rest study it because they have to. In addition, the other basic science courses with their laboratory components take up most of their time. They want to devote a bare minimal amount of time to medical statistics, pass the exam and be done with it. They do not want or expect any demanding material in this class.

If the instructor does not take steps to counter such views in the initial lectures, he will have to live with a group of bored students throughout. This had been the experience at UCLA as well. But by the time I joined the department, the faculty had worked out a good strategy to deal with the problem. It was based on the realization that we were not teaching future statisticians. There was no need to stuff the syllabus with formulas and derivations. Instead, the approach should focus on reading articles from medical journals, discussing them in a systematic way, unearthing the statistical ideas embedded therein, explaining their significance and generalizing their application. In this way, statistical notions are seen to arise from concrete medical applications. (Chapter 6).

There was a skeletal syllabus, specifying the statistical ideas and concepts of research design and interpretation that each instructor had to cover. Otherwise, we were free to select our own articles, books and other material. While a few articles were shared, each of us had our own article repository. After teaching it the first time,

I went a step further. Instead using articles for varied medical conditions as my colleagues did, each year I focused on a single ailment. For example, it could be acute earache in children, a common malady with a rising incidence in the US in those years.

This proved to be a challenging endeavor in ways more than one. I had to select ten to twelve relevant articles that would also contain the essential statistical concepts in a sequential and understandable way. It entailed spending hours in the library each summer. But in the end, it was worth it. The students became engaged sooner and discussions were more fruitful.

This approach allowed me to make the students aware that medicine was an arena filled with different diagnostic and treatment modalities, and controversies. Adopting one or the other treatment for a particular condition required evaluating the nature and quality of relevant empirical evidence. This served to underscore the importance of statistical ideas like systematic and random effects, bias and precision in health and medicine. In the case of acute earache in children, the default treatment in the US and UK was dissimilar to that in the Scandinavian countries. The former advocated routine use of antibiotics while the latter used a wait-and-see approach and a prudent recourse to anti-microbial drugs. Which was the better strategy? I gave the students journal reports of the clinical trials that had evaluated these strategies. The message was a mix-one. In this case, how do we arrive at an overall judgment? As it was a relatively common condition, the students came to realize that once they started practicing medicine, it was an issue they would have to deal with. To draw a balanced and informed judgment, they would need a good grasp of basic statistical ideas.

In the penultimate week, there was a class debate. One side would present evidence relating to one treatment strategy; the other side, the other strategy. A lively exchange decorated with cookies and juice would ensue. Later, the students would tell me they never thought statistics could be fun. They appreciated that without a basic knowledge of the discipline, they would find it harder to understand papers in medical and health journals. The other instructors were impressed by my approach. Yet, in the light of the time and effort needed, none of them adopted it.

But it was not just fun. Statistics needs thought and due attention. Each week, I gave them an article to read and a homework assignment based on it. In the first two weeks, this generated an outcry.

> The other sections get an article and homework every other week. Why are we being given extra work?

They complained to me. Some went to the head of our department who was also the course coordinator, and voiced their discomfort. He would come tell me: *Karim, go easy on them.* Every time my response was: *This is my style of teaching. They will have to live with it.*

Another condition I set for my class was not to use computer based statistical software to do the numerical problems in their assignments. You need to use a calculator and your brain, I told them. If you just enter the data in the computer and get an answer, you will not understand why a certain method is needed to tackle a certain type of problem. Often the methods are used in a routine fashion. Misuse and abuse of statistical ideas in health research proliferates as a result. Use of computers is the second step. First develop an understanding of what you are doing and why. You can use a word processor for writing your report but that is it. That was my line. Grudgingly, they accepted it.

And every year, as it became engaged in the course material, the class calmed down. At the end, a number of students would tell me:

> Thank you, professor, for taking us through the grind. While students in other sections were stumbling through the material, we really learned something.

I also taught applied and theoretical statistics course to the master's and doctoral level students at UCLA. These students did not need motivation to tackle advanced statistical material. With the medical students it was another story. The Medical Statistics course was the most challenging course I taught. Each year I felt a deep sense of satisfaction when it was over, and looked forward to the next year's class.

STATISTICS AND ERROR

Statistics is the science of error. It allows scientists studying nature, humans and societies to classify and quantify the type of errors they can make while drawing conclusions from the information they gather. It makes them aware of the potential biases, inaccuracies and imprecision in their findings and interpretation.

Errors in science derive from systematic and random sources. Over the years, scientists have formulated varied strategies to control and minimize error. Satisfactory results from giving a drug to ten consecutive patients in a clinic does not imply that a broadly usable remedy has been found. A well-designed, conducted and analyzed clinical trial is in order before such a conclusion can be drawn. And even then, the findings may have limitations. Medicine and medical research deal with issues of life and death. An uncompromising attention to control of error is essential.

In practice, however, the application of scientific method and statistics to medical research has been replete with numerous, minor and major but avoidable missteps (Altman 2002; Evans, Thorton and Chalmers 2006). These include utilization of inappropriate study designs, too small sample sizes, biased allocation of patients to treatment arms, selective or distorted reporting, underreporting of adverse effects, unjustified use of subgroup analysis, inappropriate data analysis methods, over-analysis of data, neglect of the size of treatment effects, too short a follow up period, excessive amount of missing data, replacement of clinical outcomes with surrogate markers and a host of other flawed practices (Chalmers et al. 1983; Chan et al. 2004; Chan and Altman 2005; Lagakos 2006; Persaud and Mamdani 2006; Schatz et al. 2005; Schulz and Grimes 2005; Thornley and Adams 1998).

The factors underlying such bias and error inducing practices include academic promotion criteria based on quantity, not quality of research; publish or perish climate in the academy; unduly competitive atmosphere for research funds; superficial peer-review; circular citation; too many short-cuts in research conduct; lack of training in research methods; and importantly, conflict-of-interest arising from increased reliance on drug company funds in research; misleading advertising; company control of publication decisions and not reporting research showing unfavorable findings (Angell 2005; Brody 2007; Henderson 2010; Kassirer 2005).

In all my statistical courses, be they in the US, Norway or Tanzania, I did not neglect to raise the issue of misuse and abuse of statistical methods, giving examples and pointing to their sources. The scope and type of errors always took my class by surprise. Yet, in most cases, they appreciated the fact that I made them aware of an important issue they had not considered before. It often led to a spirited discussion of the ethics of medical research and social responsibility of scientists.

But in my medical statistics class at UCLA, the matter at times raised rankles from some hyper-patriotic minded students:

> Professor, you have shown us many cases of flawed research from the US. But does such poor quality research not occur elsewhere too?

I would respond:

> You are quite right; it is a global problem. But the US leads the world in terms of clinical trials. The decisions of the US FDA have global implications. For the topic we are dealing with the US is over-represented in term of the number of trials done. What I have given you is a comprehensive list of such studies. Instead of focusing on the origin of the studies, we should become familiar with their potential flaws and possible causes of such flaws. In future, as doctors and researchers you will need the tools to enable you to identify and avoid such errors.

It was a response accepted by the class. And from then on such political diversions would not occur. It was most gratifying when years later I met the patriotic students who were now practicing physicians.

> Professor, now I understand what you were telling us. There is so much pressure on us from the drug and device manufacturers to use their products. But when I see the glossy brochures they give us and examine their citations, I see a proliferation of the types of errors you made us aware of.

UCLA is one of the elite universities in the US, and its medical school leads the way in some areas of bio-medical research. My students had a solid educational foundation and could grasp the class material without much difficulty. But they and even my departmental colleagues and most other professors in the medical school had ideological blinders which diverted their vision from systemic and broader factors. Awareness of commercial and institutional bias, which had a major effect on medical research, teaching and practice, was low. The detrimental effects of such biases on patient and public well-being were not within their otherwise logically minded purview. It was a classic instance of miseducation in an advanced capitalist nation.

Such a narrowness of perspective arises from years of immersion into the capitalist system, from the influences of parents, schools, teachers, media, business promotion exercises, war-related propaganda and the political establishment. You are taught to think critically, but only within the bounds of a specialized discipline. You learn to conform to, not question the system. (Schmidt 2001). America is the best, and that is all there is to it. You become averse to consider any notion, however factually and logically sound it may be, that places doubt on this perceived wisdom. If you doubt it, you are afflicted with irrational anti-American propaganda. Even under the comic, neo-fascistic reign of Donald Trump, the vast majority of Americans cling to it. As the socially committed, brilliant scientist observed:

> *Common sense is the collection*
> *of prejudices acquired by age eighteen.*
> Albert Einstein

AFFIRMATIVE ACTION

Earlier I noted that the entering class at the UCLA School of Medicine had 150 students. Strictly speaking, it was not so. The size of the new UCLA class was 120. The other 30 students were enrolled at the Drew Medical School across the town but were doing their pre-clinical courses at UCLA. This arrangement stemmed from the policy of affirmative action in higher education.

The history of the American society is a history of profound economic and racial injustice. Until the 1960s, the US education system was essentially an Apartheid system. Schools in the predominantly white neighborhoods had adequate facilities and qualified teachers. In the other areas, schools were overcrowded, run-down and had shortages of basic educational material. The people lived in areas with poor health, commercial, transport and other services and encountered overt and covert discrimination in housing, jobs and promotion. Their civil and voting rights were curtailed as well. Enrollment of minority students into the universities was low due to decades of ingrained discrimination.

The vibrant civil rights struggles of the 1960s produced measures to address such inequalities. Affirmative action in colleges and universities was instituted for women and minority groups as a remedy for historical exclusion and to increase their presence in professions like medicine, law, engineering, and the academia.

Drew Medical School was located in the vicinity of the predominantly African American and Latino American neighborhoods of Los Angeles and was affiliated with the adjacent Martin Luther King Hospital. But education, research and quality of patient care here hardly compared with the UCLA School of Medicine and the world class UCLA Hospital.

In order to at least partly deal with this problem, the UCLA School of Medicine assumed the responsibility of providing the first two years of pre-clinical training to the Drew medical students. Hence, the additional 30 students in our entering class. As expected, most of these students were African Americans, Latinos and South Indian Americans.

The presence of Drew students affected how the Medical Statistics course was organized. The five sections noted above were based on declared background in statistics. There was an advanced section for students with a good background in the subject; three regular sections for students who had an average level of prior exposure to it and a remedial section for students with a previously low level of exposure to statistics.

It was a voluntary, self-selective scheme. But, wittingly or unwittingly, it became a race and class based scheme. While the first four sections had mostly white and East Asian students, year after year, the Drew students tended to join the remedial section. It apparently worked well. Students and faculty were attuned to it. These underprivileged students needed special, separate attention; that was the ruling line.

During my first two years, I taught a regular section class. For the rest of my time there, I was assigned to the advanced section. The remedial section was always taught by Professor EE, a friendly old-man who was liked by his students and colleagues. There were no complaints.

But I was not comfortable with the existence the remedial section and the racial exclusivity it embodied. When I raised this issue in the staff meetings, Professor EE responded:

> Karim, these kids have led a tough life. You have to take it easy on them and give them a chance.

Everyone else nodded their heads at this condescending attitude. When I asked why there was no remedial section in the other subjects, I was told that statistics was special. I did not buy any of these arguments but was out-voted. And that was the end of the story. But things changed in 1996. Our departmental head who was also the course director was taking a sabbatical leave. So I was made the temporary course director for that year. Assignment of instructors to the five sections was now my job. I assigned the remedial section to myself and requested Professor EE to teach a regular section. He graciously accepted; after all, I was the boss.

As the course director, I had access to all the records for this course. Perusing through the cabinet, I made several revealing discoveries. I found that Professor EE had been teaching at a substandard level and setting exams that were too easy. No wonder, he was popular with the students who were more concerned about anatomy and physiology. I also found that Professor CN, a graying old lady who had joined the department a long time back and who always taught a regular section taught elementary stuff in the formula-memorization, traditional style. It did not pose a challenge to her students. With a pleasant, ever-smiling personality, she was also a popular figure among the students and the faculty. The duo did not adopt the article-based philosophy we had agreed on and stuck to the age-old alienating style of teaching statistics. But they were liked by the students since securing a good grade in their sections did not require much effort. The students emerged from their classes with the same negative attitude towards statistics they had upon entering it and did not gain much of lasting value to their career as doctors. In order not to alienate these veterans in the department, the departmental head had tolerated these substandard practices.

That year, I taught the remedial section in exactly the same fashion and with the same level of material as I had done for the regular section. And the students responded as the regular section class had done: Groans in the first two weeks but settling down to my pace and assignments, and becoming engaged with the articles from then on. The end of the course debate was as lively as ever. Some students showed an outstanding performance. They could well have breezed through the advanced section. And at end, quite a number came to thank me for educating them about the mechanics and realities of medical research. They were particularly pleased to have learned the basic tools for critical analyses of papers published in medical journals.

The Drew students had been attracted to the remedial section in the past through interactions with their predecessors. The professor is a nice fellow and you will have an easy time. Even those with an aptitude for and good background in the subject had undervalued themselves. Patronizing tendencies from the professors fed upon their own low level self-esteem. Lower expectations led to lower level of performance. But when they were challenged, they performed as the others did.

I submitted my report to the departmental head upon his return. My main recommendation was to abolish the remedial section. It was a counter-productive undertaking for the Drew students. Fortunately, with the evidence I gave, he agreed. I also asked him to urge Professor EE and Professor CN to adopt the article-based teaching method in their sections. He presented my proposal in the planning meeting for the course that summer. Only two types of sections, an advanced section and four regular sections should be adopted. And, it was accepted. The remedial section was history. And that was the last time an effectively segregated medical statistics class was taught at the UCLA School of Medicine.

At the national level, affirmative action produced mixed results. Women undoubtedly benefited from it; the numbers and proportion of women in higher education and professions is higher now than it was in the 1960s. But for African Americans, it generated marginal results, and faced on-going hostility from White and Asian Americans. The key reason for the disparate outcomes is clear: while varied social and economic trends in US society improved the position of women in many aspects of their lives, that of African Americans remained stagnant in terms of jobs, housing, health care, basic education and social security. Tampering with the system at the top produced more black doctors, lawyers and engineers, but the vast majority of their siblings continued to receive substandard basic education under a hostile learning environment. And that is where it stands to this day.

The dominant political and economic forces in the US are pitted against a genuine change in the lives of African Americans, Native Americans, Latin Americans, immigrants and other disadvantaged minorities. Such a change cannot be envisaged without a fundamental change of the social, political and economic system as a whole (Sunkara 2019). The problems they face span all areas of life: education, health care, jobs, environmental pollution, housing, law enforcement and courts, voting rights and cultural domination. They are reinforced by the corporate domination of American politics and society. Imperial actions by the US factor into this conundrum. White Americans at the bottom rung of the economic ladder are affected by similar economic problems. But racially divisive attitudes and politics keep those at the bottom from uniting for a common cause. (Chapter 15).

Affirmative action at UCLA School of Medicine was a part of the stop-gap measures that failed to address foundational issues. What was needed was a comprehensive, sustained effort by the state and federal governments to raise the standards at the Drew Medical School and the Martin Luther King hospital. And those actions should be undertaken in the context of the overall transformative efforts.

Affirmative action applied in the medical statistics course stemmed from a patronizing stand towards minorities and produced performance below what they were capable of. They could do and did much better if challenged like other students. Low expectation induces poor outcome and reinforces the expectations, and the cycle is perpetuated. Nothing short of a decisive act is needed to break this vicious cycle. I was glad to have played an instrumental role in confronting this issue for our course.

CENSORSHIP AND THE ACADEMY

During a visit to a university bookstore in San Francisco in 1996, my attention was drawn to a book with the catchy title, *Deadly Medicine*. Likely a sensationalistic work, I thought as I flipped through it. As always, my first step was to peruse the reference list. There was an abundance of papers from major health and medical journals. That was a surprise. A further scrutiny of the initial chapters induced me to purchase the book (Moore 1995).

The next two evenings were spent reading it. My training as a medical statistician have made me adopt a sharply critical attitude towards any health related assertion. On this matter, one cannot be too careful. In a field vital for human welfare, claims that are either bogus or based on flimsy evidence proliferate. I examine the reliability and extent of evidence behind any claim, subject it to a reanalysis where possible and read other papers that support or refute it. As an instructor of courses on evidence-based medicine at reputable universities and with published papers in the field, I am not easily fooled. (Hirji 2009; Hirji and Fagerland 2009; Hirji and Premji 2011).

Written by an established science investigator and writer, it dealt with the treatment of irregular heart rhythms (arrhythmias). Our heart pumps blood through our body in a regular, periodic fashion. When its electrical conduction system is disturbed, the flow pattern becomes irregular. The problem occurs in several forms that range in severity from mild to life threatening. Doctors use electrocardiograms and other tests to diagnose it.

This book focused on a drug called Tambocor widely prescribed to treat varied forms of arrhythmias. It also contained a readable history of the development of the scientific methods for evaluating the efficacy medical treatments. Tambocor was used as an example to describe the actual process of discovery, testing and approval of medical drugs in the USA.

The author gave ample evidence to demonstrate several weaknesses in this process. The shortfalls in the relevant clinical studies included too short a follow-up period, a small sample size, use of samples not representative of the population of users of the drug, use of intermediate markers like stabilization of arrhythmias instead of clinical end-points like incidence of serious arrhythmias, heart attacks or death rate as outcome measures. Data analyses had focused on statistical significance but not the magnitude and precision of the effect measure. The potential of the drug to induce serious arrhythmias was ignored. The few researchers who pointed to the existence of such an effect were not heeded. And the pathophysiologic theory underlying the use of such drugs, though seemingly plausible, had not been tested through long-term studies.

Overall, the evidence unearthed by the author indicated the existence of a strong pro-corporate bias among the university-based researchers as well as in the US Food and Drug Administration. Such biases at times lead to the approval of drugs with a potential to inflict serious harm on the patients. Often, they are withdrawn but only after years of use by a large number of patients.

By the mid-1980s, Tambocor was used for people with serious and mild arrhythmias and became one of the mostly widely prescribed drugs in the US and elsewhere. Millions of prescriptions were written annually. Nonetheless, researchers at the US National Institutes of Health initiated a multi-center, large sample, double-blind clinical trial to evaluate the efficacy of this drug using clinical outcome measures. Such a trial for a drug that has undergone recent approval is rare. Because of the wide utilization of Tambocor, it was seen as a justified and necessary study.

The results of this meticulously conducted and analyzed study came out in 1989 and took the medical community by surprise. The death rate in the placebo group was 2% while in the drug group, it was 4%. The difference was not just statistically significant but, given the large number of people on the drug at that time, was also clinically significant. The 2 percentage point difference in the death rates pointed to thousands of excess deaths on an annual basis. Immediately, a highly publicized press conference was convened by the heads of the FDA, NIH and US Secretary for Health. They jointly announced the withdrawal of the drug from common use.

The book is well-written, thoroughly documented and educative about the design and analysis of clinical trials and the possible deviations from the scientific method in the actual clinical trials. I deemed it a relevant book for a graduate level course on the ethics of clinical trials I was scheduled to teach at UCLA in the fall. Accordingly, I placed an order for copies of the book through the UCLA bookstore. Two days later, the manager called me to say that it was out of print. That was curious – a book recently published but not a block buster going out of print that soon. When our departmental secretary made a call to the publisher, she got the same response – the book was unavailable. Fortunately, I was able to track down the author, who was a senior research fellow at George Washington University's Center for Health Policy Research. He told me that I was not the first person to contact him on this question. Many others had asked him why they could not get copies of his book.

The book was not out-of-print. Thousands of copies lay untouched in the warehouse. But the publisher was reluctant to release them for sale because the drug company had threatened to sue if it continued to market the book. Both the author and publisher had been aware of such a possibility when the book was in the offing. Consequently, the manuscript had gone through a thorough review by medical experts and steps were taken to ensure that all the assertions it made were amply documented. The drug company had little evidentiary basis upon which to pursue its case.

Books of a critical nature are published every year in the US. But most are brought out by small publishing houses with a limited reach. This book from a leading publisher had, however, crossed the line. It not only took aim at a strong pharmaceutical firm but also targeted the FDA, the research community and the practicing physicians for uncritically adopting a new, poorly tested drug and prescribing it to millions. The top executives at the publishing firm had apparently weighed in to override the decision of the editor who had approved the book. It had to be shelved.

The contract allowed the author to purchase the remaining copies of his book at a very low price. And he had managed to secure a large number of boxes. Was I interested to a get a box or two? Of course, I said. The UCLA bookstore ordered two boxes and I personally ordered four boxes for future use. And my students paid $4 for a book that otherwise would have costed $25. It formed an important pillar of my course on the ethics of clinical trials. The students found it a revealing and educative text.

Dismayed at the prospect of this exemplary work going out of circulation so soon, I wrote a book review and submitted it for publication in one of the leading biostatistics journals, *Statistics in Medicine*. Much longer than the usual reviews, it addressed the methodological, practical and ethical aspects of drug testing, clinical trials and drug approval. In two weeks, I got a response. The review editor told me that even though it was not normal for the journal to accept unsolicited reviews, he found my review so impressive that he had accepted it for publication. I was elated.

Having published other papers in this monthly journal earlier, I knew that once you get the acceptance letter from the associate editor, it takes about three months before it appears in print. So I waited. Three months on it did not appear. There must be backlog, I thought. Six months later, there was nothing. Concerned, I contacted the editor. What he told me was something I thought did not occur for a scientific journal.

> Your review is being assessed in by our legal office in New York. We need to wait.

I had written a fully referenced, scientific review. What did lawyers have to with that? I waited and waited. Finally, it appeared in print fifteen months after acceptance. No explanation about the delay was given (Hirji 1997).

It seems that the campaign to bury this book was a far reaching one. And probably one corporate giant was trying to protect the reputation of another giant. But there was no legal basis to prevent the publication of my review. So the lawyers had relented and allowed it to go into print.

This experience demonstrated the existence of gate-keepers in the US social system. Their role is to exercise control over views that pose a firm challenge to the existing order and corporate interests. Though called by different names, in reality they are censors.

The term censorship denotes the existence of societal mechanisms that restrict or prohibit free movement of ideas.

Censorship can occur in overt or covert ways and can be exercised by state or non-state agencies. Usually, it is taken to mean the existence of a governmental censorship board whose task is to curtail or ban the circulation of books, movies, magazines and other entities that promote viewpoints in conflict with the official line. The nations of the West, which do not have such central boards, are thereby seen as `free' societies. It is held that censorship is a problem in the other parts of the world (Roy 2018; *Wikipedia* 2018).

That is not just a half-truth, but a profound misperception. A high level of effective censorship has operated in the US for a long time. It flourishes to this day as well (Cohen 2006; Editor 2019; Hermann and Chomsky 1988; McChesney 2008; Naureckas and Jackson 1996; Randall, Naureckas and Cohen 1995. The website www.fair.org is an excellent source for articles on this issue). The essence of ideologically derived indirect forces that shape the outlook of the people was aptly captured by Karl Marx:

> *The ruling ideas of each age*
> *have ever been*
> *the ideas of its ruling class.*
> Karl Marx

Censorship in the academy is manifested at the institutional, professional, financial and ideological levels. Voices that critique the way things are done at the institutions, deviant voices within varied disciplines, those who query the foundation of American society, capitalism and imperial foreign policy and academics who oppose the increasing role of corporations in education and research funding are muffled or silenced through varied indirect and direct ways. Such academics face greater obstacles in securing promotion, tenure, research funds, professional responsibilities, sabbatical leave and other opportunities for advancement. The stated reasons are tangential in nature. The basic reason is unstated but is well understood and serves as a warning to others. Speak up and face the fire. Shut up and prosper. One example often suffices to bring the others into line. Academics then indulge in self-censorship to protect their careers. A few hardy ones survive and persist; but they are the exception to the rule. (Chomsky et al. 1998).

During my nearly two decades of stay in the US, I saw and read about many such cases. The author of *Deadly Medicine*, for example, continued to write well researched papers and books on adverse effects of medicinal drugs but they lost the comprehensive, critical approach of his previous work. With my tendency to speak up, I too encountered such obstacles at various junctures and contexts. A small deviation and you are accused of `bringing politics into science.' For example, in my ethics class I pointed out that a major food manufacturer that had given a substantial donation to the UCLA Children's Hospital also stood accused of aggressive marketing of baby formula in African and Asian countries. It thereby discouraged breast feeding and led to higher rates of diarrheal diseases and death among infants from poor families. I questioned the ethics of accepting money from such a source. That my students could not stomach, and said it was beyond the purview of the class; it was `politics'! And they wrote about it in their evaluation for the course.

Four additional factors affect the degree of academic freedom in the US universities. The fees have risen at a rate much higher than inflation. The annual cost of an undergraduate degree to attend UCLA, even for residents, is in excess of $35,000, and if you are at an elite private institution like Stanford University or Harvard University, it will cost you somewhere in the region of $65,000 per year. A typical student emerges with a debt that is between $150,000 and $200,000. Financial pressure inhibits student activism and independence. Academic tenure enabled the faculty to independently engage in research and write on issues they felt to be important and without worries about political consequences. Of recent, the granting of tenure has been restricted and some outspoken academics have been stripped of tenure on spurious grounds. More and more of the teaching is now done by low paid, overworked, part-time adjunct faculty. They are not rooted in the academy. Job insecurity leads to a tendency to not rock the boat. Persistent attacks by conservative politicians regarding so-called `left-wing bias the academy' feeds into the conundrum. Corporate funding also adds to it. Pro-business biases permeate the courses and research and dilute the quality of education. (Brennan and Magness 2019; Cantwell and Kauppinen 2014; Childress 2019; Mettler 2014).

As a consequence of such factors, self-censorship in the academy is on the ascendance. You follow the crowd. The atmosphere of the 1960s, where a good number of independent, critical voices based on the university campuses presented engaging analyses of different aspects of society and the world is now history. Only a trace remains.

Indirect censorship operates in a subtle manner. Pervasive yet hidden from sight, it is generally more effective than direct censorship (Brody 2007; Crossen 1996; Wikipedia 2018, 2019). From 2004 to 2007, I taught a series of one to two-week long courses on Evidence Based Medicine at UCLA School of Medicine, University of Bergen and University of Oslo. The attendees were medical residents, post-graduate research fellows in public health together with consultant physicians and professors. Each time, I inquired about the book *Deadly Medicine* and the incident it covered. None of the course participants had heard of either. The drug withdrawal in 1989 had generated headlines. Yet, within a few years, it was banished from memory. It had led to a few papers in medical and biostatistics journals about the utility of surrogate markers but not much else. The impact on the drug testing and evaluation process was minimal. But such markers continue to be used in medical research. What should have been a cause for a paradigm shift in the process of drug approval and a required read for courses on the design and methods of clinical trial is virtually dead and buried. You may find a couple of copies on Internet-based outlets. That is it. I took two boxes to Dar es Salaam and gave out a few copies each year to students and colleagues. But I do not know if they were read or appreciated.

A recent case of Steven Wing, a Professor of Epidemiology at the University of North Carolina is instructive. His research had focused on the impact of large scale pig farms on human health. However, his work was under threat from the giant corporations that own these farms and fund a large amount research done by the universities in the state. It was an issue avoided by other researchers. Yet, Professor Wing was forced by corporate lawyers to reveal records that might identify his respondent and break the promise of confidentiality. Upon showing other cases of corporate pressure on academics, Kate Cox and Claire Brown state:

> But over the past 30 years, as public funding for university research has dried up, private industry money has poured in. And with industry money comes industry priorities. Agribusiness has funded research that has advanced its interests and suppressed research that undermines its ability to chase unfettered growth. The levers of power at play can seem anecdotal — a late-night phone call here, a missed professional opportunity there. But interviews with researchers across the US revealed stories of industry pressure on individuals, university deans and state legislatures to follow an agenda that prioritizes business over human health and the environment. (Cox and Brown 2019).

A large number of examples of corporate subversion and distortion of scientific, health and environmental research have been exposed. Yet, the problem is larger today than it has been in the past.

Ideas can be suppressed as effectively in a covert manner as by overt bans and aggressive state action. In the former case, people feel they have freedom of speech and expression, but that freedom is constricted within narrow bounds. Implicitly, they know where not to cross the line. On basic matters, you conform, not pose questions. Pervasive indirect censorship is thus a central pillar and driver of pro-capitalist miseducation in American academic institutions. As Noam Chomsky puts it:

> *Education is a system of imposed ignorance.*
> Noam Chomsky

9

EDUCATION AND DEBATE

SUMMARY: This essay provides an overview of the series of intellectual exchanges that occurred at or originated from the University of Dar es Salaam from 1966 to around 1990. The issues in contention included structure and function of education in a developing nation like Tanzania, formulation of relevant curricula, the need for interdisciplinary courses, the policy of Socialism and Self-Reliance, connecting education to social activism and the liberation of Africa from colonialism, racist rule and neocolonialism. My aim is to underscore the reputation of the University of Dar es Salaam as a beacon of progressive scholarship in Africa in those years. The issues raised in these debates are important today as well. Progressive intellectuals and activists need to study those debates and draw lessons for the ongoing struggle for genuine liberation of Africa. Vigorous, grounded, free-flowing intellectual exchanges in the academy, media and society are essential ingredients in the drive to combat the malady of under-education in Africa.[1]

*

---

1. This essay was initially drafted as an extension to my review of Yash Tandon's *Common People's Uganda* (Hirji 2019b). This revised version should be read in conjunction with chapters 10 and 11 which cover related material.

Change is the end result of all true learning.
Leo Buscaglia
++++++++++

AN IDEAL UNIVERSITY TRANSMITS advanced knowledge to students, taking some to the frontiers of their disciplines, and generates new knowledge in natural and social sciences and other disciplines. It is an important repository of art, literature, culture and philosophical ventures. Yet, ideas in any field do not emerge in a linear, homogenous way. The process has ups and downs, and at times, dramatic turn arounds. It is fraught with minor and major disputations. Tensions abound as the varied tendencies reflecting social or discipline based conformism come into conflict with new notions that challenge the status quo. A university, if it is not a university in name only, must be a battle ground, a factory of ideas and new horizons.

In that regard, for nearly three decades after it was established, the University of Dar es Salaam (UDSM) functioned as a university *par excellence*. From its days as a constituent college of the University of East Africa onto operating as an autonomous university, its campus was the stage of a series of extended intellectual exchanges of academic, national and Pan African import. The debates started in 1966, gathered steam in the 1970s, and went on, though at a much reduced level, into the 1980s. The issues in contention varied as did the style, venue and parties involved. (Note, in this essay, I use the name UDSM for both the incarnations of this institution.)

UDSM stood out among African universities with respect to charting out ideas of relevance to study curricula, conceptualization of the African reality and promotion of genuine social and economic transformation in the continent. The exercise pitted progressive scholars and students against their conservative counterparts, the university administration and the national political establishment. These exchanges were followed by concerned scholars and activists from across Africa and the world. As a consequence, many of them visited the university to teach and research, for short or extended periods. They were also attracted by President Nyerere's humanism, his steadfast commitment to the total liberation of African from colonial and racist domination and the nation's policy of Socialism and Self Reliance.

Today, these debates are known as the Dar es Salaam Debates. Yet, their scope and what transpired therein have not been documented with accuracy. In fact, the existing literature is strewn with misperceptions. I give two examples.

In the Introduction to a recent work by Yash Tandon, Ngugi wa Thiong'o writes of 'the Dar Debate, generated by the 1976 publication of Issa Shivji's book, *The Silent Class Struggle in Tanzania.*' (Tandon 2019b). Dan Nabudere and Mahmood Mamdani are identified as the responders to this work. But *Tanzania: The Silent Class Struggle* (the correct title) first came out in 1970 as a special issue of the student magazine *Cheche* when neither Nabudere nor

Mamdani had joined UDSM. The responders to this book were Walter Rodney, John Saul and others I mention later. Nabudere and Mamdani critiqued Shivji's second book *Tanzania: The Class Struggle Continues*, which came out in 1973.

Another misrepresentation appears in the same work. Talking of the radical student magazine at UDSM, *Cheche*, the author declares:

> In one of its early issues, Rodney criticized Ujamaa, whereupon the government banned Cheche, arguing that Tanzania did not need to import a foreign ideology; it was building its own model of socialism. (Tandon 2019b, p.192).

First, Rodney did not write any article on *Ujamaa*, let alone a critical one, in *Cheche*. Among other things, what prompted the ban was the earlier mentioned first work by Issa Shivji, which came out in 1970 as a special issue of that magazine. Rodney's comment on Shivji's paper appeared in a 1971 issue of a sister magazine, *MajiMaji* that came into existence after *Cheche* was banned. Unlike Shivji's work, it was quite conciliatory towards the policy of *Ujamaa*.

Noting such details accurately is not just a matter of simple exactitude but affects, as I will show later, the perspective you get on the debates and their changing content and style as well.

NATIONAL SERVICE

In the year 1966, the government of Tanzania floated a proposal to introduce a national service scheme under which the recipients of post-secondary education would be enrolled in a two year program of serving the nation. It would entail spending six months in a military style camp prior to joining the university or a college, and 18 months of work on a reduced salary after graduation. But the university students were, for the most part, opposed to it. A contentious exchange ensued in the national media. The student representatives had doubts about its utility. And they lacked trust in the senior government and party personalities who were championing the program (Ivaska 2003).

The tussle between the government and the students culminated in a long student march to the State House. President Nyerere received the chanting crowd. Yet, after an emotional address, he reacted firmly, expelling more than 400 students from the university. And that is how it all began.

ROUND ONE

While most of the expelled students were readmitted after about a year, the incident sparked off deep soul searching on the university campus and beyond. The main concerns were: What is the role of a university in a poor nation like Tanzania? How can higher education reflect the goals and values of the nation? Is university education a right or a privilege?

These issues gained further import after the issuance of the Arusha Declaration in 1967. By then, quite a number of socialist academics had joined the university. Together with committed socialists like AM Babu in the government, they spearheaded moves to put the academy onto to a footing that was appropriate for the nation and Africa. The key players on the staff included Walter Rodney and John Saul. A major conference on the role of the university in socialist Tanzania was held on the campus in March 1967. AM Babu and Walter Rodney, the two principal speakers, proposed that the institution be transformed into a socialist university (The Nationalist 1967a; 1967b; 1967c; 1967d).

The discipline-based courses at UDSM and other African academies, particularly in the social sciences and education, were conservative in content and biased towards Western pro-capitalist mode of thought. The overspecialization they embodied did not provide a good understanding of human history and the nature of social and economic development. In addition, students in science, law, medicine and other areas did not have any exposure to ideas relating to development and society. They would likely graduate with the conservative, elitist mindset they had when they joined the university.

The key proposal put forward was to institute a progressive, rigorous interdisciplinary course dealing with national and international social and economic development which would be compulsory for all the students. The single discipline oriented right wing academics and the conservative administration stood opposed to this proposal.

The idea of a common interdisciplinary course was put forward in various academic venues and the ensuing exchange went on for several years. Besides oral exchanges in meetings, papers and book chapters were written (Resnick 1968). The idea became a reality in July 1969. All incoming students were now required to take Development Studies (DS). An interdisciplinary course tailored for social science undergraduates, East African Society and Environment (EASE), was initiated two years on. Opposition from the conservatives, however, did not abate. Led by the head of the Department of Political Science, Anthony Rweyemamu and the historian John Iliffe, they signed a memo in 1971 calling for the absorption of the Department of Development Studies into the Department of Political Science. They were criticized by radical students in a strongly worded counter memo that questioned their rationale as well as their motivation (But I am running ahead).

ROUND TWO

The Arusha Declaration of February 1967 catalyzed the founding of the Socialist Club on the campus. Academic staff and students took part in its discussions. A few months later, it morphed into the Students' African Revolutionary Front (USARF). Students from Tanzania, Uganda, Kenya and Malawi joined the Front. Yoweri Museveni, a student from Uganda, was its founding president. Not more than three academics ever became associate, non-voting members. During the three years of its existence, the membership USARF was less three percent of the total student population of about 1,200. Yet, its impact was far in excess of numbers. In many of its activities, USARF acted together with the campus branch of TANU Youth League (TYL).

In no time, USARF distinguished itself as an activist, radical group on academic, ideological, national and Pan African arenas (Hirji 2011). An early USARF activity was a well-attended panel discussion on `The Strategy, Conduct and Tactics of the African Liberation Movements.' The speakers included members of African Liberation Movements based in Dar es Salaam and Walter Rodney (The Nationalist 1967f). Here Rodney renewed his call to convert UDSM into a socialist university. Subsequently, upon an invitation from FRELIMO, five USARF members visited the liberated areas of Mozambique adjacent to the southern border of Tanzania. Their report was circulated on the campus and among the liberation movements. Besides FRELIMO, USARF had a close working relationship with the Pan African Congress (PAC) of South Africa. In the following years, some representatives of these movements joined hands with USARF and TYL in a number of practical activities and on several controversial issues.

The birth of USARF marked a decisive turning point in the scope and contentiousness of the debates on the campus. This occurred on several fronts.

One, USARF stimulated intense exchanges with the conservative students on matters like celebrating the Rag Day, hosting US based or funded cultural groups, doing volunteer work on the university farm and villages, combining political commitment with academics, the agenda and activities of the main student organization, and so on. The venue for the debates ranged from the campus notice boards, the main student magazine, the national media to regular verbal tussles near the student cafeteria. During its life time, UASRF (jointly with TYL) frequently issued strongly worded statements relating to student, academic, national and international events.

Two, the campus TYL (whose leaders were also USARF members) organized the Second Seminar of East and Central African Youth in December 1969. The main speakers were Walter Rodney, Ahmed Gora Ebrahim (PAC), Charles Kileo (Law student and USARF/TYL member) and Nogmbale Mwiru (TYL HQ). In his presentation on the Ideology of African Revolution, Rodney labeled the independent governments in Africa as neocolonial regimes. For this, he was strongly criticized in an editorial of the ruling party newspaper. The editorial was said to emanate from the State House (The Nationalist 1969k).

Three, the student radicals joined hands with leftist academics to rally against the unending opposition from the conservative Tanzanian and expatriate academics to the common, interdisciplinary course and to general curricular reform. USARF also critiqued, in words and by militant action, the existent curricula in Law and Political Science (consult The Nationalist (1969a) to The Nationalist (1969n) for details on the issues mentioned above).

Four, an additional front opened up when USARF members began to critically appraise aspects of the national policy. One instance was the articles they wrote in the newspapers questioning the policy on tourism. People from and beyond the campus took part. When the Minister for Tourism visited the campus to defend the policy, he received a severe dressing down from the radicals. These exchanges later appeared in the book *Tourism and Socialist Development* (Shivji 1973b). The move to give loans to senior civil servants to purchase cars generated another exchange.

To address the matters being raised by USARF and TYL, President Nyerere held two public question/answer sessions on the campus. He also invited the radicals for talks at his residence. While in private he expressed sympathy with their concerns, in the public fora, he roundly ridiculed them. (Hirji 2011).

USARF began an educational forum, called ideological classes that met on Sundays to discuss ideas like capitalism, imperialism, socialism, and African liberation. It was a structured study program with assigned topics and books. Most of the sessions were led by students but once in while, a lecturer or professor was invited. The progressive Tanzanians, Kenyans and Ugandans on the campus conducted their own private discussion sessions on issues relating to the situation in their countries.

The move to change what until 1970 was a university college into an autonomous national university occasioned the submission of proposals from students and academic staff to the committee that was responsible for planning and overseeing the move. Various staff and student groups, including USARF, submitted proposals that differed in terms of structure, curricula and role of the national university.

ROUND THREE

A major leap forward in the nature of the debates on the campus was catalyzed by the establishment of the USARF/TYL magazine, *Cheche*. The first issue appeared in October 1969, and the fourth and final issue, in November 1970. In that month, both USARF and *Cheche* were banned by the government. Yet, during its short life, *Cheche* came to be known as a creative voice of radicalism whose impact extended far beyond the academia to the nation and other parts of Africa and the world (Hirji 2011).

The publication of Shivji's *Tanzania: The Silent Class Struggle* as a special issue of *Cheche* in August 1970 carried the debate on the nation's policy of *Ujamaa* and on how to conceptualize the African reality onto a higher level. Its message reverberated in the classroom as well as other venues. The next (final) issue of *Cheche* carried commentaries on it from KF Hirji, Yoweri Museveni and AS Namama. The paper was a major bone of contention at the East and Central African Social Science Conference held at UDSM in December 1970. The first issue of *MajiMaji* carried responses to *The Silent Class Struggle* by John Saul and Walter Rodney. When the paper appeared in a book form in 1973, it contained these two responses and responses from Justinian Rweyemamu and Thomas Szentes. Elsewhere Lionel Cliffe and Kassim Guruli gave their comments on the book.

On a related issue, Walter Rodney's paper depicting *Ujamaa* as a form of scientific socialism occasioned a couple of internal meetings among radical students and staff. The contentions were sharp but were carried out in a comradely fashion. Later, Rodney reversed his position on this question (Rodney 1972b; Rodney 1975).

Another phase on the debate on *Ujamaa* was initiated by Adhu Awiti's detailed research on rural stratification in the Iringa region published in *MajiMaji*. The process of class formation in Tanzania was the main topic in contention. Walter Rodney was one of the principal responders to this paper.

The debate initiated by *Tanzania: The Silent Class Struggle* gained momentum with the publication of the Institute of Development Studies paper entitled *Tanzania: The Class Struggle Continues* by Issa Shivji in 1973. The first set of comments on this report appeared in the August 1973 issue of *MajiMaji*. They were written by AP Mahiga, Adrian Foster-Carter, Walter Rodney and Kwesi Botchwey. Peter Meyns, Harko Bhagat and Mahmood Madani wrote critical comments later on. The arrival of Dan Nabudere and his Ugandan colleagues at UDSM in 1973/74 rekindled this debate, albeit in more intense manner. The exchanges at this stage were published in Tandon (1982).

ROUND FOUR

Besides what transpired in relation to *Cheche* and *MajiMaji*, many leftist academics and students, Tanzanian and non-Tanzanian, wrote books and papers analyzing the theory and practice of the policy of *Ujamaa*. The topics included the functioning of the state enterprises, agriculture, rural development, villagization, economic and manpower planning, state and private industries, and the role of the World Bank and other imperial agencies in the nation. Some of these publications sparked off internal and national debates. The journal papers and research reports are too many to list here. Some are given in the reference list of this essay. In addition to those already noted, some related books are: Cliffe and Saul (1973); Coulson (1979;1982); Kaniki (1981); Kjekshus (1977;1996); Mamdani (1976;1984); Mapolu (1976); Nabudere (1976); Othman (1980); Resnick (1968); Rodney (1972a); Rweyemamu (1973); Rweyemamu et al. (1972); Sheriff and Ferguson (1991); Shivji (1985); Tandon (1982); and von Freyhold (1979).

Exchanges on identity related issues also took place in this period. Marjorie Mbilinyi was a pioneer in raising the question of women's rights. Some other progressives, while supporting equal rights for women, differed with her in terms of the strategy to achieve it. But the two sides failed to meet halfway. AG Ebrahim addressed the contentious matter of race and class, especially in relation to South Africa, and O Parkipuni noted the plight of the Maasai people.

In addition, progressive staff in law, social sciences and the natural sciences strove to put their professional associations onto a more Africa related footing and away from the existing pro-Western influences. They organized and participated in national, regional and Pan African level conferences with such goals in mind. The debates also concerned the content and methods of teaching these subjects, and reverberated at the departmental level as well. A degree of dissent among the progressive staff, however, reduced the pace at which progress on these issues was made.

ROUND FIVE

In July 1971, the students at UDSM boycotted classes for about a week in protest at the expulsion of the leader of the students' union. The basis of the conflict was the authoritarian, inefficient and academically unsound style of operation of the new university administration installed a year earlier. It was the first and only pro-democracy uprising at UDSM. The united front of radical, nationalist and conservative students, male and female, was joined by the progressive academic staff and the campus workers. They were firmly opposed by conservative academics, the administration and the national government. (HIrji 2018a).

The onset and aftermath of this crisis stimulated a major, long-term debate on the need to democratize university governance. The student union, radical students and progressive staff forwarded their proposals in the form of memos and reports while the conservative academics and the administration continued to back the status quo. This debate took place in the national papers and campus venues. After this uprising, the academic staff put forth a petition calling for the establishment of an independent staff union. It took nearly a decade of struggle for that to become a reality.

In March 1977, students from UDSM and a few colleges staged

a street march against the surreptitious enhancement of pay and benefits of members of parliament and ministers. The protest with banner and loud chants, though peaceful, was broken up with a baton and tear gas charge by the riot police. 367 students were placed under custody and sent home. Two months later, most of them were permitted to resume their studies.

The 1980s saw the outbreak of additional contentions between the academic staff union and the administration. They tackled issues like democratic governance, academic freedom, academic standards, salaries and benefits, and the effects of the World Bank's structural adjustment program on higher education. By the end of that decade, however, the staff union and the students at UDSM had largely shed their progressive aura, and the era of debates petered.

COMMENT

What I have outlined above is a far from complete description of the intellectual ferment and contentions that transpired at UDSM in those decades. But it is an improvement, in terms of scope, on the descriptions given by Campbell (1986) and Shivji (1993a; 19993b; 1993c).

Chapter 10 of the recent work by Yash Tandon, Common People's Uganda (CPU), is devoted to the UDSM debates (Tandon 2019b). According to it, these debates consisted of four parallel debates. They are labeled: (i) Nyerere, *Ujamaa* and the debate on Socialism, (ii) The Ugandan internal party debate, (iii) AAPS and the pedagogy of social sciences, and (iv) The debate on Class, State and Imperialism.

But this classification falls quite short of what I have presented above. In the first place, it fails to cover the majority of the debates. Further, it implies that only the Ugandan progressives held internal debates, that only the Political Science department was engaged in endeavors to change the orientation of its professional association; and that the debate on *Class, State and Imperialism* essentially began with the arrival of Nabudere and his colleagues at UDSM. As noted in Round One to Round Five above, UDSM was the scene of extended debates on basic issues like class formation, class struggles, capitalism, socialism, imperialism and neocolonialism, not just in general terms but especially in relation to Tanzania and the policy of *Ujamaa*.

The four-parallel-debates scheme is too narrow in scope, biased and replete with errors. In addition to the two instances noted at the outset, I mention one other error for now. On page 205 of CPU, it is stated that the Nabudere initiated phase of the debates was prompted by 'the 1976 publication of Issa Shivji's book, *The Silent Class Struggle in Tanzania*, initially as a paper for *Cheche*.' This assertion is flawed on four counts. First, in the footnote, the title is different. The correct title is *Tanzania: The Silent Class Struggle* which first came out in 1970 as a special issue of *Cheche*. The book critiqued by Nabudere was Shivji's second book: *Tanzania: The Class Struggle Continues*. This was first published not as an issue of *Cheche* (which was dead by that time) but as a 1973 research report of the Institute of Development Studies. As noted above, the first book was discussed in *Cheche*, later in *MajiMaji* and subsequently in a new edition of book of the same name. The debate on the second book started in 1973 in *MajiMaji*. The commentary by Nabudere was in relation to the second edition of this book that was published in 1976, as clarified in the footnote on page 205 of CPU. That there were two books in contention and a series of debates on each is overlooked in CPU. The debates on the first book are totally ignored.

STYLE AND CONSEQUENCES

One basic feature of the open and internal debates among the leftists at the campus, students and staff, needs emphasis. Prior to 1975, they were carried out in comradely, cordial terms, and in a spirit of learning from each other. Despite their at times substantially discordant positions on theory and practice, the contending parties continued to cooperate as before on practical matters. The more than ten people who commented on *Tanzania: The Silent Class Struggle* did so as people engaged in a common struggle. The first round of the debate on *Tanzania: The Class Struggle Continues* involving AP Mahiga, Adrian Foster-Carter, Walter Rodney and Kwesi Botchwey reflected the same spirit. Even the strong criticisms by Meyns, Bhagat and Mamdani of this book had a positive tone. But the atmosphere changed dramatically with the issuance of Dan Nabudere's trenchantly worded, dismissive verdict on the same work.

Prior to 1973, the relationship between Nabudere and the radical students at UDSM had been a mutually supportive one. The second issue of *Cheche* had carried an article by Nabudere. And when he was unjustly detained by Milton Obote, *Cheche* campaigned for his release.

CPU admits that the post-Nabudere exchanges were `polemical' and `passionate.' But this is an understatement. They created such a rancor that comrades who had cooperated for years stopped talking to each other. The effect was felt acutely on the Tanzanian side. After Nabudere brought out his critique, I wrote a piece that questioned the logic of his arguments. But the venom it generated floored us. How can one conduct a productive discussion in such an atmosphere? It became a name-calling exercise as Shivji and his associates were branded `misguided' `neo-Trotskyists' whose writings were shallow and `bad'.

Fortunately, they decided not to respond but to continue their work of spreading socialist ideas beyond the campus into schools, colleges and later, factories. Matters of theory were not set aside.

Internal study and discussion went on and were done in the form of writing educational and analytic material using what they regarded as a scientific approach.

The post-Nabudere debate sowed confusion among the students, especially the newcomers who had developed an affinity to progressive ideas in their school days. They could not make out why people they had looked up to were now at each other's throats. Coming on top of the uninspiring political trends in the nation, the hostile atmosphere served to curtail recruitment into the progressive camp. This period marked the beginning of the slow decline of UDSM as a bastion of radical ideas and propelled it towards becoming an institution defined by apathy, and later, into a dollar-driven purveyor of puerile neoliberal ideas.

CONTENTS AND THEORY

All the debates at UDSM were primarily related to the short-term tactics and long-term strategies for the true liberation of the people of Africa. For this purpose, one basic theoretical and practical query was: In this struggle, who is/are the principal enemy/enemies and who are the allies of the people? The question was posed for both the countries that had not yet attained political freedom from racist or colonial domination and those that had achieved formal independence.

For Walter Rodney and almost every comrade in and beyond the USARF group, the answer in relation to most nations of Africa was clear. The state and leaders in nations like Zaire (Mobutu Sese Seko) and Malawi (Kamuzu Banda) operated in oppressive, corrupt ways and were firmly allied to Western imperial nations. They were not allies of the people. The struggle for liberation there had to be jointly against these rulers and their imperial backers. In Maoist terms, the struggle against such regimes was not a segment of the secondary contradictions but a part of the principal contradiction. The disputations arose for nations like Tanzania, whose leaders and governments were more people friendly, and had Pan-African, independent foreign policies.

As CPU notes, such issues are as relevant today as they were in the past. Africa is in a state of profound crisis. The World Bank steered neoliberal capitalism is not leading it to genuine development, peace or freedom. Economic insecurity, poverty and extremist ideas continue to feed into the existent societal animosities. Nations are falling apart. But more and more people are rising up to demand fundamental change. In order to formulate a viable strategy for change, they encounter the same basic question: Who are their enemies and who are their friends?

In a recent illuminating article on Sudan, Tandon shows the direction towards an answer. An essential requirement, he says, is

> [A] vanguard party that can mobilize the people to bury their internal (religious, regional, sectarian) differences to fight the Euro-American Empire and its local agents. (Tandon 2019a).

His exposition makes it clear that it is not a struggle against imperialism in the abstract, but concretely a struggle against the military which holds state power and the ultimate external backers of the neoliberal system it oversees. It will be a struggle on two fronts, internal and external.

CPU recounts Mao's distinction between the principal and secondary contradictions in the struggle. The struggle in China was waged on two fronts: against the Kuomintang regime and the local warlords as well as against the Japanese imperial forces. Both fronts were elements of the principal contradiction. The confrontation with the former was not, in any shape or form, for resolving a secondary contradiction.

Call them what you want: local agents of imperialism, comprador capitalists (CPU, page iv), comprador bourgeoisie or petty bourgeoisie; the essence is the same. This group directly or indirectly controls the state and uses it to amass considerable wealth. With no compunction in killing thousands to retain power, it is no ally of the people. And it is not a matter of personalities. The struggle to dislodge the local rulers from the seat of power will now or later face the wrath of the imperial external backers, especially if measures to fundamentally transform the socioeconomic system are adopted. If we are clear on this point, a wrangle over the `correct name' can only have a divisive, counter-productive effect.

Politicians with loyalty to powerful interests employ vitriolic labels to stifle rational discourse and create the impression that their opponent has bad intent. For example, if an activist in the US promotes increased funding for public schools in poor, minority neighborhoods, or campaigns for a state funded and controlled health insurance scheme like that in Canada or the UK, rightwing politicians quickly call him a `communist.' The label says it all. No more talk is needed. Do no not listen to that person. He/she is evil. That tactic often stymies even moderate attempts to change the prevailing system.

MORE OF THE SAME

In CPU, Tandon appropriately declares that `*it is time that ... differences that go back almost generation ago are put past us.*' (page 205). Yet, the manner in which he proceeds hardly reflects that intent. According to him, USARF comrades were `*young, idealistic, impressionable students (barely in their twenties).*' They harbored `*hopelessly illusionary dreams,*' had a bookish mentality and were disconnected from the African reality. As a result, they were easily misled by pseudo-Marxists from the West (page 196). Deploying a quote from the book *Cheche* (`We were impelled by love for humanity') to essentially ridicule them, CPU gives the impression that nothing they did was any value.

Regrettably, this book continues the name-calling, dismissive style of the Nabudere initiated debate. Nabudere alleged, without evidence other than baseless associations, that the writings of Shivji and his associates were `bad' works produced under the influence of neo-Trotskyist and neo-Marxist ideas imported from abroad. In a similar fashion, CPU employs selective, out-of-context quotations and unwarranted generalizations to imply that the student radicals were useless dreamers.

Leon Trotsky, together with VI Lenin was a co-leader of the 1917 revolution in Russia. Central to what is now known as Trotskyism is the idea of permanent revolution, a process under which socialist revolutions in advanced capitalist nations would propel the revolutions elsewhere. Trotskyism precludes, as a matter of principle, the idea that a socialist revolution can occur or be independently sustained in societies that are technologically backward and have a predominantly rural economy.

No work of Shivji, Mamdani and their comrades reflects, explicitly or implicitly, such a vision. None refers to Trotsky or any of his followers. They all supported the socialist revolutions in China and Cuba. They never said that socialist transformation in Tanzania was out of question. On the contrary, Shivji and Mamdani (like Walter Rodney and John Saul) were supportive of the effort to change Tanzania into a socialist society. Thus, Shivji opined in *Tanzania: The Class Struggle Continues* that the *Mwongozo* (a key ruling party document) had opened up the possibility of a transition to socialism in Tanzania, a patently anti-Trotskyist proposition.

But what disturbed Shivji and his fellow student radicals was the vast gap between intentions and practice. The real trends in the economy were entrenching neocolonial dependency on the West. The changes in the political sphere were strengthening an authoritarian bureaucracy and disempowering the people. In terms of management style, treatment of workers and investment decisions, the nationalized firms functioned like private capitalist enterprises. In the rural areas, the peasants were dealt with as in the colonial era. Even on its own terms, *Ujamaa* was not working. The radical students and academics strove to harmonize theory with practice by documenting this chasm and raising awareness about the need to counter it. And they worked within the rubric of the ruling party, as members of the university branch of the TANU Youth League. They did not form an opposition party, under or above the ground.

In those days, left groups in the West and elsewhere had a tendency to split into smaller and smaller factions that often derived from an obsession with theoretical purity. They typically ended up spending more time fighting with each other than confronting capitalism and imperialism. The security agencies surreptitiously fomented this practice. You had Marxists, then

Marxist-Leninists, then Marxist-Leninist-Maoists, Stalinists, Trotskyists, neo-Trotskyists, and this left tendency and that tendency. The last phase of the debate on Shivji's second book sadly saw the emergence of that phenomenon at UDSM. The consequences were similar. We need to learn from that debacle and be clear that there is no cause to continue, as CPU does, with that mode of discourse in this day and age.

Yes, we were young, and in the hopeful spirit of that era, harbored fine dreams for driving human society towards a future based on development for all, peace, equality and justice. Nonetheless, we did not stop at dreams, but also carried out detailed theoretical and empirical studies. We engaged in specific struggles on the campus and beyond, went to and worked in schools, factories and villages, engaged with the African liberation movements and visited the liberated areas of Mozambique. None of that is noted in CPU.

CRITICAL LESSONS

I draw several lessons from these debates that I think are important for the progressive activists and intellectuals of today.

- Foremost, keep in mind Che Guevera's maxim that `[t]he true revolutionary is guided by great feelings of love' and develop an internationalist spirit.Combine theory with practice, and practice with theory.
- Read extensively, especially about African and global histories, and study and apply the scientific method of analyzing societal development.
- Critically examine past and contemporary struggles, and learn from both the achievements as well as the errors of those who came before you.
- Conduct internal and public dialog on the varied perspectives that are bound to emerge and do so in comradely ways, not ways that endanger unity and impede the struggle. Focus on matters of substance, not terminology or labels. Adopt a civil tone even with your adversaries. It is not how you say it but what you say that is critical.
- Specific agendas within the movement should not be pursued in divisive ways but ways that combine the specific with the general.
- Do not lose hope; the struggle is a long term one; there are bound to be ups and downs. But ultimately, Africa and its people will triumph.

10

EDUCATION AND HISTORY I

SUMMARY: With a comparative historical perspective on two major East African universities, Professor Mahmood Madmani wrote an article in the *London Review of Books* that was aimed to determine the sources of and give remedies for the problems facing universities in Africa today. (Mamdani 2018). However, this article has numerous conceptual and factual flaws, and its recommendations are either too limited or potentially counterproductive. This essay is an attempt to set the record straight. Tackling under-education in the African academy in an effective manner requires an unbiased understanding of its roots in the past and present academic settings as well as in the socioeconomic realities. Ill-conceived, half way type of measures risk more harm than good.[1]

*

---

1. This essay was published as Hirji KF (2019) The African University: A critical comment, *Pambazuka News*, 30 August 2018 (www.pamabazuka.org). This is an edited version.

*It is possible to store the mind with a million facts
and still be entirely uneducated.*
Alex Bourne
++++++++++

UNIVERSITY EDUCATION TODAY

IN 1970, TANZANIA HAD ONE PUBLIC university with less than three thousand students. Now it has some fifty public and private universities and university colleges with a total student population of around two hundred thousand. Much of this growth has occurred in the past twenty years. A similar story prevails across Africa.

Between 1991 and 2006, the number of students in higher education [in Africa] rose from 2.7 million to 9.3 million. This was an annual rise of about 16%, but public resources for expenditure grew by 6%. (Kavuma 2012).

The expansion in numbers has, though, been accompanied by a steep decline in the quality of education, research and intellectual output. A proportionate rise in the academic staff has not taken place, class rooms are too small to accommodate the increased numbers, instructional equipment is in short supply and buildings are not well maintained.

The deleterious trend in educational quality affects not just the new institutions but also the old ones where the curricula and standards of instruction had been comparable to those at major universities in the Western world.

Apart from a few exceptions, universities in Africa now enroll students who have passed through a poorly run school system and a below-par scheme of examination. They are herded through degree programs with watered down curricula by academic staff who regard teaching as the last priority. Most courses lack textbooks or equivalent instructional material. To pass the exams, the students just memorize the electronic PowerPoint slides from the instructor. Undergraduate and graduate student research projects are shoddy in terms of design, implementation and reporting. Plagiarization, inventing data and external assistance to write reports prevail widely, yet are tolerated practices. At the end of the day, a graduate with an upper class bachelor's degree or a master's degree is unable to write a coherent, grammatical paragraph in English, handle elementary items like percentages and ratios, or give a sensible answer to a routine question from his or her area of specialization.

Professional degree programs like medicine, dentistry, engineering and agronomy are similarly afflicted. Both the theoretical and practical aspects of the training are deficient. If you ask a recently qualified civil engineer to compute the strength and direction of forces in a basic bridge like structure, a problem a good Form VI student can tackle, the answers you get will astonish you.

A person with a BA degree in English Literature or History has read only a couple of books beyond what was the norm for Form VI students in the past.

The universities, especially the private ones but also the public ones, depend on student fees to keep afloat. It is a competitive atmosphere in which the administrators seek to enroll as many students as possible. High standards generate high failure rates and create negative publicity. It is not in their interest to urge the staff to adhere to such standards. Expansion of class size without a concurrent increase in the teaching staff compounds the problem. Having paid the fees, the students feel entitled to the degree certificate. Instructors who teach elementary material and set easy exams are preferred to those who make them think and sweat. Several African nations have witnessed the emergence of unaccredited, fake universities (Chapter 6).

The academic staff deal with the huge class sizes by turning teaching into a routine task, setting easy-to-grade, simple multiple choice exams, and passing almost everyone. They are aware that if you maintain high standards, it is you who will be taken to task for unfairly penalizing the students and invite opprobrium from the administration as well as your colleagues. You are expected to conform, not stand out.

The academicians focus on lucrative consultancy projects, especially those with external funding, engage in commercial activities on the side, and seek opportunities for travel, particularly abroad. Even when they get extra pay for the task, they give lackluster guidance to the students whose research they supervise. Most do not keep up with the latest developments in their fields, or read relevant books and journal papers. Unless it is has external collaborators, their research projects usually are sub-standard. A lecturer with a doctoral degree from a European or American university may, at the outset, publish a couple of state-of-the-art papers in reputable journals. But the subsequent publications resemble what you see from post-graduate students and get published in the one of the many of poorly peer reviewed throwaway journals in existence today. One cannot but conclude that the initial papers were mostly the work of his or her supervisor, who was also a co-author.

Academic promotions are a matter of routine based on a mechanical scheme of awarding points that sidelines consideration of quality. Hastily written consultancy reports earn you points. Being a professor in Africa today does not imply that you have made a significant, novel contribution to any field.

The popular fields include business and management studies, accountancy, public relations, personnel management, journalism, mass communication, law, education and computer applications. Traditional fields like basic sciences, history and sociology attract fewer candidates.

Yet, that is not how it has always been. Up to the end of the 1980s, most African universities had adequate standards of instruction and student research. Student evaluation schemes were rigorous. Staff research and publications shone with quality output. The criteria for academic promotion were strict.

A host of internal and external factors have contributed to the decline of African education systems. The primary factor has been the inability of the African governments to reduce economic dependency and institute sound, broad-based programs of economic and social development. It generated high levels of external debt, entrenched poverty and produced chaos in the educational sector. By the time the lords of international finance came calling, there was no choice but to yield to their orders. So began the mad-rush to reduce state expenditures and privatize. In the early 1990s, health centers were closed, teachers were laid off and the educational sector starved of funds as the foreign and local investors, officials and politicians grabbed valuable national assets at giveaway prices. As universities saw a further reduction in funding, experienced professors sought jobs outside the country, and others started growing pineapples, running bars and mini-bus operations to make ends meet. In many African nations at present, remuneration for the academic staff is low. In Tanzania, academic salaries are relatively better. Yet, in terms of quality of instruction and research, it presents an equally bleak picture.

The scope of the disaster generated by this reckless drive that was cheered on by the Western governments and political pundits became evident within a decade. It could not go on. Hence another round of `reforms' was instituted, again under the aegis of the Western nations and their agencies. The entry of China gave Africa a breathing space at the outset but ultimately began to reinforce the trends that have brought about the conditions we see today in the education and other sectors.

In places, the conditions in the academia have reached extreme proportions. For example, the final exams at the historically distinguished Fourah Bay College in Sierra Leon could not be held in 2010 because there was no writing paper. (Keating 2011).

> What might appear as an absurd aberration is, however, painfully emblematic of the conditions faced by tens of thousands of university students in sub-Saharan Africa. Once considered the `Athens of West Africa', Fourah Bay, a key part of the University of Sierra Leone, is now a depleted national resource that is barely able to keep its doors open, much less provide a useful 21st century education.

> In next door Liberia, the University of Liberia is hardly in better shape. Students are crammed into overcrowded classrooms, sometimes having to share seats; there are no facilities for teaching the sciences; the medical school is little more than a name-plate and corruption reigns in far too many transactions between students, faculty and administrators. What was once a crown jewel on the Liberian cultural scene is now an underfunded mess with no rescuers in sight. (Keating 2011).

No wonder the children of the elite shun the local universities and seek education and employment oversees.

Higher education in Africa is in deep trouble. Yet, it has not garnered adequate attention. Apart from occasional empirical reports, the local and foreign experts and agencies focus on problems in primary and secondary schools. They do not realize that the rote starts at the top. Ill-qualified academics churn out uneducated graduates in a factory like fashion. But they are expected to be good teachers, managers, doctors, agronomists and engineers. The regulatory bodies, when they pay attention, do not delve into the basic issues like the quality of research and teaching. The often proposed therapies for the malady of under-qualified graduates are to impart `entrepreneurial skills' and pay more attention to computer based skills.

The mostly self-serving experts and academics from outside do not desire to offend their hosts. Though they see the serious nature of the malaise, they address a minor problem here and there. Concerned local scholars do not want to alienate their colleagues, draw the ire of the state and administration, or jeopardize their future. So they too address tangential matters. Systemic problems are overlooked.

Under this culture of silence, mediocrity at the top breeds mediocrity across the system. Education loses meaning. It is not what you know or can do, but the certificate you hold and the connections you have that will land you a good job.

MAMDANI'S CONTRIBUTION

The silence, however, is not total. Some concerned scholars, educators and citizens are voicing their dismay at the trends in the education sector. Professor Mahmood Mamdani's article, *The African University*, in the *London Review of Books* (Mamdani 2018) is a timely contribution to the ongoing debate. As it has garnered ample positive publicity, there is a need to assess its analysis and recommendations. And that is the aim of this essay.

The title of his article is a bit misleading. Mamdani actually focuses on just two East African universities that in the 1960s were two campuses of the University of East Africa, Makerere and Dar es Salaam. A decade on, they became autonomous national universities. Mamdani classifies Makerere as `*the paradigm of the European colonial university*' that retained its '*conservative, universalist tradition*' with pride while Dar-es-Salaam `*had an ambitious, nationalist sense of purpose*' and `*became the flag-bearer of anti-colonial nationalism and the home of the new, African public intellectual.*' Developing these themes further, he contrasts these institutions in terms the features noted in the table below.

Features of two East African universities

Makerere	Dar es Salaam
Universal scholarship	Intellectual commitment
Promotion of excellence	Promotion of relevance
Discipline-based approach	Interdisciplinary approach
Apolitical academia	Socialist politics
Traditional curricula	Curriculum review
Conservative orientation	Nationalistic orientation
Academic freedom	Societal engagement
De-racialization	Expatriate leftist domination

He illustrates his categorizations by contrasting two leading academics of that era, Ali Mazrui at Makerere, and Walter Rodney at Dar es Salaam. According to him, Mazrui was a `towering public intellectual` with `a strong belief in the classical model` and deeply suspicious of `socialism` and related political ideas. For Rodney, on the other hand, the university was `a space of activism in which knowledge was constituted in the here and now`, colonialism was `a raw exercise of power relations`, and African renewal lay within `a socialist framework ...` According to Mamdani, Rodney and other leftist academics at Dar es Salaam, for whom `ideology was everything` were complicit in the decline of the scholarly standards in the academia.

After dealing with other issues, and noting the current poor state of the universities in Africa, he gives a recipe for improvement that stands on three legs: usage of local languages in scholarship and instruction, reduction of fees, and `to theorize our own reality, and to strike the right balance between the local and the global as we do so.` The employment of Mazrui-identified notion of the African `mode of reasoning` is implied as a crucial element of the last task.

In this essay, I argue that Mamdani's article has significant flaws along several fronts. It derives from a simplistic version of history, contains major errors of fact, significant omissions and unwarranted generalizations. Based on unreal dichotomies, it embodies a biased and inconsistent mode of reasoning. I begin my case with an issue that forms a key part of his presentation, namely, that of interdisciplinary studies.

INTERDISCIPLINARY SCHOLARSHIP

Mamdani began his academic career in 1972 at the University of Dar es Salaam. His main responsibility was to lead a new interdisciplinary course called East African Society and Environment (EASE), a required course for undergraduates in the Faculty of Arts and Social Sciences. Those in the other faculties attended a separate interdisciplinary course, Development Studies (DS) that had been launched earlier under the stewardship of Lionel Cliffe. Previously, a few lecturers like Sol Picciotto in the Faculty of Law had infused their courses with an interdisciplinary spirit.

Each course, while catering to students with different backgrounds, had a common aim, namely to give an overall perspective on the history and functioning of human society and provide a context for specialized courses, with the focus on African societies. Each course was designed to counter the myopic vision generated by the over-specialized nature of modern education, and make the student more attuned to the local and global realities. Whether you were a social science, natural science, law or medicine major, the common courses were designed **to complement and not be a substitute for** your main discipline based study program.

Mamdani's assertion that a `radical camp, mostly non-Tanzanian ... above all ... wanted to abolish discipline-based departments' has no basis. In the lead up to the establishment of DS and EASE, no leftist document that called for the set-up of an interdisciplinary course took such an extreme position. What they stressed was the need to make the discipline based courses more relevant to the African situation.

A time-honored tactic to discredit your opponent is to ascribe an absurd stand to him and floor him with an easy swipe. Such a ploy is adopted by American conservatives and right wing academics to attack the left. It gained traction during the Cold War years. Ali Mazrui and the right wingers at the Dar es Salaam, including those in the University Council, invoked that style of reasoning to attack radical students and staff. And today, Mamdani has bought into that type of reasoning.

The two interdisciplinary courses did not materialize overnight. They were products of years struggle by left-wing members of the academic staff, expatriate as well as local, a few leftists in the ruling party, and, crucially, radical students working under the umbrella of the University Students' African Revolutionary Front (USARF). While benefiting from the socialistic climate generated by the Arusha Declaration, this and the other left initiatives faced strong opposition from the senior conservative academics, the university administration and the staunch right wingers in the government. Officials of the ruling party had an ambivalent stance. While these courses were felt to reflect Mwalimu Nyerere's call for the university to educate committed intellectuals, they viewed the orientation taken by the common courses with suspicion. What turned the tide in favor of their establishment was the consistent, militant support provided by USARF.

Yet, there were calls for dismantling them even after they came into operation. The only academic staff document that sought to abolish an existing department was a document signed by eleven prominent right wing lecturers and professors, including the head of Department of Political Science, Anthony Rweyemamu and historian John Iliffe, calling for the disestablishment of the Department of Development Studies. And these were the proponents of academic freedom and staunch supporters of Ali Mazrui at Dar es Salaam.

UNREAL DICHOTOMIES

As course directors, Cliffe and Mamdani formulated innovative programs under an integrated, political economy-based Marxist framework and recruited well qualified academic staff from varied departments to lecture on different topics. None was a replay of the doctrines of the ruling party in Tanzania, or a Soviet era text on political economy. While they formed a key part of the search for relevance at Dar es Salaam, none of these courses compromised academic excellence and rigor.

The students taking EASE, for instance, had to read a voluminous reader containing papers from varied journals and book chapters as well as other recommended papers. The effort required was comparable to that needed for the other courses, be they in sociology, or history. Essay topics and examination papers were of a similar standard and graded as rigorously.

Mamdani identifies the pursuit of universal scholarship at Makerere with academic excellence attained under the traditional curriculum. And the drive for societal commitment, relevance and curriculum review is implied to have compromised and diluted academic standards at Dar es Salaam. Not only for interdisciplinary studies but for the discipline based programs, the dichotomies he postulates do not reflect the diversity of the academic scene at these campuses. Even at Makerere, there was a degree of curriculum review, as was the case in all the universities in Africa after independence. And that was a generally a positive step, and not something to lament.

During the 1960s and 1970s, the degree programs in the natural and social sciences were similar in content and complexity at these places. Apart from courses in history, especially at Dar es Salaam, most courses had originated from similar courses offered at British universities and continued follow the same lines. At both campuses, some departments offered high quality, demanding courses and some departments had shallow offerings. There were variations within departments as well.

Consider the Department of Education at Dar es Salaam. Nearly

40% of the students, who were being trained as secondary school teachers, came under its purview. They were taught courses such as Psychology of Education, Philosophy of Education, Sociology of Education and Teaching Methods. Most of them had the traditional orientation Mamdani identifies with Makerere. Review of their curricula was minimal. Yet they were taught in a disjointed, shallow manner, hardly reflecting any notion of excellence. Some instructors used material largely borrowed from American textbooks. The course on Philosophy of Education, taught by a priest, made you feel as if you were attending a Sunday sermon.

The situation was different in the Faculty of Law. As a result of student struggles and work of the radical lecturers, some courses saw far reaching changes in their content and orientation, with the students getting a hefty dose of interdisciplinary material. Yet, most of the courses in the faculty were traditional, reflecting the unchanged capitalistic nature of the economy and society. The academic staff were a mixture of right wingers, liberals and radicals. The standard and quality of instruction did not vary according to the political orientation of the instructor. In those years, the law students took rigorous and demanding courses across the board. (Ulimwengu 2019).

At both institutions, the important determinants of quality of instruction were how long the study program had been in existence and the qualification and experience of the instructor. When the Dar es Salaam campus came into operation, Makerere had existed for four decades. At the outset, many of the academic staff at the former were just starting their academic careers. It was no surprise that in the 1960s, the courses at Makerere generally were of higher quality than the similar courses at Dar es Salaam. What was surprising was the short time it took for Dar es Salaam to catch up. Courses in the Faculty of Science and the Faculty of Arts and Social Sciences became, in a span of few years, of the equal caliber at both the campuses.

A similar situation prevailed with respect to the research and writings of academic staff. For areas like history, economics, political science, law and sociology, the numerous books and papers produced at Dar es Salaam from the 1960s into the 1980s reflected outstanding, innovative scholarship that left an international imprint. These included Shivji (1970; 1986), Rodney (1972), Rweyemamu (1973), Mamdani (1974), Mapolu (1974), Leys (1975), Kjekshus (1977), Iliffe (1979), Kaniki (1980), Coulson (1982), Sheriff (1987) and Sheriff and Ferguson (1991). Most of these books are by committed left-wing scholars who were advocating relevance in research, writing and course curricula.

The association between traditional orientation and excellence posited by Mamdani is not backed by evidence. His claim that for the left ideology was everything is negated by the generally meticulous and far-going nature of the research and the high standard of scholarship and teaching shown by the progressive academics. It is an ideologically based assertion.

WORLD BANK AND IMF

In the 1970s, Mamdani was an erudite Marxist scholar. Today he ascribes to the cultural, political analysis in the style of mainstream American political scientists. Accordingly, his writings today at most only tangentially reference economic issues and factors. Adopting an analytic method based on identity, he has dispensed with concepts like neocolonialism, Pan-Africanism, class analysis, economic dependency, imperialism and neoliberalism. But on one economic aspect, he has retained a degree of continuity. Today as then, he continues to regard two international financial institutions, the World Bank and IMF, as villains. Though, now he views them narrowly, just repeatedly noting the deleterious effects of the structural adjustment programs they initiated for Africa in the 1980s.

Both these institutions were centrally involved in economic affairs of most African nations from the day of independence. In Tanzania, the World Bank involvement did not abate, in terms of providing a direction for the economy, funding of projects and provision of advisors and experts, an iota even during the *Ujamaa* years. It was not averse to supposedly socialist schemes like nationalization and villagization. The sole project over which Nyerere's government differed with the World Bank was the construction of the railway line to Zambia. The Bank wanted the focus to be on road transport.

In his article, Mamdani invokes the World Bank to drive home the final nail in the coffin for the idea of interdisciplinary studies:

> *Anyone who still thinks of interdisciplinarity as the key to a new world should consider that it has been a working principle for World Bank teams on the ground in Africa since the Bank's inception.* (Mamdani 2018).

Consider the following Mamdani-inspired statement:

> Anyone who still thinks of education as the key to a new world should consider that the World Bank has been a major advocate, planner and funder of education projects in many African nations from the time they attained independence.

Surely, most people, including Mamdani, would dismiss it outright. That the World Bank has firmly associated itself with education is not a valid reason to not develop education. The problems lie with the nature of the education policy, the type of education projects, the terms of the funding and the type of projects ignored by the World Bank, and not with education in the generic sense of the term.

The World Bank supported the national five-year economic plans in all the East African nations after independence. Yet, Marxist economists backed the idea of economic planning too. Economic planning meant quite a different thing for the two.

The World Bank is a major driver of the neoliberal globalization that prevails today. Does that automatically imply we should oppose all modes of globalization? When Karl Marx and Friedrich Engels called on the workers of the world to unite, they were advocating globalization. But it was a pro-people mode of globalization. That prevailing today serves the interests of multinational corporations, the technologically advanced nations and the local elite, not the ordinary people or the poor nations. It entrenches dependency and poverty, and creates stupendous inequality. That is what we oppose, and not economic and cultural interactions between all nations and peoples on the basis of equality and mutual respect.

Correspondingly, the phrase `interdisciplinary studies' has a meaning for the World Bank that differs in significant aspects from that advocated by the left at Dar es Salaam. Would the Marxist political economy oriented interdisciplinary course Mamdani taught at Dar es Salaam have had the approval of the World Bank? Surely not.

The key rationale underlying the advocacy of interdisciplinary studies by the left is summed up in a simple phrase: The truth is the whole. It is the basic realization that intellectual and scientific inquiry of objects like the human body, an ecosystem and human society should delve not only into an examination of their constituent parts but be cognizant of the complexities of the relationship between the parts as well. It does not suffice to just aggregate what is known about the parts. A theoretical model for the whole is also essential. For the left, the reductionist, single discipline-based approach, as deployed by mainstream social scientists, is inadequate and misleading. Yet, the left does not seek the elimination of discipline based studies. As note earlier, the interdisciplinary courses at Dar es Salaam were designed to complement them.

In the hands of the World Bank, the interdisciplinary approach is more of a multi-disciplinary approach. It enjoins narrowly-oriented experts from diverse disciplines and makes the whole by summing the parts. Apart from ascribing to diffuse market principles, they lack a broad, explicitly formulated theoretical model of society like the political-economy based approach.

Even when the Bank advocates area studies, their premises, units of analysis, framework and specific questions differ in a major way from what its critics promote. The term `systems analysis' also appears in this context. But it has a different meaning in the writings of the Polish Marxist economist Oscar Lange than for the financially oriented World Bank policy gurus.

This topic needs a deeper inquiry into the nature of scientific method for natural sciences, social sciences and other fields. But this is not the place for them. Here, it suffices to observe that the same analytic phrase can have very different implication for people with different frameworks for analyzing society. The quoted assertion by Mamdani is oblivious of this and other relevant issues, even though he led an interdisciplinary study program in the past. Taking them into account makes its validity suspect.

IDEOLOGICAL CLASSES

Another set of leftist activities at Dar es Salaam upon which Mamdani casts a deficient light were the ideological classes and study groups.

> A group with an official imprimatur, known as the 'ideological class', met at 10 a.m. every Sunday, with the aim of offering participants an alternative to church. An informal but well organized range of after-class study groups also proliferated over the years. (Mamdani 2018).

The ideological classes were begun by the University Students' African Revolutionary Front (USARF). As a member of USARF, I was given the responsibility to organize the first set of classes. I made out the syllabus, the schedule of topics and the reading list for each class, and recruited the lecturers. They were a mix of senior members of USARF, leftist academics and people from the African liberation organizations based in Dar es Salaam in those days. But fellow students were in the majority. The first class was held in late 1969, the venue being the main lecture room of the Faculty of Law.

We did not seek or have approval from the university administration, the government or the ruling party. It was purely our own initiative. We did not even seek or have permission for the usage of the Law Faculty lecture room from the Dean of the Faculty. A leftist member of the staff opened the door for us at the designated time, and that was it. When the Dean came to know about it, he kept quiet. Most likely, he was afraid that if he did intervene, these radicals may stage a noisy demonstration in front of his office. In no way or form did these classes have `an official imprimatur'.

The central reason for holding the classes was fill in the gap in our knowledge arising from the right wing slant of the majority of the courses being taught in the Faculty of Arts and Social Sciences, and the Faculty of Law. We wanted to learn more about the history, theory and practice of socialism and how the method of Marxist Political Economy could be applied to analyze African history and society in an interdisciplinary way. When the classes began, the two interdisciplinary courses, Development Studies and East African Society and Environment, had not got off the ground. Even though we had a heavy load from our regular academic courses, we took this initiative for self-education.

For these classes and its other activities, USARF did not rely on any form of support from any external entity, be it from a socialist or capitalist nation. While interacting with media persons from some socialist nations, USARF maintained an independent stand.

When the USSR invaded Czechoslovakia in 1968, USARF was the first group to protest and hold a demonstration in front of the Soviet embassy in Dar es Salaam. When China began to consort with Mbotu Sese Seko, the dictator of Zaire, we expressed our displeasure to a visiting delegation from China in no uncertain terms. And USARF members were aghast at the theocratic cult of personality prevailing in North Korea.

Mamdani gives the impression that the classes had an anti-religious rationale. If that was the case, why target only Christianity, not Islam? The classes were held on Sunday mornings because it was the most suitable time. That many students attended Church at that time was just a coincidence. In any case, most USARF members were not in the habit of attending prayer sessions. The students who went to church looked at us with derision as they passed by. That is true. But not a single class topic focused on religion.

The study groups Mamdani mentions were a further self-education initiative among those who felt that they needed to learn in depth what they had got from the ideological classes. Again these groups did not have official blessings of any form.

While noting that *Cheche*, a radical student magazine, was banned by the government, Mamdani fails to say that it was published by USARF, the same group that was holding the ideological classes. The question is: How come one major activity of USARF and USARF itself was banned while its other principal activity, the ideological classes, received `official imprimatur'? Because of the selective and diffuse way in which he presents his case, this anomaly remains hidden from the readers.

After the ban on USARF and *Cheche*, another radical magazine, *MajiMaji*, came into being. The ideological classes were continued by the campus branch of the ruling party youth league, TYL. At that point, TYL had the same radical stance as USARF, and was often at odds with the university administration and the ruling party. I know that at least for the initial five years of their existence, the ideological classes did not secure any form of `official imprimatur' (see Hirji (2011) for details).

At one point President Nyerere maintained a dialog with the radical students. But it was more of an attempt to know what they were up to and placate them. While he did not want to be seen as a suppressor of independent socialist initiative on the campus, he did not have a special affinity towards these students. When he had to make a choice, there was no doubt what his stand was. In a public question-answer session with the university community, he roundly ridiculed their ideas. In an address to a conference of Catholic bishops after imposing the ban on USARF and *Cheche*, he told them that he had done so in order to curb the influence of communism at the campus. A devout Catholic who regularly went to Church, it is hard to imagine why he or the ruling party would allow the holding of educational sessions at the national university that had openly anti-religious aims. Mamdani's assertion about these classes trivializes their aims and is historically inaccurate.

MAZRUI AND RODNEY

In Mamdani's essay, the descriptors associated with Ali Mazrui of Makerere include: a `towering public intellectual,' a thinker who grappled with fundamental philosophical issues relating to the foundations of knowledge, a defender of academic freedom, a promoter of academic excellence in the context of classical model of the academia and a prolific writer who boldly penned `incendiary essays' that challenged the powers that be. In particular, he decried the socialist policies then being pursued by authoritarian African leaders. Overall, it is a glowing portrait from which Mazrui's unique conceptualization of the `African mode of reasoning' is presented as a possibly central aspect of the revival of African universities.

Walter Rodney, for whom the descriptor `intellectual' is not employed, stood in a sharp contrast. He was primarily an activist for whom ideological commitment and struggle against imperialism overrode all else, a `super-leftist' who sought to convert the university into an ideological college beholden to the ruling socialist government. We read:

> [Rodney's] How Europe Underdeveloped Africa was a grand excursion in dependency theory, very much in line with the premises of the Arusha Declaration, while Mazrui's discourse emphasized the growing contradiction between the promise of Arusha and the reality of social and political developments in Tanzania. (Mamdani 2018).

Rodney emerges as a prosaic empiricist lacking original ideas who visualized major historical phenomena like colonialism with simplistic notions like power and violence. Further, he was among the expatriate super-left that uncritically glorified the *Ujamaa* policy of the ruling party in Tanzania. In comparison with Mazrui, Rodney is seen as a political conformist who pandered to borrowed nations like dependency theory and not an innovative thinker.

To assess Mamdani's characterizations, we look at the global context. Those were the years during which the Cold War was raging everywhere. Under the leadership of the United States, leftist academics and students, among other pro-democracy activists, were targeted, expelled, imprisoned, tortured and murdered in their thousands in Latin America, Asia, the Middle East and Africa. Yet, they courageously continued to fight for social justice and freedom against the dictatorial regimes supported by the West. On the other hand, rightist academics, when they spoke out, mostly received a slap on the wrist.

Rodney was no conformist, in theory or practice. He boldly challenged the authorities wherever he was. He was expelled from

Jamaica, nearly thrown out of Tanzania on at least two occasions, and assassinated in his homeland.

Mazrui, it must be said, was not just a person fascinated by ideas; he too was an activist, only that he was a right-wing activist. He actively sought venues to promote his anti-socialist views and passionately promoted them. Though he crafted his own terminology, his basic views, method of analyzing society and style reflected the Cold War era anti-socialist diatribe prevalent among the mainstream American political scientists. Their substance derived from the type of material contained in conservative newspaper headlines, not good research. Beneath the surface, apart from the flowery rhetoric, his views and propositions in that time were hardly original.

It is of interest to note what Mazrui could and should have done but did not do. The suppression of potential rivals and political opposition was more intense and brutal in Kenya, his home country, than in Tanzania or Uganda. It was effectively a one-party, one-man state. Yet, Mazrui's writings did not attack those anti-democratic practices. He did not mount on a platform at the University of Nairobi or another venue to denounce them. He did not direct his ire at the shocking disparity between the opulence of the `respectable' areas of Nairobi and the stark misery in the adjacent slums; a disparity far sharper than for any city in East Africa. Had he done these things, he would have landed in real trouble.

Around December 1970, upon invitation from the Department of Political Science, Ali Mazrui gave a couple of public lectures in the main assembly hall at Dar es Salaam. For both the sessions, the hall was jam-packed with students and academic staff. That such lectures were held speaks to the level of academic freedom prevailing at this university.

Mazrui spoke in his typical titillating style, pouring artfully articulated scorn on the policy of the Tanzanian ruling party and ideas of the campus left, and roundly praising the Western societies as bastions of freedom and progress. It was the speech of a person afflicted with chronic America-philia. Entertaining the audience with verbal gymnastics, he reiterated his view that scholarship was not compatible with social commitment.

The opposition to his views was not spearheaded by the leftists on the academic staff. It was the radical students who posed tough queries and made critical comments. The next day, two of them wrote long articles criticizing his views. These were distributed among the audience at the next lecture. Munene Njagi, a Kenyan student wrote a piece with the title `Some points of disagreement with the intelligent professor, Ali Mazrui' and my piece had the title `The Mugwumpiness of Professor Mazrui' (Hirji 1970a; Njagi 1970). We took issue with his simplistic definition of an intellectual and pointed out the inconsistencies and factual deficiencies in his speech. Njagi concluded that the `[P]rofessor is an intellectual preaching the gospel of submissiveness to imperialism.' After giving an example-based alternative view of the intellectual in a detailed fashion, I stated: '*Mazrui is mistaken if he thinks he is a rebel. He is a conformist par excellence.*' We are sure these comments reached him though we never got a response.

Mazrui spared dictators like Mobutu of Zaire or Banda of Malawi from his incendiary pen. As an effective public persona standing against the '*evils of communism*', he was the darling of the US Agency for International Development. Even the Apartheid government of South Africa accorded him an invitation.

Mazrui's articles on Tanzania and Ghana mentioned by Mamdani lack substance and do not take the socioeconomic conditions in those nations or the global context adequately into account. Their superficiality makes them incendiary only in style. The truly incendiary writings about Tanzania came from the leftists at Dar es Salaam. Radical students and staff published highly critical articles that exposed concretely the gap between the promise and practice of the Arusha Declaration. These were published in *Cheche*, *MajiMaji* and other venues, including the national media. These writings, based on solid research, carried weight and could not be dismissed as simple propaganda. That is why USARF and *Cheche* were banned. While Mamdani mentions the critical writings of Issa Shivji, he fails to note other writings along similar lines. And he does not classify them in line with the glowing praise he heaps on the oppositional voice of Ali Mazrui.

It is undeniable that there was much to admire about Tanzania and Nyerere in those days. People of goodwill everywhere noted the positive contrast it presented with many African nations. Its firm anti-colonial, anti-racist stand, support for the right of nations to self-determination and humane national policy attracted many Africa-oriented academics, especially the socialists, in the West as in the rest of Africa. Nyerere was seen as a gentle, simple man of firm principles. There was a reason for Tanzania-philia.

Yet, many leftists from outside, including Rodney, once they were in Tanzania for a few years, began to develop a critical attitude towards the economic, political and social trends in the country, and wrote about it. Their writings were generally based on extensive research. Mamdani has little to say about these writings of the so-called super-left.

Mamdani's dismissal of *How Europe Underdeveloped Africa* (HEUA), one of the most important books on African history written in the twentieth century, is an unfounded ideological position. Translated into several languages, for decades it stood unrivalled in terms of usage for general African history courses in universities across African and the world. Today, as many leftwing books of that era have been forgotten, Rodney's principal work still attracts a good following from academics and others.

The leftists at Dar es Salaam, including Rodney, saw consideration of theoretical issues for analysis of human society a matter of importance. That was a principal reason for promoting interdisciplinary studies. *HEUA* is a creative blend of classical

Marxist theory, dependency theory and Pan-Africanist ideas for modeling African history. It synthesizes material from a broad range of sources to produce a coherent explanation why African societies are the way they are. Importantly, his theoretical model and analysis also provide clues for transforming the African condition.

No original work of Mazrui from that era has a comparative standing. The notion of `mode of reasoning,' which Mamdani presents as a major contribution, was stated in a perfunctory, point-scoring, debating style, and never elaborated. To have traction, it needs years and volumes of inquiry. Yet, Mamdani clings to it even though Mazrui, in his later years, appears to have dispensed with it (see below).

Since the day it came out in 1972, *HEUA* has elicited unsubstantiated hostile venom from conservative and far-right historians. Now, in a subtle way, Mamdani has joined them. Interestingly, he also fails to note, as I show later, that after the 1980s, Mazrui was quite conciliatory towards the ideas of Rodney and the `super-left' he had dismissed in his early days, and also adopted some of them.

REVITALIZING THE AFRICAN ACADEMY

The central theme in Ali Mazrui's year 2013 acceptance speech for an award given for his contribution to African education was the need to distinguish between modernization and Westernization. He called on Africans to study developments in other nations, especially India and China. For that effort, he noted three key items: ideology, intermediate technology and ways of organizing the economy. Upon this foundation, he gave a series of steps to reform secondary and higher education in Africa (Mazrui 2013). At the secondary school level, **every student** should:

- Learn three languages: an African language, a European language and an Asian language.
- Take a course on Global History of Science.

At the university level, **every student**, irrespective of specialty, should:

- Pursue an African language or an Asian language course at an advanced level.
- Study a course on Third World Civilization.
- Study a course on Great Systems of Thought.

Mamdani first blames the leftists and later declares the changes introduced under the influence of agencies like the World Bank as the key factors behind the dilution and downward slide of higher education in Africa. These included tuition fees, departmental autonomy and market-oriented studies. Consequently, he proposes three steps for lifting the African academy from its current predicament:

- Greater utilization of local languages in scholarship and instruction.
- Reduction of fees.
- Theorization of the African reality in a way that balances the local and global and possibly employs the African `mode of reasoning.'

In this context, Mazrui and Mamdani sound like the super-left of the earlier era. Mamdani decries curricula that do not reflect the `life experiences, or family and community histories' of the students. Both recognize, in their own ways, economic and educational dependency on the West as a prime factor in the deterioration of African education. And thus they come across as committed scholars who, in the search for relevance, are advocating curricular reform!

Yet, there are major differences between what they suggest. Mazrui's proposals are concrete, challenging but workable. Mamdani's proposals are diffuse, half-way type, and potentially divisive and impractical. They elicit a number of disturbing questions: What is the local language in Kenya? Should the languages of instruction for a Luo child and a Kikuyu child be different? It is one thing to emphasize the preservation of local languages and another to make them a central aspect of education. The latter will just enhance the ethnic, regional and religious divisiveness that constitutes a major malady afflicting Africa today. Further, non-usage of local languages is often used by politicians and educationists as a convenient bogey for explaining the poor state of education in Africa today. They talk about it, yet do not take concrete steps to change the situation. In Tanzania, the politicians and educators regularly stress the importance of Swahili yet send their children to English medium schools. Mazrui does not propose a change in the medium of instruction but recognizes the innate ability of children everywhere to master several languages. And he challenges those concerned with education in Africa to appreciate that fact and make it a reality.

Mamdani's invocation of the `African mode of reasoning' assumes that such a mode of reasoning exist. Does it have rules of logic that are different from those universally accepted today? Are the modes of reasoning in Ghana and Algeria identical? Do the Muslims of Nigeria employ a mode of reasoning different from that used by Christian Nigerians? Venturing in such a direction is but a recipe for divisiveness and pedagogical disaster.

The modern Mazrui has dispensed with such parochial agendas

and stresses the global nature of science and scientific thinking. The three required courses he proposes stem from a spirit and orientation similar to that behind the interdisciplinary courses developed by the `super-left' of Dar es Salaam. He has also become more reconciled to their ideas. Thus, a footnote to this paper reads:

> 11. For examples of works which have creatively used Marxist categories, see Samir Amin, "Capitalism and Development in the Ivory Coast," in African Politics and Society, Irving Leonard (ed.) (New York: Free Press, 1970), pp. 277–288; and Giovanni Arrighi and John S. Saul, Essays on the Political Economy of Africa (New York: Monthly Review Press, 1973); E. A. Brett, Colonialism and Underdevelopment in East Africa (London: Heinemann, 1972); and Colin Leys, Underdevelopment in Kenya: The Political Economy of Neo-Colonialism (London: Heinemann, 1975). (Mazrui 2013).

On the other hand, Mamdani's call to theorize `our own reality' in a balanced way gives the impression that hardly anything of that sort has been done thus far. He negates the more than half a century of creative effort and volumes of writing by scores of African and Africa-oriented scholars, even the prolific and outstanding ones like Samir Amin. Had he taken a closer look, he would have seen that in their search for relevance, balancing the local and the global in a scientific manner was a key aim of those he brands as the `super-left,' including Rodney.

It is the norm among the neoliberal scholars today to try to bury efforts to find intellectual alternatives to capitalist theories undertaken in the 1960s and 1970s. They want us to forget that crucial aspect of our past and ignore anything related to socialism. They talk as if we have to start from scratch; as if there is nothing to learn from history. Thankfully, as the above quote shows, the new Mazrui is not as narrow minded.

Mamdani's proposal to reduce fees is a step in the right direction. But, given the depth and breadth of the academic malaise, it is a small step.

OTHER ERRORS AND OMISSIONS

Earlier, I noted two clear errors in Mamdani's essay: giving an official status to the ideological classes and the call to abolish discipline based programs. His declaration that Nyerere `went on to outlaw all parties except his own' also needs to be corrected.

Mamdani does not inform his readers that in that era most African nations, whether they called themselves socialist or not, were headed on the path to effective one-party or one-man rule. Mostly that was done by decree and/or violent suppression of the opposition, as in Malawi, Kenya and Zaire, three nations closely allied to the capitalist West. In contrast, one party rule in Tanzania came about after it was overwhelmingly approved by a popular, free and fair vote. The phrase `to outlaw,' which conveys a different story, is unsuitable in this context.

In consideration of what Mamdani said about Nyerere and Tanzania in his WE Dubois Lectures, this misrepresentation is surprising (Mamdani 2012). There Mamdani presents Nyerere as an ideal leader who successfully and peacefully resolved the divisions along racial and tribal lines inherited from the colonial era. Tanzania is viewed as a model African nation where citizenship was the operational principle. I have indicated elsewhere that his assessment of Tanzania and Nyerere there was based on selective evidence and too skewed (Hirji 2017). There Mamdani is like a modern day adherent of Tanzania-philia, but in the present essay, he talks as if he suffers from Tanzania-phobia.

Thereby, Mamdani can refer to *'deracialization'* implanted at Makerere in neutral terms. The correct term is Africanization. In a bid to correct the inherited racial disparities, African academics, Mazrui among them, obtained rapid promotions under which the traditional rules of academia were suspended. The contradiction with the alleged policy of promoting academic excellence is not stated. At Dar es Salaam, academic promotions were based more on merit and citizenship, and not race.

Mamdani's has uncritical praise for the magazine *Transition* but he does not inform his readers that it was funded by the CIA. Thereby, he also gets away without noting that in those days Mazrui was the darling of the USAID and right-wingers in the United States.

Mamdani omits the University College of Nairobi, the third campus of the University of East Africa, from his essay. With a right wing atmosphere firmer than at Makerere, Nairobi represented the opposite of Dar es Salaam in a number of important ways. The stridently pro-West government of Kenya, though it had a proclaimed policy of African Socialism, detested what was going on in Tanzania, and viewed the leftist tendencies at the Dar es Salaam campus with suspicion. Kenyan students at Dar es Salaam had to be selective in terms of taking home the books and papers they had acquired in the course of their studies. They would land in trouble if they were discovered to have books from China or a work by Mao Zedong in their baggage. The few progressive Kenyan and expatriate academic staff at Nairobi had to tread with care. Student protests at Nairobi were suppressed with batons. Yet, all this was done in the name of academic freedom and excellence, and reducing the interference of politics on scholarship.

Lack of consideration of even the situation at Nairobi makes his focus too narrow. Nonetheless, Mamdani deems it fit to present his case as if it applies to the entire African continent. As Colin Leys observed in a response to his essay, many specific aspects of the universities have to be considered before one can draw the type of broad conclusions he does (Leys 2018).

Finally, Mamdani views intellectuals in a static manner, as if their views do not evolve over time. Some regress and some progress. The leftists at Dar es Salaam were educated by intellectual interactions and trends in Tanzania and Africa. And some dramatically altered their views over time. There have been two versions of Mamdani, the Marxist of the 1970s, and the anti-socialist, identity-politics driven scholar of today as there were two versions of Ali Mazrui, the rabid anti-socialist, Ameriphilia driven sloganeer Mazrui of the 1960s and the Pan-Africanist, open-minded and erudite cultural theorist of the later years.

For example, in his later days, Mazrui confessed that in the past:

> [w]e were all influenced by Marx and Lenin without necessarily becoming Marxists or Leninists. Some Africans embraced Marxism as an ethic of distribution. Others believed in Marxism as an ideology for development. Most African intellectuals were also stimulated by Marxism as a paradigm of analysis. Mazrui (2012).

That Ali Mazrui was, politically or intellectually, a Marxist to any degree in those days is a dubious proposition. Nonetheless, the fact that he made such a statement in his later years was indicative of the degree to which his views have converged towards those of the 'super-left' he had lambasted earlier.

These misrepresentations in Mamdani's essay augment those I mentioned earlier. Combined with a host of conceptual and factual flaws, they enable Mamdani to make seemingly sound case. Yet, his essay is a hollow effort based on selective evidence to support an ideologically predetermined case.

THE DOWNWARD SLIDE

The progressive picture of the University of Dar es Salaam I have painted applies to the period from the mid-1960s to the late 1970s, the period that is also the focus of Mamdani's essay. In the subsequent years, most of the progress that had been achieved through creative efforts of local and expatriate staff, most of them left-wing, and radical students, began to unravel.

The ban on USARF and *Cheche*, the first major step in that direction, represented the determination of Nyerere and the ruling party to ensure that the leftist tendencies on the campus did not go out of hand. Accordingly, key positions in the university administration were placed in the hands of party loyalists. The process accelerated after the student pro-democracy uprising of 1971. From then on left-inclined local and expatriate academic staff were removed from the campus via unjustified transfers, non-renewal of contracts and other devices. Recruitment of leftist staff was reduced. EASE was abolished and DS became a shallow version of its former self. After the middle of the 1970s, with the campus TYL dominated by ruling party faithful students, the ideological classes and MajiMaji lost their radical edge. In no time, only a few

Tanzanian academics on the campus independently promoted the idea of academic freedom, struggled against the authoritarian administration, critically analyzed the trends in the nation at large and Africa, and espoused a radical political stand.

From the early 1980s, the discipline-based study programs began a downward slide in terms of the quality of scholarship and academic standards. This deterioration, prompted in part by World Bank driven reduction in funding, was observed at UDSM, Makerere University and University of Nairobi, and other universities in Africa. (Kavuma 2011). And in the recent years, despite increased funds for research, research productivity remains low. One benchmark is the annual number of papers published by academic staff in recognized international journals. While the desired level is one to two papers a year, these days academics at Makerere only manage to publish one such paper per five years and those at UDSM, one paper per ten or more years (Cloete at al. 2011, pages xv-xxiii). And often, the papers in question have multiple foreign and local authors, with some of the latter being honorary authors who played little substantive role in the research and writing process. Distinctive papers by one or a few local authors and no foreign input are rare.

The driving factors behind such negative trends were internal as well as external, educational as well as societal. Overall, under the rule of autocrats of varied hue and economic domination by Western nations, multinational firms and financial institutions, most African states had lost the nationalistic sense of direction of the 1960s, and had become mired in debt and destitution. Unable to stand on their own feet, their educational infrastructures began to crumble as well. I talked about this at the outset.

Vast inequalities prevail across Africa. Poverty remains entrenched. Major portions of the economy are under the control of foreign capital. Levels of indebtedness are rising rapidly. Social services like health and education have become grossly unequal. The elite and their children get good but costly health care, at home and abroad, and attend well-resourced schools that charge high fees. As the universities have become universities in name only, their children go to India, South Africa, the UK and USA for further education.

WHAT IS TO BE DONE?

The problems faced by modern African universities are grave and wide-ranging. While it is daunting to visualize how and where to begin to deal with them, we need to see that they are multi-sectoral, interdisciplinary in scope. The problems of higher education cannot be resolved without tackling the problems of the education system as a whole. The problems of the education sector relate to those in the health, transportation, agriculture and other sectors. They have common roots. To resolve them, a compartmentalized approach cannot work. This task also entails restructuring the relationship between state and the people, transforming the basic internal and external economic relationships, and making the state accountable to the ordinary people, and not the billionaires, multinationals and the international capitalist system. A viable future for Africa and African education can only come through struggles to transform the neoliberal system that dominates and exploits its people and resources.

Nonetheless, it is not an either-or issue. Simultaneous struggles on all fronts are essential. The general endeavor to achieve a just, people-oriented society has to be contemporaneous with the effort to transform education, and higher education in particular.

With regard to the latter task, I deem four measures to be essential at the outset. First, Africa needs fully funded, state supported universities, where most students will get a full scholarship in return for a contract of five years of public service upon graduation. The mushrooming of private universities, many of which lack qualified staff and offer abysmal quality education, has to halt and the existing ones attached to one or the other public university.

Second, the universities should enroll only well qualified students, and award degrees to only those who demonstrate the required, high standards of achievement. The mass degree-awarding mills have to cease. Academically irresponsible conduct on the part of the teaching staff and administrators so prevalent today has to be curtailed. Given the dearth of qualified academics, this means that at the outset, we will have fewer universities with lecturers and professors who have the needed academic credentials. They will enroll fewer students but produce graduates who have mastered their disciplines. There is no running away from that unpalatable reality.

Third, reform of the curricula of the discipline-based study program is a prime necessity. The reforms should focus on enhancing excellence and making the study programs more relevant to the needs of a social system that will benefit the ordinary people, reduce mass poverty and combat inequality.

Fourth, all university students, irrespective of their specialization must attend an interdisciplinary course in each year of study. Such courses will help them locate their particular profession in the context of the society as a whole, practice it more effectively and be responsible citizens. These courses need to learn from the lessons and contents of the earlier era courses like Development Studies and East African Society and Environment, and take into account Mazrui's proposals to introduce compulsory courses on the Global History of Science, Third World Civilization and Great Systems of Thought.

Comprehensive research, interdisciplinary analysis and critical thought are the essential tools for this monumental pedagogic and practical task.

CONCLUSION

Mamdani's essay does not reveal the depth of the malaise faced by the African University. It is an ideologically biased, factually flawed, conceptually effusive and selective portrait of its history, and the causes and current of the situation. His method of analysis cannot lead to a sound course of action to resolve it. More likely, following his diffuse mode of reasoning and ill-defined recipes may just compound the problems of the African academy. His essay educates us more about what we should not do, than what we should.

While Mamdani remains a captive of the flowery Cold-War era rhetoric of the ancient Ali Mazrui, the person he admires has moved on. According to many observers, Mazrui later came to adopt positions that he had earlier identified with Rodney and other leftists at Dar es Salaam. There is much of value in his later day publications on culture, religion, language and history. In particular, his latest recommendations for improving the state of the African education are worthy of note.

In this era, the African University is a bastion of conformism to capitalist ideology and the worship of everything Western. It suffers from a dearth of erudite, independent scholarship. The academic staff struggle for better terms of service and salaries; the students seek improved terms for loans, better hostel and cafeteria facilities, and not much more. Excellence and deep learning have been put side; relevance is conceptualized in terms of enhancing entrepreneurship and market-based personal competitiveness. The political authorities have no tolerance for critical academic voices.

Changing the situation entails a major struggle. University students and academic staff must study the histories of the African and global academies, learn from the efforts of their predecessors, and embark on bold struggles to transform African education and society. The works of erudite scholars from all corners of the world need study. Not just the socialist but also the liberal academics who have done specialized but meticulous research on education and other fields need attention. Close attention to the works of the revolutionary intellectuals of the past is also essential (Shivji 2018).

In sum: while the methodology underlying the writings of the Mamdani of the 1970s retains its relevance today, attending to the mode of reasoning of the modern Mamdani, especially as embodied in his recent article on the African university, will only drive African education astray. His suggestions for are more likely to entrench under-education rather than offer a respite from the modern day academic maladies.

11

EDUCATION AND HISTORY II

SUMMARY: You can only learn from the past if it has been documented and presented without much distortion. This essay focuses on a recent rendition of the history of Tanzania during the *Ujamaa* years, and of the ideas and activities of the progressive students and academic staff at the University of Dar es Salaam (UDSM) in that time. A comprehensive, unbiased and accurate knowledge of the past is an essential component of the struggle to overcome under-education and replace it with free, relevant and quality education.[1]

*

---

1. This essay has not been published earlier. Together with Chapter 9, it was drafted as an extension to my review of the book *Common People's Uganda* (Tandon Y 2019b) that appeared in *AwaaZ Magazine* of August 2019 (Hirji 2019b). It should be read in conjunction with chapters 9 and 10 which cover related material.

It is the mark of an educated mind
to be able entertain a thought
without accepting it.
Aristotle
++++++++++

WE OFTEN SAY THAT IT IS IMPORTANT to learn from history. But that is possible only if historical events, ideas and processes are known with reasonable accuracy and without significant bias. As Marx said, the dominant ideas of any age are the ideas that serve the interests of its ruling class. The representation and teaching of history are not neutral acts. They are colored by the existent social structure and class interests. Even when material that sheds a better light on the past exists, it is generally absent from or distorted in the mainstream versions of history. What the person in the street comes to know is what reinforces the prejudices and values of the present era (Zinn 1990). Those seeking to transform the status quo have thus to seek out less biased and more comprehensive historical material and employ scientific methods to untangle and analyze it. But that task is made more difficult if and when the progressive activists of the earlier days render the past in ways that misrepresents it in critical ways.

Consider the case of the *Ujamaa* era in Tanzania. In these neoliberal times, it is common for media pundits and intellectuals to declare that it failed because socialism is not a workable option for human society. For example, they look at the problems of the education system today and assert that their roots lie in the misguided socialistic policies of that era. Such views are based on a flawed view of history, factually deficient foundation and elitist, pro-capitalist prejudices.

On the other, for the common man, the current neoliberal reality is so unpalatable that a sort of nostalgia towards the Nyerere era prevails. At least, he was an honest leader who tried his best to improve the lives of the people. Such nostalgia also prevails among the progressives who fail to employ scientific analysis to understand the realities and dynamics of the *Ujamaa* era. A salient instance of such a tendency is seen in the book *Common People's Uganda* by Yash Tandon (Tandon 2019b). It has a dual personality in that the history of Uganda is analyzed within a Marxist framework using ample empirical documentation but that of Tanzania relies on official declarations and subjective perceptions. It just confounds the task of learning from history.

ANALYZING *UJAMAA*

The assessment of *Ujamaa* in CPU is deficient at the conceptual level. It is stated that since Nyerere did not profess to be a Marxist, it was not appropriate, as the radical students did, to criticize him for not adhering to the scientific socialist line. The CPU line is: Tanzania was building a unique brand of socialism that had no relation to scientific socialism or foreign brands of socialism.

Consider the case of the Christian Evangelists in the US who campaign for the removal of the theory of evolution from school curricula. According to the logic of CPU, since they do not profess to be scientists, it is not valid to criticize them for not adhering to science. That, clearly, is an illogical proposition.

The idea of 'scientific socialism' has its roots in a work by Friedrich Engels that distinguished scientific socialism from utopian socialism. The latter places primary stress on intentions but the former links socialism to concrete trends in history with the help of concepts like economic base, superstructure, production and class relations and class struggle. Since then it has become a part of the lexicon of Marxism and denotes the framework for societal analysis and the vision deriving from the works of Marx, Engels, Lenin, Mao and others.

Among other places, it is well described in the first chapter of Walter Rodney's *How Europe Underdeveloped Africa*. He later stressed its import in a paper that is referred to on page 192 of CPU:

> Russia, China, Vietnam, Korea, Cuba – i.e., every successful socialist revolution has borne out the truth of Engels' observation that Scientific Socialism is the fundamental condition of all reasoned and consistent revolutionary tactics. The mobilization of the producers, the defense of revolutionary gains and the advance of the struggle against modern monopoly capitalism are not tasks that can be accomplished by good intentions alone. Rodney (1972b).

Chapter 5 of CPU deals with the Marxist scheme of dividing society into the base and the superstructure and the exhortation by Mao Zedong to put politics in command. These ideas are related to the long and short term perspectives on history. CPU posits them as the guiding principles of the analyses of the situation in Uganda and across the world. Though CPU does not label them as such, they form the basis of the scientific socialist approach. Most readers of CPU will not know the meaning of this term. By adopting an ambivalent stance, CPU does not induce clarification.

CPU thus implies that the scientific method of analysis deemed valid everywhere is not applicable to Tanzania. For this nation, it suffices to rely on the declarations of the philosopher statesman and the author's subjective perceptions. Noble ideas, not socioeconomic trends and analysis, enable us to adequately assess the direction of development and long term future of this nation.

Yet, CPU further qualifies this rule. On page 192, Walter Rodney's one time claim that *Ujamaa* was a manifestation of scientific socialism is quoted in approving terms. Thus, it is valid to apply the ideas of scientific socialism to Tanzania so long they are seen to be in line with *Ujamaa*. But if they are of a critical bent, then scientific socialist analysis is suspect. That is akin to saying that the method of investigation employed by a scientist should not depend on its intrinsic validity but on the type result expected from the investigation. I talk more on Rodney and this issue later.

There is a further conundrum. Demagogic ruling party functionaries in Tanzania regularly asserted that scientific socialism was not applicable to Tanzania. It was also common for the reactionary politicians in Africa to assert that Marxism was irrelevant for Africa because it was a foreign ideology. But they at the same time rejected all the Marxists ideas upon which the analysis given in CPU rests too.

THEORY AND PRACTICE

CPU says that the ruling party document, *Mwongozo*, was a means of giving power to the people not just in factories but principally in the rural areas. The main success story noted thereby is the relocation of millions of the rural residents into villages where they would get services like health, education and water. But the actualities and consequences of this process, which totally violated the spirit and words of *Mwongozo*, are attended to in a cursory fashion.

Just after the Arusha Declaration, the rural residents were willing to move into the *Ujamaa* villages or start collective farms at their current locations. Many did so spontaneously. But that support waned once they saw that the promises were not followed by deeds. By 1973, the project had stalled. It was then that the order to move them by force was issued. The exercise was conducted in a harsh manner, with many people killed or injured. Much property was looted by the rampaging militias. The real numbers are not known as much of the information was suppressed. Apart from rosy reports from regional officials, there is no evidence that the lives of the peasants improved after the exercise. In all likelihood, it deteriorated as the peasants lost access to their original water sources without having a new one in place, incidence of contagious diseases rose due to unplanned congregation of people and so on. Agriculture productivity and output did not increase, nutritional levels remained as before and rural incomes stagnated as the peasants had no option but go on planting the traditional export crops in the same old fashion ways. No wonder that the president of the World Bank was supportive of this `socialist' program.

Mwongozo declared that the people should be involved in running their affairs, there should be work place democracy and accountability, and leaders should shed their arrogant, authoritarian modes of conduct and become humble servants of the masses. These fine words were taken seriously by workers in private and state owned factories, and students in schools, colleges and the university. In one place after another, they stood up to demand their implementation. Everywhere, the official response was the same: riot police were sent in to force them into submission. The so-called ring leaders were expelled. Life after *Mwongozo* remained as it was before *Mwongozo*.

Progressive students and staff at the University of Dar es Salaam held Julius Nyerere in high esteem for the way in which he had led the nation peacefully to Independence, his principled stand against inherited racial and ethnic divisions, his policy of using merit, not race or tribe as the basis for educational opportunity and job allocation, his firm support of African unity and his outstanding endeavors to eliminate colonial and racist rule in Africa. Where they differed with him was on the issue of socialism. But unlike others, they were not opposed to socialism. On the contrary, they were dismayed by the clear signs in all sectors that the manner of implementation of *Ujamaa* was driving the nation onto a path that was not socialistic in anyway except fine declarations.

These assertions were based on a large number of investigations by the progressive academics and students, visits to schools, factories and villages, and conversations with people from different parts of the nation. They derived from concrete analyses of concrete conditions.

BASIC FACTS

At this juncture, I note a few basic facts about radicalism at UDSM. The UDSM Socialist Club was launched soon after the promulgation of the Arusha Declaration in February 1967. But it was replaced by the University Students' African Revolutionary Front (USARF) in November 1967. USARF had two categories of members, regular and associate. Both paid the dues and attended internal meetings, but the latter could not vote or hold an office. Regular membership was open only to students. Membership at the associate level was for the academic staff.

The USARF magazine *Cheche* was founded in October 1969. But USARF and *Cheche* were banned in November 1970. USARF was thus in existence for three years and its magazine, for a year. It is incorrect to refer to the radical students at UDSM after this date using the name USARF. This review uses the terms radical students, USARF members or former USARF members as the context demands.

It is generally overlooked that during its entire life, USARF worked hand in hand with the campus branch of the youth wing of the ruling party, TANU Youth League (TYL). Only Tanzanian students could join TYL. But all the leaders of TYL in that period were active members of USARF as well. After the magazine *Cheche* was proscribed, the campus TYL launched the successor magazine *MajiMaji* that for several years reflected the same radical spirit. It died a natural death in early 1980s.

The word *Cheche* refers to the USARF magazine and to a book about this magazine that was published in 2011. This essay refers to the latter as `the book *Cheche*.' CPU lacks clarity on all the above points.

HOME GROWN MARXISTS OR WESTERN TROTSKYISTS?

CPU makes a series of strong assertions about the association between student radicals and the progressive academics and persons beyond the campus. It affirms that these youthful comrades had a tendency to prefer Western Trotskyists rather than home grown Marxists. The former are held responsible for leading the impressionable minds away from sound analyses of the African reality. For example, on page 203, it says that:

> One of the sorely missing pages in Hirji's Cheche is a consideration of the contributions of great Tanzanian scholars in the Marxist tradition such as Justinian Rweyemamu, Mohamed Babu and Haroub Othman (CPU, page 203).

Let us examine such assertions on a case by case basis.

AM Babu

Assertion: `Other Tanzanian scholars in the Marxist tradition that were ignored by the USARF included Mohamed Babu and Haroub Othman.' (CPU, pages 202–203).

Reality: AM Babu's association with the university unfolded in March 1967, when, as one of the principal speakers at the conference on the role of the university in socialist Tanzania, he proposed that it be transformed into a socialist institution. Upon the founding of USARF later that year, its members developed close working and personal relations with him. As an erudite Marxist and Minister who eschewed bureaucratic fanfare, he was a major inspirational figure for them. He gave a couple of campus public lectures they organized and participated in at least one ideological class. It was from him that we came to appreciate that the problem with foreign `aid' was not just that it was insufficient but that its basic function was to cement imperial dependency. His ideas on building a nationally integrated economy helped clarify our views on socialist economic development.

His association with the campus radicals extended well beyond the lifetime of USARF. It was common for former USARF members to visit him at his home in Upanga. When he and his fellow Zanzibari comrades were unjustly detained in 1972, it was they who initiated internal and external campaigns for his release. He remained on close terms with us after he was freed and during the time he was abroad. He wrote the concluding chapter for a book on the history of Zanzibar edited by two academics with close ties to former USARF members. I often went to his home in Upanga. When he was teaching at Amherst, USA in the 1980s, Ahmed Gora Ebrahim of the PAC and I paid him a couple of enjoyable day-long visits to savor his exquisite cooking and talk about African issues.

Babu is one of people to whom my book *Cheche* is dedicated, and his name appears in approving terms a further fourteen times. The details of what is stated above are given therein. What is claimed about Babu in the two quotes from CPU therefore has no factual value.

In his Introduction to the book on the Dar es Salaam debates that was edited by Tandon, Babu ascribes equal weight to the books by Shivji, Mamdani and Nabudere, calling them `three most important books to come out of East Africa.' This point, noted in CPU, begs the question: How come Babu, a person well admired by Tandon, accords such importance to the works of Shivji and Mamdani, works which according to Yash Tandon and Dan Nabudere came from the pens of neophyte, externally influenced neo-Trotskyists who lacked real knowledge of the African condition? CPU does not provide us a clue about how to resolve this paradox.

Haroub Othman

Assertion: `Other Tanzanian scholars in the Marxist tradition that were ignored by the USARF included Mohamed Babu and Haroub Othman.' (CPU, pages 202–203).

Reality: In the days of USARF, Haroub Othman was the Assistant Dean of the Faculty of Law. It was he who made the Faculty of Law lecture room available on Sundays for the purpose of holding the ideological classes organized by USARF. And it was because of him that we had access to the Law Faculty cyclostyling room for printing and binding the issues of *Cheche*. He also wrote a book review for the second issue of *Cheche*.

When he became the Head of the Institute of Development Studies, he recruited three former USARF associates to join the academic staff. He was our close comrade all along. We read and discussed his papers with interest. Accordingly, he is one of the person's to whom the book *Cheche* is dedicated. Three of his books are referenced in that book as well. It is of relevance to note that Haroub's photo with my family and me appears in a book I recently wrote about Walter Rodney. That is an indicator of how close we were.

The assertions in CPU that there was some sort of estrangement between him and USARF and he is ignored in the book *Cheche* lack a valid foundation.

Justinian Rweyemamu

Assertion: Justinian Rweyemamu `never participated in the various

Dar debates' and his books were never `among the books prescribed for reading in the study groups of USARF and Cheche' who favored 'European Marxists to a home-grown Marxist like Justinian.' (CPU, page. 204).

Reality: J Rweyemamu arrived at UDSM in 1972. The books referred to in this quote are:

- Book 1: Rweyemamu JF (1973) *Underdevelopment and Industrialization in Tanzania: A Study of Perverse Capitalist Industrial Development*, Oxford University Press, Nairobi.

- Book 2: Rweyemamu JF, Loxley J, Wicken J and Nyirabu C (editors) (1972) *Towards Socialist Planning: Tanzania Studies No. 1*, Tanzania Publishing House, Dar es Salaam.

Book 1 is a technical work filled with data on different economic activities and sectors analyzed with elaborate statistical models and methods. It is a challenging read even for a final year economics undergraduate. One cannot expect radical students from varied disciplines to engage with it. Yet, a number of former USARF members who joined the academic staff at least perused it. Rweyemamu's chapter in Book 2, based on the final chapter of Book 1, is more accessible.

CPU ascribes Book 2 solely to him. That is in error. He was one of its four editors and one of its eight contributors. Further, since USARF and *Cheche* were banned in 1970, there is no way USARF study groups could have used his works. Yet, both books are approvingly referenced in the book *Cheche*.

All the claims as to what books and writers were preferred by USRAF in CPU derive from the syllabus of the ideological classes for its initial year, that is, 1969/1970. That syllabus is reproduced in the book *Cheche*, which is the source for Tandon. By the end of 1970, USARF was no more but ideological classes continued, albeit under the purview of the university TYL, the publisher of *MajiMaji*. The classes were in operation during the time Tandon was at the university but it does not seem that he attended a single class, or knows anything about the books used therein.

Even though he was a late arrival on the scene, Rweyemamu did participate in one of the Dar es Salaam debates. His commentary on Shivji's *Tanzania: The Silent Class Struggle* appeared in a later edition of this work. It was just that he did not take part in that phase of the debate initiated by Nabudere. Why he did not is a matter of speculation. Perhaps he was put off by its harshly polemical tone. CPU appears to place the blame for his non-participation on former USARF members. Why not on Nabudere's side?

Rweyemamu was a progressive academic but not a political activist. He did not participate in the activities of the radical students. Yet, they held him in respect and his contributions on the academic front were appreciated by them.

Tandon's admiration for his two books has some paradoxical

aspects. First, the other contributors of Book 2 were Lionel Cliffe, John Saul, academics who worked closely with them, or who held a position on Tanzania that was in line with their position. In CPU parlance, it was run over by neo-Trotskyists. All these eight contributors, while expressing sympathy with and hopeful towards the socialist endeavors in Tanzania, were also critical of the actual trends on the ground. They raised serious concerns about industrial development, political organization, economic, financial and manpower planning, rural and regional development, management of parastatal firms and health policy.

Upon noting major deficiencies in the post-Arusha industrial strategy, Rweyemamu ends his chapter in Book 2 by warning about the danger of rekindling perverse mode of state capitalist development to the detriment of the people of Tanzania (Book 2, pages 47-48). In a similar vein, after an instructive survey of health policy after Arusha Declaration, Malcolm Segall concludes:

> The present health policy of Tanzania is the same as that of non-socialist developing countries; it should be different. Health is an area of society which has not yet been penetrated by socialism. The country can `plan and chose' a people's health service. (Book 2, page 160).

These are the very types of criticisms Shivji and his comrades were advancing. It seems that for CPU who says it is more important than what is said. Also, its stand on these two books is not consistent with the blanket praise for Nyerere and *Ujamaa* given therein.

As noted in Chapter 9, the endeavors to reform the curricula in arts and social sciences (and Law and Education) began years before Justinian Rweyemamu joined UDSM. And he was not the main initiator of the East African Society and Environment course. He played an important role in both these endeavors. CPU does not well represent his role on these issues.

LIONEL CLIFFE AND JOHN SAUL

The political scientists Lionel Cliffe (UK) and John Saul (Canada) who taught at UDSM in that period were quite sympathetic to *Ujamaa* and Nyerere. They carried out many studies on the political changes and social conditions in Tanzania, and produced insightful books. Their two volume compilation, *Socialism in Tanzania*, is an indispensable work for understanding what transpired in that era. But their backing for Nyerere and his policies was not a blind one. It was tempered by they observed.

Though none became an associate member of USARF, both were very supportive of the magazine *Cheche* at the practical level. While they did not attend the ideological classes, both wrote commentaries on Shivji's first book. Saul's commentary appeared in the inaugural issue of *MajiMaji*.

According to CPU, the `young' USARF students:

> ... were led to their idealistic dreams by mature ideologists of 'scientific socialism' who came, mostly, from Europe, Canada and the United States – among them John Saul and Lionel Cliffe, who imported the writings of Euro-American Marxists, especially Paul Baran and Paul Sweezy. Baran and Sweezy were the real 'gurus' most cherished by the USARF and Cheche in their 'ideological classes'. (CPU, page 196).

Taken together with what is stated on page 208 of CPU, we infer that Saul, Cliffe, Baran and Sweezy were the neo-Trotskyists who influenced Shivji and his associates into pandering `bad' and groundless notions like the `bureaucratic bourgeoisie.'

Lionel Cliffe, a firm socialist, did not ascribe to Marxist ideas. John Saul stood more to his left, but was not a thinker devoted to scientific socialism. None of their writings appeared in the reading lists of the first four years of the ideological classes. While they were our comrades, to say that USARF comrades or Shivji were primarily influenced by them is a laughable proposition. If anything, it was the other way around.

Baran and Sweezy were well grounded Marxists but their ideas were not linked to Trotskyism. Their writings are among the more than thirty books in the first syllabus for the ideological classes. It is dominated by works written in the classical Marxist framework, and includes the works of Marx, Engels, Lenin and Mao. The five books accorded special importance in this list, and which are noted in CPU, included, in addition to two books by Baran and Sweezy, works of Fanon, Nkrumah and Engels. Were the latter books neo-Marxist or neo-Trotskyist as well?

If you look at the complete list, it is apparent that the assertions made in CPU have no basis. The list derives from traditional type of Marxist writings from all over the world. I note that three: Mir Publisher, *Fundamentals of Marxism-Leninism;* PI Nikitin, *Fundamentals of Political Economy* and P Sweezy, *Theory of Capitalist Development* are expositions of classical Marxist ideas that accord with the theoretical framework of CPU (Chapter 9). No book by Leon Trotsky or a known Trotskyist appears in this list and, with one exception such books did not appear in the reading lists of the next three years of the ideological classes.

Trotsky was a major leader of the Russian revolution. His works are a part of the Marxist legacy. There is no *a priori* reason to ignore them. A number of comrades read a couple of his articles and the three volume stellar biography written by Isaac Deustcher. But they were among the hundreds of articles and books we read. We learnt a lot about the Russian revolution from them. But they exercised no decisive influence on our thinking. We never subscribed in any shape or form to the notion of `permanent revolution,' that is identified with modern Trotskyism.

The activists of today must keep an open mind. They should not censor what they read and select what they discuss based on simplistic, emotive labels. And, importantly, they should make up their own mind about what is and is not relevant for their struggles.

WALTER RODNEY

The Guyanese born scholar, activist Walter Rodney taught at UDSM for seven years. His path breaking book *How Europe Underdeveloped Africa* reverberated globally from the day it came out. It is beyond doubt that he was the preeminent Marxist, Pan-Africanist personality to have graced this campus.

After a brief, tumultuous stint at the University of Jamaica, he returned to UDSM in June 1969 and stayed there until early 1974. In no time, his influence on instructional and research methods and content was felt not just in history but also well beyond. And he was one of a handful of academics who became intimately linked to radical student activism at this university.

During his initial stay, he was a prime catalyst for the Socialist Club which subsequently transmuted into USARF. Rodney immediately joined it at the associate level, being one of the two academics who ever did. He attended USARF meetings, gave public lectures it organized, often came to and once in a while conducted an ideological class, took part in practical work like staying and working in *Ujamaa* villages and supported *Cheche* by contributing an article on African labor for its first issue. If we have to single out one Marxist who deeply and decisively influenced the student radicals at UDSM, it has to be Walter Rodney. That is clear from the book *Cheche*, which forms the primary source used by Tandon to lampoon them. (see Chapter 9 for further details).

What does CPU say about Walter Rodney? In the Introduction to CPU, Ngugi wa Thiong'o calls *How Europe Underdeveloped Africa* 'a classic of Pan-African thought.' In the main text, it is stated:

> One of the luminaries at the campus, then, was Walter Rodney from Guyana, who wrote his influential book, How Europe Underdeveloped Africa (1972), whilst at the University (CPU, page 190).

Two pages later we read:

> In one of its early issues, Rodney criticized Ujamaa, whereupon the government banned Cheche, arguing that Tanzania did not need to import a foreign ideology; it was building its own model of socialism. (CPU, page 192).

This paragraph was reproduced in Chapter 9 as well where I showed the host of errors it contains. Though CPU does not state the source, it apparently is from a 2013 paper by Shivji in C Chung (editor) (2013) *Walter A Rodney: A Promise of Revolution*, Monthly Review Press, New York. Compare what is in CPU with the following:

> The issue [of Cheche] that followed carried commentary on my long essay. One of the comments was by Walter Rodney, and after that the journal was banned and the organization [USARF] deregistered. (Shivji 2013).

On this point, Shivji is in error and CPU reproduces that error. This is easily checked by looking at the tables of contents of all the issues of the magazine *Cheche* that are given in the appendix of the book *Cheche*. And Tandon wrote a review of this book for *Pambazuka News*.

The footnote for the quote on Rodney from CPU given above reads:

> Later, Rodney wrote a piece for the journal African Review, reviewing his assessment arguing that Ujamaa was a 'localized manifestation of the principles underlying scientific socialism.' Quoted in Hirji, Cheche, op.cit. p 149

I discussed the inconsistencies in CPU related to this footnote in Chapter 9. I further note that here Rodney's remark is put under quotation marks. But Rodney never said these exact words. In the book *Cheche*, they are given as a paraphrasing of what Rodney said. CPU converts that into an exact quote. A small, but revealing error. Further, CPU does not say that later on Rodney made an about turn on this point.

> In Tanzania, as elsewhere, the strengthening of the state has gone hand in hand with the emergence of privileged classes who themselves depend inordinately on the state machinery for power and accumulation (Rodney 1974).

Elsewhere, in relation to Tanzania also, he said:

> And at the present time the petty bourgeoisie, although small in number, is in control of the state. It is reproducing itself. It still retains certain kinds of links with the international monopoly capitalist world. Rodney (1975).

Remarkably, other than what is in on page 192 as quoted above, CPU has nothing else on this illustrious Marxist and Pan Africanist academic and revolutionary. What was the nature and extent of his influence on student radicalism at UDSM? What role did he play in the various Dar es Salaam debates? Were his ideas of a neo-Marxist, Trotskyist mode or were they more in line with the finance capital perspective of Nabudere? He was the principal player in these debates. He commented on each of Shivji's books, wrote comments on related papers by others at UDSM, and penned his own papers on these issues. And he played a critical role in several exchanges about university curricula, professional associations and African liberation. That he did not take part in the Nabudere phase of the debates was because he had departed for Guyana by the time it got off the ground.

Why does CPU maintain a total silence on these questions? Is it for the sake of not taking on a real heavyweight of Pan-African and Marxist thought? CPU's avoidance of Rodney, his influence and ideas smacks of political opportunism. It is indicative of the uncomfortable corner you can land in if you rely on emotive labels and selective quotes, not logic and evidence to drive your case.

Another related scholar ignored by CPU is the distinguished Marxist economist Guyanese Clive Thomas. A write of influential texts, he taught at UDSM in those years and was held in high esteem by the radical students. He lectured in the ideological classes. To this day he remains the most prolific and people-oriented economist of the Caribbean region. His ideas on imperialism and underdevelopment are a far cry from the simplistic line advanced by Nabudere.

HENRY MAPOLU

Henry Mapolu was a USARF member who served on the editorial board of *Cheche* and later was the founder-editor of *MajiMaji*. On graduation, he joined the Department of Sociology at UDSM but continued with his radical activism. He wrote well researched, clearly articulated original papers on Tanzania and *Ujamaa* right from his student days. His focus was on rural development and the relationship between workers and management in private and state factories. He subsequently edited a well-received book on the latter topic. He was the only local academic to voluntarily abandon a promising career in the academia and join a large industrial enterprise as a worker education officer. Jointly with Shivji, he wrote papers and a book on workers struggles in Tanzania. (Mapolu 1972; 1976; 1986; 1990).

Yet this dedicated, erudite scholar and activist is mentioned only once, and in passing, in CPU? Why ignore this genuinely home-grown Marxist? Is that because his ideas were in line with those of Shivji and his comrades?

While CPU mentions Babu, it has nothing on Ngombale Mwiru, the other ranking Marxist in Nyerere's administration. As a senior official in TYL, he helped the student radicals at UDSM to launch the magazine *MajiMaji* as a way of countering the ban on *Cheche*. He wrote articles on Tanzanian politics and addressed a conference on African youth they organized.

AHMED GORA EBRAHIM

Ahmed Gora Ebrahim, a leading figure in the Pan Africanist Congress of South Africa, was exiled in Tanzania. A Marxist with a particular affinity to the Chinese revolution and Mao, he was a frequent presence at the UDSM campus. He taught in the ideological classes and spoke at USARF sponsored public lectures. With his unique ability to combine humor with serious analysis, he always attracted overflowing crowds. His weekly column in a national paper was eagerly awaited. A major figure of influence on USARF comrades, he was also in very good personal terms with them. We now and then used to visit him at his home in Upanga. In ideological terms, he was a comrade as far apart from Trotskyism as you can get. CPU has nothing to say about him.

THE INFLUENCE MAKERS

The CPU line on the intellectual influences on the UDSM student radicals is biased and simplistic. The actual story was more complex involving a wide variety of thinkers, writers, cultural personalities and freedom fighters. The left-inclined students who joined the university in the years 1967 to 1971 had been inspired by Patrice Lumumba, Julius Nyerere, Kwame Nkrumah, Nelson Mandela, Martin Luther King, Malcolm X, J Odinga Odinga and other luminaries from the time they were in school.

Upon joining the university, they came into contact with second and third year radicals. The veterans were their main mentors at the outset. Through them, they connected with the progressive academic staff and others who were closely tied to USARF and TYL. They were Walter Rodney, AM Babu, Ahmed Gora Ebrahim, JL Kanyiwanyi, K Ngombale Mwiru and Haroub Othman. Their mentors and such contacts introduced them to the writings and lives of Frantz Fanon, Amilcar Cabral, Karl Marx, Friedrich Engels, VI Lenin, J Stalin, Mao Tse Tung, Ernesto Che Guevara, Fidel Castro, Ho Chin Minh, Rosa Luxemburg and G Plekhanov. The USARF organized public lectures and ideological classes were also instrumental in this regard.

In the class room, they encountered academics of nationalistic, rightist, progressive and radical persuasion. The leftists were small in comparison with the centrists and conservatives. But they carried a voice. Varying over time, they included MA Bienfeld, Lionel Cliffe, Andrew Coulson, Jaques Depelchin, Ed Ferguson, Kassim Guruli, Grant Kamenju, Joe Kanyiwanyi, Helge Kjekshus, John Loxley, Andrew Lyall, Archie Mafeje, Mahmood Mamdani, Marjorie Mbilinyi, Ahmed Mohiddin, Haroub Othman, Abdul Paliwala, Sol Picciotto, Walter Rodney, Justinian Rweyemamu, Abdul Sheriff, Thomas Szentes, Arnold Temu, G Tschannel, Michela von Freyhold, Wamba dia Wamba and others. The radicals also benefited from the lectures given by visiting progressive academics from all over the world who graced the campus in that era. Of course, not all radicals came in touch with all these academics. But they constituted our collective source of progressive ideas.

In the process and through their own initiative, they came to read works of leftists like Eqbal Ahmad, Tariq Ali, Samir Amin, G Arrighi, Paul Baran, Waldon Bello, JD Bernal, Charles Bettleheim, J Bronowski, Amilcar Cabral, Aimé Césaire, Noam Chomsky, Oliver

C Cox, Josue de Castro, Basil Davidson, Angela Davis, Simone de Beauvoir, Regis Debray, Maurice Dobb, Ruth First, Paulo Freire, Andre Gunder Frank, Erich Fromm, Eduardo Galeano, Roger Garaudy, W Gordon Childe, Michael Harrington, William Hinton, Eric Hobsbawm, Joshua Horn, Leo Huberman, George L Jackson, Pierre Jalee, CLR James, Gabriel Kolko, RD Laing, Oscar Lange, Colin Leys, Henry Magdoff, Bernard Magubane, Ernest Mandel, Herbert Marcuse, Albert Memmi, Félix Moumié, Vance Packard, James Petras, Bertrand Russell, Edward Said, Jean-Paul Sartre, Ronald Segal, Edgar Snow, Paul Sweezy, Eric Williams, Jack Woddis, and Howard Zinn. They also devoured the left oriented journals available in the university library.

On the literary front they were attracted to Ayi Kwei Armah, James Baldwin, OR Catillo, Nawal El-Saadawi, Nadime Gordimer, Maxim Gorky, Nazim Hikmet, Ibrahim Hussein, Yashar Kamel, Alex LaGuma, Gabriel Garcia Marquez, Sembene Ousmane, José Saramago, Adam Shafi, Upton Sinclair, Hamza Soko, Wole Soyinka, Nguugi wa Thiong'o, and Robert Tressell. And this is an incomplete list.

Reading habits and what was read varied among comrades. Some were attracted to these authors; some to others. But they talked among each about other their readings.

I can say with confidence that we always critically engaged with what we read and what we were taught. Our line was a simple line: to search for the truth and serve the people. Other than that we were beholden to no one, on the campus, in East Africa or beyond. I am sad to see that CPU fails to notice this. And while more can be said, I now wrap up this essay.

CONCLUSION

Yash Tandon is a progressive scholar and activist with many well read books and papers to his credit. His analyses of imperial interference in Africa and of the political and economic situation in the African countries brim with keen insight. Mahmood Mamdani is another distinguished, progressive scholar on the African scene with several books that have captured a wide market in Africa and beyond. While Tandon continues to adhere to the Marxist analytic framework, Mamdani has abandoned it for identity based analytic methods (see Chapter 10). Nonetheless, both exercise a signal influence over the visions and ideas of the emerging African youth.

What transpired in Tanzania during the Nyerere era is a topic that attracts attention form activists and progressive intellectuals, young and old, in Africa and beyond. What does it have to say about the prospects of socialism in Africa? Despite their erudition, both Tandon and Mamdani have a blind spot on these questions. As documented in Chapter 9, Chapter 10 and this essay, their stands on Tanzania under *Ujamaa* and the role and perspectives of the radicals at the University of Dar es Salaam in that era are seriously flawed. While their stands on *Ujamaa* are different, they are unified in their castigation of the leftist activities at the UDSM. Their writings on these issues are more likely to misinform and mislead than to elucidate and illuminate. And while Tandon's *Common People's Uganda* has the potential to be a standard work on the political economy of Uganda, the biased material on Tanzania it contains form a blot that undermines its quality and utility. An accurate representation of what transpired in Tanzania during *Ujamaa* and of the vibrant debates at UDSM is of interest to Tanzanians and people elsewhere in Africa and the world. A distorted representation can only undermine the progress towards the genuine liberation of Africa.

In Chapter 2, we identified two contending tendencies towards the policy of Education for Self-Reliance (ESR) during the *Ujamaa* era. The idealists reflexively celebrated ESR while the realists pilloried it on the basis of evident problems but without taking the socioeconomic context into account. An alternative mode of analysis that was empirically based and examined education in terms of broad societal conditions and trends was presented. In the recent works of Mamdani and Tandon, we also observe such conceptually and factually flawed tendencies. And here too a scientific approach that is logical, factually valid and reflects a coherent framework of social and historic analysis is called for.

There are several lessons from those times that the activists of today need to attend to. These include:

- Knowledge is a weapon. Read broadly and extensively, local and international books and papers. Do not impose restrictions of an arbitrary nature on the kind or sources of material you read.

- Examine history, social issues and political claims using scientific analysis and empirical evidence and not simply ideals and intent or an ideologically distorted dismissive style.

- Discuss and debate, on an ongoing basis, what you read and observe. Knowledge is not a static but an ever evolving entity.

- Always employ a civil tone, whether among your comrades or with your political adversaries. The force of your argument lies not in how loudly you can say it but in its logic and content.

- Combine theory with practice. Knowledge ultimately derives from practice and has to be examined and tested in the light of practice. Knowledge is a congealed form of practice of others, alive or dead.

- No matter what happens, keep hope alive.

The activists and progressive intellectuals of the past adhered, at least in part, to some of these precepts but sidelined the others. The activists and academics of today must do better.

12

EDUCATION AND READING

SUMMARY: Until recently, books have been a major pillar of education, enlightenment, culture and social intercourse. Yet, in Africa book reading in general has been on a steep decline. Educational facilities, especially the higher learning institutions are affected in a major way by this trend. Since the potential alternatives, the computer and the Internet, are not employed as they should be, the lacuna further diminishes educational quality and enhances under-education. This essay explores the manifestations and likely causes of this problem.[1]

*

---

1. The initial portion of this essay was first published as Hirji KF (2014) The sweetness of a fake book, in *Pambazuka News*, 3 December 2014 (www.pambazuka.org). The remaining portion is new to this book. This essay represents a continuation and elaboration of the material in Chapter 7.

*Reading is to the mind
what exercise is to the body.*
Richard Steele
++++++++++

Books are a uniquely portable magic.
Stephen King
++++++++++

*Keep reading books,
but remember that a book is only a book,
and you should learn to think for yourself.*
Maxim Gorky
++++++++++

The wise man reads both books and life itself.
Ling Yutang
++++++++++

*Once you learn to read,
you will be free forever.*
Fredrick Douglas
++++++++++

*To read without reflecting
is like eating without digesting.*
Edmund Burke
++++++++++

*The ink of timeless books
transmutes in tinge and shade
from one century to another
but classic words never fade.*
Terri Guillemets
++++++++++

AT ONE LEVEL, IT SEEMS that the emphasis on books and reading has never been greater. Newspapers frequently carry stories about them. Politicians ponderously pontificate to encourage students and the public to read books. Joining the cacophony are educationists, local and external, business moguls, media editors, and civic leaders. You read of the establishment or refurbishment of school and public libraries in the regions and see photos of primary school children engrossed in books in a new library. A few districts have started a mobile library service.

At another level, complaints about the decline of reading culture in the nation abound. Teachers, educationists, parents, publishers and others express dismay at the amount of time students spend with electronic entities – television, cell phones, computers and video games, even in the rural locations. In the modern age, college and university students are disinclined to touch books beyond that which is absolutely necessary to pass an exam.

In this essay, I reflect on this paradox. Where is our nation headed in terms of books and book related learning? I begin with a curious but real life tale.

FAKE BOOKS

You shop in Dar es Salaam at your own risk. Purchase a `quality' light bulb at a stiff sum; three days later, it goes `poop.' Get breakfast cereal in an attractive box; inside you find coarse, odd tasting stuff, and perhaps, a crawly bug or two. Buy a high-priced door lock upon a solemn assurance that it is the genuine item; after four months of use, it jams.

Fakeness is now integral to our lives. Fake promises by our bigwigs: that we are acclimatized to. Our lives are enlivened by all manner of fake goods, fake education, fake medicines, fake news, fake friends, among a pervasive litany of fakes. We grumble, we complain. But the moment an opportunity arises, we inject our own brand of fakeness into the fertile arena.

I thought I was a savvy guy, aware of all the varied brands of double deed. Sadly, I was wrong. A recent experience has made me realize that searching for the fakest of the fakes is like searching for the largest number; for any you have at hand, a bigger one exists. And it has features even your wildest dreams cannot foresee. It is an experience worth sharing.

I was in a supermarket. My shopping list comprised sorghum flour, tea bags, honey and the like. A stand strewn with books distracted me. Disregarding my list, I eagerly scanned it from top to bottom. Virtually all were books of fiction. Looking like new, each bore the same price: TSh 6,500/=. A few classics aside, most were recent products.

I am addicted to books. Mostly I read the serious stuff: current affairs, history, biography, science, health, mathematics, etc. I do not watch TV or the movies. Compromised health prevents me from dining out. For entertainment, I listen to music, stroll along the seashore and gobble up novels from a wide spectrum of genres.

A good mystery makes my day. Apart from the usual fare — Agatha Christie, Arthur Conan Doyle, Ian Rankin, PD James, Ruth Rendell and Henning Mankel — I am also a fan of Arthur Upfield (Australia), Robert van Gulik (China), Tony Hillerman, Sarah Paretsky and Margaret Coel (USA), Kwei Quartey (Ghana), James McClure (South Africa) and Ernesto Mallo (Argentina).

A Coel tale relaxes you with a gentle romance and Native American history while keeping you on the edge for a few hours. The escapades of the enigmatic half-breed sleuth Napoleon Bonaparte concocted by Arthur Upfield generate tension and pleasure as they give you insights into life in that continent down under, and especially into the Aborigine culture. I can go on, but it will divert us unnecessarily.

It being my lucky day, two enticing tales of detection were available: *Death and the Dancing Footman* by Ngaio Marsh, and *The Shape of Water* by Andrea Camilleri. I seized both. Anticipating Farida's complaint about my book mania, I added a bar of dark chocolate to the basket.

I was on the mark: She smiled brightly as her eyes fell on her favorite after dinner treat. But she had a question: What did this box of biscuits cost? Only rarely do I relook at the sales receipt. And I was astonished at what I saw. The last item was two kilos of sugar. I had bought honey, which was itemized, but not sugar. Moreover, no book item was listed.

How can one confuse books and sugar? That was my first thought. The probable reason why the salesgirl had made the substitution then came to mind. The books lacked a bar code. To enter it on the sales register, she would have had to look it up and enter it manually. Entering two kilos of sugar instead saved her the trouble. Consequently, I paid TSh 3,400/= for items worth TSh 13,000/=. It looked like a twice over lucky day for me, though at the expense of her employer. Yet, more often than not, such mistakes result in customers being overcharged.

When I lived in Los Angeles in the 1990s, I regularly shopped at a large grocery store near our home. The sales clerks earned about $7.50 per hour, or $60.00 for an 8-hour shift. The sales girls in Dar es Salaam, who do exactly the same job, are lucky to secure $4.00 a day. With the daily wage, the latter can buy 4 kilos of sugar while the former can get 30 kilos (at $2 per kilo). Is it reasonable to expect our super exploited workers to be loyal employees, or work with diligence? Cost of living has been globalized, but real wages of ordinary workers remain as they were 50 years back.

Another crucial difference: In Los Angeles, I was invariably greeted at the sales counter with a big smile: `How are you today? Did you find everything you wanted?' and was sent off with a cheerful `Have a good day.' Here it is a low key affair; at times you pay and depart with your stuff in silence.

One day, outside a nearby bank, I came upon that Los Angeles sales clerk who had cheerfully served me for years. She did not display even a hint of recognition, and calmly passed by as if I did not exist. Those wide smiles and pleasant words, I understood, were fake smiles and words. They were the automated postures of a depersonalized, corporatized, money-driven society.

Not so here. Our home born salesgirl had that day greeted me with a polite `*Shikamoo Babu*' (My respects, grandfather). It was a genuine utterance; there was nothing fake about it.

To return to my tale: That night, I eagerly seized my Nagio Marsh find, intending to go from cover to cover before falling asleep. It was then that I uncovered a truly unprecedented brand of fakeness. Despite its authentic front and back covers, this was not a Ngaio Marsh work. From the first to the last page, it was a year-2003 autobiographical novel by Samira Serageldi, namely, *The Cairo House* (Harper Perennial, London, 2003).

Thou shall not judge a book by its cover – how true. Books with frayed, half-torn or missing pages; those I have bought. Receiving by mail a book other than the one ordered; that I have experienced. But buying a book that misrepresents itself in such a fantastic way; now that was a truly novel event.

Probably the print runs of the books had overlapped. Some copies had mixed up the covers. The mishap was likely discovered at the final inspection. Yet, instead of discarding them, the company sent them to a charity or institution through which they ended up in Africa. The loss was mitigated by itemizing the donation on the tax return and getting a tax deduction. The local supplier probably got them free or almost free. Perhaps they were part of a lot for free distribution to schools and libraries. But through dubious channels, they ended up in shops, earning a handsome profit for the local supplier, and a cut for the public officials involved.

Anything is good enough for Africa. On a continent mired in poverty, something is always better than nothing. That is how we end up buying fake books. In what is already a decidedly barren landscape for books and book reading, external forces and their local allies never cease placing new twists to compound our dilemmas. It is an ancient story: if they ban a potentially carcinogenic pesticide, the stocks are shipped to us, not destroyed. If the date of sale of some commodities has passed, they are adroitly repackaged and bestowed on to us.

Dejected a bit, I read Andrea Camilleri. It was a spicy who-done-it in which Inspector Montalbano invokes his usual tact to paddle through the rough waters of the Italian police bureaucracy and confront the political and business elite to reach a surprising conclusion. He made my day, though he did not leave as sweet a taste in my mouth as Ngaio Marsh would have. *The Cairo House* has been set aside for now. One of these days, I will get to it. Will it be as sweet as a kilo of sugar? I wonder.

BOOKS IN THE WESTERN WORLD

The Industrial Revolution in Europe and North America brought with it a tremendous expansion of book writing and publishing. Smoke spewing paper mills enabled the production of affordable newspapers, magazines and books for the masses. Compulsory education and growth of public education systems enhanced literacy and the affinity to books. Book reading, an activity only the well-to-do could hitherto indulge in, became a popular past time and an indispensable tool for learning. Many public libraries were built and bookstores, small and large, mushroomed. While much of the literary output was of a cheap thrills variety, outstanding works that have stood the test of time also came into being. Books on science, health, technology, business, politics, history and arts among other subjects came to embody the cumulative repository of knowledge.

The onset of the neoliberal era in the 1980s set into motion strong forces that are gradually but inexorably undermining this state of affairs. The number of publishers has shrunk as well established small and not-that-small publishers have been gobbled up by giant conglomerates. As competition has gone down, these oligopolies have greater freedom to set prices for the bookstores and purchasers, and terms for the authors. Measures instituted by conservative politicians have stultified admirable public education systems and closed public and school libraries. The rise of mega-bookstores and more recently, of economically powerful online purveyor of books have proved fatal for a large number of independent bookstores in these nations.

While book writing was never a reliable venue for earning a living, let alone prospering, now the situation of the authors is even more onerous. The publishers set their sights on the few authors who generate best-sellers. While they make big bucks, the other authors have a harder time getting their work into print. And when they do, they have to live with pitiful royalty levels. Alternative channels are few. Self-publishing and independent publishing offer a respite but marketing the books brought out in these ways poses a major challenge.

In the world of academic publishing, a scandalous situation prevails. Publication of academic journals and books is now controlled by a few corporations. The subscription prices, even for electronic journals, are so high that major universities in the West are forced to curtail the number of journals in their libraries. Science, medicine, engineering and social science textbooks sell at previously unimaginable prices. For example, in the US, you cannot find the latest edition of popular textbooks in physics or chemistry that are under a hundred and fifty or two hundred dollars. It is a racket. A new edition of a commonly used text appears every two or three years. In most cases it differs but a little from the earlier edition. Yet, the instructor uses the latest edition, which is stocked in the college bookstore. This discourages recycling of books and forces the student to buy the more expensive edition. The authors of the blockbusters reap dollars while new authors, however creative, face a truly uphill battle to enter the field.

The electronic era has further reduced the scope for the printed book. E-books and e-book readers have the potential to give readers a level of access to book material not encountered before in history. Monopoly marketers like Amazon.com have not only increased the death rate of the independent booksellers but have, through popularization of e-books made the printed book face the possibility becoming a rare, costly item.

Nonetheless, the book culture remains vibrant in the wealthy nations. With a solid historic, cultural and economic foundation, their utilization in education, leisure and other purposes continues unabated. Book prices in general are not outrageous. Globally, hundreds of thousands of new and old titles see the light of the day. It looks as if the print book still has a long lease of life. (Fisher 2004a, 2004b; Manguel 1997).

READING, BOOKS AND UNDER-EDUCATION

In Africa, as indicated at the outset, books and book reading face graver problems. I take the case of Tanzania.

People want to know; they want to read. Newspapers are expensive. Each day, you see crowds near newsstands, straining their necks to see the front page material. They want to look at the sports page. They talk about what they have managed to see. I cannot forget a 1994 photo of a beggar with polio-shrunk limbs sitting on the bare pavement in the hot sun. Having put aside extending his arms for money, he was engrossed in a newspaper discarded by a passerby. That photo inspired me to start a book review column which came out every other week for about four months.

The system of neoliberal under-education instituted in the 1990s has been driving, gradually but on a sustained basis, students, teachers and the public away from the world of books and reading, especially leisure reading. It is an undisputed reality. I elaborate below.

LIBRARIES

The news stories about establishment of new libraries rarely mention the fate of the old libraries. From the mid-1960s, a well-functioning, well-stocked national library system developed in Tanzania. With the main branch in Dar es Salaam, it had branches in almost all the major towns. The former was housed in an impressive, two-story structure. Students and general readers were attracted to the temples of knowledge in good numbers. They could savor a wide range of fiction and non-fiction books, locally published and imported, and an array of magazines and journals on the shelves.

Decent libraries operated at all the colleges, teacher training institutes and many secondary schools. Where teachers with an affinity to books and motivated librarians were present, the quantity and quality of the material on the shelves was decidedly impressive. On a visit to Mkwawa Secondary School in Iringa in 1973, I was floored by the range of books on science, general knowledge, literature and history in its library. The UDSM library was, if not the best, among the best university libraries in Africa. Dar es Salaam also had British Council Library, US Information

Agency Library and three locally run private libraries. All except one of the local libraries were open to the public. The reading rooms of most of the libraries were usually crowded. Reading was taken for granted. The situation was far from ideal but was a far cry from what prevails now.

From my past visits and a recent informal survey done for this book by a research assistant, the following picture of the current situation emerges.

The once stellar public libraries remain crowded, but with pupils who use them as quiet study areas. No one browses the shelves. There is hardly anything new. Other people rarely visit them. New issues of a few magazines are occasionally seen. The few new books are from external donations. Old books and journals are brown and dusty. Book borrowing is basically non-existent.

Consider the National Library in DSM. It retains the three sections: a kindergarten to primary school section, a secondary school section and a general public section. A graduated but affordable annual fee is levied. Many working parents keep their young children in the first section. As such, it is always full. Activities for the kids are, however, not as well organized as in the early days.

Attendance in the secondary school section, the largest in terms of space, ranges from 300 during term time to about 450 during school holidays. The shelves are stocked with textbooks and novels. Few books are new. Usage is low; the shelves are dusty. It is mainly a quiet study area for the students.

The public section is stocked with novels and an assortment of old books on general topics. A reference section with archival material also exists. The visitors mainly read newspapers or work on their computers. The books, arranged in a disorganized manner on the dusty shelves are hardly read. Many shelves are half empty. Yet, there is a large stock of uncatalogued books in the storage area. An occasional researcher uses the archival material, which is as well in a state of disarray.

In 2017, an American section was set up with US funds in one corner of the library. It provides information about studying in the US, has few inspirational books, conducts sessions to promote American culture and provides Internet access to the users.

The University of Dar es Salaam campus now has, in addition to the old Chagula Library, a fabulous library structure built with Chinese funds. Deriving from its stellar historic legacy, the former has all types of books, pamphlets, manuscripts, newspapers, government publications and UN and other agency reports. Recent issues of academic journals are few. Material is organized as the Law Collection, Science Collection, Arts and Social Science Collection, Engineering Collection and the Africana Collection. The last collection has archival material for access by the students, staff and others for research purposes. It also has many leftist and socialist books from the early days. But this valuable, one-of-a-kind resource is poorly maintained, and contains large gaps.

Online access to a scholarly material from international sources is available. There is an electronic catalogue of material as well. Access to the Internet can be, though, for purposes other than that connected with the courses.

Though many students come to the library, few use the books on the shelves. Books recently acquired through donations suffer a similar fate. Shelves are dust laden. The occasional book placed by a user on a desk remains there for ages. And when it is re-shelved, chances are that it will end up in a different place. Engineering and law students refer to some books as directed by their lecturers. Else, the place is a quiet study area where students work on their own computer. In some corners, students groups engage in discussions. Independently browsing the shelves and borrowing books for self-study are extremely rare.

The Chinese-built UDSM Library is an impressive structure with fine furniture that can accommodate up to 2,000 users at a time. A host of computer work stations exist. About 13,000 books have been acquired. But there does not seem to have been much coordination between the academic departments and the library in this exercise. The books here suffer the same fate as those in the old library, as the students use the comfy space mostly for self-study and work on their own computers. It is a well maintained, shiny place but in terms of transmitting knowledge and intellectual inquiry, it looks like a white elephant in the making.

Dar es Salaam is home to around fifteen universities and colleges now. Each has its own library, some new, mostly old. Their collections are more specialized, though a number have fine general collections inherited from the 1970s. But the usage and functioning of these libraries is similar to what has been described above. The bleak conditions at the Muhimbili University library were described in Essay 4 and Essay 7. The libraries at the Law School of Tanzania and the Center for Foreign Relations, however, are an exception. Adequately stocked with relevant material, their upkeep is good. Individuals from the relevant professions use the books and other documents for work related consultation and study. The latter also has a good stock of progressive material from the 1970s.

Overall, college and university libraries are places where the students go for self-study or work on their own or library computers. Books remain untouched, literally for decades. Valuable historic material rots. Teachers do not visit the libraries and rarely assign the students to consult a library book or journal. The little new material is from external donations. Of the three community-based libraries in Dar es Salaam, two have shut their doors. One remains open for a couple of hours a day as a magazine and newspaper reading room, a hollow version of the past.

There is, though, something to applaud. After the 1990s, a number of nationalistic or progressively oriented NGOs were founded, mostly under the initiative of some leftists of the 1970s, to promote human and social rights in varied societal arenas. They include the Tanzania Gender Networking Program (TGNP), Haki

Elimu, Haki Ardhi (Tanzania Land Alliance), Nyerere Resource Center and Twaweza. Each has a reading room or a library that is open to the public. The quality and types of books and documents at these places are an ocean apart from that available elsewhere. Here, while the reliance on foreign funds persists, what is on the shelves is determined primarily by local activists. Local funds are also raised. Measures to gather and preserve progressive material from the 1970s are taken. The material is placed systematically on the shelves and maintenance is as it should be. But these are small places with limited sitting capacities. Their existence is not well known and only a few students, academics, activists and professionals come to examine the material. Yet, these are among the few places where books and material documenting the efforts of the earlier days to combat under-development and under-education are found. Much of that is of relevance to modern day counter-neoliberal transformative efforts. These organizations also have educational seminars covering issues like social, economic rights and human development.

In 2012, the management of the Institute of Adult Education in Dar es Salaam took a decisive action that was in line with the spirit of the times. The rotting material in the library, meaning a gigantic portion of the stock of books that had been untouched for decades, had to go. The space was needed for computer stations. A major store of knowledge found its way into the dumpster overnight. Fortunately, some enterprising street vendors got the word and rescued a good number of the books. The library stock now graced the makeshift street stalls behind the New Africa Hotel. And that is where I found fine books at giveaway prices. On these rickety shelves, I saw books deemed rare by global standards. For the equivalent of two dollars I bought a thick biography of Karl Marx that was published in 1930. On Amazon, it was priced over two hundred dollars. While it is not unusual for a library to dispose some of its books as it acquires new material, an instantaneous ejection of a huge and valuable part of the stock only occurs under the purview of under-education.

The stories in the media about new libraries do not give a full picture. You see photos of primary school but not secondary school students or adults glued to books. These are photo-op shots made for the launch. The libraries are funded by external entities. No coordination exists. Each entity provides material it has gathered or feels is needed. Pupils read books the teachers are not familiar with and are unlikely to read. Their operation of these libraries depends on availability external funds.

An American student and a Tanzanian academic working in the US were in the news in early July 2019. They had obtained donations to the tune of US$110,000 to support two libraries in Arusha. Ten computers were also provided. The two were lavishly praised by media editors and others were urged to emulate their spirit. (Editor 2019; Ubwani 2019). Not much gets done without charitable efforts from abroad.

Sending books and magazines to Africa from the West is an industry. Organizations like Book Aid, School Aid and STEM Book Project collect books from individuals, schools, colleges, publishers and libraries and package them for shipment. Funds for transport are raised from the public and companies. Most books are used books but some are new surplus stock. Not much thought or effort goes into determining exactly what is needed and where. Only a rough grouping of the books is done. At the destination, what is provided is accepted without any queries. The recipient expresses the consignment with gratitude. After all, books are books.

In the mid-2000s, a local NGO liaised with one such charitable group. Books for schools and colleges were requested. Sometime around 2008, at least four large containers stuffed with books of all kinds were delivered. External funds to hire staff and convert a residential structure into a storage and distribution place were secured. The books were not for sale but had to be distributed cost-free to educational institutions.

A friend and I visited the place on three occasions. The moment we entered, we had to wade through pile upon pile of books on the bare floor. One large room had books on the shelves and the floor. Placed in a semi-organized fashion, we went from room to room to find the books we were looking for.

The NGO had sent out information brochures to schools and colleges in the city. But the response had been disappointing. It needed a teacher or two to visit the place, identify the books appropriate for their school, and do the necessary paperwork for delivery. It was not clear who would cover the transport charge. Only a few teachers had come and a couple of hundred books were sent off. Though not allowed, some teachers and students had purchased books for themselves. My friend and I bought a few books at throwaway prices. I think some of these books found their way to the booksellers, supermarkets and street vendors in the city.

Otherwise, the enormous stock gathered dust. Two containers were untouched; their contents rotting away in the tropical humidity, heat and rain. But the staff did not seem concerned. There was no oversight from the suppliers. NGO funds paid their salaries whatever the outcome. After a few years, the place ceased to operate. No one knows what happened to the books.

In 1997, I subscribed to two secondary school level magazines I felt were suitable for Tanzania. They were sent directly to the main branch of the National Library. But the magazines never appeared on the shelves. They were not to be found in the basement storage area either. No one at the library had come across them. But they had been mailed. With the help of some library employees, they must have been sold in local books stores or the street vendors. After a frustrating couple of years, I stopped the subscriptions. About ten books on medical statistics I had procured from abroad and given to the library at the Muhimbili University suffered a similar fate. Some students had decided to have their own copies. If you do not do it, someone else will; that is the prevailing philosophy.

But the situation is not all disheartening. I had also sent a boxful of books and two magazine subscriptions to the Zanzibar Library. When I went there a year later, the books and magazines had been catalogued and were neatly placed in accessible locations. Compared to the Dar es Salaam library, it was a well-organized and utilized place. The senior librarian had continued to adhere to his commitments to his profession and the reading public. It was a refreshing visit.

BOOKSTORES

In the 1970s, apart from the world class UDSM bookstore, there were five major well-stocked bookstores in the city. The range of material was wide. Today, apart from one exception, the other older bookshops are either in a stagnant state or have folded. The Dar es Salaam Bookstore near the Samora Avenue is nowhere near where it was; the Catholic Bookstore behind the former Avalon Cinema now mostly sells religious books; the Dar es Salaam Printers Store on Jamhuri Street has a good stock of school books but a random assortment of other books, most which have been there for years. The UDSM bookstore remained in a morbid state for a long time. It is now under private ownership. (see below). And there was a popular second-hand book store near the main post office. Established in the colonial era and run by an elderly, friendly man, the fiction and non-fiction titles numbering in the many hundreds were systematically arranged on the clean shelves. The prices were less than a fifth of the original. Until I joined the university, this place was my sole source of personal books.

The former Tanzania Publishing House bookstore on Samora Avenue is an exception. Now it operates under the auspices of Mkuki Na Nyota, a private publisher. With its variety of recent and past books, it is the only place in the city where you feel that you are in a real bookstore. But it too has felt the crunch of under-education. The customer base is poor. Quite a few are tourists who can afford the pricey books; to attract locals it has to supplement its fine collection on African literature and books on Africa by cheap thrills from local authors and the West. School books drown out the other stuff. Yet, it is having a hard time keeping afloat.

Mkuki na Nyota had opened a new bookstore on the campus of the recently established University of Dodoma. It was the only bookstore on the campus of the second largest university in the nation with a student population over 10,000. But the customers were too few. Lecturers did not use it for course books; they and their students had little interest in independent reading. Book prices were too high. It was not easy to meet the operating costs. My last information was that it was on the verge of collapse.

Between years 2006 and 2015, several new bookshops opened in the city and a few smaller bookshops of the past expanded their business. The main impetus behind this growth has been the rapidly expanding population of the city. A city with less than half a million residents in the 1970s is now home to some five million people. The demand for primary and secondary school books has risen accordingly.

Apart from outlets that only sell religious books, now there are some nine bookstores in or near the city center, four stores in the Kariakoo area and six, including the UDSM bookstore, in the outlying suburbs. They mostly stock children's books, school books and trashy novels. There are Swahili and English books on the shelves. When schools are in operation or there is a specific order from a school or an institution, business is adequate; else, the customers are few. Other than self-help books or a few practical, work related books, the demand for current affairs, general knowledge, good literature, history, biography, and science books is pretty low. Book prices for the most part are on the high side; medical and law books can be marked up as high as 500,000/=. However, the prices are negotiable, and a 10% reduction is often possible.

The privately owned UDSM bookshop, University Elite Bookshop, is a branch of the Elite Bookshop in the Mbezi area. The renovated place has shiny floors and well-arranged books on university level subjects from different publishers placed in an ordered fashion on the immaculate shelves. But it also has a sizeable stock of children's and school books. Students mainly buy books that are used to prepare for exams. Though the student population has grown more than six fold from the 1970s, the volume and quality of books sold is below that of the earlier times. Hardly anyone, including the members of the academic staff, purchases books for the sake of reading, entertainment or independent intellectual inquiry.

In addition to the TPH bookstore, there are two other new bookshops of some distinction. Novel Idea started with two branches, one in the city center and another in an upscale shopping center in Masaki. Both branches had an admirable range of local and imported fiction and non-fiction titles. Some were very recent publications. The city center branch was in operation for nearly one and a half decades. But the paucity of buyers led to its demise. The other branch, which is visited by tourists and well-to-do locals, continues in business, though the sales volume is not that high.

The Soma Bookstore and Café in Mikocheni is an exceptional place. It is a medium size store with a good range of books, used and new, on many subjects by local and external authors. Unlike the other stores, it does not carry school books. An adjacent café provides tea, soft drinks, snacks and a decent meal. A fine garden and an outdoor covered area provide venues for book launches, discussion groups and meetings on issues of national interest. An adult reading group, a children's group and a poetry club meet here on a regular basis. Its customer base consists of activists, scholars, tourists, and a smattering of students. It assists community libraries to undertake a needs assessment exercise as well. Yet, for this commendable bookstore, meeting operating costs has been a major challenge.

Other than the city center branch of Novel Idea, I know of four other stores selling books and stationary in city and outlying malls that had to close their doors. In 2010, I saw two new outlets that sold used books published abroad. I visited the one not far from the main entrance of the Muhimbili University on five occasions. The books on the shelves and in the storage area included serious as well escapist novels from varied genera, books on science, health, psychology, nature studies, cooking, and business skills for popular as well as educational consumption. The prices were affordable. For TSh 5,000/= you got a hard cover book and for TSh 3,000/= a paperback. Yet, it suffered from a dearth of customers. No university student visited the place. In a couple of years, the owner decided to close the doors for good.

When I visited the one near the junction of Indira Gandhi Street and India Street, I was quite astonished. The tall shelves were full of college and university level material in the natural and social sciences, medicine, law and engineering, and literature and the arts. The mathematics shelf had excellent undergraduate and post-graduate level books on most of the branches of this subject; a truly rare thing in this part of the world. And the prices were well below the typical prices for such textbooks. The books, from USA and Europe, were an edition or two prior to the latest edition. But that is not a problem. It matters little if you have a year 2000 edition of a text on psychology, sociology, physics or health instead of the latest one when the alternative is no edition.

Owned by a company from India, it had opened a second similarly stocked store near the campus of the University of Dar es Salaam. On each of the four occasions I was at the city center branch, I was the sole customer. The manager told me they had sent out publicity material to educational establishments but had not yet got a response. University students and staff did not visit this or the campus area branch. Lecturers did not use books from here as reference books. One lecturer I met from the Mathematics Department was unaware of its existence. Predictably, after a couple years of operations both the stores closed down. Another new bookshop near the main Post Office stocked with cheap but good books from India met a similar fate. No buyers, the manager told me. Indeed, Dar es Salaam is not a friendly place for bookstores other than those that cater for primary and secondary school needs (Dalali 2019).

Today the street vendors of the city have a better range of books than the bookstores. Some eight vendors operate around the city center, two in Kariakoo and about three in the outlying areas. But they have used copies, and some are worn out. Yet, if you search hard, you find hidden gems. Their sources are people who have accumulated a large number of books during their studies some decades ago but now need to get rid of them. They also get throwaway copies from bookstores. Once in a while, as noted above, they get a major portion of a library. They also have used copies of school textbooks of the past; some of these are not available elsewhere. Prices are highly negotiable but hard bargaining is in order. An initial quote of TSh 10,000/= can be reduced to TSh 3,000/=. Customers are few. Many browse but few buy. Passing by tourists offer some respite. Income from street vending only permits a poverty level life. Yet, they are a part of our repositories of intellectual resources.

ON WRITING AND PUBLISHING

A vibrant culture of book reading is hard to imagine without there being a solid tradition of writing and publishing. In the 1960s and 1970s, many African nations including Tanzania witnessed an upsurge of authors writing fiction and non-fiction books. Budding Tanzanian authors wrote a range of plays, poetry and novels in Swahili and English (Mazrui 2000). There was a blooming output of books on politics, economics, history, education and social analysis by local and expatriate academics at the University of Dar es Salaam. The books were published by the Tanzania Publishing House, East African Publishing House, East African Literature Bureau and reputable external publishers. Books, cheap and plentiful, were read widely. Libraries stocked a good range of local and imported books that were frequently accessed.

Neoliberalism has brought forth drastic and at times, paradoxical changes in the world of books. In Tanzania, books now are too costly. Even parents with a reasonable income think twice before buying books for their children. Oddly, despite the additional cost of shipping, locally published books are more expensive if they are printed here than if the printing is done in Turkey or China. The quality of the local product is often lackluster. After wallowing in years of lucrative but corrupt official contracts, the local printers are addicted to super-profits. The publishers and book sellers maintain too high a profit margin. It is a vicious cycle that feeds onto itself. High prices mean fewer buyers which becomes a reason to increase the prices, and on and on. Only the street vendors present a respite; but their stock has no reason or rhyme.

High prices for books do not translate into increased royalties for the author. Far from it. If you are an independent author, you find that you are the biggest loser. Only a few authors can earn a living from writing. In Tanzania, the situation for all except a select group of NGO-blessed authors is bleak in the extreme. There is no money in writing.

There are two categories of books – sponsored and non-sponsored. Authors of the former have a smooth sailing in terms of earnings and ease of publication while the latter face major obstacles on both fronts (see below for elaboration). There is no shortage of books on religion. A reasonable number of authors try their hands at children's novel, short stories, poetry and primary school books. Books on entrepreneurship, self-improvement and business capture the attention of budding authors. Such books are a mish-mash of standard ideas from external sources peppered with local examples. Given the plethora of such works in the market, and unless funded by an NGO, their cliental is distinctly a narrow one.

Apart from just a few of the books noted above, the quality of writing and output are far from commendable. In the world of African literature, Tanzania stands near the bottom. Other than two Tanzanian authors who have of recent garnered awards for African short stories, there is not much to take pride in. In the non-fiction arena, a handful of local but older generation authors continue to write works that are well-regarded here and abroad. One or two young scholars, Chambi Chachage among them, demonstrate efforts to generate high quality work. In the arena Swahili literature, Adam Shafi has brought out a memoir that entertains, informs and reflects outstanding literary and linguistic merit. Even though his earlier books are required reading in secondary schools, he is, like Ebrahim Hussein, now an almost forgotten personality in our media. Yet both remain celebrated scholars beyond our borders (Hussein 1970; Shafi 1978, 1979, 1999, 2003, 2013).

The web blog http://udadisi.blogspot.com/ run and edited by Chambi Chachage is an encouraging, bright spot on the local literary scene. It regularly carries informative, illuminative and well-written essays, articles and commentaries in English and Swahili on a wide range of topics. The critical spirit embodied in these articles and the accompanying creative cartoons is a refreshing change from the usual apologetic or sycophantic and shallow material you find in the local media.

Two annual or biennial short story and poetry competitions, one in the honor of the contributions Ebrahim Hussein are held. Despite a good number of entries, the quality is mostly lackluster. No winner has made a national, Africa-wide or international impact. Both events operate from an external stimulus and funds. Modern Tanzanian authors have yet to make a faint mark on the African literary scene, and remain miles behind Kenyan and Zimbabwean authors.

It is the same story everywhere you look. Under the influence of the mentality induced by under-education, the media and the politicians, not much gets done without an external god-father. And even then, the outcome is far from what it should be.

A PERSONAL JOURNEY

My experiences in the process of publishing my previous seven books with four different publishers illustrate the points made above. I recount them now.

Chapman & Hall, UK and USA: After completing my doctoral studies in 1986, I published a series of papers dealing with the statistical methods for analysis of small sample discrete data. In 1989, a paper on the topic of which I was the main author was awarded a prestigious international prize. After a track record of more than a decade in this line of research, I was commissioned by the statistical editor of Chapman & Hall, a distinguished statistics publisher, to write a book on this subject. Entitled *Exact Analysis of Discrete Data*, it was published in 2005 (Hirji 2005).

Writing was done over a seven year period. A great deal of my work and leisure time in those years was consumed by it. During this period, Chapman & Hall was taken over by a larger entity, CRC Press (Taylor & Francis) of Florida. But the imprint remained and my contract and contact editor were the same.

This book is for students pursuing master's and doctoral degrees in statistics and biostatistics, and professional statisticians who deal with analysis of small sample data. The reviewers in two leading international journals recommended it highly.

As the publisher and I were aware, the annual sales would be limited. But being the first book on this topic, it would have a guaranteed market for years. Thus far it remains the only one. The list price is $155, though on Amazon.com, you can get it at $76. The investment on the part of the publisher for such a work is small. The author uses a scientific word process, LATEX, to bring out a formatted, printer ready computer file for the book. The software package has a steep learning curve. Apart from a few general comments from two reviewers and the contact editor, the author does the editing and copy-editing tasks. He also provides a fully formatted index. In the past the author submitted a complete draft of the text and the publisher provided the expert manpower to finalize the print version. Now such tasks are farmed out to the author, thus doubling the time spent on the manuscript. In this age of print-on-demand publishing, publishers do not maintain a large stock, thus reducing inventory costs. And for each book sold, there is a handsome profit to be made.

In financial terms, there is not much for the authors as the royalty is pitifully small. The out-of-pocket expenses I incurred for writing the book were not reimbursed. In the first five years after publication, I got about $200 per year from the sales, and in recent times, about $100 per year. The benefits are indirect. They include professional prestige, invitations to conferences and the like. At UCLA, where I was stationed when I wrote the book, books do not count towards promotions; only the papers published in peer-reviewed journals in your own field do.

Unless you are one of the few whose books become standard texts for commonly taught courses at many universities, academic publishing of quality texts is essentially a labor of love; and a backbreaking one too. In the setting of the universities in Tanzania today, expecting a professor to devote the unremunerated, extensive time and effort required in such a task is literally to expect a miracle. The commercial ethic drives him or her into well reimbursed consultancy projects or team-research projects where the time investment is hardly onerous.

I give one example. I was approached by a colleague at MUHAS to take part in a WHO funded evaluation exercise about malaria research. It required a team of three experts, a malaria specialist, a public health expert and a biostatistician. I was to serve in the latter capacity. Our job was to evaluate and write a report on WHO funded projects in Tanzania. I inquired about the mechanics of on-site visits. That was not necessary, I was told. We get written reports for the projects and we would write a report on these reports. For a two-week exercise, the amount available was $10,000. My share would be $3,000. Yet, without site visits, it is not possible to evaluate such projects. Was the study protocol adhered to? Were quality control measures in place? Were the personnel adequately trained? Did any major obstacle arise? Was data entry done accurately? You need to compare what is in the forms and research logs with what is in the computer file and the report. Otherwise, the job is a superficial and possibly misleading one. Why did WHO set such low standards for assessing the quality of the work it funds? As these questions were not resolved, I declined to participate in the project.

Yet with two weeks of minimal desk-bound effort, I could have earned more than I have got so far for the book on which I spent seven years. Indeed, under-development and academic under-education do not augur devotion to academic excellence.

Media Council of Tanzania, Tanzania: After I started teaching statistics courses at the UDSM in 1971, I took a keen interest in the reporting of education, health, economic and agricultural statistics in newspapers. Between 1975 and 1980, I focused on transport statistics and from then on, on health and medical statistics. I kept a large pile of relevant reports from local papers. They became my sources of examples on the use and misuse of statistics in the media. Over this time, I wrote commentaries on this issue for some local papers and magazines (Hirji 1993a; 2007a; 2007b; 2007c).

Especially after 2005, I was disturbed by the extremely poor quality of the reports containing education, health, economic and other statistics in the Tanzanian papers. Basic items like sums, percentages, rates and indices were erroneously presented. Interpretations did not reflect the data and varied from paper to paper. For example, after the release of National Form IV exam results, the headline in one paper would say *'Girls trounce boys'* while another paper would claim the exact opposite. Each had selected its own data subset and way of summarizing it.

The Media Council of Tanzania (MCT) is a non-governmental body mandated to monitor the ethics, rights and conduct of media personnel, quality of reporting, and the relationship between the media and state agencies. All media entities in Tanzania, private or public, are associated with the MCT. It publishes a quarterly magazine, periodic reports and booklets. Each year, it presents awards to journalists, media workers and media entities judged to have shown good performance on relevant matters. A part of its annual budget comes from the local media firms and other companies but the bulk is from grants from European nations and organizations.

In 2011, I approached the executive secretary of MCT to discuss my concern on the quality of statistics in the media. It was then decided that I should write an educational text on basic statistics for journalists. MCT would publish it and use it for training purposes. After expending two to three hours daily over fifteen months, it became a reality. The title was *Statistics in the Media: Learning from Practice* (Media Council of Tanzania, Dar es Salaam, 2012).

Unlike my previous book on statistics, the main part of this book was devoid of mathematical symbols and formulas. These were relegated to a short appendix. Each chapter had a good number of examples of local media reports with statistical information that were used to explain key ideas like percentage, ratio, average and variation. The quality of data interpretation in the reports was analyzed and explained. My aim was to make it accessible to journalists with a secondary school level exposure to basic mathematics.

My work involved research, organizing media material, acquiring and reading relevant books and papers and planning and writing the book. But I went a step further. I used my knowledge of LATEX to format and typeset the final computer file that would be sent to the printer. This was a time consuming task. Close attention was needed to ensure that the printed pages would emerge without a minor blemish. I also produced the index. A computer graphics expert at MCT designed and formatted the book cover. I interacted with him to modify his initial proposals. And instead of transmitting the print ready file to the printer by email, I went to their plant in person and worked with the technician for a couple of days to make sure that the printed work was of the desired quality. Only after I had an initial sample in hand did I rest my laurels. There is no point in leaving the final step to chance. In our setting, you run the risk of undoing all your efforts.

As a non-commercial entity, MCT does not pay royalties to authors. It gives a lump sum fee for completion of assigned tasks. I had no idea as to the total budget for this project. My contract entitled me to a fixed fee of $5,000 for the delivery of the manuscript. I was not compensated for the additional formatting, typesetting and other tasks though they were separately budgeted for. But I had no complaints.

The task of copy-editing the final document was to be assigned to an expert editor. At first, I asked a professor of linguistics to assist us. She said she normally charged Tsh 30,000/= (approximately $15) per page. For a book of three hundred pages, that would come to roughly $4,500. I was astounded. In two weeks, she would get about as much as the author. I knew her well and she was willing to reduce her normal charges by a third. But even that was too much. Then

I contacted an editor from a local publisher I had worked with on another book (see below). He was from the US but he charged only $800 and did a fine job. This incident indicated to me the extent to which local university experts are now conditioned to easy money from foreign funded NGOs. Had I not insisted on reducing the costs, she may well have secured what she had asked for.

My impression was that there was a generous budget for this project. Besides printing costs, the MCT official overseeing this work and others probably secured handsome compensation. Two external experts were asked to evaluate the book in professional terms. One was a veteran Tanzanian journalist and another, an academic from the UK who had a good level of familiarity with agricultural and economic statistics and had taught at UDSM years back. Their task was to write a brief overall report on the manuscript. Both gave highly glowing reviews. Each was paid $1,000. But the British academic found himself in a dilemma. Should he charge a poor nation such an amount for work that did not consume that much of his time? He told me that he did not want any compensation. But the funds were there. If not him, someone else would get the sum. So I advised him to accept the check and use it for some worthy causes here.

I recall one incident. I had gone to the MCT for routine consultations. As the meeting ended I was asked: `Professor, how did you come here?' I said I had come by public transport and would return home by it as well. I did not need a refund as the total cost would just be TSh 800/= (less than a dollar). My hosts were aghast. Why do you take such trouble? I was admonished. Immediately, I was ushered to the cashier's office and handed TSh 100,000/= for future transport needs. And for that day, a taxi cab was summoned and paid for, making the ride home a comfortable one.

Once the printer had delivered the goods, a launch event sponsored by the MCT was held. There were speeches and good food. The event secured good publicity in the local media. I was hopeful. The effort to improve the quality of statistical reporting in our media could begin in earnest.

As this book was fully paid for, there was no question of making a profit. As an umbrella media organization, it was the responsibility of the MCT to distribute copies in sufficient numbers to the local media groups and newspapers free of charge and provide copies to students taking journalism related courses, their instructors and members of the public at a low price. At the outset, I was informed that this indeed was the plan. But some months on, I found that none of that was being implemented. Journalist after journalist informed me he or she had not seen the book. I had told the MCT officials that I was ready to lead educational seminars at various media establishments to introduce the book. And I would do it free of charge. Yes, professor, we are working on it, I was told that each time I contacted them. After a while I learned that MCT was selling the book at TSh 20,000/= per copy. Why? The money was needed to print a few hard bound copies. But that too never happened.

Predictably, there were no buyers. No student or instructor would pay that amount. At most, they would pay one-fourth of the price. The only bookstore in the city which had a few copies on the shelf sold it at TSh 30,000/=. After a year, it had sold only a couple of copies and did not order more.

Essentially, the stock gathered dust in the MCT storage area. I had to do something. The UK based academic reviewer had handed his $1,000 compensation to me for use as I pleased. I used it and my own funds to buy, at 50% wholesale discount, seven boxes of the book. They were distributed free of charge to journalists, students, teachers and other interested people. I attended public gatherings on national and media affairs to distribute fee copies. Other than through such efforts, hardly anyone has got a copy. Other than a brief mention in a short course on media statistics, no educational event relating to it has been held. The quality of statistics in much of the media has hardly improved, though I have the impression that one editor took note of my criticisms and tried to remedy the quality of statistical reporting in his paper.

Why the lack of progress? Organizations like the MCT which get their funds mostly from foreign sources in the form of grants work from project to project. Once the funds for a particular project are utilized, they move on to the next one. Unless the activity has long term funds, the incentive to continue does not exist. It is a logic accepted by the funders and the recipients. For the local experts and officials, it is a money-making game. Do the work, get your check and move on. It is not your job to deal with the effects on the ground. You did your job as per your contract. That is what counts. And too often, it is a substandard job.

On my part, I remain a frustrated statistician. I have a high opinion of this book. I have not found another book that presents statistical practice and theory in an African setting in an accessible way, has a progressive, scientific perspective, and has a wide range of examples from African and international media. It secured good reviews in the local media and the Pan-African Pambazuka News. It pains me to see all that effort come to a naught.

Mkuki na Nyota Publishers, Tanzania: I have published three books with this publisher. The first was as the editor of essays about the history of a radical student magazine at UDSM (*Cheche: The Reminiscences of a Radical Magazine* – 2011). The second was my childhood memoir (*Growing Up With Tanzania: Memories, Maths and Musing* – 2014) and the third was my first novel (*The Banana Girls* –2017). I retired from my teaching work in July 2012, and thus had more time for the books I had desired to write for quite some time.

Mkuki na Nyota Publishers (MNP) is the successor of the state owned Tanzania Publishing House (TPH). But the management has remained the same. From the 1960s, TPH made a local and international mark by bringing out a good number of high quality fiction and non-fiction books in Swahili and English. The former included works by Adam Shafi, Ibrahim Hussein and Hamza Sokko.

The latter included numerous scholarly works on African and Tanzanian history, culture, society and economics. It co-published the path breaking work by Walter Rodney, *How Europe Underdeveloped Africa* (Rodney 1972). The books in the Tanzanian Studies Series shone in terms of progressive orientation as well as scholarly analysis.

In recent times, MNP has published literary works for children and adults in Swahili and English, and memoirs by local authors and political personalities together with scholarly books on the history and social and political situation in Tanzania. Some of them are of a Pan-African scope. In addition there have been a few science and medicine oriented books. Other books have addressed legal, educational, cultural, traditional and religious topics.

MNP has in some ways adhered to the foundation laid by TPH, but it has also been affected by the commercial pressures of neoliberalism and the phenomenon of under-education. Books sales have plummeted. Not many bookstores carry what it publishes. While its flagship shop on Samora Avenue remains the best bookstore in Dar es Salaam, the customer base has gone down sharply. Books are costly; books do not sell; priced are raised; sales go down further. Apart from short novels for children, other books are priced above TSh 10,000/=. More and more, it is the tourists and visitors, and less and less the locals who buy books at the MNP store.

A major problem is the cost of printing books locally. Despite the extra shipping charges, it is cheaper to have books printed in Turkey or China than in Dar es Salaam. The overseas printers are more dependable and provide books of a better print quality. A book from Kenya normally costs less than a comparable book published and printed here. The absence of import duties on books is a key factor. In order to deal with this issue and reduce warehousing costs, MNP installed a good print-on-demand machine. But it is manufactured according to US specifications and often malfunctions with regard to the type of paper and ink available, quality of binding and photography. The reliance on external printers has thus not abated.

The books published by MNP fall into two categories: sponsored books and non-sponsored books. The first types of books do not entail a financial risk. The sponsor, usually an externally funded NGO, or at times, a local business or political foundation, pays an upfront fee to the author, and covers the printing and related costs. The outlay is minimal. The publisher secures an adequate profit even before a single book is sold. Such books are a gold mine. MNP tends to bring them out as a matter of priority.

The non-sponsored books emanate from manuscripts submitted by the independent authors who lack a big daddy. If accepted, they face greater delays and are often not as well attended to. None of the books I published with MNP had a sponsor. For each, I incurred out of-pocket expenses ranging from $700 to $1,500. I had to contact people from my past, photocopy old records from the dusty trunks in my house, produce photographs, pay research assistants and buy computer supplies.

My overall experience with this publisher has been a positive one. I worked with its staff closely to ensure that each book was of the desired quality. Its cover designer did a splendid, creative job in each case. An American editor based then in Dar es Salaam was contracted by MNP to edit the first book. His charges were reasonable and I was satisfied with the job. But for the second book, his quote was more than twice of that for the first. Apparently, he had got wind of the super payment the NGOs gave to local editors and did not want to be short-changed. Instead, an editor resident in Beijing was contacted. She had worked in Tanzania a few years ago. Her charge was $700. Yet, her editing was thorough and meticulous. No detail escaped her attention. I was truly impressed at the time and quality of effort she put into the task.

I am told that that has been the usual MNP experience: local editors charge an arm and a leg but their work leaves a lot to be desired. Editors from South Africa and elsewhere provide a better service for half or less the charge. MNP looks out for promising young graduates for training to edit manuscripts and other publishing associated tasks. But apart from graphics work, the experience has been a mixed one. Some high school graduates from private schools do a better job than the UDSM graduates who have on-paper fine bachelor's degrees in English or Swahili. The interns are with the firm for short periods. And those hired on a full time basis tend to move on once they have obtained the experience to land a better paid job with an NGO. MNP cannot compete with such deep pocketed entities.

After their launch, my first two books secured a good exposure in the media. But the subsequent sales were disappointing. Marketing was a part of the problem. MNP does not send copies to potential reviewers. Its website is not maintained. The sale prices were beyond the budgets of teachers, university students, professionals and members of the public, the potential local market. My first two books are priced at TSh 25,000/= and TSh 30,000/=. In these trying times, only a rare Tanzanian will fork out such a sum for a book not related to a study program or a specific work related task.

The outcome for the third book, a short novel based on the plight of the street vendors of an African city, has been more disappointing. The final manuscript was delivered on time in May 2017. Cover design and a printer-ready pdf file were produced within two weeks. According to the contract, printed copies would be available in Tanzania in four months. MNP markets its books internationally via the African Books Collective (ABC) platform. On demand printing makes it possible for MNP books to appear in the global marketplace within a week of the delivery of the pdf file. And that is what happened with all my books including *The Banana Girls*. By July 2017, you could buy this novel directly from ABC or from outlets like Amazon.com.

Hence a person in the US can get it readily. But it is hardly an option for a Tanzanian reader. The price ($25), even by US or UK standards, is too high for a short novel. Shipping cost would increase the amount by 50% or more. More than two years on, it is not on sale in any bookstore in Tanzania. I think just a hundred copies have been sold, mostly in the US. Why the delay? The key reason is that it is not a sponsored work. During this time, MNP has brought out many sponsored books. A book meant for readers in Tanzania and East Africa thus faces the possibility of never seeing the light of the day here. As the author, there is nothing short of taking costly legal action I can do to correct this clear violation of contractual obligations.

Another problem I encountered with MNP was on royalty statements and royalties. Each year, I got them only after repeated reminders. And it takes a special effort to get a royalty account for the ABC sales. In the past two years, I have lost the energy to pursue it and have not received anything from MNP.

Not that it makes a major difference. For the first two MNP books my annual check never exceeded 300,000/= (or $150). At today's prices it barely suffices to cover the grocery bill for my family for a single month.

Daraja Press, Canada: My last two books *The Enduring Relevance of Walter Rodney's How Europe Underdeveloped Africa* (2017) and *The Travails of a Tanzanian Teacher* (2018) have been published by Daraja Press formerly based in Montreal, but now in Ottawa, Canada. The present book has the same imprint as well.

Daraja Press, a small publishing house essentially run by one person, thus far has twenty five titles on its website. Specializing in books about Africa, they cover issues relating to Africa and Africans in diaspora, African and Soviet history, progressive novels, poetry, cultural affairs, oil politics and climate change. A few titles are in French, Portuguese and Swahili. The distinctive feature of the books is the solid, progressive perspective they present. A number use the Marxist analytic framework.

With limited resources, it depends upon the author to deliver an error-free manuscript. I sent my first book with Daraja Press to an editor who charged a nominal fee. For the next book, my daughter, my wife and two unpaid reviewers pitched in. I also sent a reasonable sum to Daraja Press to help defray the cost of cover design and waived my royalty.

The first book was reprinted locally under an agreement with MNP and is available in its bookstore. But printed copies of the second one are not available here; the transport cost is prohibitive. There is, though, a fine silver lining. The basic goal of Daraja Press is to bring out and disperse broadly progressive visions and analysis for the liberation of Africa as well for cultural enrichment. It allows authors to distribute the e-versions of their books free of charge to anyone they like. Where authors are agreeable, the books are placed on commonly accessed book websites. I have used that opportunity to circulate both my books with Daraja Press widely across Tanzania, East Africa and beyond.

Otherwise, Daraja Press has to improve its performance with

regard to sending review copies and making effort to get wider publicity for the fine books it has been bringing out.

THE NEW MEDIA

Books demand attention and concentration. You venture in a book in a paragraph by paragraph, page by page fashion. They encourage deeper thinking. Even escapist fiction requires a systematic read, a disciplined approach.

The electronic devices with on screen material, Internet access and social media connections, on the other hand, not just enable but also encourage the reader to dispense with such traits. You momentarily are on a page, then jump to a hyperlink, then to another until you lose track of where you began. Or you are swept aside by a WhatsApp chat, an SMS, or a call. Or you return to the video game or music video you had been glued a while back. Unlike the book you hold in your hand, the slick device has too many attractions for you to resist for long. You tell yourself that you will take a temporary break from the electronic book or article but end up shelving it for days or months.

The discipline required for reading books is a learned activity. It has to be cultivated at a young age. But the young ones now are exposed to electronic devices — video games console, television, smart phones and computers – around the same time as they begin to touch books. The former are more exciting. Books are boring, unless someone reads them to you in an entertaining style. The too-busy adults are also ensnared by the electronic media. After a stressful day, they would rather have the naughty kid do something that will keep it quiet and out of mischief than demand their undivided attention. The electronic devices are the modern day baby sitters, perhaps more dependable than the human ones.

The extent of exposure to electronic devices at a young age worries child psychologists, educators and neuroscientists. Is it affecting brain function in a profound manner? Is it rewiring the brain? Will the ability to focus on a physical or mental task be seriously impaired? Will what they believe and how they think be shaped by the few corporate behemoths whose basic aim is not to inform or educate but to entertain and make a profit?

These issues are an increasing focus of scientific research. While we cannot draw clear cut conclusions, a consensus is emerging on some effects on human cognition and memory. Information overload and a fast flow impair attention span and in-depth contemplation. New information provides a thrill but if acquired regularly reduces retention and adversely affects memory. In 1998, about 10,000 Goggle searches were done per day. Now that number is close to 5 billion. Why remember when you can get all you want instantly?

Modern technology improves multi-tasking skills and the speed at which tasks are completed but at the expense of creativity and long term intellectual growth. Ever immersed in it, we fail to observe and gain from the richness of social and physical environments. Social media are as addictive as addictive chemicals; approvals from our contacts provide the highs. More contacts are gained but the singular benefits of close personal interaction are lost. The human brain adapts to regular use of electronic media and the Internet. Brain circuitry is changing. Excessive usage of smart phones and computers may increase the incidence of Attention Deficit Hyperactivity Disorder.

Computers enable students to create a polished product that does not represent the underlying effort. They become dependent on technology for the smallest task. Their spelling, grammar and handwriting skills are impaired. Most students do not back up their data. Software or hardware problems thus entail a loss of all that the student has. Students from well to do families have better machines and Internet access at home. Use of computers has brought forth new forms of academic dishonesty that can be suspected but difficult to prove. Being fixated to the screen for hours is socially isolating and deprives the students from benefits of interactive learning (Schreiner 2019; see also Chapter 7).

While groups like the isolated elderly may benefit from exposure to the goings on in the outside world, children and young adults are at a greater risk from the negative impact of modern technology. Overall, the evidence emerging from studies on such issues is not encouraging, to say the least (Burnett 2016; Carr 2008, 2010; Perry 2016; Simpson 2008; Small and Vorgan 2008).

In the under-developed nations, the children do not have as much of an exposure to electronic devices as those in the richer nations. But here the book culture is weak, the system of under-education denigrates and deprives them of books, and depravation on all fronts stunts mental development. Yet, the trend is that households struggling to make ends meet have a cell phone. Donor funds pour electronic devices into the system of education without due thought and an overall plan. An actual experiment in chemistry is replaced by watching a screen simulation. In this setting the effects are, in some ways, more deleterious. Modern media in schools and colleges in Africa fail to make up for the loss caused by the absence of textbooks, reference books and practical activity.

A couple of years back I had an occasion to converse with a lecturer in English Literature at UDSM. She told me that when she was pursuing her undergraduate and post-graduate studies in Germany, it was normal for the professor to begin a course by handing out a list of ten to twelve required readings and a few additional recommended readings. Some of these books were daunting to paddle through. She had taken four not-that-voluminous books, two of which the students should have read in Form VI, to her class at UDSM. Immediately, a groan of disquiet ensued. `How come the other classes set only two books?' They asked. But that was not the case at the same university in the 1970s.

Over the past twelve years, in the addition to the students at MUHAS, I interacted in person with many students and recent graduates from UDSM and some high schools in Dar es Salaam. They had degrees in journalism, law, mathematics, statistics, and engineering. I gave books to some of them and requested them to write reviews and reports in English. Yet, I did not find a single instance where I was satisfied with the grammar, mode of expression, consistency and logic in what they wrote. Mostly, it was strewn with an odd form of the language.

A Tanzania athlete, who had performed well in a long distance race in London in 2018, was interviewed by a TV reporter there. The manner in which he framed his reply embarrassed the Tanzanians living in London and left the athletes from neighboring Kenya in titters. Compare that with what was said by the Tanzanian marathoner John Stephen Akhwari at the 1968 Olympic Games in Mexico City. He had courageously reached the finish line despite sustaining a serious injury mid-way. His spirit and fine words made him an international symbol of bravery in sports and earned him the title: *A King Without a Crown*. (Hirji 2014, page 246). As some commentators have observed, over these fifty years, we have developed a unique language, Swanglish, which is heard not just in the street but also from politicians, journalists and academics (Macha 2008; Msemo 2018).

The Tanzania Commission for University (TCU) has the mandate, among other things, to set and protect the academic standards at the universities in Tanzania. When you visit its website, you find a short welcome message from Professor Charles D. Kihampa, the Executive Secretary of TCU. The first paragraph of this message is reproduced below:

> It is my pleasure and gratitude to welcome you to our website. We at Tanzania Commission for Universities (TCU) trust that you will find this website superbly informative, educative and appealing to the high growing demand for knowledge about university education in Tanzania and beyond. (www.tcu.go.tz, accessed 16 May 2019).

The reader may judge what this extract (and the entire message) reveals about the usage of English language in this nation.

THE BOTTOM LINE

Reading and writing are complementary human activities; one cannot flourish without the other. Together with the printed book, they form a crucial component of the intellectual and technical foundation of human society. Without these three components, the education system as we know it could not have come into being. In the three decades past, however, each one of them has come under a strong attack due to the proliferation of computers, small electronic communication devices, the Internet and social media platforms. (Fisher 2004a,2004b; Manguel 1997).

With nearly five thousand universities and two year colleges enrolling millions of students each year, the US leads the world in terms of access to higher education and utilization of electronic technology. Though this system is afflicted with profound ideological miseducation, it provides rigorous training in discipline based areas like natural science, medicine and related fields, mathematics and statistics, engineering, languages and literature to hundreds of thousands of undergraduates, has cutting edge post-graduate programs and conducts advanced class research. Yet, the deleterious effects of neoliberalism and misuse of computers are evident here as well. By leaving undergraduate instruction to under-paid, overworked adjunct faculty, costs are cut but at the expense of pedagogic quality. Other than at a few, mostly elite, institutions the study programs inhibit critical thinking, complex reflection, reading and writing. Studies show that in 1961, college students spent on average 25 hours per week studying beyond the classroom. By 1981, it had gone down to 20 hours per week and presently it is at 12 hours per week. Reading requirements have been lowered as students spend longer times online. Most of the spare time is devoted to non-educational pursuits. Attrition rates have increased and now on average it takes a longer time to get a first degree in US. Yet, fees have skyrocketed as the administration arm has grown faster than the academic arm. The upshot is that education related debt in the US now stands in excess of $1 trillion, more than national credit card debt. (Grafton 2011).

In Africa, the academic situation is at the bottom of the barrel. The universities barely function as universities, and reading and writing skills are weak across the board. Nonetheless, talk is cheap here. Everyone pontificates on the importance of reading, writing and books in education and society. But these activities face great obstacles that are far from being addressed. Local funds are not provided to improve the situation. Without an external savior, little is done. I surmise:

- Administrator and bureaucrats lacking vision or commitment in conjunction with external funders who have their own agenda set policy priorities.

- Educators and students, especially at the higher levels, are paying much less attention to the printed book and academic journals than is required for sound education.

- University students learn from PowerPoint projections, Internet browsing and fast perusal of computer based material than from books.

- The high cost of books, poor state of bookstores, types of books at hand and the manner of usage of the libraries are key parts of this conundrum.

- The NGO culture fosters intellectual and material dependency, and distorts the flowering of an autonomous, indigenous book culture.
- It does not pay to write. Serious writers without a financial backer face such a stiff battle that only a few venture in that direction.
- Seasoned academicians have abdicated writing books in favor of lucrative consultancy and report generation projects.
- The volume, quality and contents of the English language books written by local authors in Tanzania are deficient compared to that in many other nations of Africa.
- We have an abundance of Tanzanian hip hop (bongo flava) music stars. But we do not have literary stars. Modern Tanzanian authors do not stand out even in terms of what they write in Swahili.

Yet, at the end of the day, it is a mistake to blame technology for these problems. Technology is wielded by humans. Technology can be used for a good purpose or be abused to serve narrow or shallow interests. I liberally employed computers and Internet sources for teaching courses in universities in Tanzania, the US and Norway. However, the manner in which teachers prepare their class material is not necessarily the way by which students should learn it. I directed my class towards reading the course books and course notes, and related papers so that they would grasp the essential concepts, be able to apply them where needed and understand the finer aspects of various topics.

I was brought up and educated in a setting where book reading and serious reflection were essential ingredients of education. The university students of today lack that background and, on their own, are unable to exercise the needed prudence. They are directed into avenues that stifle intellectual growth and independent learning. Memory and cognitive skills are adversely affected. Creativity and adapting what is learned to nonstandard conditions is compromised. Neither theory nor practice of any value ensues. Only under-education prevails.

While the population of Dar es Salaam has grown more than five-fold compared to that in the 1970s, the number of bookstores and libraries, and the availability and quality of books has not kept pace. Except in a few corners, use of books in higher education and independent reading of books is almost dead. They have been supplanted by social media chats and superficial surfing of the Internet. University graduates lack critical reasoning skills, originality of expression and practical work, and are unable to write in a cohesive, logical manner in any language.

Ultimately it is the system of neoliberal, dependent capitalism that has brought us where we are. The dominant positions of computer and electronic communication and information conglomerates in the global and local economies together with the positions on these issues adopted by senior educators and policy makers who are subservient to that state of affairs are propelling us into an educational and developmental abyss. A balanced, practical utilization of books and traditional venues together with computers and Internet sources for basic and higher education thereby cannot be conceptualized and put into practice without tackling the broader political, economic and social tendencies.

13

EDUCATION AND EDUCATORS

SUMMARY: Many educators and experts in pedagogy have postulated what they regard as the basic tenets of good teaching. After decades of standing against the blackboard, I too have formulated what I consider as six key principles of sound teaching. Recognizing that teaching is an evolving profession, I present them to stimulate a debate on the role of teachers in transforming the prevailing system of under-education into one that will produce the critical thinkers, and competent professionals needed by Africa.[1]

*

---

1. This essay was first published as Chapter 10 in Hirji KF (2018) *The Travails of a Tanzanian Teacher*, Daraja Press, Montreal. This is a revised and edited version.

*The best teachers
teach from the heart,
not from the book.*
Author Unknown
++++++++++

NO SET-IN STONE GOLDEN RULES for good teaching exist. Teachers with diverse and even contrasting approaches manage to deliver sound, sustainable education to their students. Yet, anyone who has stood in front of a blackboard for decades tends to develop what he or she sees as key principles of effective teaching. While the recipe will vary from teacher to teacher, much common ground will exist.

In 1987, AW Chickering and ZF Gamson enunciated seven principles for good undergraduate level teaching that have garnered extensive publicity (Chikering and Gamson 1987). They are: (i) Encourage contact between students and faculty; (ii) Develop reciprocity and cooperation among students; (iii) Encourage active learning; (iv) Give prompt feedback; (v) Emphasize time on task; (vi) Communicate high expectations; and (vii) Respect diverse talents and ways of learning. The Walker Center for Teaching and Learning at the University of Tennessee at Chattanooga has generated a detailed guide for university instructors which is based on these principles. With numerous case studies of teaching at different colleges, it is a valuable tool for instructors in the institutions of higher learning everywhere. (Walker Center 2019).

After teaching for over four decades in such places, I have formulated my own set of basic principles of good teaching. While I generally concur with the Chikering and Gamson principles, I have come to place a rather different emphasis on the issue. Their principles focus on how to teach; I bring in what to teach as well. In my book, sound teaching is based on: (i) Love your subject; (ii) Respect your students; (iii) Maintain high academic standards; (iv) Practice and require ethical conduct; (v) Integrate theory with practice; and (vi) Inject extraneous material. They are elaborated below. In addition, I delve into the specific challenges to effective teaching in the environment of under-education. I do not expect universal agreement with what I present, or with the relative stress I put. Rather, I offer it as a contribution to the dialog on teaching that needs to continually go on among educators, students, parents and citizens. Teaching is a dynamic profession.

1. LOVE YOUR SUBJECT

A teacher with a deep attachment towards his or her subject is not easily forgotten by the students. They can sense whether you teach because you have to or because you want to. Your demeanor in the classroom will reveal how enamored you are with the topic. And that spirit will also infect your students.

The love of what you teach will keep you learning about it for as long as you teach, and later on as well. It will lead you to avoid teaching in a routine fashion. You will be driven to introduce fresh perspectives on the topics you cover as you go along. And occasionally you will relate some material beyond the curriculum and stray into novel realms.

I strove to keep up with the developments in the field of theoretical and applied medical statistics. During the long vacations, I upgraded my lecture notes and changed the reading material. It never seemed like a burden but just a part of who I was. I can thereby confidently affirm that:

> *I was still learning when I taught my last class.*
> Claude Moore Fuess

2. RESPECT YOUR STUDENTS

As a teacher, you have a responsibility to play your part in the process of the development of your students as human beings. Your job is to shape their knowledge base and skills, and mold their attitudes towards their profession and the world at large.

Your students are your second family. You have to be attentive to their pedagogic problems and personal concerns, and be flexible when it is warranted. They should know that you care, and are always willing to listen and act appropriately. A teacher who just comes to class, says what he has to say and disappears neglects a basic part of his job, namely, to engage with the students after class. It is only through such interactions that you can come to know your students well, monitor their progress and modify your pace and style accordingly. Each group has its own characteristics. Do not assume that what worked last year will suffice this year.

I informed my students that my job was to help them learn the course material. I had a designated two-hour period each week when they could come to my office for individual or group consultation. Those who could not make it during that time because of clinical duties or other reasons made separate appointments. It was an unusual thing at the Muhimbili University of Health and Allied Sciences (MUAHS). Because of the large size of the class, a line of students would regularly form at my door. If a student failed to take a test due to family emergency or illness, I would set a separate test for him or her.

Ensure that you fulfill what is expected from you. Prepare and give out course material, electronic or printed, ahead of time. Do not deviate from the schedule announced in class. Be punctual; be present in your office during the class office hours and appointment times. Correct and give feedback on assignments and tests in a timely way. With a large class size and no teaching assistants, it is a tall order. But when you do what you are supposed to do, the students will tend to keep their side of the bargain. They will know that you respect them and in turn they will respect you. Overall, I agree that:

> *The secret in education lies*
> *In respecting the student.*
> Ralph Waldo Emerson

3. ADHERE TO HIGH ACADEMIC STANDARDS

Being helpful to the students as much as possible does not, however, imply compromising academic standards. While you go the extra mile, at the end of the day, they have to demonstrate that they have put in the effort needed for the subject. If they do not, they bear the consequences. There can be no exceptions on this issue.

Substandard, easy exams were routinely set at MUHAS. But I did not set easy tests or exams, and my grading was strict. As a result, I was able to exercise a distinct effect on student performance. After the initial year, they realized that in my course it was possible to fail the second supplementary final exam, and be disbarred from the degree program. It was an unheard of phenomenon. Word filtered down to the new batches. Attendance in lectures in the following years rose to almost 100%, and the students took the course material more seriously than when passing this course was a guaranteed thing. A few lecturers were heard to complain that the students were paying excessive attention to my course and neglecting other courses.

At the outset, many students, at UCLA as well as MUHAS tended to be unhappy at my demanding requirements. They would complain but to no avail! But once the course was over, quite a number would thank me for making them undergo the arduous drill: 'Professor, we really learned something.'

Teaching statistics as a series of routine numerical techniques to be applied to standard settings inhibits intellectual development and opens the subject to misuse in practice. While medical and health students need not know how to mathematically derive the formulas, they should understand the meaning and rationale behind their use. In my class, I told the students that I did not want them to just memorize the formulas but to grasp the basic principles underlying the application of statistics to health and medicine.

At UCAL and MUHAS, my tests and the mid-term exam were thereby always open book, open-notes exams. They could bring in any printed or written material for the exam. Though, computers and cell phones were not allowed. Especially at MUHAS, that took the students by surprise. However, after the first test, when their expectation that it would be plain sailing were shattered, they began asking more questions in class and more attended the office hours. Though setting such tests entailed more work on my part, it was a necessary aspect of teaching the subject as it should be taught. If the university regulations had permitted, even my final exams would have been open-book exams.

At both universities, I saw instructors who taught easier material and gave substandard exams with routine type of questions. It lessened their work and earned them cheap popularity. Because of the breakdown of the system of external examiners at MUHAS and lack of student evaluation, they easily got away with a poor job. Many of today's students prefer such instructors. Those who make them sweat become quite unpopular.

Once a group of students approached me to complain about the final exam given for a course I was not involved in. They claimed that it did not reflect the material that was taught and wanted me to raise the issue in the meeting of the Examiners' Board. My reply was:

> I know that nearly a third of the lectures in this course were not given. At that time, none of you complained. Now that the exam is not to your liking, you are upset. I am doubtful about your seriousness towards education. Sorry, I cannot help you.

In comparison, in the 1960s and 1970s, maintenance of standards of instruction and examination were not sidelined at UDSM. The instructors in all the faculties and disciplines demanded a lot from their students. It was the norm. There was no grade inflation. Though the pass grade was 40%, it required hours of backbreaking work on a daily basis to pass any course. A First Class degree was a rare event. With a bachelor's degree from UDSM in those days, you could compete with graduates from the best global universities.

Sadly, that is no more. In these high-fee paying days of instant gratification, instructors face strong pressures to compromise quality and inflate grades from parents, students and administrators as well as from their own colleagues. Diploma mills abound. Academic transcripts that indicate distinctive performance are common. Yet, even a person with a doctoral degree from UDSM or MUHAS now generally demonstrates a level of intellectual attainment and maturity that is more deficient than an honors level undergraduate of the earlier era.

And lax grading of degrees is a world-wide trend that also affects the hallowed universities in the UK as well. In the past, a first class degree was an uncommon mark of distinction. Nearly 30% of the graduates in the UK are now being awarded a first class degree. Commentators see this as an implicit way to justify the exorbitant fees charged to students these days. You paid for it, so you get it. It also attracts more students to the institution. (Gill 2019).

In India the practice has reached an extreme level. Thus, the Dean of Law School at Delhi University, a well-regarded university, tendered her resignation because her efforts to alter the anti-academic and unethical practices of the administrators had failed to bear fruit. She said that student assessment bore little relation to performance. You passed no matter what you did.

> *The professor alleged, among other things, that students with as low as 31% attendance were being allowed to take exams and were being given marks for attendance in the name of tutorials never conducted.* Jain (2019).

Particularly in this era of unbridled commercialism in education, it is very important to underscore that:

> *What all good teachers have in common, however,*
> *is that they set high standards for their students*
> *and do not settle for anything less.*
> Marva Collins

4. PRACTICE AND REQUIRE ETHICAL CONDUCT

As a teacher, it is your fundamental obligation to advocate a high standard of ethical conduct and adhere to it. You should never engage in favoritism, be it for financial, personal or other reasons. You should not cut corners in research or misrepresent your work. Your conduct inside and outside of class has to be guided by uncompromising intellectual and moral integrity.

Sad to say, breakdown of ethical norms is a common affliction in the modern academy. Not just the students but the academic staff too fall prey to that pernicious bug. I note one example.

In the year 2000, a student in the Master of Public Health program at MUHAS approached me for assistance in relation to her research project. It concerned people receiving antiretroviral drugs for HIV infection. I do not lecture in this program and was not her supervisor. But I usually do not decline to help a student. I soon realized that though she was one of the top students in her cohort, her knowledge of research methods and data analysis was poor. Given the number and types of lectures they had been given, one could not expect more. Thus I spent many hours instructing her on the basics, and improving her research proposal. There was no *bahasha* (supervisory allowance in the form of an envelope stuffed with cash) for me for this work. That was for her designated supervisor.

Then she went off into the field. Three months later, she was back in my office, now with a thick report in hand. She wanted me to read it and give comments before it was finalized. As I perused it, I was astonished. It was a first class, well organized report with a fairly large number of subjects. Data analysis, illustration and interpretation had been done in an appropriate manner. A novice had accomplished in three months what it would take a team of qualified professionals a year or more to do.

I was not fooled. It was not her work. She had obtained outside help. Perhaps the data were in large measure manufactured. I politely told her that I had already provided sufficient assistance to her and it was the responsibility of her supervisor to comment on and approve her report. She passed with flying colors and I never heard from her again. As for myself, I was demoralized and dejected. All that effort ground to dust. As I walked home that evening, I wondered if the leadership of public health in our nation is falling under the hands of experts who have been educated in this style. Where are we going?

5. INTEGRATE THEORY WITH PRACTICE

When teaching any subject at any level, it is essential to maintain a balance between ideas and facts, between the general and the specific, between theory and practice. This precept applies whether you are teaching carpentry or surgery, mathematics, history or biology. And the balance has to be maintained in a dynamic fashion from beginning to end.

The manner in which a discipline or craft is visualized or practiced by professionals in the field does not necessarily represent the ideal way through which newcomers should be taught. Both for slow learners and the bright students, a one-sided emphasis on one aspect or the other of the subject interferes with the learning process. It can also be counterproductive.

Applied Statistics (medical statistics, transport statistics, education statistics, business statistics or agricultural statistics) is typically taught as a series of standard techniques for handling a set of numbers. The instructor outlines a statistical procedure, applies it to an example, and proceeds to the next one. You waddle through one hour of drudgery to another. Most examples are routine and contrived. The student is tasked with memorizing and applying the techniques when needed. For most students, the subject is banished from the mind as soon as the exams are over.

And this is the alienating approach under which medical statistics is taught in all the study programs at MUHAS, and in general, across the world. Yet, it can be taught by organically integrating it into the applied field. Both at UCLA and MUHAS, I taught Medical Statistics with a subject matter article based approach. Each lecture took off from perusal of one or two health related papers, electronic copies of which had been distributed beforehand. The required readings had reports of research on conditions like polio, malaria, childhood diarrhea, ear infection and so on. A key criterion for selecting an article was that it had in some fashion utilized the statistical tool or method I wanted to cover in class on that day.

I did not begin my lecture with formulas or numbers. Instead, I would discuss the substantive issues in the article. Given their medical or health related background, the students would be readily drawn into the discourse. The statistical issues and numbers would naturally arise in the process. It was a means to make the students realize that they were essential for a complete understanding of the article and the health questions at hand. And often I would critically analyze it to indicate how the study and data interpretation could be improved. My ultimate goal was to convince the class that a basic grasp of the major principles of statistical thinking was a prerequisite for the sound and effective practice of their professions. On this matter, most students were skeptical at the outset. But, by the end of the course, I felt that many had changed their attitude towards statistics (see Chapter 8 for details).

6. INJECT EXTRANEOUS MATERIAL

While subjects are taught separately, reality is not compartmentalized. The biological and physical realms, including human life at the individual and social levels, exist and develop as integrated processes. Human health embodies physics, chemistry, biology, numbers, psychology, economics and sociology as a complex, dynamic entity.

When teaching any subject, especially at the university level, it is imperative to make the students aware of the wider ramifications, even as doing it may entail stepping beyond the formal curriculum. I hold that such digressions are a necessary part of understanding the subject. It also promotes the evolution of the student as a socially responsible and competent professional.

My courses on medical statistics at UCLA and MUHAS integrated the actuality of statistics in the real world. I informed my class about the numerous cases of misuse and abuse of statistics in medical research and published papers. I showed how a poor grasp of research methods, conflict of interest, the drive for fast promotion and commercial motives compromise research quality even in industrialized nations. I stressed that statistics is about seeking the truth about a usually complex reality. Without strict adherence to the ethical norms in research and reporting, the ensuing numbers are not just worthless but potentially harmful to human health too.

Dealing with such issues engaged them at a personal level and improved their critical thinking skills. A number of students I met years later thanked me for making them aware of the deeper realities of health research.

In addition, I dealt with the history of medical research and the major contributions of statisticians in the development of research methods and addressing ethical matters like fairness, balancing risk and benefit, and informed consent. The central role played by statisticians in the discovery of the placebo effect in medicine was covered as well.

And I did not neglect to mention the role played by some statisticians in undermining good quality research. I recall the Discrete Data Analysis course I taught at UCLA in 1996. The twenty five or so students were either in the Master of Science in Biostatistics or Master of Public Health program. In one lecture, I reviewed a published paper on assessing the efficacy of a drug for the treatment of a particular chronic condition. The study, done at a US university, was funded by the drug manufacturer and its statistician had been involved in data analysis and interpretation. By a detailed reanalysis, I showed them that the method used for data analysis was inappropriate, and interpretation of the results was biased. Data were analyzed using an outcome measure that exaggerates the benefits but masks the adverse effects of the drug. Commercial considerations had skewed the study.

At this juncture, two students, one an American and the other from China, raised a question:

> *Professor, are you not bringing politics into the classroom?*

I responded in a forthright manner:

> *Well, it depends on what you mean. The pharmaceutical sector is one the largest employers of statisticians today. When you graduate, you may land a job in that industry. In your data analysis, will you compromise the interests of the patients to those of your employer? Will you violate your ethical obligation to adhere to the norms of scientific integrity in research? My job as a teacher is to show you sound methods of analyzing data and make you aware of analysis methods that can produce misleading results. If you call that `politics,' then I am guilty of injecting politics into statistics.*

The class found my response satisfactory. After that the other instances of scientific misconduct I gave generated an engaged discussion. And once in a while, doses of humor and fascinating episodes from the history of medicine punctuated a technical presentation. Well chosen, timed digressions produced a richer learning process. I enjoyed them and the students did too.

> *The best teachers are the best story tellers.*
> *We learn in the form of stories.*
> Frank Smith

TACKLING UNDER-EDUCATION

In the modern African academy, especially the Tanzanian academy, the state of under-education makes the task of the instructor doubly difficult. In the courses I taught at UCLA, the students, with the exception of one class, had a good educational background and were well motivated. My lectures could start at the required level without doubts on my part about their ability to comprehend what I was saying.

But that assumption did not apply to my recent MUHAS classes. The grades on a student's high school or undergraduate transcripts bore little relation to his or her knowledge of the prerequisites. The majority lacked the ability to write a paragraph in a coherent, logical manner. Their grasp of the English language was deficient. If I gave a paper from a journal of pediatrics to a student in a post-graduate degree program, I could not assume that he or she would understand it. If set a memory-based exam that required reproducing the basic facts, most would do well. But if I added questions needing interpretation of material from a journal paper and writing a comment, the scribbled answers often made little sense.

At all the stages of the course, I faced a major dilemma:

- How do I present ideas like absolute risk and correlation coefficient to students who have difficulties even with percentages and simple averages?
- How do I critically review a paper when what it says has not been understood by the majority?
- How do I set a test that not just tests memory but comprehension as well when I cannot understand the answers they give for the latter type of questions?
- How I raise broader issues relating to ethics and society when the foundation is so poor?

I dislike spoon feeding. It is a bad teaching style. But at times, I had no choice. The students at MUHAS had been conditioned to sailing through their studies with minimal effort. It was a given that most would get the degree. Only those showing extremely poor performance or attendance found themselves in trouble. Many instructors complained about the performance of their students. But at the end of the day, all passed. And more than the truly deserving ones secured high grades.

Effective teaching and maintaining high standards was a daunting but not an impossible task. I had to work doubly hard, and find ways and means to make the students also put in the necessary effort.

The Walker Center guide recommends team teaching as a device to improve the effectiveness of instruction. (Walker Center 2019). It is done in two ways: (i) A group of instructors under the direction of the course coordinator do the teaching. Each gives one or more lectures on his or her topic(s), sets a question or two for the exam and grades that part of the exam. (ii) A large class is split up into sections and each section is taught independently by one instructor.

The coordinator ensures that the instructors follow the syllabus and teach at the required level.

In the first way, the instructor is usually well versed in the topic he or she teaches. But responsibilities are diffuse and instructors do not come to know the students well and may teach at below or above the required standard. It needs an awareness of what came before and what will come after your lecture(s). Many basic science courses at MUHAS were taught in this fashion. And it was the preferred way. In practice, however, the way it was done was far from satisfactory. The coordinator handed out topics to anyone willing to teach them; meetings to plan, assess the progress and discuss the outcome were not held. You did not know the relative performance of the students with respect to what you taught. No lessons were learned as the cycle was repeated year after year.

Many instructors had a fixed set of slides they used to teach a topic in this or another course, at MUHAS or in an external class elsewhere. Not much attention was paid to the level of the course. It minimized our work. You gave the lectures, met your teaching responsibility for the semester and were free to travel for research and consultancy. If anything went wrong, you could always say that you were not responsible; you did what you were assigned to do. For the student, there were no office hours or means for further help. The coordinator did not take adequate steps to maintain academic standards in teaching and the exams. It worsened the problems of under-education, not resolve them.

The second way of team teaching was the one used for the medical statistics course I was involved in at UCLA (see Chapter 8). It reduced the problem of a large class size and enabled more individualized and level specific attention. The instructor was with the same students for a whole semester, came to know them well, could adjust what and how he taught by monitoring their progress, and bore the full responsibility for what transpired in his or her section. We held meetings to plan, monitor and evaluate the course as a whole and made recommendations for the new class. The coordinator supervised all these activities. Yet, some teachers did not follow the basic philosophy laid down and there were issues with adhering to the required standard. This way of team teaching was not adopted at MUHAS because it required the instructors to be present on the campus throughout the semester. It meant a loss of revenue from travel and the lucrative consultancy projects. Further, the academic staff numbers were insufficient for this purpose.

Well aware of the limitations of team teaching and the impossibility of having several sections, I always taught my courses at MUHAS on my own, even with the very large classes in the latter years. It gave me the opportunity to maintain the academic standards in a uniform way and I came to know the students well. It was an exhausting job but worth it.

Additionally, in a situation where the other instructors were inclined to set routine, substandard examinations and were lax in their evaluations, I faced a moral quandary as well:

- Was I treating my students in an unfair manner?
- Was I unnecessarily hindering their future careers?
- Could a person not be a good doctor even if he or she had poor understanding of medical statistics?
- How could one function in an ethical manner in an environment where ethical norms were sharply curtailed?

At the end of the day, I concluded that compromise of teaching quality cannot in the long run benefit our nation and the people. It was essential for all academics to adhere to high ethical and educational standards. And, I had to do the best I could. So I plowed on with my usual style.

At the end of the day, what I found distinctively encouraging was the presence of a fair number of motivated, diligent and able students. After each continuous assessment test, I gave a book prize to each of the four best performing student. It encouraged them further and others to do better in the coming tests. Over time, I saw them bloom into specialists who were compassionate and treated their patients with the best means at hand.

What was most discouraging was the lack of cooperation from other instructors. There was little concerted, common effort to adhere to the basic standards in teaching, student research and evaluation. Too busy with consultancy projects, they were discouraged by the large number of students in the class. The university administration gave little assistance. For example, with teaching assistants drawn from the pool of senior post-graduate students, one can easily handle a class numbering in the hundreds. But the big bosses refused to entertain such a proposal.

Keeping up that effort on your own, year after year, is emotionally and physically exhausting. It drains you. Thereby, due to age and illness, and a fast expanding class in which the background of the students was poorer year after year, I could not go on. I threw in the towel in 2012, and retired from formal teaching to focus on writing from then on.

Despite the minimal resources available in educational institutions in Tanzania and Africa, by standing together the academicians can tackle sub-standard student performance in the courses and research. The electronic medium can be utilized in a planned manner to deal with the dearth of books and instructional material. Strict standards in setting, supervising and marking exams can go a long way towards making the students aware that if they do not sweat, there will be no degree at the end of the day.

Being an effective teacher in the environment of under-education requires not just adherence to the basic tenets of teaching but also going an extra mile. Yet, it can be done. When you decide to call it a day, you can then say that you tried your best.

14

EDUCATION AND ACTIVISM I

SUMMARY: Learn to learn but also for change. Trying to change without learning will lead you astray. Historically, students have played key roles in the struggles for social justice. It has been a worldwide phenomenon. In Africa, the students of today mainly engage in two forms of activism: Work with NGO type of entities to assist disadvantaged groups in society and identity politics. This essay deals with the first form. Invoking an historic confrontation between the supporters and opponents of Rag Day at the University of Dar es Salaam, it formulates a radical critique of NGO type of philanthropic work. To move Africa towards social justice, equality and decent living for all, the students and academics should not just engage in reformist, palliative actions but need to challenge the prevailing neoliberal order and its progeny, under-education, at their roots.[1]

*

---

1. This essay derives from Hirji KF (2019a) Raggers versus radicals: Who prevailed? *Pambazuka News*, 5 February 2019, www.pamabazuka.org. This is an edited version.

I'm for truth, no matter who tells it.
I'm for justice, no matter who it is for or against.
I'm a human being, first and foremost,
and as such
I'm for whoever and whatever benefits humanity as a whole.
Malcolm X
++++++++++

THE YOUTH DREAM AND HOPE. Unhappy at what they see around them, they desire a better world. It is as true today as it was yesterday. But what they dream about and how they try to achieve their dreams change over time and place. The struggles of the youth of South Africa in the 1980s is distinct from their struggles today; students and academic staff in the UK, Germany, France and Mexico have staged protests against hikes in fees and reduced state funding in the recent years, but in the 1960s they fought for peace and social justice.

The African youth of today are attracted to charitable activities to help people in need. Life in Africa is permeated with philanthropic efforts that are pursued under the umbrella of non-governmental organizations (NGO). Numbering in the hundreds, they deal with a myriad of causes that range from support for street and disabled children, assisting persons with HIV infection, empowering women and girls, improving education and health services, giving free legal service to the poor, supporting marginalized communities, protecting Albinos and the elderly, and providing health education to promoting civil rights and media freedom.

The existence of NGOs is now seen as a natural state of affairs. In this era of high unemployment, young people, especially university graduates, compete to land an NGO job. University professors and experts yearn to land a consultancy assignment with them, as it needs little effort and is quite lucrative. You take part in the activities of an NGO not because you believe in the cause but for the benefits it confers. These NGOs, which function in a fragmented manner, get most of their funds from Western nations, UN agencies, international organizations and individual donations abroad. In addition, most African nations are highly dependent on external funding in the form of grants, soft loans and foreign investments for their economic development and social projects.

On the domestic front, fund raising activities for schools, health clinics, disabled children, people affected by natural disasters and a host of other causes occur on a regular basis. Newspapers feature stories of politicians and ministers soliciting donations for schools. Banks, mining companies and other firms build classrooms and donate school supplies; religious bodies urge their followers to remember the poor on special occasions; wealthy individuals visit shelters for blind and disabled kids; office workers have fund raising walks to help children with disabilities, and so on.

The better off should help those who have been left behind. The fruits of economic progress should be shared among all members of society, locally and globally. This spirit, which pervades the charitable activities, is accepted by the providers and recipients, and permeates our national fabric. I call it the humanitarian spirit.

Others disapprove. Conservatives proclaim that regular assistance to the poor and needy, especially by state bodies, only makes things worse. The poor are behind because they avoid hard work and sacrifice. Automatic handouts make them lazier and drive them towards anti-social conduct. This is the conservative spirit.

The progressives, for their part, declare that the poor need jobs and investments and provision of right kind of training to meet the challenges of modern life, not just charity, public or private. On the international front, they say that aid should be supplanted by trade and investments from abroad. That is the only way to raise living standards in the poor nations. This is the progressive spirit.

There is, however, a fourth spirit towards charity which I denote the radical spirit, which differs in a critical manner from these three spirits. But it is now largely forgotten, in Africa as elsewhere, even though it had begun to gain prominence in the 1960s and 1970s.

The first part of this essay aims to illuminate the nature of the radical critique of philanthropy through a discussion of an event that occurred in 1968 at the University of Dar es Salaam (UDSM). I hold that only the radical approach can lift Africa out of the state of underdevelopment and mass poverty. This event shows a concrete manifestation of this spirit at an African university.

RAG DAY

On this Saturday, the 9th of November 1968, a cool breeze blows on the hilly campus of the University College, Dar es Salaam. With no lectures today, the place remains sleepy. Though, there is a major exception: some 300 students, nearly a quarter of the student body, are wide awake by 6 am and stand at the cafeteria door as it opens for breakfast. From their attire and demeanor, it is apparent that they are not a unified group. The majority have put on torn or funny looking clothes while those in a smaller sub-group, about a tenth, are dressed as students here usually do. The two groups have contrasting intentions. The former are set to embark on a festive, seemingly virtuous course of action while the latter have a plan to sabotage, in a decisive way, these festivities.

I refer to Rag Day, by now an established, much anticipated annual event at this campus. It is a day set aside for the students to raise funds for a worthy charitable cause. They plan to march through city streets, a tin in hand, to solicit donations from passersby and merchants. Dressed in tattered clothing or clownish costumes, they will shout, sing, bang their tin cans, dance here and there, as they beg for money. It is for a good cause, they say. And they have official sanction, from the city offices and the university administration. The latter provides the vehicles that will transport them to and from the city center.

Before examining what transpired at this campus on that fateful day, let us first look at the general history of Rag Day.

ORIGIN AND ESSENCE

The wiki-dictionary, (en.wiktionary.org), defines Rag Day as a day on which `*university students do silly things for charity.*' It appears to have originated in England in the later part of the nineteenth century. The name stems not so much from the rags adorned by the students but by their tendency to rag (hassle, pester) members of the public in the process of eliciting money.

By the 1960s, Rag Day was a regular event in universities across Britain and some other parts of the world. The first Rag Day in Africa was held at the University of Pretoria, South Africa, in 1925. After the former British colonies gained independence and established their own universities, they too began to hold Rag Day.

Rag Day continues to be staged at many universities today. At times, it is a part of a larger event called Rag Week. Though the way in which it unfolds varies from place to place, the essence is the same, to raise funds for charity. In the UK, annual funds raised during Rag Day are estimated to range from five to ten million pounds. At the University of Pretoria, Rag Day is staged with musical and festive events and raises funds that are allotted to about 200 charities. Means other than a street march are also employed. In Singapore, Rag Day is enjoined with major national celebrations (National University of Singapore 2011; Orr 2012; University of Pretoria 2012).

In the past, Rag Day was associated with rowdy, drunken, disorderly and anti-authoritarian behavior. This type of conduct has been brought under control in most places. Rag Day has gained more respectability. Some universities in Nigeria, though, are an exception. Their students tend to be quite unruly. Many dress in a shocking style. Allegations are rife that instead of being channeled to charity, the money they raise is pocketed by the students (Buzznigeria 2018; EduAfrica 2015).

Yet, in Africa today, Rag Day persists only in a few nations. In several places, it died a natural death. It is only at University of Dar es Salaam that it died a sudden death. And that happened not due to an edict from an authority but stemmed from a defiant act on the part of that smaller of group of students.

It is to the story of the why and how of the undoing of Rag Day at this university that I turn to. My aim is to highlight the distinctive stands on charity emerging from this episode and underscore their relevance to the problems of economic and social development of African nations today.

THE UNDOING OF RAG DAY

We return to 1968. Rag Day at the Dar es Salaam campus is organized by the Tanzania chapter of the World University Service (WUS). In the week preceding the event, cyclostyled posters advertising the event are pinned on all noticeboards:

> UNIVERSITY COLLEGE RAG DAY
> HARK! W.U.S. IS SPEAKING!
> The World University Service (Tanzania) Committee has sought and obtained permission to hold a RAG DAY on
> Saturday, November, 9th 1968.
> The event will consist of a fund-raising procession for the benefit of the Msimbazi Children's Centre. Some students will adorn and ride floats, while others will solicit offerings from Embassies, Government Offices and Business concerns along the route.**Departure:** Opposite the Cafeteria at 7.30 a.m., on buses and lorries.
> **Itinerary:** Upanga Road, Jamhuri St, Uhuru St. to the Cloak Tower, Independence Avenue to the Askari Monument, Azikwe St., City Drive, Shaaban Robert St., Independence Avenue back to the Askari Monument, Makunganya St., India St., Upanga Road back to the University College.
> STAFF STAFF STAFF STAFF STAFF STAFF
> University College Staff will be visited in their offices and at their homes on the previous day, Friday. Please note: paper money is easier to handle.
> STUDENTS STUDENTS STUDENTS STUDENTS
> At least 150 students are required to carry out this good work. Sign up IN THE COMMON ROOM OF YOUR HALL so that you will find place in one of the vehicles which is[?] provided for transport, and be PUNCTUAL on Saturday morning. The more, the merrier!
> Dress in RAGS of every color and description! Rehearse your calls and songs! Plenty of noise is required! Name tags and tin cans will be provided to collectors.
> Only twenty percent of the proceedings[?] will be retained to cover incidental expenses and to promote other worthy causes.
> EIGHTY PERCENT GOES TO MSIMBAZI.

An interview with WUS (Tanzania) chairman, S. Amos Wako (a student from Kenya, later to become the Attorney General of that nation), is prominently featured in the student magazine, *The University Echo*:

> Mr. Wako stated that the `Rag' celebration was an important event in most universities of the World.
> It had two aims one, to provide room for relaxation for the students, staff and administrators, and the other to raise funds, 80 percent of which went to the needy, he said.
> Mr. Wako stated: *The World University Service believes, as its name implies, that the university should serve the community in which it is created.'* The Standard (1968a).

This promotion of Rag Day does not sit well with a small group of radical students organized under the umbrella of the University Students' African Revolutionary Front (USARF) and the campus branch of the youth wing of the ruling party, TANU Youth League (TYL). In the evening before the event, USARF holds a meeting in which Rag Day is the sole topic on the agenda. After an extended debate, they resolve in unison that it is not compatible with African culture and the desire of Tanzania to build a society based on socialism. Rag Day needs to be stopped, one way or another.

In the morning of Rag Day, they are the first ones at the cafeteria door. After the meal, they head to the parking area nearby where the vehicles that will transport the Raggers stand. They gather chairs, wooden logs, dustbins and other objects to erect a makeshift barrier at the exit of the parking lot.

A few set about deflating the tires of the parked vehicles by letting out air. One has a sharp pocket knife, which he uses to puncture one tire of a mini-bus. The drivers of these vehicles, who are gathered in a corner of the parking lot, do not intervene or say anything. Having done their deed, the radicals stand in a defiant mood in front of the barrier.

My memory has it that these anti-Raggers included Jonathan Kamala, Andrew Shija, Bernard Mbakileki, Ally Mchumo, Salim Msoma, Ramadhan Meghji, Issa Shivji, Karim Hirji, Charles Kileo, S Mdundo, J Moronda (Tanzania), Yoweri Museveni, Eriya Kategaya, James Wapakabulo (Uganda), Kapote Mwakasungura (Malawi) and Kabiru Kinyanjui (Kenya).

As the Raggers enter the parking area, they are in for a shock. Their vehicles cannot move; the exit is blocked by a human, physical barrier. An extended confrontation between the two sides ensues. But it is all a verbal exchange; there is no physical contact or violence. The Dean of Students appears on the scene about an hour later. His attempt to make the radicals stand down is met with deaf ears. Though he can order the campus guard to dismantle the barrier, he is in two moods about it. On the one hand, he opposes what the radical students have done. On the other hand, he fears the political consequences if he acts harshly. After all, these defiant fellows are shouting in the name of the official policy of socialism, and he may be seen as an opponent of that policy.

A short while later, two vehicles with armed policemen descend at the site of the fracas. Their commander tells the radicals to move aside so that the barrier can be removed. But they remain defiant. Andrew Shija, the TYL chairman, is bold enough to lecture him about the Arusha Declaration and why Rag Day is incompatible with the national policy of Socialism and Self-Reliance. Like the Dean of Students, he is unsure of how to deal with the situation. His training tells him that he should arrest these troublemakers and remove the barrier by force. But what will his superiors think? Will be accused of violating the national policy?

Reluctantly, he makes a decision. There is a threat of public disorder here, he says. Rag Day is suspended. The stunned Raggers have no recourse but to return to their halls of residence. Fearing further defiance from the radicals, the Dean of Students also cancels the Rag Day dance party that was to be held that evening. It is a total victory for the radical students. After this day, no Rag Day was celebrated at this campus.

When land was requisitioned for the university campus, it came with a large cashew nut farm (*shamba*) on the outskirts. The farm shows signs of years of neglect. Of recent, USARF and TYL members have started working at the *shamba* during weekends. It is a purely voluntary effort, clearing weeds and overgrowth, and harvesting the nuts. The proceeds from the sales are donated to the African Liberation Committee based in Dar es Salaam. In the aftermath of the Rag Day debacle, USARF/TYL invites all members of the university community to participate in this and similar efforts. The funds raised could be sent to the needy children's center in the city as well.

To help others, students should show their commitment by engaging in ongoing practical work rather than just begging in the streets once a year, they declare.

The radicals stood against Rag Day without seeking approval from any authority, on the campus or beyond. It was a risky decision as we could have faced serious disciplinary action from the administration or even arrest by the police. We stood for our principles and were saved by the prevailing spirit of socialism in the nation and not by any person in high authority.

PROS AND CONS

During the next two weeks, the controversy about Rag Day and its demise takes center stage at the campus and in the national print media. Most students, academic staff and administrators oppose the action of the radicals. While the official media maintain a discrete silence on the matter, the main (British owned) English language daily (*The Standard*) pens a strongly worded editorial castigating them as political saboteurs who have no concern for disadvantaged children. These two weeks feature a lively but heated exchange between the two sides in the Reader's Forum section of this paper. To its credit, despite its editorial stand, the paper gives adequate space to both sides. Thus, the issue of 17 November 1968 has four letters, two for each side. The longest letter gives a militantly worded defense by the USARF chairman, Yoweri Museveni.

The principal points presented by those who support Rag Day are:

- The Raggers are motivated by a desire to help needy children.
- There is nothing wrong if they also have fun in the process.
- The radicals are a bunch of ideologically blinded, self-serving political opportunists.
- Instead of mounting a dramatic action, they should have worked with the organizers of Rag Day and reached a compromise acceptable to both sides.
- Moreover, they have been misled by a few foreigners with no

concern for the people of Tanzania.

The last accusation is ironic: The accusers are not Tanzanians. It is not pointed out that WUS, the Rag Day organizing group, is a foreign funded entity whose local chairman hails from Kenya and whose local patron is a British academic at UDSM. While WUS officials receive financial support from abroad, USARF has no internal or external funder.

Such nationalistic proclamations are but a ruse to divert attention from the main issue. Being a part of the young University of East Africa, this campus has students and staff from many nations. USARF/TYL members have an internationalist spirit and know that no nation or race has a monopoly over good or bad conduct.

The arguments advanced by the radical students and their few supporters among the academic staff note the following points:

- USARF/TYL members support the provision of assistance to needy children.
- But that assistance should be provided by the rest of the society as a matter of right and not in the form of occasional handouts by the privileged.
- And it should certainly not be done in a way that makes a mockery of the destitute children.
- The main long term aim should be to struggle to eliminate poverty, not just occasionally throw crumbs to the poor.
- Charitable actions like Rag Day actually to underpin an unjust and unequal social system by providing a safety valve to release the built up pressure, and give legitimacy to those who have amassed ill-gotten gains.

The case for the radical side is cogently summarized by Andrew Lyall, a law lecturer, in a letter to *The Standard*. It is reproduced in full below.

> If socialism is an attitude of mind, it is clearly an attitude which editorial writers, in spite of their nominal adherence to national policy, are totally unable to comprehend. Your leader on `Rag Day' leaves this beyond doubt.
>
> Charity has a necessary function in Western countries only because of the defects of the capitalist system. Socialism certainly does not preclude charity. If we are interested in making the lives of the Msimbazi children not merely `a little more comfortable, a little brighter' but in solving the problem, that will not be done by people dropping a few shillings in a tin. It serves only to indulge the hypocritical emotions and deepen the hypocrisy of those whose concern for the plight of the orphans goes so far as the change in their pocket, but stops short of any policy that would make a real impact on their standard of living.

To be an orphan is to feel left out of society, a feeling that is increased not lessened by receiving donations from charity. The children of Msimbazi need to be adopted by the nation, to feel that everyone is their father.

If existing Government funds are not sufficient to solve the problem, one does not have to look far to find additional sources. The more fortunate members of society will have to become somewhat less fortunate.

Your statement `it is not shameful to wear rags to solicit funds from others' misses the point. It is not shameful to wear rags if that is all you have to wear. But for others to put them on as fancy dress for a carnival when they are surrounded by those for whom they are, of necessity, daily wear displays at the very least gross insensitivity to their feelings.

The children of Msimbazi have their dignity too. It is not to be insulted by patronizing handouts from the `fortunate'. Nor should attempts be made to divert revolutionary students from their purpose by a squalid appeal to bourgeois sentimentality.

Andrew Lyall
University College
Dar es Salaam
The Standard (1968b)

In advancing their views, USARF/TYL stood together with the eminent the US civil rights leader, Dr. Martin Luther King, Jr.

True compassion is more than flinging a coin to a beggar; it comes to see that an edifice which produces beggars needs restructuring.
Martin Luther King

WHO WON?

Did the action taken by the radical exercise a long term impact?—That is the question. And the answer is a resounding `no'. While that battle of 1968 was won by USARF/TYL, looking around Africa today, it is abundantly clear that the supporters of Rag Day have prevailed. Even in Tanzania, where no Rag Days are held, the spirit enshrined in Rag Day has taken a firm hold among the youth, the intelligentsia and the political establishment.

The punitive conservative spirit, which blames the poor for their own predicament also makes itself felt now and then, as when the authorities round up beggars and street children and repatriate them to their home villages. Some voices in the media concur with such harsh deeds (Mwita 2010). But overall they have a limited scope, and do not affect the prevalence of the patronizing Rag Day type of spirit in the social fabric.

The socialistic spirit whereby people join hands in mutual

solidarity to construct a society founded on the principles of social justice and equality, where adequate nutrition, good housing, clothing, appropriate health care and education are enshrined and implemented as basic human rights, where people with disabilities and special needs are adequately taken care of by the state, where grassroots democracy prevails, and where the people of Africa stand on their own feet, and not be dependent on the crumbs from external entities, sadly that spirit has waned considerably.

The ethic of capitalism, neoliberalism has triumphed. Africa continues to be dependent on largess from the so-called donor nations and institutions. To members of USARF, begging was an affront to human dignity. Yet today our leaders perpetually stand in front of the `donors', with their hands outstretched without any sense of shame.

An example: Former President Jakaya Kikwete of Tanzania proudly declared in October 2010 that he was the first leader from Africa to gain an audience with the US President Obama. He went on to say with elation that President Obama had promised to `*flood our nation with assistance*'. (Mwendapole and John 2010). Earlier, after being criticized for making too many trips abroad and that with a large contingent, he defended himself by claiming that it was because of his trips that the previous US president George Bush had promised to give sufficient mosquito-protecting bed nets to cover each and every Tanzanian child.

The economic policies of African nations are geared to attract external funds on a continuous basis, further entrenching the tentacles of dependency which extend to all facets of society, agriculture, industry, transport, education, health, media, culture and political organization. External entites lay down how things should be for us in all the aspects of our lives. Once in a while, an NGO finds itself in trouble with the state authority. Yet, it is always a transient situation and does not affect the NGO culture as such.

Walter Rodney noted that the enhancement of the ability of a people to determine their own lives is a basic feature of economic development. Despite a modicum of economic growth, Africa has become more and not less underdeveloped over the past three decades. The little industrial capacity built up after independence was dismantled as a result of the neoliberal onslaught. Tanzania is one of the world's largest producers and exporters of cashew nuts. But the nuts are exported in raw form as most of its cashew nut processing factories were idled after privatization. It has as well not developed the capacity to extract the valuable oils and chemicals from the nuts. Many such examples exist.

The current embrace of aid has a profoundly negative impact on how we view our own capabilities. Instead of instilling confidence in our ability to determine our future, attitudes of meekness and submissiveness towards outsiders prevail (John 2010). A word from a foreign entity to provide a basket of funds is portrayed in the private and state media in exaggerated, celebratory terms. For instance, the *Nipashe* Special Supplement (2010) depicted an agricultural loan from India as the savior of our farmers. Today the prediction remains far from being a reality. But no one talks about it anymore.

In reality, such loans and grants are a means for the external powers to secure a greater economic foothold and market for their companies, gain investment opportunities and enhance their image, especially in this era of a highly competitive climate between China and the West. And the `aid' always damages the capacity of African nations to determine their own destiny.

> Aid has never been just about helping people. It is also realistically about gaining influence in the world and exercising soft power. Providing aid money can generate valuable access and generate a sympathetic cohort of people who can be called upon to further down the line. Chesseman (2019)

A large body of literature on the deleterious effects of foreign `aid' exists. The pioneering work of Hayter (1971) depicts its structural impact while Hancock (1994) has numerous illuminating cases that demonstrate the fundamentally flawed nature of `aid' projects. Of the many other works of relevance, I note a few: Bah (2014), Barker (2017), Caufield (1997), Chery (2012), Hudson (2003), Lagan (2018), Moseley (2015), Nyikal (2005), Polman (2011) and Serumaga (2017).

Even the devoted promoters of foreign `aid' proclaim that it is of major benefit to the providing nations (Cheeseman 2019, Gates 2017).

> A more stable world is good for everyone. But there are other ways that aid benefits Americans in particular. It strengthens markets for U.S. goods: of our top 15 trade partners, 11 are former aid recipients. It is also visible proof of America's global leadership. Popular support for the U.S. is high in Africa, where aid has such a dramatic impact. Gates (2017).

This actuality is hidden by the mass media. People in Africa regard the `aid' as a heavenly blessing. More than half a century after attaining political independence, the majority in Africa states live under insecure and substandard economic conditions. The small scale farmers remain at the mercy of a volatile external market while the urban dwellers, even the educated ones, find it extraordinarily difficult to land a reasonable, long term job and try to eke out a living from a highly competitive, unreliable petty trading environment.

The blame for Africa's predicament is placed wholly and solely on the shoulders of its corrupt leaders, past and present. People say that the out of goodwill, `donors' from outside have poured hundreds of millions of dollars into Africa. But instead of utilizing them for the benefit of the nation these leaders squandered them for their own benefit or used them in inappropriate and inefficient ways.

But, it is forgotten that the `donors', like the World Bank, the UN agencies, the bilateral organizations and other agencies of the West have been with Africa since the first days of independence. They have been centrally involved in policy making and determination of the type of economic projects but they have little to show in terms making a major difference in Africa and much to show in terms of how their nations and organizations benefitted. If there is blame to be placed, they deserve at least half of it. Further, hardly anything is said about the havoc created on the continent by the myriad of external military `assistance' programs.

The NGOs often have `experts' from the 'donor' nations who lack qualifications and experience for the tasks involved, and who come to Africa ease their conscience. Their intentions notwithstanding, they live in exclusive compounds, enjoy the tropical holiday and accumulate good sums to fund a mortgage back home. Yet, the ordinary people, officials and intellectuals here treat them as if they are demi-gods—the bearers of the mighty dollar. What ensues is a progressive cycle of dependency, denigration of our own experts and expertise, self-recrimination and loss of self-confidence (Hirji 2007a, 2007b; John 2010; The Citizen Reporter 2010).

Such attitudes are reminiscent of the attitudes towards the rich and charity among the working people of Britain that were aptly captured by Robert Tressel a century ago (Tressel 1914; 2012). The workers were resigned to whatever the fate held in store. Any talk of an alternative to the existing state of affairs was rejected outright.

SYSTEM CHANGE NOT CHARITY

Charity, aid or philanthropy at the international and domestic levels, serves an essential long-term purpose by providing legitimacy to an unjust and exploitative socioeconomic system. Whatever the stated intentions of the providers, it functions like a pressure release valve of steam engine to prevent explosive occurrences. Their stranglehold over the economies of Africa and its people go on. Foreign funding in the education sector primarily functions to produce graduates with who have limited intellectual, practical and political horizons, and perpetuates under-education. (Iqbal 2019; Moloo 2018; Moseley 2015; Todhunter 2012).

The talk about creating jobs or focusing on trade and investments for poor nations also misses the mark. Neo-liberal capitalism thrives on low wages. It needs a large pool of unemployed or semi-employed people. The types of trade and investment opportunities offered to poor nations are meant to extract resources and economic surplus and enhance their dependence on external forces.

Meaningful African liberation requires a decisive severance of the bonds of material and intellectual dependency. And, in that matter, an essential point must be stated with clarity. Although one talks of `them' and `us', it should be understood, as the radicals of the past did, that the question is not that one of race or skin color. It is one of basic economic structures, international and national; of class relations and social systems. Africa needs internally propelled system change, not external charity (Hirji 2017; Rodney 1971b).

African liberation has to be founded on three basic principles: socialism, regional cooperation and regional self-reliance. Instead of being mired in seeking solutions within the confines of the current neoliberal system, African youth must have bold dreams and think in terms of a fundamental transformation (Tandon 2019). That was the vision of the radicals of the earlier era, and it is a vision that the youth of today must adopt.

The technological capacity to resolve all the critical problems facing humanity have been present at least for half a century. But it is the strangle-hold of the rich and powerful classes and nations over the state, politics, media and thought process that have prevented that capacity from being utilized (King 2010; Sunkara 2019).

The anti-Rag Day action of the radical students of that era was a part of their struggle to confront the prevalent system of under-education and the neocolonial political and economic system that gave birth to it. It was founded upon a concurrence with the vision of the great American civil rights champion:

> *The time has come for us*
> *to civilize ourselves by the total,*
> *direct and immediate abolition of poverty.*
> Martin Luther King

Let this be the cry of the African youth of today as well. For, the future of Africa and indeed, of humanity, lies not with the modern day do-gooders—the NGOs, local and external philanthropists, `aid' donors and their employees but with those who will boldly mobilize and organize the masses for a fundamental transformation of the neoliberal, capitalist economic system.

15

EDUCATION AND ACTIVISM II

SUMMARY: This essay continues the discussion of student activism begun in Essay 14. The focus here is on identity politics, the other major form of activism prevalent in society and university campuses today. After defining the notion of identity politics, describing its manifestations, it presents a radical critique of such politics, especially its tendency to fragment the people. African liberation requires broad grassroots level unity. Confrontations along ethnic and religious lines have created much havoc on the continent. Such divisions have come to the fore due to the hopelessness generated by the abject failure of the neoliberal system to improve the lives of the people. Instead of succumbing to such divisions, African students and academics need a unifying vision that promotes social justice and equality. Instead of identity politics and identity based social analysis, they need a scientific framework that will challenge both the prevailing neoliberal order and its progeny, under-education, at their roots.[1]

*

---

1. This essay derives from Hirji KF (2019b) Deconstructing identity politics, *Pambazuka News*, 16 April 2019, www.pambazuka.org. It has been edited extensively and some parts not related to student activism have been removed.

> *Our true reality is in*
> *our identity and unity with all life.*
> Joseph Campbell

++++++++++

IN FEBRUARY 2019, an Egyptian soccer team was scheduled to play a Tanzanian team for an Africa-wide championship. In the lead up to the match, the headlines in our papers declared: We will teach these Arabs a lesson. I wondered: Is Egypt not in Africa? Or, is only a person with a black skin truly African? In the 1970s, it was unthinkable for a Tanzanian newspaper to display such a racialist stand. Today, with the vibrant spirit of Pan Africanism of those days a distant memory, it is quite acceptable. It is an era of looking inwards, professing loyalty to people who are like you in one fashion or another, and forming narrower and narrower social circles.

Historically, people everywhere have located themselves, socially and psychologically, within distinct social groups. In this era of globalization, which was supposed to have brought people together, the practice has paradoxically reached a higher level. Other than race or color of skin, people are divided by gender, religion, ethnicity, language, community, politics, nation, and even things like profession, sports team and favorite cold drink. The pervasive electronic devices and social media multiply and entrenches such identities.

That persons with similar characteristics cluster is not a disconcerting outcome. Due to shared beliefs and practice, a Muslim or a Christian will generally associate with persons of his or her own faith. But when these clusters turn into arenas for hostility and conflict and when many hostile divisions prevail, it becomes a serious issue. All aspects of life are then framed in terms of us (the good ones) versus them (the bad ones). The desire to find common ground and compromise is constricted as people are embroiled in continuous conflicts over the rights, role and social status of their own identity groups. When not checked, antagonisms of this sort boil over into violent conflict with deadly outcomes.

This essay aims to disentangle the notion of identity politics, explore the justifications behind it, discuss the criticisms voiced against it and promote a socialistic perspective on the matter. After laying the basis of the topic, the attention for the most part is on identity politics at university campuses.

IDENTIFYING IDENTITY POLITICS

Besides personal identities, people as well possess a collective identity. You identify with those who share some feature(s) of your personal identity. They are your **identity group**. And you may have more than one group. Such groups have deep roots in history, social and economic structure and politics. Many identity groups emerged from long, genuine histories of exclusion, domination and discrimination in society. People from these groups unite to struggle for their rights and removal of social barriers they face. Not just the victims but those on the other side, the dominant groups, also form identity groups. Modern identity groups are a product of the history and nature of politics and social divisions within the national and global capitalist systems.

Some identity groups are active and some are passive. The former engage in what has come to be known as **identity politics**. According to the online Merriam-Webster dictionary, identity politics is:

> politics in which groups of people having a particular racial, religious, ethnic, social, or cultural identity tend to promote their own specific interests or concerns without regard to the interests or concerns of any larger political group.

Identity politics is contrasted with traditional party-based politics and is said to have attained its present form after the 1950s. But this formulation is unduly narrow in terms of scope and history. In the same dictionary Catherine R Stimpson gives a broader definition:

> Identity politics is contemporary shorthand for a group's assertion that it is a meaningful group; that it differs significantly from other groups; that its members share a history of injustice and grievance; and that its psychological and political mission is to explore, act out, act on and act up its group identity.

Identity politics plays a prominent role in the political arena, particularly in the Western nations. When women organized and began to struggle for equality and the right to vote, they engaged in identity politics; and so did people with disabilities when they united to demand better access to services and facilities. Identity groups based on race, ethnicity, gender, sexual orientation and immigration status have become more vocal and assertive. They hold public protest marches to voice specific grievances, demand their rights and official recognition of their status as equal to those of the others, and restrict their electoral support to politicians who explicitly declare sympathy with their cause. And the same holds for the majoritarian identity groups that are opposed to these set of identities, such as fundamentalist Christians and white nationalists in the US.

Both personal identity and social identity are not fixed, biologically constituted entities; they are complex, effusive social constructs, which moreover, transmute over time. Some personal and social identities are relatively more stable; but that is not due to genetics but reflects their social and economic positions in society. Accordingly, not all identity groups engage in identity politics. An identity group active at one time may cease to be so later. An identity group designation that has come to the fore of recent is

'People of Color.' Striving to unite dominated racial groups, it thus far is more of a conceptual construct that a practical reality.

EXAMPLES

A few examples of identity politics are in order. We start with the case of Tanzania. Decades of exploitative and unjust colonial rule led the people to unite and organize the struggle for independence. A shared language facilitated the evolution of a sense of territorial unity. Asserting their national identity, they now demanded the actualization of their right to self-determination. But there were complexities in this process as well. British colonialism, which utilized the policy of divide and rule, had generated significant social and economic divisions within the society. These divisions, based on race, ethnicity, region, gender and religion, persisted after colonial rule ended. Progress to counter these divisions and the resultant inequalities was made in the early days after attaining independence, yet they persist to this day. The chasm between Christians and Muslims, for example, comes to play in an underground form during the national elections.

Another case is that of African-Americans in the US. From the days of slavery to the present day, they were, and still are, victimized by varied forms of discrimination, overt and institutional, that leave most of them at the bottom rung of social ladder, lagging far behind the white majority in terms of income, jobs, education, health status and services, political and civil rights, treatment by the justice system and the quality of residential life. From those days onto today, they have fought against discrimination and for their basic rights. They are opposed by groups among the white majority who openly or subtly seek to retain the *status quo*. In their own ways, both are engaging in identity politics.

The year 2015 saw extensive eruption of xenophobic violence in the cities and towns of South Africa. Immigrants from other African nations, especially those running small shops, faced violent attacks, and their properties were looted. Many died. As it made front page news, the rest of Africa stood in shock. Tanzania had for decades supported, politically and materially, the struggle of the South African people for liberation. Even its citizens were not spared the vicious mob attacks. As South African politicians employ jingoistic rhetoric to garner votes, the attacks go on. It is a toxic form of identity politics. (Chutel 2019; Editorial 2019b).

In March 2019, an armed white supremacist stormed two Islamic mosques in New Zealand, killing 50 worshipers and injuring 41 others. As the killer's online manifesto indicated, he was driven by a hatred of Muslims and immigrants. The gruesome incident made headlines across the world. He was asserting his white European identity. His deeds were celebrated by extremists of similar persuasion in Europe and the US.

These examples underscore a critical point: Identity politics is a two-sided affair. It is broader that what is presented in dictionary definitions. Those at the bottom of the social ladder and those from the dominant social group engage in identity politics. In fact, the latter form of identity politics has a longer history, is more prevalent and often takes extremist or violent forms. The Ku Klux Klan in the US and the skin heads in the UK are two prime examples. The mainstream discourse on identity politics neglects this key point.

UNIVERSITY BASED IDENTITY POLITICS

The 1960s witnessed a robust outbreak of struggles against injustices of a diverse nature at university campuses across the world. Students in Latin America, Africa and Asia rallied against dictatorial regimes. In the US and Europe, they fought against the manifestations of capitalism and imperial military adventures. Within these overall struggles, there were sub-struggles conducted by specific groups. Women and disadvantaged minority groups, for example, strove to confront the injustices affecting them. These struggles were not confined to college campuses but were a part of overall struggles for social justice and in places, of the struggles for national self-determination. But the academia formed a key venue for the struggles (Ali 2005; Legum 1972).

At the university campuses today, the broader struggles have not only taken a back stage but have essentially been erased from memory. In a reflection of the political and economic transformation at the national and global levels, modern day students are involved in actions that relate to (i) NGO type of work; (ii) concerns about fees and living conditions; and (iii) identity group issues. This last form of action constitutes their primary political work. And that too is a two-sided affair with conservative and progressive factions pushing their opposing agendas.

One well publicized instance relates to historic monuments. Students in South African and British universities have demanded the removal of statues of Cecil Rhodes; students in Ghana and Malawi have called for pulling down of the statute of the Indian independence leader Mohandas Gandhi; African American students and activists in the US have agitated to dismantle the statues and monuments of figures from the civil war era who supported racist oppression; Native American communities and students have campaigned, successfully in some cases, for removal of symbols like mission bells and paintings of Christopher Columbus on university campuses in California and other states of the US that serve to glorify the genocide against the indigenous nations.

The demands by historically disadvantaged minority groups for equal opportunity and representation in higher education, well-paying jobs, the media, political institutions and other venues constitute another form of identity politics in the Western nations. Such demands are articulated on university campuses on a regular basis.

Restricting `hate-speech' is also a rallying point for identity based agitation. Should the academia provide a platform to people who have espoused extremist, derogatory views towards immigrants, Africans, Muslims, women, gays and lesbians? Identity activists want them to be banned, and quite a few universities have complied (Shah 2019).

At the universities of Tanzania and other nations of East Africa, identity politics has not assumed the degree of prominence it has garnered in the West. But the under-currents exist. Self-help groups based on regional origin and religion operate. A few years ago the students from mainland Tanzania at UDSM decried the perceived better financial assistance given to students from Zanzibar. The deep ethnic schism in Kenya that became a violent frenzy after the flawed elections in 2007 is also manifested in the academia.

THE CONSERVATIVE CRITIQUE

As it began to achieve prominence, identity politics came under attack from the left and right sides of the political spectrum. First consider the latter. It features predominantly in the media and political landscape. It declares that demands of minority groups have become unreasonable and stray into the realm of absurdity and social confusion. These groups are accused of wanting to `rewrite history' and rejecting compromise, even when it is reasonable. They just want their stand to prevail. In the process, they divide society into tiny enclaves, shatter cultural cohesiveness, pit ordinary people against one another and set the stage for unending social instability.

Aram Bakshnian, an American conservative, declares that his nation faces a divisive `*identity crisis*' as a result of `*identity politics run amok*.' (Bakshnian 2019). Ramnik Shah provides a lengthy, conservative attack on identity politics (Shah 2019) and declares that we live in `*bleak times*.' He also decries the importation of Western identity politics to Africa.

The conservative stand against identity politics has a degree of validity. I expand on this below. First, I note its limitations. One: It does not acknowledge the historical legitimacy of the demands for justice and equality and the generationally harmful effects of exclusion and under privilege on minority groups and dominated nations. Today, even when discriminatory practices are proscribed by law in the West, they continue in hidden forms and have a similar harmful effect. Institutionalized discrimination in education, housing, health services, employment, commercial services, shopping, etc., is an ingrained facet of life in the US and UK. (For details about schools, see Chapter 5 and 8).

Two: The right wing vision of identity politics is too narrow and uses a double standard. It only sees the strivings of African Americans, Latinos, women, Muslims and people of alternate sexual orientation as identity politics. Identity based political activities of the dominant groups are excluded from consideration.

Conservatives condemn violent extremism of the Islamic variety. But Christian, Hindu and Jewish religious fanatics do not elicit equivalent opprobrium or calls for combative action. Islamophobia prevails, overtly and covertly and in some cases in a virulent form, in all Western nations. Right wing politicians rally against Islam and Islamic culture. The ban or calls for the ban of the head gear worn by Muslim women is a typical example. At the same time, the manner of coverage accorded to Islam in the main media fans the flames of aversion. No wonder that a survey reported in February 2019 indicated that about a third of Britons felt that Islam is a threat to their way of life. Such xenophobic attitudes, which emanate from an illogical attachment to European identity, are however excluded from the rightist discourse on identity politics (Editorial 2019a).

Extremist white-race identity movements have a long history. With the rise of anti-immigrant hysteria, Islamophobia and fascistic political tendencies, they have increased in strength and influence, leading often leading to deadly ends. In his manifesto entitled General Identity, the New Zealand killer described himself as a person with a European identity and European blood. The two pillars of his white nationalism were hatred of immigrants and Muslims. For him, they were invaders who had to be eradicated.

Though the demands of the minorities and their rationale are opposed to those made by the majoritarian groups, philosophically the two views have the same basis: an exclusive loyalty to a particular group in society. By omitting the latter from the discourse, the conservative vision clearly employs a double standard.

HISTORIC MONUMENTS

There is no doubt that the statues and symbols of the past which have come under attack celebrate injustice, insensitivity and oppression. Yet, they are a record of the past. A plain removal simply erases memory; it does not serve to more accurately present the past. And it indicates the lack of confidence in the ability of people to make valid judgements about the past.

By just focusing on removal of such symbols, a golden opportunity is being lost. In my view, even the most egregious monument should be left in place. But its message should be countered with a prominent plaque stating the misdeeds of the person and describing the event in question. Other monuments that serve to give a balanced picture should be erected in prominent places. Further, universities in the US should run courses giving an accurate history of the genocidal efforts against Native Americans, slavery and its aftermath, suppression of working classes, imperial wars and the problems faced by modern day minority groups. They should be a part of the general studies requirements for undergraduate degrees. It would assist to counteract the miseducation embodied in the education system.

At times, the calls to demolish historic items stray into the realm of disbelief. Pulling down the statutes of the unrepentant imperialist Cecil Rhodes is understandable but removal of Gandhi's statues is not. It is true that in his early days in South Africa, he expressed racist attitudes towards Africans. But later, he became a person respected by leaders of the African independence struggles. He inspired the American civil rights leader, Martin Luther King. No one is born with the mature stand he/she later promotes; views evolve over time. And that holds for the heroes of Africa as well. Ideas that will justifiably offend someone somewhere can always be found.

Charles Dickens, the British novelist whose books elegantly and starkly brought to life the dark side of capitalism and the plight of those at the bottom at the same time held racist views towards colonized people. Should school children not read his books because of that fact? It came to light in the 1980s that one of the best textbooks on human anatomy being used for medical training had utilized the findings from the abominable research done by Nazi doctors on concentration camp inmates during World War II. Should the book be banned? In both cases, the best option is to continue using them but to also highlight their negative aspects in a prominent manner in the new editions and through other means.

Progressive intellectuals and activists worldwide struggled in the 1960s and 1970s to overcome the pro-capitalist and pro-imperial biases in history and the other social science disciplines. They did so through scientific research and writing more accurate renditions of history and society. It was a battle of ideas. The University of Dar es Salaam was a key venue in such efforts. It is a tradition the students and academics of today need to remember and uphold.

Historical structures, sites and symbols are under attack across Africa today. Deterioration and destruction of these embodiments of the past is not a result of a conscious agenda but arises from neglect or commercial factors. Pre-colonial era settlement sites, colonial era buildings and places of archeological value are either not maintained or have been demolished to make way for new high rise structures. National museums and archives are in poor conditions. Records of historical import gather mold and rot away.

For example, in doing research for a previous book, I had to look at the 1968 to 1975 copies of the main English language daily in Tanzania. At the UDSM library and the central branch of the national library, they were not well maintained and had large gaps. The company owning the newspaper had placed the pre-1980 copies in a large container that was not opened for ages. And when it was, it was seen that rain water and tropical humidity had made the whole lot unusable even for recycling. The Hoover Institution at the Stanford University in California has, I am told, a complete record of the Tanzanian newspapers from that era.

Yet, local authorities and members of the historical profession do not act until donor funds materialize. Instead of agitating to remove this or that statue, the university based activists should divert their energies into the preservation of our history. It is an indispensable component of our national identity.

FREEDOM OF SPEECH

Prior to the 1960s, university campuses across the globe were basically monopolized by right wing perspectives that rationalized capitalism and Western cultural tendencies. Left wing perspectives were in a minority and faced regular opposition from conservative scholars and the political establishment. The 1950s McCarthy era in the US, for example, witnessed a witch hunt against real and alleged communists in the government, media, entertainment industry and the academia.

In the 1960s, winds of change began to blow on university campuses. It was a world-wide affair. Leftist academics and students asserted their right to be heard without intimidation. The Free Speech Movement at the University of California, Berkeley was a prime example. Thousands of students protested for the right to organize political activity on the campus and for freedom of speech and academic freedom. They were influenced by the struggles against the war on Vietnam and for civil rights. Students in France took over universities. African universities were affected by this trend as well.

The struggles at UDSM conducted by USARF and leftists academics have been described in Chapters 9, 10 and 11. USARF was banned in 1970s, and the new Vice Chancellor began the process of removing leftists from the campus. Today, that process is complete as socialist and radical voices have virtually been extirpated from the academia everywhere. Only a rare campus and a few academics are the exceptions to the rule. Across the world, the radical voices of the past have been replaced by voices espousing identity related causes.

At this stage of neoliberalism, the democratic aura that accompanied its inception is being super ceded by populist authoritarian or fascistic regimes. The trend is evident in both the technologically advanced and the poor nations. Restrictions on the media and freedom of expression generally and in the academia are an integral part of this scene. Brazil, India, the Philippines, Eastern Europe, Egypt are prime examples. In that respect, they are falling in line with the traditional theocracies of the Middle East. In India,

Bangladesh and Pakistan, reporters, wayward academics and free thinkers are being targeted by extremist forces that apparently have official imprimatur. Many have been murdered in broad daylight. Often, the perpetrators have avoided capture.

Restrictions on what the media can say or print, what is allowed on social media and the activities that are allowed at university campuses are seen across Africa. Tanzania, for example has recently passed a highly restrictive media law that curtails media freedom to a significant degree. Further, it also passed a law that made it illegal to disseminate social, economic and health statistics that did not have the blessings of the National Bureau of Statistics. A minor infringement and you face large fines and jail time (Hirji 2014). Several newspapers alleged to have violated these laws have been suspended for short or long periods. The message has sunk in. Many websites and blogs have ceased operation and dissenting voices in the media, social media, parliament, academy and elsewhere have been muted. While freedom of expression is enshrined in the constitution, the political authorities, police and the courts operate as if no such basic law exists. These types of practices can be observed across Africa. The statistics law was modified only after the World Bank weighed in and withheld funds for some projects. (Eyakuze 2019).

Political activities, vaguely defined, are proscribed by law at the university and college campuses in Tanzania. It is a far cry from the heady days when the UDSM was a leader in radical political thought and activities. In early 2019, progressive activists were seeking a venue to hold a meeting to discuss the books written by a local leftist writer. Upon approaching UDSM officials for a meeting space, they were asked to show the list of presenters. The officials said that it contained two people associated with an opposition party. That was not permitted. Either change the list or go elsewhere. That was the line. The meeting was held in another place. Double standards also prevail; on the campus as well as in general. Members of the ruling party often hold meetings; while opposition parties are denied permission to hold internal meetings. The latter are targeted unfairly and repeatedly; many spend weeks and months behind bars only to be released without cause later on. Journalists disappear without a trace. And opposition members of the parliament come to learn that parliamentary immunity is, for them, an illusion.

Restricting the right of any person to express his or her views, be they from one side or the other side of the socio-political spectrum, is wrong as a matter of principle. As such, even those who have positions that are clearly offensive to the members of certain communities, that denigrate some cultures or religious faiths, that insult Africans or immigrants, that condemn gays or lesbians, have the right to say what they want to say, on college campuses, the media or other public venues. Furthermore, given the deleterious trends noted above, these are the worst times to call for restrictions on people who have such views. There are laws on the books that can and should be employed for people who directly call for inflicting bodily harm on others. There are laws that apply in the case of making patently wrong accusations. Otherwise, restrictions on speech just rigidify extremist views, attract others to such offensive views, drive the adherents underground and encourage violent action.

Let them say what they want to say, but counter it effectively through education and debate. State officials, main media, academics of good will and prominent personalities should take a lead in that effort. Instead, what happens in the Western mainstream media is that the hatemongers get more space than they deserve while the other side is restricted to a soundbite (Malik 2019).

A SOCIALISTIC PERSPECTIVE

The analysis and critique of identity politics from a progressive, socialist vision of society has been given by many authors. (Gray 2018; Haider 2018; Hirji 2019; Lancaster 2017; Manji 2019). Here I summarize the main points.

Our primary identity is the human identity. First and foremost, we are members of the great human family and should behave as such. As expressed by Amilcar Cabral (and quoted in Manji 2019):

> We talk a lot about Africa, but we in our Party must remember that before being Africans we are men, human beings, who belong to the whole world. Amilcar Cabral

The fundamental root of the major problems people everywhere face is neoliberal, imperial capitalism, a system characterized by corporate domination of the economy and society, a vast wealth gap between those at the top and the broad majority, the division of the world between affluent and poverty stricken nations, a plutocratic or symbolic form of democracy and, of recent, trends towards fascism. Integral to them are imperialistic conduct by the rich nations and entrenchment of social and economic dependency in the poor nations (Manji 2019).

Racist, misogynistic, jingoistic, homophobic, fundamentalist and anti-immigrant ideas and movements must be firmly opposed in theory and practice. And the merits of and claims for redress and reform made by long discriminated groups in the industrialized and underdeveloped nations need full support.

The transformative strategy has to systemic, namely to organize to overturn, nationally and globally, the capitalist, imperial domination and work towards attaining a society based on social and economic equality, grassroots democracy, social justice, mutual trust and cooperation, full accountability and total non-violence. In its place, we need to strive for a society based on respect for the dignity and rights of all minority and majority groups. And their struggles ought to be integrated within the overall transformative strategy. It is not a question of fighting capitalism first and then dealing with racism but of recognizing the two problems as two sides of the same coin, and confronting both simultaneously.

The struggles against capitalism and imperialism need a broad based united front of the commoners, the working people, the exploited and the disadvantaged, that is, the 99% who presently are divided into disparate groups and subgroups. The process of attaining a peaceful, just coalition between these groups and the majority should be a democratic, consultative process based on mutual respect.

A long historic view shows that the formation of political identities is not a fixed but a dynamic phenomenon. A once discriminated group may no longer be so marginalized later on, as the cases of Irish Americans and Jewish Americans illustrates. Once upon a time they were excluded from renting apartments in `respectable' neighborhoods but that is no longer the case. Identities are a social and historic construct and not an immutable fact of nature.

Thus, appearance or rhetoric and actuality differ. The problems faced by minority groups do not just derive from cultural issues or skin color but have an economic basis. Immigrants are attacked not just because their cultural practices differ from that of the majority but also due being the most exploited segment of the labor force. The locals are made to believe the immigrants have `stolen their jobs.' The real culprits, the corporations which benefit from immigrant labor, are absolved of blame. When there is an economic downturn, these foreign workers become a politically demonized and readily expendable part of the labor force.

While accepting the just basis of their cause, the socialist perspective on identity politics questions the narrow vision and the divisive tactics of the dominated groups who struggle within its framework. Single-minded identity politics pursued in a disjointed way has counterproductive and harmful consequences. Take the case of the US. The African American and Latino communities live in neighborhoods with abysmal educational, health, commercial, transport and other services. Institutionalized discrimination in housing, jobs and work promotion affects their quality of life. Yet, when African Americans march against police brutality, you do not see many brown faces; and when Latinos march in relation to immigration issues, you do not see many black faces. Viewing each other as adversaries, they fail to benefit from the fact that unity is strength.

The stand of some influential African American leaders has been: Fight racism first and deal with capitalism later. It is a self-defeating strategy that not only plays into the hands of capitalist oriented (liberal and conservative) politicians but also creates sharp divisions between the different identity groups each of whom wants to place its cause at the top of the political agenda.

Hence, when a political candidate with relatively progressive policies emerges, challenges the hold of corporate power on the political system and advocates wide ranging changes in health, education, investment and taxation of benefit to the majority, white or black, male or female, not just the major politicians but also the leaders of the dominated identity groups rally against him or her because he or she does not adequately articulate their demands. Identity politics then effectively functions as a protector of the capitalist system. Progressive candidates for presidency in the US like Ralph Nader and Bernie Sanders were opposed by African Americans for similar reasons. And when Martin Luther King extended his agenda to fighting for poor people and opposing the US aggression on Vietnam, he was accused by some African American leaders of betraying the civil rights struggle.

Narrow policies emerging from identity agitation lead to stop-gap remedies that backfire in the long run. Affirmative action in the field of higher education in the US illustrates the down side. Due to other socioeconomic trends, it was of benefit to women. But for African Americans, it has had marginal results. (Sunkara 2019).

Consider the gender question in relation to Tanzania. Education for Africans was not a priority under colonial rule. Within this limited setup, the representation of women was abysmally low. It underwent a major change after Independence. Thus, by the 1970s, some twenty percent of university students in the nation were female. Though gender parity is a ways off, today there are proportionately and numerically more women doctors, engineers, lawyers, business and state executives and political personalities, including members of parliament. And that is the direction along which further progress is essential.

But there are two not-that-laudatory aspects of this trend. First, there is no evidence that the greater presence of women in the professions, business, high state office and politics has in any way affected the basic dependent, inefficient, unaccountable and politically authoritarian neoliberal system in the nation and the poverty mired, disempowered state of the majority, including the millions of women at the bottom. The institutions where the elite women operate run as before. The hostility of some women politicians of the ruling party to political pluralism and the opposition parties, for example, matches that of their male colleagues. Gender parity at the top does not, in itself, promote efficiency, economic justice or democracy. Second, the issue of gender parity (mostly at an elitist level) is championed by the politicians, the Western embassies and the `donor' agencies at the expense of serious effort to empower the people, uplift their social and economic conditions and place onto the nation of the path of reducing external dependency and instituting substantial, sustainable progress in the economy and social services. Many foreign funded NGOs promote gender balance and combat violence against women; most funding agencies place promotion of gender parity as a condition for securing their funds. Yet, no NGO deals with why multinational firms and the big local businesses do not pay a living wage to their workers, how the workers can organize to secure a better deal for themselves or why the banks charge exorbitant interest to the customers. Yet, women too are affected by the latter set of problems (O'Hagan 2019).

In almost each departmental meeting I attended at my university, the issue of gender balance was stressed. Not that these academics, who paid scant effort to teaching and standards of instruction, had suddenly become champions of women's rights. It was that the external agencies who funded their research and consultancy endeavors needed at least verbal stress on the matter.

At the international level, the election of women to the high office in nations like the US, the UK, Sri Lanka, Israel, India, Pakistan, Bangladesh, Burma and Liberia did not make their politics more just, humane, or change the economic set up that favors corporations and the very wealthy. How did the first African American president, who was as pro-business and imperialistic as his Republican predecessor, alter the day to day conditions of African Americans or promote better US policies towards Africa? Not much or not at all. Yet, African Americans and Africans rejoiced when he was elected (Cohen 2019; Mahdawi 2019; Stoller 2017).

Narrowly pursued identity politics endangers the wellbeing of people elsewhere. Members of one minority groups are enrolled in the service of dominating other people, within the nation or abroad.

Identity politics leads to emergence of identities within identities, as exemplified by the notion of intersectionality. A person with multiple discriminated identities faces discrimination arising each of these identities, and in a compounded form (Crenshaw 2015). A black, Muslim woman in the US is subjected to social biases arising from being black, a Muslim and a woman. An Albino woman in Tanzania faces gender bias as well as the prevalent prejudice against Albinos. There is no doubt that such persons encounter quite daunting obstacles in life. Yet, the practical effect of treating them as a separate group is to say, these people are special, their problems have first priority. Instead of unifying the identities, it turns into a divisive process that exacerbates existing divisions among the people at the bottom. Another division is formed by colorism which pits dark skinned black women against light skinned black women. Decades of conditioning under capitalism and clever marketing strategy of skin lotion manufacturers have led them to believe that the latter is more desirable than the former. You are less likely to get married if you have a dark skin (Greenidge 2019). Real and cruel as such divisions are, the solution does not lie in tackling each by itself. What is needed is a sustained, overall, unified struggle against all forms of prejudice, discrimination and inequality (Anonymous 2013; Mahdawi 2019).

Utilizing an identity based framework for social and historical analysis is the academic counterpart to identity politics. It employs social identity as the key conceptual unit, sidelines or disjointedly considers economic factors and ignores primary matters like imperialism and neoliberalism. Having displaced the socialist and Marxist modes of social analysis, it is now the dominant framework in African, Western and other universities. Even progressive scholars employ race, ethnicity, gender and cultural factors as pillars of their explications of society and history. The rich heritage of the former forms of scholarship from the 1960s and 1970s is treated as if it never existed. Modern scholars know that if your research proposal is based on a Marxist framework, you will have a hard time securing funds. Instead, they construct proposals based on a market friendly, identity based framework in which human and social rights are conceptualized in a stultified bourgeois fashion. Their vision is limited to poverty alleviation and not elimination of poverty and inequality.

The capitalist system at its foundation is a class based system. Those at the bottom, the 99%, are dominated and exploited for the benefit of the owners of wealth and capital, the 1%. Yet, the presence of socially divided and politically adversarial identity groups is a basic feature of the system (Gerard 2019; Kumar 2018; O'Hagan 2019). Capitalism cannot operate in a stable manner if those at the bottom unite to struggle against the system. When they become aware of the nature of the system, its very existence is threatened. Hence, for capitalism to remain in command, the masses must be divided into mutually hostile groups. Divide and rule thus has been a basic feature of the system since its inception. Afraid of the possibility of poor white laborers uniting with the slaves, the slave owners in the US promoted disharmonies between them by throwing crumbs to the former and giving some poor whites supervisory work that made them feel superior to the African slaves. (Haider 2018). Divide and rule, as we saw in Chapter 1 and 2, was an essential ingredient of colonial rule in Africa.

Racism was a fundamental feature of nascent capitalism and later a fundamental feature of the emergence of capitalism and the subsequent period of colonization that subjugated vast sections of humanity across the globe to its voracious need for increasing the rate of accumulation of capital. Manji (2019), page 54.

Divide and rule operates today as well. So long as humanity is divided along racial, religious, ethnic and other grounds, corporations continue to reap super profits, the 1% can continue to reap enormous wealth and their environmentally harmful actions remain unchallenged. If Muslims and Christians in Africa are at each others throats, global corporations and imperial powers will continue their plunder and domination of Africa.

Identity based political and social affiliation (and identity based social analysis) mask the actual nature of capitalism and imperialism, divert attention away from key economic relations to other issues and present superficial choices to the electorate. Electoral choice becomes a seesaw that swings from one neoliberal, pro-corporate party to the other party of the same bent as the politicians fan the flames of cultural hostility between the groups at the bottom. The differences among the 99% are highlighted while what they share, which covers almost all aspects of life, is ignored. This money-run democracy has no room for those who seek to unify the people at the bottom against corporate power and the ruling elite. Disjointed identity politics thus complements the capitalist tendency to divided and rule and, in the long run, harms the well-being of the very groups that practices it.

The year 2007 presidential election in Kenya was, according to many observers, a patently flawed process. Widespread frustrations about the outcome subsequently generated gruesome violence along ethnic lines. About a thousand died, more were injured, and more than half-a-million people were internally displaced.

Yet, to simply ascribe the violence to `tribal hatred,' as the media did, is misleading. Besides benefiting multinational firms, the economic policies of the government have produced a wealthy internal elite that strives to monopolize state power. While this elite is predominantly from one ethnic group, the vast majority of that ethnic group live under the same conditions and share the same problems as the rest of the people of Kenya. But astute and persistent manipulations of ethnic identity and dishing out a few crumbs now and then by the elite leadership has made them regard other ethnicities as their political and social enemies. And the neoliberally inclined politicians in the opposition groups have as well played the ethnicity game to drum up support. Ultimately, as Susskind (2007) cogently argued, `*it's the inequality, not the tribal identity*' that drives conflict and violence.

In Tanzania, the schism between Christians and Muslims tends to manifest itself in the public arena now and then. The spokesmen for the Muslims complain that people of their faith are not accorded equal opportunities in education, jobs and higher office appointments. While there is a modicum of truth to this charge, these spokesmen tend to distort history, exaggerate the situation and ignore the numerous serious problems afflicting the bulk of the members both faiths (Hirji 2014b).

Africa not only needs cohesive internal strategies but the struggle for equality, justice and progress has, of necessity, to be Pan African in scope. Contemporary African leaders at best pay lip service to the idea. In practice, they focus on cultivating economic ties with Europe, America and Asia. In the 1960s, Pan Africanism was viewed not only as continent wide unifying force but was at the same time the basis for solidarity with oppressed people everywhere. African people need to unite, go beyond narrow nationalism and resolve historic internal racial, ethnic and other divisions justly and amicably. Else, the imperial and neoliberal tendency to divide and rule will keep us at the bottom in perpetuity. Let us heed the lessons not just from South Africa and Kenya but also Chad, Niger, Nigeria, Sudan, among other places.

DARE TO DREAM

Obsession with narrowly construed social identities is driving humanity towards divisiveness and mutual antipathies. As people at the bottom bicker about their grievances in restricted ways, the local and global economic, political and military overlords continue to rule over humanity. Perpetually peddling exclusive identity politics will convert our struggles into a grand illusion. Like the frog that boiled to death as the water in which it floated was heated gradually, humanity will remain unperturbed as the planet burns up politically, socially, economically, militarily and physically. Our narrowmindedness will render us clueless and powerless to confront the mighty corporations and governments that control the world for the benefit of a few billionaires. This is as true in Africa as it is in Asia, Latin America and the Western nations.

In Africa, the system of education under neoliberalism and other ideological apparatuses like the media and political establishment do not promote a sound understanding of the social and economic realities. They mask the fundamental issue: the economic exploitation of the people and the nation by large internal and external capitalist entities and the drainage of wealth abroad. They do not show that the ensuing, enduring poverty produces intense frustrations that spill over into other social differences. Ethnic groups, immigrants and religious communities become the scapegoats, and nowadays such differences assume violent proportions. Such differences are taken to be rigid and unchangeable. Thus, influenced by under-education, neoliberal ideology and ensuing intellectual myopia, university students turn to identity politics as the academics wallow in factually deficient identity based social, political and historical analyses.

Africa does not need fragmented visions. It needs unity and system change. Justice, equality and progress for Africa, including the minorities and the majority will not come from the illusions of liberal democracy. For human liberation, a solid grounding in the universal human identity has to be the primary basis for political and social endeavor. The fight of the rights of the discriminated identity groups, which reflects real problems, is not side-lined, but should be conducted within a universal framework that will unite the hitherto conflicting identities. As people work within specific identities, they must also transcend such identities and organize a broad coalition to conduct their struggles.

Because racial, ethnic and religious divisions have existed for a long time, they have formed roots apart from the economic factors underlying them. Racism in the US society and the academy, for example, is firmly embedded within the social psyche (Sidel 1995). Religious divide in India and Africa is a second nature. To overcome such prejudices and form a united front is a daunting task. Yet, it has to be done; there is no other way. Both sides have to reach a common ground based on justice, dignity and mutual respect.

In sum, our fundamental operating principle for political and social action ought to be that embodied in the universalistic ethic espoused by Che Guevara:

Above all, always be capable of feeling deeply
any injustice committed against anyone,
anywhere in the world.
Ernesto Che Guevara

16

EDUCATION AND LIBERATION

SUMMARY: This essay summarizes the key features of under-education uncovered by our long journey from the colonial times to the present beguiling neoliberal era. It also presents suggestions about how to tackle the malady of under-education and its root, the neoliberal system, at the personal and political levels.[1]

*

---

1. This essay has not been published previously.

In the middle of difficulty lies opportunity.
You never fail until you stop trying.
Albert Einstein
++++++++++

OUR JOURNEY FROM THE DAYS of harsh colonial rule to the hopeful early post-Independence times and onto the painful modern neoliberal era has underscored the entrenchment of economic underdevelopment and social malaise in Africa. The forms have changed, but the essence, the domination of the continent by external forces and their local allies and persistence of widespread misery remains. This process has been accompanied by the evolution and persistence of under-education in the education systems of African nations. Though our focus was mostly on Tanzania, what we observed applies in general to the rest of Africa.

In the present age, under-education is the principal form of education in Africa. Arising from economic and social underdevelopment, it in turn fosters underdevelopment. With the primary attention to university level education, under-education was observed to have the following features:

- Rapid expansion of institutions of higher learning and their student populations. Establishment of many for-profit private universities in a poorly regulated environment is an integral part of the trend. In some nations, unaccredited and fake universities have also come into being.

- Markedly low levels of quality of instruction and scholarship at both the old and new, public and private, universities.

- Prevalence of deep educational inequality whereby a few acquire decent conventional type of education but the majority wallow in a state of profound pedagogic penury and do not grasp elementary linguistic, numerical and logical skills even after completion of university level studies.

- A common tendency to neglect teaching and concentrate on easy-money generating consultancy projects and commercial activities on the part of the academicians.

- Excessive reliance on external entities for resources to plan and conduct academic activities. External entities also exercise a major influence on the organization, contents and future direction of the education system.

- General reverence and desire for ideas and things that are foreign in origin and a knee-jerk negative attitude towards those that are local.

- Generally low quality of the research work done by undergraduate and postgraduate students. Main research focus is on superficial issues and examination of systemic issues is avoided.

- Unless done in partnership with foreign academics and experts, the research conducted by the academic staff is also tainted with similar features.
- Compromised ethical norms among students and academics in the classroom and research activities. Plagiarization, cheating in tests, manufacture of research data and reliance on other parties to write research reports are on the ascendance.
- Remarkable decline in the utilization of books and printed material for instruction and learning. Only a few academics write books of internationally recognized high standards.
- Uses of computers, electronic technology and the Internet in ways that are counterproductive and which discourage both in-depth and broad based-learning. Technology facilitates unethical conduct.
- General veering towards intellectual superficiality and mediocrity without being aware of it. A common striving for quick rewards with little concern for the quality of the output.
- Preponderance of identity based social analysis among the social and political scientists who generally neglect to study the historic, structural and economic dimensions of the current malaise.
- A profound mismatch between educational output and the state of the economy and investment resulting in high levels of joblessness among the university graduates, including those with advanced degrees.
- Preoccupation in the academy with the struggles to lower fees, get higher pay and benefits, and secure better living conditions.
- A general focus on NGO based charitable activities and identity politics with consequent abandonment of systemic level struggles or formation of broad united fronts with common people.
- Lip service to the notion of academic freedom in an environment dominated by unquestioning political conformism.
- A profound degree of mis-education that places strong ideological blinders on the educated and makes them lose confidence in their and their nation's ability to solve social and national problems with internal resources.

Under-education is neither theoretical learning nor mastering a skill but a certificate in your hand. A reward for attending a diploma mill, it takes you nowhere intellectually and professionally but you expect it will take you somewhere financially. It is a systemic malady, not due to individual shortcomings only.

STUDENT AND ACADEMIC STRUGGLES

In November 1969, radical students in the Faculty of Law at UDSM joined by supporters from other faculties staged a two-day occupation of the Law Faculty building. The blocked the entrance and, instead of going to class, held their own study sessions. Their demands were centered on opposition to an American inspired change in the law curriculum and for reorientation of legal studies towards a socialistic, Pan African mode.

There was a similarly inspired but more inclusive occupation of school buildings when I was a student at the London School of Economics in 1971. The premises were taken over by students for nearly a week. The basic demands were similar: greater student participation in the university affairs and removal of the pro-capitalist and pro-imperialist biases in the social science disciplines, business studies and economics. A whole week of alternative teaching conducted by students and progressive staff took place. It was a refreshing moment. In those days, student struggles went in tandem with struggles for overall progressive social change.

In the present neoliberal era, what the students study and concern with social transformation have taken the back seat. Instead, the attention is mostly on reduction of fees, opposition to state funding cuts and increasing staff and student benefits. Accordingly, the year 2010 witnessed wide-scale outbreaks of student protests at British universities. Affected institutions included Cambridge University, Manchester University, University of Plymouth, University College London, London School of Economics, King's College, London, School of Oriental and African Studies, Slade School of Fine Art, University of Sheffield, Newcastle University and University of York. The students staged sit-ins, building occupations and class boycotts to oppose education cuts and higher tuition fees, and sought bursary increases. In some cities, they gained support from local celebrities. School students marched in solidarity and lecturers also went on strike. A number of students were arrested by the police. (Smith 2010).

In 2018 and early 2019, teachers in major American cities staged strikes that, in some cases, lasted for weeks. Going beyond the demands for pay raises and job security, they asked for reduction of class size, more support for public education, less funding for private, charter schools, reduced emphasis on standardized tests and more resources for schools in minority areas. Having greater public, parental and media support than in the past, they secured significant concessions from the school district authorities in many school districts.

It was in the South American nation of Chile that students demonstrated exemplary insight and resolve not seen elsewhere in the recent times. Under the American installed and supported brutal dictatorship of Agosto Pinochet, intellectuals, students, academics and civic leaders showing any opposition to the state were rounded up and tortured. Many were murdered and disappeared. A stringent neoliberal economic policy which affected the education sector was also installed. An unequal, elitist education system came into being.

After the fall of Pinochet, neoliberalism was not reversed but reinforced. Privatization gained pace as the quality of education and job prospects for the university graduates declined. These market oriented policies led to the consolidation of vastly unequal but lackluster education. Dropout rates for the low income groups were on the ascendance. In 2011, the students said enough is enough. Under the bold, charismatic, visionary leadership of a university student, Camila Vallejo, tens of thousands at all levels of the system took to the street for six months. Attempts by the authorities to neutralize them by force, or to coopt and intimidate their leaders failed. Operating under the banner of `Educate, don't profiteer,' they demanded a comprehensive roll back of the neoliberal agenda in education and society. With their popularity on the decline, the national leaders had to make concessions. But it was a first step and a long road lies ahead. (Cabalin 2011).

In Africa in the recent years, while students have played a role in the fight against authoritarian regimes in many nations, they have yet to show an inclination to confront the structural manifestations of neoliberalism in education and society. In addition to agitating for fee reductions and better conditions in hostels and cafeteria, their societal and political efforts have been redirected into NGO types of activities and in places, identity politics.

In Tanzania, however, students are involved in a novel form of activity to confront the life problems induced by the neoliberal reality. The 23 June 2019 issue of *The Citizen* reported a mass prayer event organized by the Evangelical Lutheran Church in Tanzania. Held at the Uhuru Stadium in Dar es Salaam, it attracted tens of thousands of youngsters of secondary school and higher education level age. A photo of a jam-packed stadium in which they are congregated is given. With arms raised to the heavens they are earnestly, as the reporter put it, `beseeching God' for assistance in their arduous efforts to `secure jobs'. (*The Citizen* 2019).

While turning to extra worldly authority for hope and prayers may not harm, the salient question is whether the youth of Africa will bank mainly on such assistance to solve the problems facing them and the nation at large? Or will they also embark on concrete worldly struggles?

CONFRONTING UNDER-EDUCATION

In my view, countering under-education has to done simultaneously with struggles to counter under-development and efforts to build a society based on social justice, equality, democracy and progress for all. It is a long term task but has to begin now as a matter of urgency. In that effort, it is imperative for the students, academics and concerned activists to attend to the following foundational ideas and tasks:

- Engage in a program of self-education through wide reading and discussion of historical, professional and general material that is not confined by the conceptual limitations imposed by the current education system. Utilize modern technology in ways that promote and balance in-depth learning and reflection with ease of access.

- Develop a critical, progressive interdisciplinary, holistic perspective through reading and discussion of books and papers that embody such visions. Modify what you gather from such sources to fit with the changed social, educational and economic circumstances. Have a broad-based reading program.

- Generally avoid engaging in narrow identity based struggles. But when valid concerns to redress burdens on specific social groups exist, address them in the context of promoting fundamental social change. Extend immediate assistance where needed but then go beyond that to deal with fundamental causes.

- Practice what you preach. Banish ethnic, racial, religious and gender based association and favoritism from the activist groups.

- Adhere to high ethical and professional norms in personal life, the classroom, research activities, working environment and beyond.

- Raise critical issues in academic and public venues without fear or favor and avoid pandering to opportunistic political conformism.

- Link educational issues with general societal issues and strive to form broad united fronts with other activists and common people in their strivings for improvements on educational, health, life and other matters. Learn from the strategies, successes and failures of the past and ongoing worldwide struggles in such endeavors.

- Develop and foster an internationalist spirit of solidarity with people and students everywhere but avoid undue reliance on external funds and ideas, especially from capitalistic sources.

- Bear in mind that the struggle for change in Africa and the world is a long term struggle. Do not despair but remain hopeful no matter the immediate consequences.

PERSONAL MATTERS

It was commonly said among the activists of the 1960s that the personal is the political. For efficient, long-term engagement in the cause towards to which they are committed and enrich their personal lives, the activists (and the youth in general) need to live in prudent, health promoting and balanced ways. Progressive activists should there by:

- Live simple lives but healthful lives. Avoid junk, packaged food and mostly eat fresh whole grains, beans, lentils, vegetables and fruits. Limit intake of sugar, fried and fatty foods, and red meat.
- Wake up early, exercise before breakfast, and retire to bed early with a book or magazine in hand. Be physically active. Play field games when you can.
- No cell-phone use between 6 pm and 6 am. Use that time for face to face interaction with family, friends, children and neighbors.
- Never smoke. Strictly limit alcohol intake. Sodas and sugary drinks should be restricted. Drink plenty of water instead.
- Take preventive measures for diseases like malaria and viral and bacterial infections. Maintain good standards of hygiene.
- Conduct yourself with grace and dignity and be respectful to all. Always be truthful, honest and above board. Do not be greedy or engage in behind the back rumor mongering.
- Remember that laughter is the best medicine. Entertain yourself and family with stories, good music, dance and nature walks.
- Be ready to assist other activists and people in need. Participate in informal solidarity networks that undertake such work.

From a young age onwards, the influences on the youth are driving them away from healthful lifestyles. As a result, there has been an increase in the prevalence of obesity and manifestations of chronic disease among them. A sound education system needs to cover basic health education. But in Africa as elsewhere, the commercial forces emanating from food and soft drinks manufactures and the methods of taxation do not favor them and the education authorities thereby neglect to include such vital matters in the school curricula.

Other than taking basic general and personal measures, there are no predetermined or strategies or tactics in the struggle for educational and social change. What exist are the records of viewpoints and struggles of the past and present times. The current generation has to learn from that history, here and elsewhere, and devise its own methods of reaching the set goals. Many nations in Africa and across the world have recently witnessed or are witnessing nation-wide outbreak of the struggles for freedom and justice. Students and academics in some places play a critical role in such efforts. There is a need to be inspired by and emulate them.

REFERENCES

There are worse crimes than burning books.
One of them is not reading them.
Joseph Brodsky
++++++++++

Chapter 1

Abdulaziz MH (1972) Tanzania national language policy and the rise of political Swahili culture, In L Cliffe and J Saul (1972) (editors), Volume 1, pages 155-164.
Amin S (1971) *Modes of Production and Social Formations*, mimeographed copy, University of Dar es Salaam.
AR (1901/1902) *Annual Report on Development in German Tanganyika*, 1901/1902, English translation typescript, Department of History, University of Dar es Salaam.
AR (1902/1903) *Annual Report on Development in German Tanganyika*, 1902/1903, English translation typescript, Department of History, University of Dar es Salaam.
AR (1907/1908) *Annual Report on Development in German Tanganyika*, 1907/1908, English translation typescript, Department of History, University of Dar es Salaam.
AR (1908/1909) *Annual Report on Development in German Tanganyika*, 1908/1909, English translation typescript, Department of History, University of Dar es Salaam.
Arnold D (1980) External factors in the partition of Africa, In MHY Kaniki (editor) (1980), Chapter 2.
Barrette DB (editor) (1971)*African Initiative in Religion*, East African Publishing House, Nairobi.
Bottomore TB and Rubel M (editors) (1967) *Karl Marx: Selected Writings in Sociology and Social Philosophy*, McGraw Hill Books, London.

Cameron J and Dodd WA (1970) *Society, Schools and Progress in Tanzania*, Pergamon Press, Oxford.
Cliffe L and Saul J (1972) (editors) *Socialism in Tanzania*, Volumes I & Volume II, East African Publishing House, Nairobi.
Gwassa GCK (1972) *On Colonial Labor Force and Labor Market in Tanzania*, East African Publishing House, Nairobi.
Helbert CJ (1965) *Missions on a Colonial Frontier West of Lake Victoria; Evangelical Missions in North-West Tanganyika to 1932*, Gleerups Publisher, Uppsala.
Hirji KF (1973) School education and underdevelopment in Tanzania, *MajiMaji*,University of Dar es Salaam, 12:1-23.
Hornsby G (1962) A brief history of Tanga School up to 1914, *Tanganyika Notes and Records*, Dar es Salaam.
Hornsby G (1964) German educational achievements in East Africa, *Tanganyika Notes and Records*, Dar es Salaam.
Iliffe J (1969) The age of improvement and differentiation (1907 – 1945), In Kimambo and Temu (editors), 1969, page 131.
Iliffe J (1972) *Tanganyika Under German Rule, 1905-1912*, Cambridge University Press, Nairobi and Cambridge.
Kaniki MHY (editor) (1980) *Tanzania Under Colonial Rule*, Longmans, London.
Kimambo IN and Temu AJ (editors) (1969) *A History of Tanzania*, Heinemann Educational Books, Nairobi.
Lubestsky R (1972) *Sectoral Development and Stratification in Tanganyika, 1890-1914*, Paper presented at the Social Science Conference, University of Nairobi, 1972.
Mapunda OB and Mpangara GP (1972) *The MajiMaji War in Ungoni*, East African Publishing House, Nairobi.
Marx K (1971) *Capital*,Volume I, Progress Publishers, Moscow.
Mbilinyi M (1972) *The Decision to Educate in Rural Tanzania*, PhD Dissertation, University of Dar es Salaam.
Mgonde LYC (1966) *Mission Education and the Kaguru*, Student Research Paper, Department of History, University of Dar es Salaam.
Nolan FP (1971) The changing role of catechists in Tabora, In DB Barrette (editor) (1971).
Oliver RA (1969) *The Missionary Factor in East Africa*, Longmans, London.
Pierard D (1967) The Dernberg reform policy and German East Africa, *Tanganyika Notes and Records*, Dar es Salaam, page 33.
Rodney W (1980) The political economy of colonial Tanganyika, 1890 – 1930, In MHY Kaniki (editor) (1980), Chapter 4.
Schadler K (1968) *Crafts, Small Scale Industries and Industrial Education in Tanzania*,IFO African Studies, No. 4, Munich.
Schlunk M (1964) German education policy: The school system in the German colonies, In DG Scanlon (editor) (1964) *Traditions of African Education*, Teachers College Press, New York.
Sheriff AMH (1980) Tanzanian societies at the time of partition, in MHY Kaniki (editor) (1980), chapter 1.

Shivji IG (1976) *Class Struggles in Tanzania*, Monthly Review Press, New York.

Smith A (1963) The missionary contribution to education in Tanganyika to 1914, *Tanganyika Notes and Records*, March 1963, Dar es Salaam.

Wright M (1968) Local roots of policy in German East Africa, *Journal of African History*, 9(4).

Wright M (1971) *German Missions in Tanganyika, 1819-1914: Lutherans and Moravians in Southern Highlands*, Oxford University Press, Oxford.

Chapter 2

A Correspondent (1973) Frustrating our teachers, spoiling our education, *Daily News*, 19 April 1973.

A Sixth Former (1972) Crisis at Pugu Secondary School, *MajiMaji*, No 4, University of Dar es Salaam.

Affected (1973) Letter, *Daily News*, 16 April 1973.

Althusser L (1971) *Lenin and Philosophy and Other Essays*, New Left Books, London.

Bienfeld MA (1972) Planning people, in J Rweyemamu et al. (editors) (1972).

Cameron J and Dodd WA (1970) *Society, Schools & Progress in Tanzania*, Pergamon Press, Oxford.

Cliffe L and Saul J (editors) (1972) *Socialism in Tanzania*, Volumes I & II, East African Publishing House, Nairobi.

Daily News (1973) 71m/- boost to education, *Daily News*, 16 May 1973.

Engels F (1968) *The Origin of the Family, Private Property and the State*, Progress Publishers, Moscow.

Holness M (1972) *Origins and Development of World Socialism*(print version of text of radio broadcast), Radio Tanzania, Dar es Salam.

Hunter G (1972) Manpower, employment and education in the rural economy of Tanzania, in L Cliffe and J Saul (editors) (1972), Volume 2.

lliffe J (1972) Tanzania under German and British rule, in L Cliffe and J Saul (editors) (1972), Volume 1, pages 8-17.

Kibwana FJ (1973) Letter, *Sunday News*, 13 May 1973.

Kikubatayo AT (1973) Letter, *Sunday News*, 11 February 1973.

Lema AA (1973a) I hate it attitude is fast disappearing, *Sunday News*, 14 April 1973.

Lema AA (1973b) *Old Attitude Die Hard, Studies in Curriculum Development*,Institute of Education, University of Dar es Salaam, 1973.

Mbiru GK (1973) Letter, *Daily News*, 19 January 1973.

Mtaita MSO (1973) Letter, *Daily News*, 2 May 1973.

Mtui MJ (1973) Letter, *Daily News*, 18 April 1973.

Mwanafunzi Mfiahaki (1973) Letter, *Daily News*, 5 February 1973.

Ndamagi C (1973) Language, root of school ills (letter), *Daily News*, 4 June 1973.
Nyerere JK (1967) *Education for Self Reliance*, Ministry of Information and Tourism, Dar es Salaam, 1967.
Raza JH (1973) Education: The case for curriculum review, *Daily News*, 3 May1973.
Resnick IN (editor) (1968) *Tanzania: Revolution by Education*, Longmans of Tanzania Limited, Arusha.
Rodney W (1972) *How Europe Underdeveloped Africa*, Tanzania Publishing House, Dar es Salaam.
Rweyemamu J et al. (editors) (1972) *Towards Socialist Planning*, Tanzania Publishing House, Dar es Salaam.
Seidman A (1972) *Comparative Development Strategies in East Africa*, East African Publishing House, Nairobi.
Shikoyoni IMJ (1973) Letter, *Daily News*, 5 April 1973.
Shivji IG (1970) *Tanzania: The Silent Class Struggle*, ChecheSpecial Issue, University of Dar es Salaam, August 1970.
Shivji IG (1973) *Tanzania: The Class Struggle Continues*, Institute of Development Studies, University of Dar es Salaam.
Tanganyika (1953) *Muhatasari ya Mafundisho kwa Shule za Primary za Waafrika*, Government Printer, Dar es Salaam.
Tanganyika (1955) *Muhtasari ya Mafundisho Katika Middle Schools*,Government Printer, Dar es Salaam.
Tanzania (1972) *The Economic Survey, 1971-1972*,Government Printer, Dar es Salaam.
Tegambwage N (1973) Focus on education: The problem of falling standards, *Daily News*, 8 May1973.
Thomas CY (1972) *The Transition to Socialism*, Economic Research Bureau Paper, University of Dar es Salaam.
True Patriot (1973) Ministry should look into rural schools (letter), *Daily News*, 29 January 1973.
Van de Laar A (1972a) Growth and income distribution in Tanzania since Independence, in L Clife and J Saul (editors) (1972), Volume 1, pages 106-117.
Van de Laar A (1972b) Towards manpower development strategy in Tanzania, in L Clife and J Saul (editors) (1972), Volume 2.
von Freyhold M (1972), *The Workers and the Nizers*, Department of Political Science, mimeographed copy, University of Dar es Salaam.

Chapters 3, 4, 5, 6, 7 & 8

Ajay C (2012) List of blacklisted universities in USA, *msinus.com*, 19 February 2012, http://msinus.com/content/black-listed-universities-usa-427/
Altman DG (2002) Poor-quality medical research: What can journals do? *Journal of the American Medical Association* 287:2765–2767.

Andoh H (2019) Varsities must assess, measure grants, *The Citizen*(Tanzania), 6 July 2019.

Angell M (2005) *The Truth About the Drug Companies: How They Deceive Us and What to Do About It*, Random House, New York.

Anonymous (2008) Half of Cambridge students admit cheating, *The Independent*, 31 October 2008, www.independent.co.uk.

Brennan J and Magness P (2019)hCracks*in the Ivory Tower: The Moral Mess of Higher Education*, Oxford University Press, Oxford.

Broad W and Wade N (1982) *Betrayers of the Truth: Fraud and Deceit in the Halls of Science*, Simon & Schuster, New York.

Brody H (2007) *Hooked: Ethics, the Medical Profession, and the Pharmaceutical Industry*,Rowman & Littlefield Publishers, Inc., Maryland.

Burnett P (2006) Internet censorship on the rise? *Pambazuka News*,No 253.

Cantwell B and Kauppinen J (editors) (2014) *Academic Capitalism in the Age of Globalization*, John Hopkins University Press, Baltimore.

Carr N (2008) Is Google making us stupid? *The Atlantic Monthly*, July/August 2008, www.theatlantic.com/doc/200807/google.

Chalmers TC, Celano P, Sacks HS and Smith HJ (1983) Bias in treatment assignment in controlled clinical trials. *New England Journal of Medicine*, 309:1358-1361.

Chan AW, Hrobjartsson A, Haahr MT, Gøtzsche PC and Altman DG (2004) Empirical evidence for selective reporting of outcomes in randomized trials: Comparison of protocols and published articles. *Journal of the American Medical Association*, 291:2457-2465.

Chan AW and Altman DG (2005) Epidemiology and reporting of randomized trials published in PubMed journals, *Lancet*, 365:1159-1162.

Chan AW (2008) Bias, spin, and misreporting: Time for full access to trial protocols and results. *PLoS Medicine*, 5(11):e230.

Childress H (2019) *The Adjunct Underclass: How America's Colleges Betrayed Their Faculty, Their Students, and Their Mission*, University of Chicago Press, Chicago.

Chomsky N et al. (1998) *The Cold War & the University: Toward an Intellectual History of the Postwar Years*, The New Press, New York.

Cohen J (2006) *Cable News Confidential: My Misadventures in Corporate Media*,Polipoint Press, New York.

Collyns D (2019) Telesup school's fake facade called 'a symbol of Peruvian university system,' *The Guardian*(UK), 8 June 2019, www.theguardian.com/world/2019/jun/08/telesup-schools-fake-facade-called-a-symbol-of-peruvian-university-system

Collini S (2012) The threat to our universities, *The Guardian*(UK), 24 February 2012.

Cloete N, Bailey T and Maassen P (2011) *Universities and Economic Development in Africa: Pact, Academic Core and Coordination (Synthesis Report)*,Centre for Higher Education Transformation (CHET), Wynberg, South Africa.

Cox K and Brown C (2019) US academics feel the invisible hand of politicians and big agriculture, *The Guardian*(UK), 31 January

2019, www.theguardian.com/environment/2019/jan/31/us-academics-feel-the-invisible-hand-of-politicians-and-big-agriculture

Crossen C (1996) *Tainted Truth: The Manipulation of Fact in America*, Touchstone Books, New York.

Davis PJ and Hersh R (1986)*Descarte's Dream: The World According to Mathematics*, Houghton Mifflin, Boston, pages 58-59.

DeAngelis CD (2006) The influence of money on medical science (editorial), *Journal of the American Medical Association*, 296:E1-E3.

Editor (1988) Editorial, *World Health Forum*, 1988, 1(9):322.

Editor (2019) Class of 0000' campaign denounces 'cowardly' censorship of student call for climate action, *Common Dreams*, 7 June 2019, commondreams.org/news/2019/06/07/class-0000-campaign-denounces-cowardly-censorship-student-callclimate-action.

Editorial (2019) Heed Mkapa on varsities, *The Citizen*(Tanzania), 4 July 2019, page 6.

Evans I, Thorton H and Chalmers I (2006) *Testing Treatments: Better Research for Better Healthcare*,British Library, London.

Garner R (2008) Exam chiefs turn to Bond-style gadgets to defeat cheats, *The Independent*, 27 May 2008, www.independent.co.uk.

Garner R (2010) Classroom attacks left 44 staff in hospital last year, *The Independent*(UK), 20 November 2010.

Greenfield S (2008) *ID: The Quest for Identity in the 21st Century*, Hodder & Stoughton, New York.

Griffey H (2018) The lost art of concentration: being distracted in a digital world, *The Guardian*(UK), 14 October 2018, www.theguardian.com/ lifeandstyle/2018/oct/14/the-lost-art-of-concentration-being-distracted-in-a-digital-world

Head S (2011) The grim threat to British universities, *New York Review of Books*, 13 January 2011.

Henderson M (2010) End of the peer review show? *BMJ*, 340:739-740.

Herman ES and Chomsky E (1988) *Manufacturing Consent: The Political Economy of the Mass Media*,Pantheon Books, NY.

Hirji KF (A Correspondent) (1980) Democracy and education, *The Transporter*, National Institute of Transport, Dar es Salaam, 4:11-17.

Hirji KF (1990) Academic pursuits under the Link, *CODESRIA Bulletin* (Senegal), 2:9-16, In CB Mwaria, F Federici and J McLaren (editors) (2000), Chapter 6.

Hirji KF (1993) A tale of two cities, *Business Times* (Tanzania), 5 May 1993.

Hirji KF (1997) Review of Thomas J Moore (1995) *Deadly Medicine: Why Tens of Thousands of Patients Died in America's Worst Drug Disaster, Statistics in Medicine*,16:2507-2510.

Hirji KF (2007) A tale of two universities, unpublished manuscript, April 2007, Muhimbili University of Health and Allied Sciences, Dar es Salaam.

Hirji KF (2009) No short-cut in assessing trial quality: A case study, *Trials*, 10:1, www.trialsjournal.com.

Hirji KF and Fagerland M (2009) Outcome based subgroup analysis: A neglected concern, *Trials*, 10:9, www.trialsjournal.com.
Hirji KF and Premji Z (2011) Pre-referral rectal Artesunate in severe Malaria: A flawed trial, *Trials*, 12:188, www.trialsjournal.com.
Hirji KF (2018) *The Travails of a Tanzanian Teacher*, Daraja Press, Montreal, Canada.
Ibrahim K (2012) Crisis at private universities in Nigeria, *Pambazuka News*, Issue 571, 22 February 2012, www.pambazuka.org/ en/ category/features/80146
Kamagi D (2017) Ban on 19 universities remains in force, as academic year opens, *The Citizen*, 20 October 2017.
Kassirer JP (2005) *On the Take: How Medicine's Complicity With Big Business Can Endanger Your Health*, Oxford University Press, Oxford.
Kavuma RM (2011) In Africa's universities, quantity threatens quality, *The Guardian*(UK), 9 September 2011, www.theguardian.com/ global-development/poverty-matters/ 2011/sep/09/africa-university-funding-crisis
Kotlowitz A (1991) *There Are No Children Here*, Anchor Books, New York.
Kozol J (1991) *Savage Inequalities: Children in America's Schools*, HarperPerennial, New York.
Kozol J (2006) *The Shame of the Nation: The Restoration of Apartheid Schooling in America*, Broadway Books, New York.
Lagakos SW (2006) The challenge of subgroup analyses – reporting without distorting, *NEJM*, 354:1667-1669.
Llanos C (2008) Technology elevates cheating to an art form, *Whittier Daily News*, California, 26 February 2008, www.dailynews.com.
Lopez Obrador AM (2018) Privatization is theft, *Jacobin Magazine*, November 2018, jacobinmag.com/2018/11/
McChesney RW (2008) *The Political Economy of Media*, Monthly Review Press, New York.
Mettler S (2014) *Degrees of Inequality: How the Politics of Higher Education Sabotaged the American Dream*, Basic Books, New York.
Moore TJ (1995) *Deadly Medicine: Why Tens of Thousands of Patients Died in America's Worst Drug Disaster*, Simon & Shuster, New York.
Morford M (2008) You are not reading enough: Has the Internet killed the joy of sitting down with a good book, *San Francisco Chronicle*, 9 July 2008, www.commondreams.org/ archive/2008/ 07/09/10224.
Mwaria CB, Federici S and McLaren J (editors) (2000) *Africa Visions: Literary Images, Political Change and Social Struggle in Contemporary Africa*, Praeger Press, Westport, Connecticut.
Naureckas J and Jackson J (1996) *The Fair Reader: An Extra! Review Of Press And Politics In The '90s*(Critical Studies in Communication and in the Cultural Industries), Westview Press, New York.
Persaud N and Mamdani MM (2006) External validity: The neglected dimension in evidence ranking, *Journal of Evaluation in Clinical Practice*, 12:450-455.

Pitts L Jr (2008) Reading a book – An act of sedition? *The Miami Herald*, 16 June, 2008, www.commondreams.org/archive/2008/06/16/9663.

Pocock SJ (1983) *Clinical Trials: A Practical Approach*, John Wiley & Sons, New York, 246-247.

Randall S, Naureckas J and Cohen J (1995) *The Way Things Aren't*, The New Press, New York.

Ravitch D (2014) *Reign of Error: The Hoax of the Privatization Movement and the Danger to America's Public Schools*, Vintage; New York.

Rim C (2019) Why wealthy parents are increasingly choosing public over private schools, *Forbes Magazine*, 3 July 2019, www.forbes.com/sites/christopherrim/2019/07/03/why-wealthy-parents-are-increasingly-choosing-public-over-private-schools

Roy A (2018) Amid arrests and killings, Bangladesh and India must fight censorship, *The Guardian*(UK), 15 November 2018, www.theguardian.com/books/2018/nov/15/bangladesh-india-democracy-pen-international-day-imprisoned-writer-shahidul-alam

Safi M (2018) India's 'cheating mafia' gets to work as school exam season hits, *The Guardian* (UK), 3 April 2018.

Salutin R (2011a) Saving public education: Why teachers matter, *The Toronto Star*, 25 March 2011, www.thestar.com.

Salutin R (2011b) Saving public education: Too many choices, *The Toronto Star*, 25 March 2011, www.thestar.com.

Salutin R (2011c) Standard tests: More questions than answers, *The Toronto Star*, 1 April 2011, www.thestar.com.

Salutin R (2011d) Why old-school teaching fails new Canada, *The Toronto Star*, 2 April 2011, www.thestar.com.

Salutin R (2011e) The ultimate public school advantage: Democracy, *The Toronto Star*, 8 April 2011, www.thestar.com.

Schatz P, Jay KA, McComb JR and McLaughlin JR (2005) Misuse of statistical tests in Archives of Clinical Neurology publications, *Archives of Clinical Neuropsychology*, 20:1053-1059.

Schmidt J (2001) *Disciplined Minds: A Critical Look at Salaried Professionals and the Soul-battering System That Shapes Their Lives*, Rowman & Littlefield Publishers, Boston.

Schulz KF and Grimes DA (2005) Multiplicity in randomized trials I: Endpoints and treatments, *Lancet*, 365:1591-1595.

Singer S (2018) The Necessity and importance of teachers, *Common Dreams*, 30 June 2018, www.commondreams.org.

Shivji IG (1988) Professional standards, professional ethics, professional conscience, *UDASA Newsletter/Forum*, University of Dar es Salaam, 9:3-9.

Small G and Vorgan G (2008)*iBrain: Surviving the Technological Alteration of the Modern Mind*, Collins Living, New York.

Stoll C (1999) *High Tech Heretic: Why Computers Don't Belong in the Classroom and Other Reflections by a Computer Contrarian*, Doubleday, New York.

Sturdy G (2019) Mickey Mouse degrees: selling out education, *Spiked*

Online, 11 June 2019, www.spiked-online.com/2019/06/11/mickey-mouse-degrees-selling-out-education/

Sunkara B (2019) Martin Luther King was no prophet of unity. He was a radical, *The Guardian*(UK), 21 January 2019, www.theguardian.com/ commentisfree/2019/jan/21/martin-luther-king-jr-day-legacy-radical

Thornley B and Adams C (1998) Content and quality of 2000 controlled trials in schizophrenia over 50 years, *British Medical Journal*, 317:1181-1184.

Turner C (2019) First higher education institution is stripped access to student loans amid concerns over low quality degrees, The Telegraph, 4 July 2019, www.telegraph.co.uk/news/2019/07/04/first-higher-education-institution-stripped-access-student-loans/

Weale S (2017) Exam board makes last-minute changes to two A-level papers after leak, *The Guardian*(UK), 26 June 2017, www.theguardian.com/education/2017/jun/26/exam-board-makes-last-minute-changes-to-two-a-level-papers-after-leak-further-pure-maths-statistics-edexcel-pearson

Wikipedia (2018) Censorship, https://en.wikipedia.org/w/index.php?title= Censorship&oldid=86663394.

Wikipedia (2019) List of unaccredited institutions of higher education https://en.wikipedia.org/w/index.php?title=List_of_unaccredited_institutions_of_higher_education&oldid=901921881, accessed 15 June 2019.

Chapters 9, 10 & 11

Ali T (2005) *Street Fighting Years: An Autobiography of the Sixties*, Verso, New York.

Amara HA and Founou-Tchuigoua B (editors) *African Agriculture: The Critical Choices*, Zed Books, London.

Amin S (2010) *Global History: A View from the South*, Pambazuka Press, UK.

Awiti A (1975) Ismani and the rise of capitalism, L Cliffe et al. (editors) (1975).

Babu AM (1981) *African Socialism or Socialist Africa?* Zed Press, London.

Babu AM (1991) The 1964 Revolution: Lumpen or vanguard? In A Sheriff and E Ferguson (editors) (1991):220-247.

Botchwey K (1973) Class, state and the relationship between the African petty-bourgeoisie and the international bourgeoisie, *MajiMaji*, 11:34-39.

Campbell H (1986) The impact of Walter Rodney and progressive scholars on the Dar es Salaam school, *Utafiti* (Journal of the Faculty of Arts and Social Sciences), University of Dar es Salaam, 8(2):59-77.

Chung C (editor) (2013) *Walter Rodney: A Promise of a Revolution*, Monthly Review Press, New York.

Cliffe L (1972) Planning rural development, in J Rweyemamu, J Loxely, J Wicken and C Nyirabu (editors) (1972):93-118.
Cliffe L and Saul JS (editors) (1972) *Socialism in Tanzania: A Reader*, Volumes I & II, East African Publishing House, Nairobi.
Cliffe L (1973) The Policy of *Ujamaa Vijijini* and the class struggle in Tanzania, in L Cliffe and J Saul (editors) (1972), Volume 2.
Cliffe L et al. (editors) (1975) *Rural Cooperation in Tanzania*, Tanzania Publishing House, Dar es Salaam.
Cloete N, Bailey T and Maassen P (2011) *Universities and Economic Development in Africa: Pact, Academic Core and Coordination (Synthesis Report)*,Centre for Higher Education Transformation (CHET), Wynberg, South Africa.
Chomsky N et al. (1998) *The Cold War & the University: Toward an Intellectual History of the Postwar Years*, The New Press, New York.
Coulson A (editor) (1979) *African Socialism in Practice: The Tanzanian Experience*, Spokesman, Nottingham.
Coulson A (1982;2014) *Tanzania: A Political Economy*(second edition), Oxford University Press, Oxford.
Derber C, Schwartz WA and Magrass Y (1990) *Power in the Highest Degree*, Oxford University Press, New York.
Foster-Carter A (1973) The sounds of silence: Class struggle in Tanzania, *MajiMaji*, 11:12-24.
Hirji KF (1970a) The mugwumpiness of Professor Mazrui, mimeographed copy, University of Dar es Salaam.
Hirji KF (1970b) Salient implications of `The Silent Class Struggle,' *Cheche*, 3:23–34.
Hirji KF (1971a) Militancy at the Hill, *MajiMaji*, 2:6-13.
Hirji KF (1971b) Crisis on the campus: Diagnosis and implications, *MajiMaji*, 3:7–12.
Hirji KF (1973) School education and underdevelopment in Tanzania, *MajiMaji*, 12:1–23.
Hirji KF (1980) Colonial ideological apparatuses in Tanganyika under the Germans, in HY Kaniki (1980) (editor).
Hirji KF (1990) Academic pursuits under the link, *CODESRIA Bulletin*,Senegal, 2:9-16. (New version in CB Mwaria, S Federici and J McLaren (editors) (2000), Chapter 6.)
Hirji KF (2009) Liberating Africa with laughter: Ahmed Gora Ebrahim at the University of Dar es Salaam, *Awaaz Magazine*, 6(1): 26-27.
Hirji KF (2011) *Cheche: Reminiscences of a Radical Magazine*, Mkuki na Nyota Publishers, Dar es Salaam.
Hirji KF (2014) *Growing Up With Tanzania: Memory, Musings and Maths*, Mkuki na Nyota, Dar es Salaam.
Hirji KF (2017) *The Enduring Relevance of Walter Rodney's How Europe Underdeveloped Africa*, Daraja Press, Montreal.
Hirji KF (2018a) *The Travails of a Tanzanian Teacher*, Daraja Press, Montreal.
Hirji KF (2018b) The African University: A critical comment, *Pambazuka News*, www.pamabazuka.org, 30 August 2018

Hirji KF (2019a) Raggers versus radicals: Who prevailed? *Pambazuka News*, www.pamabazuka.org, 5 February 2019.
Hirji KF (2019b) Review of *Common People's Uganda, Awaaz Magazine*, 16(2), August 2019, www.awaazmagazine.com.
Iliffe J (1979) *A Modern History of Tanganyika*(African Studies), Cambridge University Press, Cambridge, UK.
Ivaska A (2003) Of students, `Nizers' and a struggle over youth: Tanzania's 1966 National Service crisis, *Africa Today*, 51(3):83-107.
Kamenju G (1972) In defense of a socialist concept of universities, in L Cliffe and JS Saul (editors) (1972), Volume 2, pages 283–288.
Kaniki MHY (editor) (1980) *Tanzania Under Colonial Rule*, Longmans, London.
Kavuma RM (2011) In Africa's universities, quantity threatens quality, *The Guardian*(UK), 9 September 2011, www.theguardian.com/ global-development/poverty-matters/ 2011/sep/09/africa-university-funding-crisis
Keating M (2011) Sierra Leone paper scandal underscores plight of African universities, *African Arguments*, 2 September 2011, https://africanarguments.org/2011/09/02/sierra-leone-paper-scandal-underscores-plight-of-african-universities-michael-keating/
Kimambo IN, Mapunda BBB and Lawi YQ (editors) (2008) *In Search of Relevance: A History of the University of Dar es Salaam*, Dar es Salaam University Press, Dar es Salaam.
Kjekshus H (1977;1996) *Ecology Control and Economic Development in East African History: The Case of Tanganyika, 1850–1950*(Eastern African Studies), Heinemann and James Curry, London.
Legum C (1972) *Africa: The Year of the Students*, Rex Collings Ltd., London.
Leys C (1975) *Underdevelopment in Kenya: The Political Economy of Neo-Colonialism*, 1964-1971, University of California Press, California.
Leys C (2018) The African university (letter), *London Review of Books*, 40(15): 2 August 2018.
Lueshcher TM, Klemencic M and Jowi JO (editors) (2016), *Student Politics in Africa: Representation and Activism*,African Minds, Cape Town.
Mahiga AP (1973) Review of `Tanzania: The Class Struggle Continues', *MajiMaji*,11:1-11.
Mamdani M (1976) *Politics and Class Formation in Uganda*, Monthly Review Press, New York.
Mamdani M (1984) *Imperialism and Fascism in Uganda*, Africa World Press, New York.
Mamdani M (2005) *Good Muslim, Bad Muslim: America, the Cold War and the Roots of Terror*, Harmony, New York.
Mamdani M (2012) *Define and Rule: Native as Political Identity* (The WEB Du Bois Lectures), Harvard University Press, Cambridge, MA.
Mamdani M (2014), Mazrui defined the terms of politics, *The Citizen* (Tanzania), 19 October 2014.

Mamdani M (2018) The African university, *London Review of Books*, 40(14), 19 July 2018.
Mapolu H (1972) The organization and participation of workers in Tanzania, *The African Review*, 2(3):381-415.
Mapolu H (editor) (1976) *Workers and Management*, Tanzanian Studies Series No. 4, Tanzania Publishing House, Dar es Salaam.
Mapolu H (1986) The state and the peasantry, in IG Shivji (editor) (1986):107-131.
Mapolu H (1990) Tanzania: Imperialism, the state and the peasantry, In HA Amara and B Founou-Tchuigoua (editors), Chapter 8.
Mazrui AA and Mazrui AM (1995) *Swahili, State and Society: The Political Economy of an African Language*, East African Educational Publishers, Nairobi.
Mazrui AA (2012) Occupying the academy: A postcolonial individual perspective, Acceptance Address for the Distinguished Scholar Award from the International Studies Association, California, April 2012, *Institute of Global Cultural Studies*, State University of New York at Binghamton, New York.
Mazrui AA (2013) Towards modernizing African education, *Institute of Global Cultural Studies*, State University of New York at Binghamton, New York.
Mbilinyi M (1979) The Arusha Declaration and Education for Self-Reliance, In AC Coulson (editor) (1979), pages 217-227.
Museveni Y (1969) Why we should take up rifles, *Cheche*, 1:32-36.
Museveni Y (1970a) My three years in Tanzania, *Cheche*, 2:12-14.
Museveni Y (1970b) On `*The Silent Class Struggle*,' *Cheche*, 3:35-38.
Nabudere DW (1970) The role of youth in the African revolution, *Cheche*, 2:3-11.
Nabudere DW (1976;1997) *The Political Economy of Imperialism*, Tanzania Publishing House and Zed Press, London.
Ngirwa CC, Euwema M, Babyegeya E and Stouten J (2014) Managing change in higher education in Tanzania: A historical perspective, *Higher Education Management and Policy*, 24(3):127-144.
Njagi M (1970) Some points of disagreement with the intelligent professor Ali Mazrui, mimeographed copy, University of Dar es Salaam.
Njagi M (1971) The upheaval against bureaucratic arrogance, *MajiMaji*, 3:1-6.
Nyerere JK (1961) Groping forward: The opening of Kivukoni College, In JK Nyerere (1966a):119-123.
Nyerere JK (1963) Inauguration of the University of East Africa, In JK Nyerere (1966a):218-221.
Nyerere JK (1966a) *Freedom and Unity: A Selection of Writings and Speeches, 1952–1965*, Oxford University Press, Dar es Salaam & Oxford.
Nyerere JK (1966b) The role of universities, In JK Nyerere (1966a):179-186.
Nyerere JK (1967) Education for Self-Reliance, In JK Nyerere (1968): 267-290.

Nyerere JK (1968a) *Freedom and Socialism: A Selection of Writings and Speeches, 1965-1967*, Oxford University Press, Dar es Salaam & Oxford.

Nyerere JK (1968b) Implementation of rural socialism, In JK Nyerere (1973):5-11.

Nyerere JK (1968c) *Ujamaa: Essays on Socialism*, Oxford University Press, Dar es Salaam & Oxford.

Nyerere JK (1970) Relevance and Dar es Salaam University, In JK Nyerere (1973):192-203.

Nyerere JK (1973) *Freedom and Development: A Selection of Writings and Speeches, 1968-1973*, Oxford University Press, Dar es Salaam & Oxford.

Omari JM and Mihyo PB (1991) *The Roots of Student Unrest in African Universities*, Man Graphics Limited, Nairobi.

Othman H (editor) (1980) *The State in Tanzania: Who Controls It and Whose Interests Does It Serve?* Dar es Salaam University Press, Dar es Salaam.

Othman H (editor) (2001) *Babu: I Saw the Future and It Works*, E&D Limited, Dar es Salaam.

Othman H (2005) Walter Rodney – A revolutionary intellectual, In SY Othman (editor) (2014):299-302.

Othman H (2010) Mwalimu Julius Nyerere: An intellectual in power, In C Chachage and A Cassam (editors) (2010):28-43.

Othman SY (editor) (2014) *Yes, in My Life Time: Selected Works of Haroub Othman*, Mkuki na Nyota & CODESRIA, Dar es Salaam & Dakar.

Packard PC (1972) Management and control of parastatal organizations, in J Rweyemamu, J Loxley, J Wicken and C Nyirabu (editors) (1972):73–91.

Peter C and Mvungi S (1986) The state and the student struggles, In IG Shivji (editor) (1986):157–198.

Resnick IN (editor) (1968) *Tanzania: Revolution by Education*, Longmans of Tanzania Limited, Arusha.

Rodney W (1967) Declaration: Implementation problems, *The Nationalist*, 19 August 1967.

Rodney W (1968) Education and Tanzanian socialism, In IN Resnick (editor) (1968):71-84.

Rodney W (1969a) African labor under capitalism and imperialism, *Cheche*, 1:4-12.

Rodney W (1969b) Ideology of the African revolution: Paper presented at the 2nd Seminar of East and Central African Youth, *The Nationalist*, 11 December 1969.

Rodney W (1969c) Letter to editor: Dr. Rodney clarifies, *The Nationalist*, 17 December 1969.

Rodney W (1971a) George Jackson, black revolutionary, *MajiMaji*, 5:4-6.

Rodney W (1971b) Some implications of the question of disengagement from imperialism, *MajiMaji*, 1:3-8.

Rodney W (1972a) *How Europe Underdeveloped Africa* (first edition),

Bogle-L'Ouveture Publications, London and Tanzania Publishing House, Dar es Salaam.

Rodney W (1972b) Tanzanian Ujamaa and scientific socialism, *African Review*, 1(4):61-76, www.marxists.org/subject/Africa/Rodney-walter.

Rodney W (1973) State formation and class formation in Tanzania, *MajiMaji*,11:25-32.

Rodney W (1974) Some implications of the question of disengagement from imperialism, In IG Shivji (editor) (1973a).

Rodney W (1975) Class contradictions in Tanzania, in H Othman (editor) (1980):18–41, www.marxists.org/subject/africa/rodney_walter.

Rodney W (1980) The political economy of colonial Tanganyika 1890 – 1930, In MH Kaniki (editor) (1980).

Rodney W (2011) *How Europe Underdeveloped Africa*(third edition), Pambazuka Press, Oxford; CODESRIA, Dakar; Black Classic Press, Baltimore; and Walter Rodney Foundation, Atlanta.

Rweyemamu J, Loxely J, Wicken J and Nyirabu C (editors) (1972) *Towards Socialist Planning*, Tanzania Publishing House, Dar es Salaam.

Rweyemamu J (1973) *Underdevelopment and Industrialization in Tanzania: A Study of Perverse Capitalist Development*, Oxford University Press, Nairobi.

Saul JS (1968) High level manpower for socialism, In IN Resnick (editor) (1968):93-105.

Saul JS (1971) Who is the immediate enemy? *Majimaji*,1:9-15.

Saul JS (1972) Radicalism and the Hill, In L Cliffe and JS Saul (editors) (1972), Volume 2:289-292.

Saul JS (2009) *Revolutionary Traveler: Freeze-Frames From a Life*, Arbeiter Ring Publishing, Winnipeg, Canada.

Schalk DL (1991) *War and the Ivory Tower*, Oxford University Press, New York.

Segall M (1972) The politics of health in Tanzania, in J Rweyemamu, J Loxley, J Wicken and C Nyirabu (editors) (1972):149-165.

Semonin P (1971) Nationalization & management in Zambia, *MajiMaji*, 1:16-24.

Sheriff A (1987) *Slaves, Spices, and Ivory in Zanzibar: Integration of an East African Commercial Empire into the World Economy, 1770-1873*, (Eastern African Studies), Ohio University Press, Ohio.

Sheriff A and Ferguson E (editors) (1991) *Zanzibar Under Colonial Rule*(Eastern African Studies), James Currey, London.

Shivji IG (1970) The Silent Class Struggle, *Cheche*No 3, Special Issue.

Shivji IG (1973a) *Tanzania: The Silent Class Struggle: With Commentaries by Walter Rodney, John Saul and Thomas Szentes*, Zeni Press, UK.

Shivji IG (editor) (1973b) *Tourism and Socialist Development*, Tanzania Publishing House, Dar es Salaam.

Shivji IG (1976) *Class Struggles in Tanzania*, Heinemann, London.

Shivji IG (editor) (1986) *The State and the Working People in Tanzania*, CODESRIA, Dakar, Senegal.

Shivji IG (1987) Debates at the Hill? In IG Shivji (1993a), 129-155.
Shivji IG (1993a) *Intellectuals at the Hill: Essays and Talks 1969-1993*, Dar es Salaam University Press, Dar es Salaam.
Shivji IG (1993b) Rodney and radicalism at the Hill, 1966–1974, In IG Shivji (1993a):32-44.
Shivji IG (1993c) What is left of the left intellectual at the Hill, In IG Shivji (1993a):200-209.
Shivji IG (2010) The village in Mwalimu's thought and practice, In C Chachage and A Cassam (editors) (2010):120-133.
Shivji IG (2012) Remembering Walter Rodney, *Monthly Review*, 64(7).
Shivji IG (2013) Chapter 8, In C Chung (editor) (2013).
Shivji IG (2018) Revolutionary intellectuals, afracaasacountry.com/2018/05/revolutionary-intellectuals
Svendsen KE (1995) Development strategy & crisis management, In C Legum and G Mmari (editors) (1995):108-124.
Swai B (1981) Rodney on scholarship and activism – Part 1, *Journal of African Marxists*, 1:31-43.
Swai B (1982) Rodney on scholarship and activism – Part 2, *Journal of African Marxists*, 2:38-52.
Tandon Y (editor) (1982) *University of Dar es Salaam Debate on Class, State & Imperialism*, Tanzania Publishing House, Dar es Salaam.
Tandon Y (2019a) The common people of Sudan at a strategic crossroad, *Pambazuka News*, 24 April 2019, www.pambazuka.org.
Tandon Y (2019b) *Common People's Uganda*, Zand Graphics, Nairobi.
TANU (1967) *The Arusha Declaration and TANU's Policy of Socialism and Self-Reliance*, TANU Publicity Section, Dar es Salaam.
TANU (1971) *Mwongozo: TANU Guidelines*, National Printing Company, Dar es Salaam.
TANU Youth League (1973) Commentaries on *Tanzania: The Class Struggle Continues* (MajiMaji Special Issue No. 11), University of Dar es Salaam, Dar es Salaam.
TANU Youth League (1980) Special Issue on Walter Rodney, *MajiMaji*, No. 43, University of Dar es Salaam, Dar es Salaam.
Temu AJ and Swai B (1981) *Historians and History: Africanist History Examined*, Zed Press, London.
The Nationalist (1967a) Turn College into socialist institution: Babu calls for complete transformation at `the Hill', *The Nationalist*, 13 March 1967.
The Nationalist (1967b) University must produce socialist people, *The Nationalist*, 13 March 1967.
The Nationalist (1967c) Varsity to undergo structural changes, *The Nationalist*, 14 March 1967.
The Nationalist (1967d) Stress on socialism at the University, *The Nationalist*, 15 March 1967.
The Nationalist (1967e) Expel US Peace Corps: TYL resolves, *The Nationalist*, 2 October 1967.
The Nationalist (1967f) Seminar on African Freedom Struggle: USARF panel discussion on `The Strategy, Conduct and Tactics of the African Liberation Movements,' *The Nationalist*, 16 November 1967.

The Nationalist (1967g) Teach revolution at Varsity call: Rodney at the USARF conference, *The Nationalist*, 20 November 1967.

The Nationalist (1967h) Students resolve on EA affairs, *The Nationalist*, 28 December 1967.

The Nationalist (1969a) Students reject new curriculum, *The Nationalist*, 5 March 1969.

The Nationalist (1969b) Law students stage protest, *The Nationalist*, 14 March 1969.

The Nationalist (1969c) Dar college authority speaks out, *The Nationalist*, 15 April 1969.

The Nationalist (1969d) Students challenge lecturer, *The Nationalist*, 31 July 1969.

The Nationalist (1969e) University Visitation meets, *The Nationalist*, 6 August 1969.

The Nationalist (1969f) Sack lecturer – students demand, *The Nationalist*, 8 August 1969.

The Nationalist (1969g) Youth condemn U.S. imperialism: Rally held to honor Vietnamese hero, *The Nationalist*, 17 October 1969.

The Nationalist (1969h) Visitation report presented, *The Nationalist*, 4 November 1969.

The Nationalist (1969i) African revolution `must be accepted,' *The Nationalist*, 10 December 1969.

The Nationalist (1969j) No liberation `without armed struggle,' *The Nationalist*, 11 December 1969.

The Nationalist (1969k) Editorial: Revolutionary hot air, *The Nationalist*, 13 December 1969.

The Nationalist (1969l) Work with masses, youth urged, *The Nationalist*, 15 December 1969.

The Nationalist (1969m) Hill students denounce U.S. imperialism, *The Nationalist*, 22 July 1969.

The Nationalist (1969n) Dar Students' Front snubs liberal Americans, *The Nationalist*, 17 November 1969.

The Nationalist (1970a) The Hill examined: Just what is the balance of forces at the Hill? *The Nationalist*, 13 February 1970.

The Nationalist (1970b) Msekwa to head Dar Varsity, *The Nationalist*, 22 June 1970.

The Nationalist (1970c) Independent Varsity of Dar born today, *The Nationalist*, 1 July 1970.

The Nationalist (1970d) Hill Students' Front asked to cease, *The Nationalist*, 13 November 1970.

The Nationalist (1970e) Editorial: Students' Front, *The Nationalist*, 14 November 1970.

The Standard (1970) Ban claim by USARF, *The Standard*, 13 November 1970.

USARF (1969) A Paper Presented to the Visitation Committee Prepared by the University African Revolutionary Front (USARF), mimeographed copy, 26 August 1969 (signed by K Mwakasungura).

USARF (1970) Our Last Stand, mimeographed USARF statement, 12 November 1970, University of Dar es Salaam.

Vestbro DU & Persson G (1970) How socialist is Sweden? *Cheche*, 2:16-22.
von Freyhold M (1979) *Ujamaa Villages in Tanzania: Analysis of a Social Experiment*, Monthly Review Press, New York.
Wamba dia Wamba (1980) Walter Rodney and the role of the revolutionary intellectual in the neo-colonial countries, In TANU Youth League (1980).
Zinn H (1990) *The Politics of History* (second edition), University of Illinois Press, Illinois.

Chapter 12

Brunett D (2016) Is the internet killing our brains? *The Guardian*(UK), 8 October 2016, www.theguardian.com/education/2016/oct/08/is-the-internet-killing-our-brains.
Carr N (2008) Is Google making us stupid? What the Internet is doing to our brains, *The Atlantic*, July/August 2008 Issue.
Carr N (2010) *The Shallows: What the Internet is Doing to Our Brains*, WW Norton, New York.
Dalali M (2019) Dar es Salaam is not a paradise for book lovers, *The Citizen* (Tanzania), 5 June 2019, page 5.
Editorial (2019) Kudos, US student Hladczuk, *The Citizen*(Tanzania), 2 July 2019, page 6.
Fisher R (2004a) *A History of Reading*, Reaktion Books, New York.
Fisher R (2004b) *A History of Writing*,Reaktion Books, New York.
Grafton A (2011) Our universities: Why are they failing? *New York Review of Books*, 24 November 2011.
Hirji KF (2005) *Exact Analysis of Discrete Data*, Chapman and Hall/CRC Press, Boca Raton.
Hirji KF (editor) (2011) *Cheche: Reminiscences of a Radical Magazine*, Mkuki na Nyota, Dar es Salaam.
Hirji KF (2012) *Statistics in the Media: Learning from Practice*, Media Council of Tanzania, Dar es Salaam.
Hirji KF (2014) *Growing Up With Tanzania: Memories, Musings and Maths*, Mkuki na Nyota, Dar es Salaam.
Hirji KF (2017a) *The Enduring Relevance of Walter Rodney's How Europe Underdeveloped Africa*, Daraja Press, Montreal.
Hirji KF (2017b) *The Banana Girls*, Mkuki na Nyota, Dar es Salaam.
Hirji KF (2018) *The Travails of a Tanzanian Teacher*, Daraja Press, Montreal.
Hussein E (1970) *Kinjikitele*, Tanzania Publishing House, Dar es Salaam.
Macha F (2008) Tanzania: Let us talk about the rise of Swanglish, *The Citizen* (Tanzania), 3 October 2008.
Manguel A (1997) *A History of Reading*, Penguin Books, UK.
Mazrui AM (2000) Socialist-Oriented literature in post-colonial Africa: Retrospective and prospective, Chapter 15 In CB Mwaria, S Federici and J McLaren (editors) (2000).

Msemo m (2018) Kiswahili: An African pride under siege, *Pambazuka News*, 13 April 2018, www.pamabazuka.org.

Perry P (2016) Cognitive offloading: How the Internet is changing the human brain, *Big Think*,bigthink.com/philip-perry/cognitive-offloading-how-the-internet-is-changing-the-human-brain, 24 August 2016.

Schreiner E (2019) The disadvantages of computers in education, www.theclassroom.com/disadvantages-computers-education-6562938.html

Shafi A (1978) *Kasri ya Mwinyi Fuad*, Tanzania Publishing House, Dar es Salaam.

Shafi A (1979) *Kuli*, Tanzania Publishing House, Dar es Salaam.

Shafi A (1999) *Vita n'Kuvute*,Mkuki na Nyota, Dar es Salaam.

Shafi A (2003) *Haini*,Mkuki na Nyota, Dar es Salaam.

Shafi A (2013) *Mbali na Nyumbani*, Longhorne Publisher, Nairobi.

Simpson A (2008) Internet 'speeds up decision making and brain function,' *The Telegraph*, 26 October 2016, www.telegraph.co.uk/news/3262597/Internet-speeds-up-decision-making-and-brain-function.html.

Small G and Vorgan G (2008) *iBrain: Surviving the Technological Alteration of the Modern Mind*,William Morrow, New York.

Ubwani Z (2019) 17-yr-old US student raises Sh100m for the Arusha library, *The Citizen* (Tanzania), 1 July 2019, page 5.

Chapters 13 & 14

Bah CAM (2014) *Neocolonialism in West Africa: A Collection of Essays and Articles*, iUniverse, https://www.iuniverse.com/

Barker M (2017) *Under the Mask of Philanthropy*, CreateSpace Independent Publishing Platform.

Buzznigeria (2018) Origin and meaning of Rag Day for Nigerian universities, buzznigeria.com/origin-meaning-rag-day-nigerian-universities.

Caufield C (1997) *Masters of Illusion: The World Bank and the Poverty of Nations*, Henry Holt & Co, New York.

Cheeseman N (2019) Why there's a case for aid to dictatorships, *The Citizen*(Tanzania) 16 January 2019.

Chery D (2012) USAID: The soft arm of imperialism, *News Junkie Post*, 24 November 2012, http://newsjunkiepost.com/2012/11/24/usaid-the-soft-arm-of-imperialism/

Chickering AW and Gamson ZF (1987) Seven principles for good teaching in undergraduate education, *AAHE Bulletin*, 39:3-7.

EduAfrica (2015) Why students re-invent Rag Day for their personal gain, www.edufrica.com/2015/10/photo-speaks-why-students-re-invent-rag-day-for-their-personal-gain/

Gates B (2017) How foreign aid helps Americans, *Gates Notes*, www.gatesnotes.com/Development/How-Foreign-Aid-Helps-americans, 17 March 2017.

Gill C (2019) Universities are destroying the value of their own degrees, https://capx.co/universities-are-destroying-the-value-of-their-own-degrees/, 16 July 2019.
Hancock G (1994) *Lords of Poverty*, Grove Press/Atlantic Monthly Press, London and New York.
Hayter T (1971) *Aid as Imperialism*, Pelican Books, UK.
Hirji KF (1993) Criminal statistics, *Business Times* (Tanzania), July 1993.
Hirji KF (2007a) HIV and poverty: Posing the right question (HakiElimu Column), *The Citizen* (Tanzania), 15 February 2007.
Hirji KF (2007b) Media bias in Tanzania: Myth or reality, *Media Watch*, Newsletter of the Media Council of Tanzania, serialized in issues No. 87, 88, 89, June, July & August 2007.
Hirji KF (2007c) Questioning assumptions (HakiElimu Column), *The Citizen* (Tanzania), April 2007.
Hirji KF (2017) *The Enduring Relevance of Walter Rodney's How Europe Underdeveloped Africa*, Daraja Press, Montreal, Canada.
Hirji KF (2019a) Raggers versus radicals: Who prevailed? *Pambazuka News*, 5 February 2019, www.pamabazuka.org.
Hirji KF (2019b) Deconstructing identity politics, *Pambazuka News*, 16 April 2019, www.pambazuka.org.
Hudson M (2003) *Super Imperialism: The Origin and Fundamentals of U.S. World Dominance*, Pluto Press, Boston.
Iqbal N (2019) Woke washing? How brands like Gillette turn profits by creating a conscience, *The Guardian*, 21 January 2019, www.theguardian.com/media/2019/jan/19/gillette-ad-campaign-woke-advertising-salving-consciences
Jain A (2019) Ved Kumari, Dean of Delhi University's Law Faculty, resigns, *NewsClick*,18 June 2019, www.newsclick.in/Ved-Kumari-Dean-Delhi-University-Law-Faculty-Resigns
John D (2010) Foreign science teachers can boost students' performance, *The Citizen*(Tanzania), 12 September 2010.
King ML (1965) Martin Luther King Quotes, www.goodreads.com/quotes/19814.
King ML (2010) *Where Do We Go From Here: Chaos or Community?*Beacon Press, Boston.
Langan M (2018) *Neo-Colonialism and the Poverty of 'Development' in Africa*,Palgrave Macmillan, London.
Moloo Z (2018) The problem with capitalist philanthropy, *Catalyst*, 2 June 2018.
Moseley WG (2015) The dark alliance of global philanthropy and capitalism, *Al Jazeera*(www.aljazeera.com), 1 Dec 2015.
Mwendapole J and John E (2010) Kikwete: Obama kuimwagia misaada Tanzania, *Nipashe*, 3 October 2010.
Mwita P (2010) It is time beggars were prosecuted, *Sunday News* (Tanzania), 7 November 2010.
National University of Singapore (2011) NUSSU Rag Day 2011 to Join Singapore in Celebrating National Day, newshub.nus.edu.sg/pressrel/1104/130411.php

Nipashe Special Supplement (2010) Mabilioni ya India kunufaisha wakulima Tanzania, *Nipashe*, 5 November 2010.

Nyikal H (2005) Neo-colonialism in Africa: The economic crisis in Africa and the propagation of the status quo by the World Bank/IMF and WTO, web.stanford.edu/class/e297a/Neo-Colonialism%20in%20 Africa.pdf

Orr G (2012) Bad behavior that's all in a good cause: Students are carrying on the RAG tradition, 2 February 2012, *The Independent*, www.independent.co.uk/news/education/higher/bad-behaviour-thats-all-in-a-good-cause-tudents-are-carrying-on-the-rag-tradition-6298083.html,

Paget KM (2015) *Patriotic Betrayal: The Inside Story of the CIA's Secret Campaign to Enroll American Students in the Crusade Against Communism,* Yale University Press.

Polman LS (2011) *War Games: The Story of Aid and War in Modern Times,* Viking, London.

Rodney W (2011) *How Europe Underdeveloped Africa*(third edition), Pambazuka Press, Oxford; CODESRIA, Dakar; Black Classic Press, Baltimore; and Walter Rodney Foundation, Atlanta.

Serumaga M (2017) Hunger, foreign debt and Uganda's fairytale budgets, *Pambazuka News*, 7 December 2017, www.pambazuka.org/ democracy-governance/hunger-foreign-debt-and-ugandas-fairytale-budgets

Sunkara B (2019) Martin Luther King was no prophet of unity. He was a radical, *The Guardian*(UK), 21 January 2019, www.theguardian.com/ commentisfree/2019/jan/21/martin-luther-king-jr-day-legacy-radical

Tandon Y (2019) 2019: A year of revolutionary rupture? Looking beyond the curve, *Pambazuka News*, 15 January 2019, www.pambazuka.org/global-south/2019-year-revolutionary-rupture-looking-beyond-curve

The Citizen Reporter (2010) Donors: Why Dar suffers huge deficit, *The Citizen* (Tanzania), 7 December 2010.

The Standard (1968a) College TYL cancels `Rag Day', *The Standard* (Tanzania), 10 November 1968.

The Standard (1968b) Reader's Forum: The sabotaging of Rag Day, *The Standard* (Tanzania), 17 November 1968.

Thompson MA (1982) *Unofficial Ambassadors: The Story of International Student Service*, International Student Service, New York.

Todhunter C (2012) Dollar billionaires in poor countries: India's `Philanthrocapitalism,' *Global Research*, September 10, 2012, www.globalresearch.ca/dollar-billionaires-in-poor-countries-indias-philanthrocapitalism/

Tressel R (1914;2012) *The Ragged Trousered Philanthropists*, Wordsworth Classics, London.

University of Pretoria (2012), Rag Day, http://web.up.ac.za/default.asp?ipkCategoryID=7688.

Walker Center (2019) *Seven Principles for Good Practice in Undergraduate Education*, Walker Center for Teaching and

Learning, www.utc.edu/walker-center-teaching-learning/teaching-resources/7-principles.php, accessed 11 June 2019.
Wikipedia (2018) Rag (Student Society), en.wikipedia.org/wiki/RAG_(Student_society)
Wikipedia (2019) World University Service, https://en.wikipedia.org/w/index.php?title=World_University_Service&oldid=812574376

Chapters 15 & 16

Ali T (2005) *Street Fighting Years: An Autobiography of the Sixties*, Verso, New York.
Anonymous (2013) I am a woman and a human: A Marxist-Feminist critique of Intersectionality Theory, *Unity and Struggle*, 12 September 2013 (www.unityandstruggle.org/2013/09/).
Appiah KA (2018) *The Lies That Bind: Rethinking Identity*, Liveright Publisher, NY.
Armitstead C (2019) 'Identity is a pain in the arse': Zadie Smith on political correctness, *The Guardian*(UK), 2 February 2019, www.theguardian.com/books/2019/feb/02/
Bakshnian A (2010) Identity politics in wonderland, *The American Conservative*, 5 March 2019, www.theamericanconservative.com/articles/identity-politics-in-wonderland/
Blum W (2014) *Killing Hope: US Military and CIA Interventions Since World War II*, Updated Edition, Zed Books, Boston.
Buell J (2017) Rural consciousness and democratic politics, *Common Dreams*, 1 May 2017, www.commondreams.org/views
Cabalin C (2011) The student movement has shaken Chilean society to the core and it will continue to shape the country's future, *The Guardian*(UK), 2 December 2011.
Chutel L (2019) Xenophobic attacks in South Africa ahead of elections, Quartz Africa, 2 April 2019, hhtp://tinyurl.com/y5cpff45
Cohen J (2019) Let's not restore or mythologize Obama, *Common Dreams*, 22 March 2018, www.commondreams.org/views
Crenshaw K (2015) Why intersectionality can't wait, *Washington Post*, 24 September 2015, www.washingtonpost.com/news/in-theory/wp/2015/09/24/
Driver A and others (2016) An open letter on Identity Politics, to and from the Left, *Medium.com*, 13 July 2016, medium.com/@We_Are_The_Left/
Editorial (2019a) The Guardian view on Tory Islamophobia: inaction speaks volumes, *The Guardian* (UK), 28 March 2019, www.theguardian.com/profile/editorial/2019/mar/28/
Editorial (2019b) Xenophobia by any name is still appalling, vicious, *The Citizen* (Tanzania), 2 April 2019, page 6.
Eyakuze A (2019) Govt deserves praise for statistics law amendment, *The Citizen* (Tanzania), 8 July 2019, page 7.

Gerard L (2019) How billionaires are using hate to divide us, 22 March 2019, www.commondreams.org/views

Gray B (2018) Beware the race reductionist, *The Intercept*, 26 August 2018, theintercept.com/2018/08/26/

Greenidge K (2019) Why black people discriminate among ourselves: the toxic legacy of colorism, *The Guardian*(UK), 9 April 2019, www.theguardian.com/lifeandstyle/2019/apr/09/

Haider A (2018) *Mistaken Identity: Race and Class in the Age of Trump*, Verso Press, New York.

Hirji KF (1993a) Criminal statistics, *Business Times* (Tanzania), July 1993.

Hirji KF (2014a) Criminalizing statistics is both undemocratic and unscientific, *The Citizen* (Tanzania), 19 November 2014.

Hirji KF (2014b) Beating the drum on one side: Confusing the people on both sides, *Awaaz Magazine*, 11(3):36-41, www.awaazmagazine.com.

Hirji KF (2019) Raggers versus radicals: Who prevailed? *Pambazuka News*, www.pambazuka.org, 5 February 2019.

Kumar R (2018) How identity politics has divided the left: an interview with Asad Haider, *Monthly Review Online*, 29 May 2018, mronline.org/2018/05/29/

Lancaster R (2017) Identity politics can only get us so far, *Jacobin Magazine*, August 2017, jacobinmag.com/2017/08/

Lawler S (2008) *Identity: Sociological Perspectives*, Polity Press, Cambridge, UK.

Legum C (1972) *Africa: The Year of the Students*, Rex Collings Ltd., London.

MacDougald P (2019) A different way to think about white identity politics, *New York Magazine*, 1 March 2019, nymag.com/intelligencer/ amp/2019/03/

Mahdawi A (2019) Don't get your hopes up about Chicago's first black lesbian mayor, *The Guardian*(UK), 6 April 2019, www.theguardian.com/ world/commentisfree/2019/apr/06/

Malik K (2019) Silencing Islamophobes is as futile a response as banning the Qur'an, *The Guardian*(UK), www.theguardian.com/commentisfree/2019/mar/24

Manji F (2019) Emancipation, freedom or taxonomy? What does it mean to be African? In V Satgar (editor), Chapter 3.

Michaels WB, Mills CW, Hirshman L and Murphy C (2016), What Is the Left without identity politics? *The Nation*, 16 December 2016, www.thenation.com/article/

O'Hagan EM (2019) Feminism without socialism will never cure our unequal society, *The Guardian*(UK), 8 March 2019.

Satgar V (editor) (2019) *Racism After Apartheid: Challenges for Marxism and Anti-Racism*, Witts University Press, South Africa.

Shah R (2019) Bleak times, *Awaaz Magazine*, 15(3), 5 February 2019, www.awaazmagazine.com

Sidel R (1995) *Battling Bias: The Struggle for Identity and Community on College Campuses*, Penguin Books, New York.

Smith S (2010) Andy Martin: My students have had a political awakening. And I'm with them, *The Independent*(UK), 6 December 2010.

Stoller M (2017) Democrats can't win until they recognize how bad Obama's financial policies were, *The Washington Post*, 12 January 2017, www.washingtonpost.com/posteverything/wp/2017/01/12/

Sunkara B (2019) To fight racism, we need to think beyond reparations, *The Guardian*(UK), 28 March 2019, www.theguardian.com/ commentisfree/2019.mar/28/

Susskind Y (2008) Inequality, not identity, fuels violence in Kenya, *Common Dreams*, 10 February 2008, www.commondreams.org/views

The Citizen (2019) Beseeching God: Youths turn to prayers to secure jobs, *The Citizen* (Tanzania), 23 June 2019.

The Economist (2018) Identity politics are stronger on the right than the left, *The Economist*, 1 November 2018, www.economist.com/united-states/2018/11/01/

AUTHOR PROFILE

Karim F Hirji is a retired Professor of Medical Statistics and a Fellow of the Tanzania Academy of Sciences. A recognized authority on statistical analysis of small sample discrete data, the author of the only book on the subject, he received the Snedecor Prize for Best Publication in Biometry from the American Statistical Association and International Biometrics Society for the year 1989. He has published many papers in the areas of statistical methodology, applied biomedical research, the history and practice of education in Tanzania, and written numerous essays on varied topics for the mass media and popular magazines.

He is the author of *Exact Analysis of Discrete Data* (Chapman and Hall/CRC Press, Boca Raton, 2005), *Statistics in the Media: Learning from Practice* (Media Council of Tanzania, Dar es Salaam, 2012) and *Growing Up With Tanzania: Memories, Musings and Maths* (Mkuki na Nyota Publishers, Dar es Salaam, 2014). He also edited and is the main author of *Cheche: Reminiscences of a Radical Magazine* (Mkuki na Nyota Publishers, Dar es Salaam, 2011). His most recent books are *The Enduring Relevance of Walter Rodney's How Europe Underdeveloped Africa* (Daraja Press, Montreal, 2017), *The Banana Girls* (Mkuki na Nyota Publishers, Dar es Salaam, 2017) and *The Travails of a Tanzanian Teacher* (Daraja Press, Montreal, 2018).

He resides in Dar es Salaam, Tanzania, and may be contacted at kfhirji@aol.com.

*

www.ingramcontent.com/pod-product-compliance
Lightning Source LLC
Chambersburg PA
CBHW051528020426
42333CB00016B/1831